Law and Humanities

Law and Humanities

Edited by
Daniel Newman and Russell Sandberg

ANTHEM PRESS

Anthem Press
An imprint of Wimbledon Publishing Company
www.anthempress.com

This edition first published in UK and USA 2024
by ANTHEM PRESS
75–76 Blackfriars Road, London SE1 8HA, UK
or PO Box 9779, London SW19 7ZG, UK
and
244 Madison Ave #116, New York, NY 10016, USA

British Library Cataloguing-in-Publication Data
A catalogue record for this book is available from the British Library.

Library of Congress Control Number: 2023915555
A catalog record for this book has been requested.

ISBN-13: 978-1-83999-036-6 (Hbk)
ISBN-10: 1-83999-036-8 (Hbk)

This title is also available as an e-book.

CONTENTS

PREFACE

Interdisciplinary approaches to law are now commonplace at least in terms of legal research. Although in the Anglo-American world at least such work has tended to be predominantly social scientific in focus, there has also been an increase in interdisciplinary scholarship on law that draws upon the humanities. This is most notable in the large literature on law and literature as well as the development of a number of further 'law and' fields. Some of these (e.g. law and history, law and religion, law and philosophy) have been long-lasting but have been revived in recent years by increased interdisciplinary collaborations while other areas (e.g. law and television, law and comics, law and music) represent new areas of interest that have seen legal scholars interact with academics from other parts of the university and with practitioners, artists and producers. These 'law and' fields, however, tend to exist in isolation from one another and this limits their development in that they are not able to draw upon each other's intellectual and methodological developments and because this means that they exist as small disparate fields at the margins of law as an academic discipline.

There is now a growing number of works that pay attention to 'law and humanities' as a field, including a small number of specialist journals, but these typically take a thematic approach and are not particularly accessible to newcomers and to a student readership. This edited work, therefore, fulfils a real and pressing need to provide an accessible, introductory but critical guide to law and humanities as a whole by exploring how various disciplinary 'law and' fields have developed. *Law and Humanities* contributes to further scrutinising the content and role of law, and how it can contribute and be enriched by being understood within the law and humanities tradition as a whole.

This edited collection provides an accessible introduction to law and humanities. It is designed to be the first port of call for students and scholars interested in particular 'law and' fields and law and humanities in general. It examines a number of 'law and' interactions in turn (ordered alphabetically). Each chapter is written by an expert in the respective field and will explore the nature, development and possible further trajectory of that particular disciplinary 'law and' field. As editors, we have encouraged each contributor to conceptualise their own discussion of their field. This has meant that a number of different approaches have been taken. Some authors focus on the intellectual development of their fields, sometimes providing a critique of its current state; others explore new and emerging developments, suggesting new approaches or conceptualisations; others still attempt to survey the terrain, often simultaneously elucidating but also critiquing the ideas of a canon or common approach within that field. The autonomy given to authors also means that some chapters overlap, tell differing stories about the development of law as a discipline and/or take different interpretations to each other. Yet, although the chapters in this collection are all very different reflecting the contrasting 'law and' fields and the interpretation of each particular author, the objective of each chapter and the collection as a whole is to explore what these different fields can learn from each other and what this reveals about the law and humanities approach in general.

We are delighted that this is one of the first books to be published in the Anthem, Law and Society Series. We are indebted to the staff at Anthem as well as to the peer reviewers for their enthusiasm and support for this collection. As with any edited collection, we are grateful first and foremost to the contributors who have made our role as editors very easy. It has been a treat to explore with them the respective 'law and' fields, focusing on not only what has been achieved to date but what can be accomplished in the future.

This book is particularly timely for us as two academics based in Wales where the new curriculum being introduced for all children of compulsory school age includes the humanities as one of the six Areas of Learning and Experience (AoLEs) that underpin the curriculum. Although the humanities AoLE is understood as encompassing geography, history, religion, values and ethics, business studies and social studies, law is listed as a complementary discipline that learners can be introduced to. Moreover, issues of governance, justice and equality are central in the 'What Matters' statement of the Humanities AoLE while learning about and learning through human rights is one of the cross-cutting themes. It is to be hoped that children and young people will be increasingly introduced to law and its interaction with other humanities subjects not only here in Wales but around the world.

Daniel Newman and Russell Sandberg
July 2023

LIST OF CONTRIBUTORS

Cristy Clark is Associate Professor at the University of Canberra.

Norman Doe is Professor at Cardiff University.

Steve Greenfield is Professor of Law at University of Westminster and Extraordinary Professor at North-West University.

Barbara Hughes-Moore is Lecturer at Cardiff University.

Daniel Newman is Reader at Cardiff University.

Emma Nottingham is Senior Lecturer at the University of Winchester.

Angus Nurse is Professor at Anglia Ruskin University.

Guy Osborn is Professor at the University of Westminster.

John Page is Professor at the University of Canterbury.

Ashley Pearson is Lecturer at the University of the Sunshine Coast.

Sara Ramshaw is Professor at the University of Victoria.

Peter Robson is Professor at the University of Strathclyde.

Russell Sandberg is Professor at Cardiff University.

Kieran Tranter is Professor at the Queensland University of Technology.

Jennifer Schulz is Professor at the University of Manitoba.

Robbie Sykes is Visiting Researcher at De Montfort University.

Ian Ward is Professor at Newcastle University.

Chapter One

INTRODUCING LAW AND HUMANITIES

Daniel Newman and Russell Sandberg

Introduction

In 1901 in his Rede lecture the distinguished English legal historian Frederic William Maitland was pondering about how the common law had survived the Renaissance.[1] Looking at the Year Books of Henry VII and Henry VIII, he remarked that these 'ancient law reports are not a place in which we look for humanism or the spirit of the Renaissance: rather we look there for an amazingly continuous persistence and development of medieval doctrine'.[2] Indeed, while Renaissance-era writers were generally contemptuous of anything medieval, Renaissance-era legal writers were not only continuing to use but were actually praising medieval texts. Maitland questioned:

> How was it and why was it that in an age when old creeds of many kinds were crumbling and all knowledge was being transfigured, in an age which had revolted against its predecessor and was fully conscious of the revolt, [that] one body of doctrine [...] remained so intact? [3]

Maitland's argument was that the common law survived because it was taught, studied and perpetuated by the Inns of Court and those they trained.[4] As Maitland commented it was 'difficult to conceive of any system better suited to harden and toughen a traditional body of law than one which, while books were still uncommon, compelled every lawyer to take part in legal education and every distinguished lawyer to read public lectures'.[5] Legal education served to fossilise the law, bestowing a sacred aura upon what would otherwise seem archaic. As he put it:

> Law schools make tough law.[6]

***

1. F W Maitland, *English Law and the Renaissance* (Cambridge University Press, 1901).
2. Ibid 3.
3. Ibid 4.
4. Ibid 26.
5. Ibid 27–28.
6. Ibid 25.

Over a hundred years after Maitland's lecture and many hundreds of years after the Renaissance, the common law continues to thrive. Attributing this persistence to the continuing role of legal education provokes a 'chicken and the egg' controversy as to causation. Yet, the role of Law Schools in making and perpetuating 'tough law' is so fundamental that it is taken for granted. Though there are exceptions, legal education remains characterised by doctrinal legal studies. The first stage of legal education focuses on the learning of legal principles, with a focus on their application. Law students are trained to operate as jurists. As Lord Goff commented extra-judicially, the prime task of jurists 'is to take the cases and statutes which provide the raw material of the law on any particular topic; and by a critical re-appraisal of that raw material, to build up a systematic statement of the law on the relevant topic in a coherent form, often combined with proposals of how the law can be beneficially developed in the future'.[7] This task includes criticising the law but crucially only on its own terms. Law is presented as an autonomous system that can be studied in its own right.[8]

This dominant form – in some cases the only form[9] – of legal education has an effect upon law students. Law students are taught to 'think like lawyers' and employ reasoning and interpretative skills that are different from elsewhere in the academy. As Anthony Bradney argued, doctrinal legal study (defined as an 'attempt to explain law solely through the internal evidence' provided by primary legal sources) leads law students not only to 'assimilate' but also to 'accept the values of the community that they are studying'.[10] At first, these ways of seeing are 'at odds with what law students have previously experienced and continue to experience outside their studies'. However, throughout the law degree what was once odd becomes normalised. And certain questions and ways of looking become excluded from the law student's gaze. As Bradney put it, 'doctrinal study explicitly identifies questions outside the doctrinal range as being something not relevant for the doctrinal student. It implicitly devalues such questions and treats them as not being worthy of consideration within the precise, objective word of the law school.' Bradney has gone as far as to say that in order to 'become a law student the student must forget who he or she is'.[11]

Bradney is not alone in raising these concerns. As the US scholar Robin L. West noted, 'law students and lawyers are trained to identify certain kinds of problems'.[12] They are taught to spot gaps in the law rather than looking at the issue 'on a systematic or structural basis'. Law students are not 'taught to think in a proactive way about

7. Lord Goff of Chieveley, 'Judge, Jurist and Legislature' (1987) *Denning Law Journal* 79, 92.
8. See B Bix, 'Law as an Autonomous Discipline' in P Cane and M Tushnet (eds) *The Oxford Handbook of Legal Studies* (Oxford University Press, 2003) 975.
9. Particularly in respect of those for whom Solicitor Qualifying Examination (SQE) courses or handbooks constitutes their 'academic' legal education.
10. A Bradney, 'Law as a Parasitic Discipline' (1998) 25(1) *Journal of Law and Society* 71, 79, 73, 76.
11. Ibid 77.
12. R L West, *Teaching Law: Justice, Politics and the Demands of Professionalism* (Cambridge University Press, 2014) 114.

problems of social justice and whether law might be part of their solution'.[13] Law students find this initially counterintuitive. West noted that 'legalism', 'the moral way of being into which students are accultured while in law school', led 'to the common complaint that law school renders law graduates amoral'.[14]

This is not simply a debate about the academic versus vocational nature of legal education. The 'tough law' that dominates the Law School syllabus often has little resemblance to law in practice, especially the kind of legal practice that law students would face for much of their early careers. The focus on the compatibility of senior court decisions and determining questions of law means that the so-called academic stage of legal education is actually preparing law students to think as appellate court judges. The way in which legal education is in a constant tug of war between the academic and the vocational, between the Law School's places in the wider university versus the professions, means that the final compromise satisfies no one.

The dominance of doctrinal legal studies in the lecture halls has not gone unchallenged.[15] The critical turn felt in Universities since the 1960s together with an increased focus on research in Law Schools, which in the UK can be attributed to otherwise undesirable developments such as the Research Excellence Framework (REF), has led to an increase in the depth and breadth of legal studies. This includes not only the study of new areas of law but also crucially a number of interdisciplinary approaches. This book explores one such development: the growing interaction between law and humanities subjects and approaches. It explores the way in which doctrinal methods are complemented – and corrected – by methods, ideas and approaches that arise from the humanities. In seeking to provide a collection that introduces the various students to these literatures and approaches, this book explores a number of humanities disciplines in turn reflecting on how they have and can be used to transform understandings of law and also how legal approaches can shed further light upon each respective discipline.

This introductory chapter explains why the study of law and the humanities requires more attention and why this approach has been employed. It falls into two parts. The first part introduces the interaction between law and the humanities, suggesting that while interdisciplinary approaches are now prevalent in relation to legal research (as opposed to Law School teaching), this interdisciplinary turn has largely been interpreted as requiring interaction with the social sciences. Against this backdrop, this chapter surveys the development of law and humanities, paying particular attention to attempts to define and classify the field. It contends that the recognition of the heterogeneous nature of humanities disciplines and approaches is not so much fatal to the

---

13. Ibid 115.
14. Ibid 64. For a classic statement also in a US context see Duncan Kennedy's pamphlet 'Legal Education and the Reproduction of Hierarchy: A Polemic against the System', first self-published in 1983 but republished with critical commentaries in see D Kennedy, *Legal Education and the Reproduction of Hierarchy: A Polemic Against the System* (New York University Press, 2004).
15. Cf. R A Posner, 'The Decline of Law as an Autonomous Discipline 1962-1987' (1987) 100 *Harvard Law Review* 761.

quest for definition and classification but rather underlines the main characteristic of this approach.

Following the work of Sara Ramshaw,[16] who reflects upon the volume as a whole in our concluding chapter, law and humanities is understood as a dynamic interdisciplinary interaction that defies canonisation and categorisation. Law and humanities draws upon the rich and varied approaches from a number of humanities disciplines to transform our understandings of law while at the same time returning the favour by using legal methods (predominantly doctrinal and socio-legal approaches) to enrich the objects of study at the centre of humanities disciplines. This underscores the need to introduce law and humanities by exploring a range of 'law and' interactions in turn from a number of humanities disciplines. This is intended as a starting point that will document how different disciplinary approaches have already been used to study law (and vice versa), enabling greater inter- and trans-disciplinary work to develop from this.

As the second part of this chapter will argue, studying the disciplines that make up law and humanities will enable focus on how the interaction between the two can operate in both directions. This will be achieved by introducing and exploring the use of what we will call the 'x as law/law as x' distinction. Exploring each disciplinary interaction with law reveals the potential for an interdisciplinary study of law and the object of study of that discipline blending legal methods with the disciplinary frames of analysis common within the other non-legal discipline.

The overall purpose of this chapter and indeed this collection is to provide an accessible exploration that introduces law students and scholars to law and humanities, showing that interdisciplinary approaches to law are not limited to the social scientific and that the study of a range of 'law and' disciplinary fields reveals a number of different methods, approaches and ideas that can enrich the study of law while also showing that a legal perspective can return the favour by transforming in turn the other disciplines studied. This is designed to be the first book that those interested in exploring law and humanities, or aspects of law and humanities, pick up. It is designed to whet the appetite and point them to further reading and research both within the 'law and' field of their choice but also within law and humanities broadly underscoring that particular 'law and' studies are enriched by placing them within the wider law and humanities context.

The Development of Law and Humanities

There is a sense in which Maitland's statement that 'Law schools make tough law' seems more applicable than ever.[17] In England and Wales, the long-established Qualifying Law Degree (QLD) has appointed seven subjects which dominate the undergraduate law degree. Although there are now no prescriptions as to the content of these seven

16. S Ramshaw, 'Law and Humanities: A Field without a Canon' (2023) 19(1) *Law, Culture and the Humanities* 77, 79.
17. F W Maitland, *English Law and the Renaissance* (Cambridge University Press, 1901) 25.

subjects, the shelves of textbooks on each of the subjects have led to a common syllabus existing by default: one that is doctrinal and focuses on legal principles as expounded in the senior courts. It is divorced from both the reality of law in practice and the rigorous academic analysis of law given that it largely amounts to the study of law as an autonomous body, the study of law out of context. Matters have worsened in recent years, however. While the study of the seven QLD subjects is still required as the academic stage for those who wish to become barristers, they are no longer obligatory to those who want to go down the solicitor route. That route now requires no academic legal qualifications at all but obliges would-be solicitors to pass the Solicitors Qualifying Examination (SQE). This comprises two stages: the academic SQE 1 (which effectively replaces the QLD requirements) and the vocational SQE 2 (which replaces the Legal Practice Course (LPC)). SQE 1 not only includes a greater number of areas of what it terms 'functioning legal knowledge' than the QLD but also is extremely prescriptive in terms of the content that will be assessed as part of each of them. A common syllabus now exists akin to the specifications published by exam boards for examinations in secondary schools. Moreover, SQE 1 assesses this legal knowledge by means of a multiple choice test akin to the driving theory exam. Law, it seems, is simply a set of rules and principles to be learnt and applied. There is always a best answer that should be selected and the idea that there is any nuance, any debate or any criticism is simply outside the scope of its study. What effect this will have upon future generations of solicitors and their ability to creatively understand and analyse the law remains to be seen. While most Law Schools at the time of writing are not teaching to the letter of SQE 1 in their undergraduate law degrees, its influence cannot be dismissed. Most Law Schools continue to cling to the QLD model, but this is likely to be increasingly infused with SQE expectations as to content and approach as textbooks pay increased attention to the SQE requirements and since most of their students who go on to enter the legal profession will now have to complete the SQE assessments.

This narrowing of academic legal education and the dominance of doctrinal legal studies is particularly odd given that outside the lecture hall and classroom Law Schools have never been so interested in interdisciplinary approaches. Since the end of the twentieth century, a number of different approaches to the study of law have developed in addition to (and sometimes instead of) the dominant doctrinal paradigm. In the Anglo-American world at least a number of 'law and' fields have prospered, in part due to the legacy of the critical turn, aspects of which have now entered the mainstream of academic legal research. The most common 'law and' fields, however, have been tended to be those that are social scientific in focus. Indeed, these have become so prevalent that they are now often regarded as being within the discipline of law itself: the label of socio-legal research denoting research drawing upon social science research methods and the ideas within the sociological, economic, criminological, political science and social theory literatures.[18] Socio-legal approaches are now perhaps dominant in terms

18. Conventionally a distinction was drawn between the sociology of law and socio-legal studies (based on a conception of the sociology of law as a theoretical 'understanding of the nature

of legal research, though doctrinal study continues hold sway in relation to the Law School's teaching.

Although socio-legal studies have become ubiquitous in terms of legal research, particularly in the UK,[19] there has also been an increase in interdisciplinary scholarship on law that draws upon the humanities.[20] While socio-legal approaches tend to understand law as a social system, approaches from humanities subjects can provide a richer understanding of the nature of law. David Nelken has written of the need to develop 'a much more complex picture of law' where 'analogies are more likely to be drawn between law and theology or law and literary theory than between law and the social and policy sciences'.[21] Sionaidh Douglas-Scott has written that 'law is as much a matter of culture as it is a system of rules' and has maintained that law 'has its own aesthetic and may be envisioned as a creative art form as much as a science'.[22]

Law and humanities has grown as a field, not only in the United States where the *Yale Journal of Law and the Humanities* was the first scholarly journal devoted exclusively to the field but also subsequently on this side of the pond.[23] Law and humanities continues to defy categorisation but as the introduction to the first issue of the *Yale Journal of Law and the Humanities* put it, the general aim is 'to restore to legal studies a proper place for the question of values'.[24] For Austin Sarat et al., in the law and humanities 'critical impulses abound, not looking to save or humanize law or lawyers, but to expose their hidden assumptions that structure their work, the values that privilege some views and silence others, the identities that law privileges and those it pushes to the margins and, in doing so, to call law and lawyers to account'.[25]

---

of social order through a study of law' and of socio-legal studies as the empirical study of the 'actual operation of law and its effects upon people': C M Campbell and P Wiles, 'The Study of Law in Society in Britain' (1976) 10 *Law and Society Review* 553), such a distinction is no longer sustainable: see, e.g., R Banaker, *Merging Law and Sociology: Beyond the Dichotomies in Socio-Legal Research* (Galda and Wilch Verlag, 2003) 14–15.

19. A decade ago, Mathias Siems and Daithí Mac Síthigh argued that legal scholars in the UK were faced by a choice as to 'whether to "go American" in moving closer to social sciences, or "go German" in remaining closer to the humanities': Mathias M Siems and Daithí Mac Síthigh, 'Mapping Legal Research' (2012) *Cambridge Law Journal* 651, 673. See also the essays in C Hunter (ed) *Integrating Socio-Legal Studies into the Law Curriculum* (Palgrave, 2012), D Feenan (ed) *Exploring the 'Socio' of Socio-Legal Studies* (Palgrave, 2013) and as means of response, D Cowan and D Wincott (eds) *Exploring the 'Legal' in Socio-Legal Studies* (Palgrave, 2016).
20. The continued existence of these two options is reflected by the way in which funding for legal research projects is available from both the Arts & Humanities Research Council (AHRC) and the Economic and Social Research Council (ESRC).
21. D Nelken, 'Can Law Learn from Social Science?' (2001) 35 *Israel Law Review* 205, 211.
22. S Douglas-Scott, *Law after Modernity* (Hart, 2013) 253.
23. Research centres or clusters titled as 'Law and Humanities' exist at Birkbeck, Warwick and Northumbria Universities, being parts of Law Schools. Journals include *Law and Humanities* and *Law, Culture and the Humanities.*
24. O M Fiss, 'The Challenge Ahead' (1988) 1 *Yale Journal of Law and Humanities*viii, x.
25. A Sarat, M Anderson and C O Frank, 'Introduction: On the Origins and Prospects of the Humanistic Study of Law' in A Sarat, M Anderson and C O Frank (eds) *Law and Humanities: An Introduction* (Cambridge University Press, 2010) 1, 11.

In their exploration of how the 'law and humanities field' has developed, Sarat et al. posit the origins of law and humanities in the United States in the law and literature movement and, in particular, James Boyd White's seminal book *The Legal Imagination*.[26] This led to a focus on the language of law and on law as a language. As Sarat et al. put it:

> If this point of view could be reduced to a maxim, it might be this: Law is a language and language matters. Another way to put it would be to say that the education of lawyers should include the cultivation of a meaningful appreciation of law as rhetoric practice – not just in the sense of an art of persuasion, but of a disciplined, textual self-directed habit of reading, speaking, and above all, writing, that has at its root critical understanding of the links among language, consciousness, and power.[27]

The strong literary focus in the law and humanities movement has been countered, however, most notably by Robin L. West,[28] on the grounds that such an approach would 'leave out much that is nontextual in our interaction with actual people'.[29] There has been a call for perspectives which 'pushes beyond the literary' and raises the question of 'how would a study of the way in which law constitutes persons proceed'.[30] Steven Cammiss and Dawn Watkins have stated that humanities label refers to 'the branch of learning concerned with human culture' and reflects the 'cultural turn'.[31] Yet, the word 'cultural' here can become as generic and meaningless as the word 'social' often becomes in socio-legal studies.

Simon Stern et al. have argued that 'to practice the humanities is to approach, with certain attitudes and sensitivities, a multitude of practices of making (of making things, making meaning, making senses) including relations between those practices of making and the values that may be at stake in such practices and their relations to each other'.[32] Crucially they note that these 'attitudes and sensitivities' include 'sensitivity not so much (and certainly not only) to the regular and patterned, but instead to the irregular and unpatterned' paying attention to 'the unpredictability of human behavior'; 'sensitivity to the blind spots in our abilities to sense who is in anger, suffering or vulnerable'; and 'sensitivity to the apparently superficial, superfluous, unnecessary, insufficient,

26. J Boyd White, *The Legal Imagination* (University of Chicago Press, 1973).
27. A Sarat, M Anderson and C O Frank, 'Introduction: On the Origins and Prospects of the Humanistic Study of Law' in A Sarat, M Anderson and C O Frank (eds) *Law and Humanities: An Introduction* (Cambridge University Press, 2010) 1, 4.
28. R L West, 'Communities, Texts and Law: Reflections on the Law and Literature Movement' (1988) 1 *Yale Journal of Law and Humanities* 154.
29. A Sarat, M Anderson and C O Frank, 'Introduction: On the Origins and Prospects of the Humanistic Study of Law' in A Sarat, M Anderson and C O Frank (eds) *Law and Humanities: An Introduction* (Cambridge University Press, 2010) 1, 7.
30. Ibid 7–8.
31. S Cammiss and D Watkins, 'Legal Research in the Humanities' in D Watkins and M Burton (eds), *Research Methods in Law* (2nd edn, Routledge, 2018) 86, 87.
32. S Stern, M Del Mar and B Meyler, 'Introduction' in S Stern, M Del Mar and B Meyler (eds) *The Oxford Handbook of Law and Humanities* (Oxford University Press, 2020) xxi, xxii.

marginal, or-by-the-by'.[33] As Stern et al. note, while conventionally a law and humanities approach has 'associated law with legal doctrines and rhetoric, in particular, and have looked to the humanities for representations of legal actors and dilemmas, and for ethical resources that can shed light on legal problems', humanities needs to be more widely drawn to 'encompass not only history, literature, art, and philosophy but the whole range of fields that use interpretative methods to study creativity, expression, and the imagination'.[34] They noted:

> These include many fields – such as architecture, geography, book history, cognitive studies, science and technology studies, and performance studies – that influence, and are influenced by legal concepts and methods, but that appear only sporadically, if at all, in law journals.

This heterogeneous list of what studying the humanities or law and humanities includes underscores the lack of a clear definition. Sarat et al. referring to the 'field of law and the humanities' have noted that 'neither institutional attempts to define it (merely as a group of disciplines not found in the social and natural sciences), nor efforts to identify a common methodological foundation (for example, in interpretation) could succeed because they were either too restrictive or too broad'.[35]

Yet, this idea of a heterogeneous cluster of subjects that are not scientific (or perhaps wholly scientific) in outlook is useful in that it provides a loose understanding of what the humanities are, and this looseness is apt given that this also reflects the nature of the grouping itself. Sara Ramshaw has argued that law and humanities exists 'not as a "canon" per se, but as a "field without a canon" or a canon that resists canonization'.[36] For Ramshaw, by its very nature law and humanities needs to 'leap ahead fearlessly to properly defy disciplinary boundaries and move the field beyond siloed thinking', this 'is one of the preliminary aims of law and humanities scholarship and pedagogy'. This requires using the rigour found within humanities disciplines,[37] without insisting upon disciplinary distinctions. Situating law as part of the humanities, then, encourages the

33. Ibid xxiii.
34. Ibid xxiv.
35. A Sarat, M Anderson and C O Frank, 'Introduction: On the Origins and Prospects of the Humanistic Study of Law' in Austin Sarat, Matthew Anderson and Cathrine O Frank (eds) *Law and Humanities: An Introduction* (Cambridge University Press, 2010) 1, 9. Compare: 'Since the nineteenth century the humanities have generally been defined as the disciplines that investigate the expressions of the human mind' (Rs Bod, *A New History of the Humanities* (Oxford University Press, 2013) 1).
36. S Ramshaw, 'Law and Humanities: A Field without a Canon' (2023) 19(1) *Law, Culture and the Humanities* 77, 79.
37. The risk is otherwise that 'Law and Humanities courses end up entertaining and lightening the heavy load of law students as well as giving them a useful cultural gloss': C Douzinas, 'A Humanities of Resistance: Fragments for a Legal History of Humanity' in A Sarat, M Anderson and C O Frank (eds) *Law and Humanities: An Introduction* (Cambridge University Press, 2010) 49, 56.

subversive thinking about boundaries, disciplines and methods. A humanities understanding of law emphasises that a rich methodological toolkit is needed to understand the various dimensions of law and that this extends beyond seeing law as a social science.

It follows from this that introducing law students and legal scholars to law and the humanities requires exploring the various humanities subjects which law can connect with. This is not to entrench disciplinary distinctions but rather to highlight the different approaches that can be taken to understand law. From understanding the often bi-disciplinary approaches of 'law and' fields, comparisons and contrasts can be made that would permit an inter- or even trans-disciplinary approach to be taken. Beginning this way is also desirable given that the experiences of these fields have varied and also differ among jurisdictions. The Anglo-American experience, for instance, has been that the study of law and literature has become well established as a critical perspective on law. The study of law and popular culture has grown from that of law and literature and has been conceptualised in various different ways.[38] It is possible to talk of interactions between the law and particular mediums (law and comics, graphic novels, film, television, computer games and so on) or by genre, while the interactions between law and art and law and music transcend the focus on 'popular' culture. In addition, the study of legal history is long standing but has tended to be institutionalised within Law Schools with much work on interactions between law and history being done elsewhere, either in history departments or by law academics identifying as socio-legal researchers. Much ink has been devoted to law and religion but the field has only crystallised as a specialism fairly recently at least in part in response to increased controversies about the place of religion in the public sphere. Research into law and geography, variously named, has blossomed in recent years and, unlike law and history and law and religion, law and geography has developed very much as an interdisciplinary endeavour. By exploring experiences from different 'law and' experiences in turn it is hoped that this collection will allow comparisons to be made that will further inter- and trans-disciplinary approaches and will underscore the value of seeing these 'law and' fields under the law and humanities umbrella.

The 'X as Law/Law as X' Distinction

By introducing the study of law and humanities through examining various 'law and' interactions in turn it should be possible to highlight their commonalities and differences not with the intention of developing a distinct law and humanities approach but rather of helping those who study particular fields to learn from one another and to benefit from conceptualising their 'law and' field as being under the law and humanities umbrella. This is likely to be particularly advantageous in terms of developing inter- and trans-disciplinary approaches by exploring how the various 'law and' fields compare.

38. See M Leiboff and C Sharp, 'Cultural Legal Studies and Law's Popular Cultures' in C Sharp and M Leiboff (eds) *Cultural Legal Studies: Law's Popular Cultures and the Metamorphosis of Law* (Routledge, 2016) 3.

This can be explored by examining whether and how the various fields employ variations of what may be referred to as the 'x as law/law as x' distinction. This refers to the way in which the interdisciplinary study of law includes the two objects of study and the frames of analysis which cross over. The study of 'x as law' refers to the study of the non-legal discipline from a legal standpoint, while the study of 'law as x' covers the study of law from the standpoint of the other discipline.

The 'x as law/law as x' distinction is most often attributed to the law and literature movement. However, the original and most common distinction is phrased slightly differently as being between 'law in literature' (the examination of 'the possible relevance of literary texts [...] as texts appropriate for legal scholars') and 'law as literature' (which 'seeks to apply the techniques of literary criticism to legal texts').[39] This distinction shows the two objects of study and the frames of analysis: law and literature includes the study of literature through the frame of law ('law in literature') and the study of law through the frame of literature ('law as literature'). The study of law in literature includes the analysis of 'the appearance of legal themes or the depiction of legal actors or processes in fiction or drama';[40] this involves 'looking at how legal issues, legal institutions, and legal actors are portrayed in literature, as well as symbolic uses of law in literary texts'.[41] The study of law as literature involves the 'parsing of such legal texts as statutes, constitutions, judicial opinions, and certain classic scholarly treatises as if they were literary works';[42] this includes examination of 'how legal texts, like court decisions, utilize literary devices, as well as the study of legal hermeneutics'.[43] Robert Weisberg referred to law as literature as 'the more elusive part of the law-literature enterprise' and contended that it included 'legal writing in terms of style and rhetoric' as well as what he referred to as 'hermeneutic subpart', that is, 'the contemporary interest in the techniques of literary criticism being applied to judicial opinions and statutes in order to discern their meaning'.[44] The field can be interpreted very broadly indeed. As David S. Caudill questioned, 'is every law school classroom discussion of the holding in a case as

39. I Ward, *Law and Literature: Possibilities and Perspectives* (Cambridge University Press, 1995) 3.
40. R Weisberg, 'The Law-Literature Enterprise' (1989) 1(1) *Yale Journal of Law & the Humanities* 1.
41. N P Ho, 'Literature as Law? The Confucian Classics as Ultimate Sources of Law in Traditional China' (2019) 31(2) *Law & Literature* 173.
42. R Weisberg, 'The Law-Literature Enterprise' (1989) 1(1) *Yale Journal of Law & the Humanities* 1.
43. N P Ho, 'Literature as Law? The Confucian Classics as Ultimate Sources of Law in Traditional China' (2019) 31(2) *Law & Literature* 173.
44. R Weisberg, 'The Law-Literature Enterprise' (1989) 1(1) *Yale Journal of Law & the Humanities* 1, 36, 2. Robin L West has noted that the law and literature movement comprises the 'literary' (reading literature for 'the value of its insights into the nature of law') the 'jurisprudential' (exploring the 'literary narrative root' of law) and the 'hermeneutic' (using literature to 'glean meaning from legal texts'): R West, 'Literature, Culture and Law at Duke University' in A Sarat, C O Frank and M Anderson (eds), *Teaching Law and Literature* (Modern Language Association, 2011) 98.

a judicial choice between two alternative narratives, one of which was more persuasive, an exercise in law as literature?'[45] For Mary Jane Schenck:

> Law 'as' literature has come to mean not mere reading to appreciate style, but reading legal documents or opinions, analyzing metaphors as socially constructed language, with the goal of deconstructing them. Reading law texts from a neo-Marxist or gender studies perspective, for instance, reveals the historical context of the law and hence a contingency that may justify social change.[46]

Despite the potential breadth of the conventional dichotomy employed in law and literature, the two terms are tended to be interpreted narrowly. As a result, a number of other forms of law and literature have been identified. The study of law and literature has also been said to include the study of 'law of literature': the study of 'laws which impact the production and dissemination of literary texts, such as American laws on free speech';[47] this focuses on 'the regulation of literature by law (e.g., copyright, defamation, and obscenity) and its socio-ideological aspects'.[48] For Norman P. Ho, a fourth way of looking at the law and literature field is the focus on 'literature and legal reform', that is, 'how literature and literary movements have affected the development of law)'.[49] Conversely, a number of scholars have maintained that 'literature in law' is the third category that has emerged following after 'law in literature' and 'law as literature'.[50] This involves the study of how legal sources use literature. This involves the study of how literature is used 'to attain various objectives – as means of persuasion, to make the facts understandable, to invoke empathy, to support legal reasoning, to foreshadow the ultimate decision, derive meanings to words, and sometimes just as a literary embellishment'.[51]

It will be noted, however, that the study of 'literature as law' is missing from these schemas. Although the term is used by some scholars,[52] where it is defined it is often

45. D S Caudill, *Stories about Science in Law: Literary and Historical Images of Acquired Expertise* (Ashgate, 2011) 13.
46. M J Schenck, 'Reading Law as Literature, Reading Literature as Law: A Pragmatist's Approach' (2013) 25 *Cahiers de Recherches Médiévales et Humanistes/Journal of Medieval and Humanistic Studies* 9, 23–24.
47. N P Ho, 'Literature as Law? The Confucian Classics as Ultimate Sources of Law in Traditional China' (2019) 31(2) *Law & Literature* 173.
48. J Gaakeer, 'Law And Literature' in M Sellers and S Kirste (eds), *Encyclopedia of the Philosophy of Law and Social Philosophy* (Springer, 2022).
49. N P Ho, 'Literature as Law? The Confucian Classics as Ultimate Sources of Law in Traditional China' (2019) 31(2) *Law & Literature* 173.
50. A Mittal and V Chaudhary, 'Law and Literature: Interpretation of the Constitution' (2020) 1 *Bennett Journal of Legal Studies* 151, 154–155; G Gadbin-George, 'To Quote or Not to Quote: "Literature in Law" in European Court Decisions and Legal English Teaching' (2013) 64 *ASp* <http://journals.openedition.org/asp/3842>
51. A Mittal and V Chaudhary, 'Law and Literature: Interpretation of the Constitution' (2020) 1 *Bennett Journal of Legal Studies* 151, 154–155.
52. J D Wright, 'Transcending Law and Literature: Literature as Law in Plato, Vico, and Shelley' (2017) 29(2) *Law & Literature* 291; N P Ho, 'Literature as Law? The Confucian Classics

understood narrowly as understanding the legal force of literature rather than the study of literature through a legal lens more broadly. Norman P. Ho, for instance, defines 'literature as law' as the study of 'the use of what are considered literary texts as sources of law for judicial decision-making'.[53] Robin West has argued that while the term has been narrowly used to describe how cultural authorities such as Blackstone can be viewed as having legal authority,[54] it echoes in the term 'culture as law' that can be understood as the analysis of 'culture of all descriptions, high, low, and mid-brow – *Law and Order, Perry Mason, LA Law, CSI, Alley McBeal* and so on – that constitute an irreducible if often ignored or unseen part of our law'.[55] Even this understanding, however, is a narrow interpretation that takes a very literal interpretation of the 'as'. West noted that examining literature as a form of law can shed light upon debates concerning legal pluralism by highlighting how a 'firm distinction between positive law on the one hand and imaginative literature on the other is at best a (slightly overdrawn) contingent truth about the law, and the literature, of our times, and not a necessary truth about the essence of either'. Such an approach, he maintained, would underscore how 'the various distinctions that seem clear and intuitive to us between law and imaginative literature were likely not always so clear, and might not always be so in the future'.

However, the study of 'literature as law' can go further than this. Studying literature through a legal lens does not necessarily require studying literature as a legal authority. It follows from Weisberg's definition of law as literature as 'parsing of such legal texts as statutes, constitutions, judicial opinions, and certain classic scholarly treatises *as if* they were literary works'[56] that the study of literature as law is the study of literary works *as if* they are legal texts. This involves not only studying literature as if it has legal authority but also as if it was interpreted like a legal text. Studying literature through law can, therefore, highlight the commonalities of the two. As West noted:

> Law, like literature, is textual. Law, like all texts, literary and otherwise, therefore requires interpretation. And, for there to be interpretation, there must, in turn, be a community of to some degree like-minded interpreters. Positive law of all forms – statutory, common, and constitutional – and imaginative literature share enough of a 'to-be-interpreted' textual

---

as Ultimate Sources of Law in Traditional China' (2019) 31(2) *Law & Literature* 173; M J Schenck, 'Reading Law as Literature, Reading Literature as Law: A Pragmatist's Approach' (2013) 25 *Cahiers de Recherches Médiévales et Humanistes/Journal of Medieval and umanistic Studies* 9.

53. N P Ho, 'Literature as Law? The Confucian Classics as Ultimate Sources of Law in Traditional China' (2019) 31(2) *Law & Literature* 173, 174.
54. R L West, 'Literature, Culture and Law at Duke University' in A Sarat, C O Frank and M Anderson (eds), *Teaching Law and Literature* (Modern Language Association, 2011) 98.
55. This has been developed and exemplified in W P MacNeil, *Lex Populi: The Jurisprudence of Popular Culture* (Stanford University Press, 2007).
56. R Weisberg, 'The Law-Literature Enterprise' (1989) 1(1) *Yale Journal of Law & the Humanities* 1 (emphasis added).

> essence that it is fruitful to think of law and literature as forms of the same thing – texts requiring interpretation – at least with regards to how we distill meaning.[57]

As Jarrell D. Wright put it, the study of literature as law establishes 'equivalence between the poet and the legislator'.[58] Combining this with the established study of 'literature in law' allows law as literature to be understood as the study of literature from a legal perspective. This allows law and literature to be conceptualised as including both the study of literature as law (the study of literature from a legal perspective) and law as literature (the study of law from a literature perspective). This underscores the commonalities of both law and literature and the two modes of analysis. If the word 'as' is seen as requiring just the narrower study of literature as a source of law, then the word 'through' could be used instead. The field could be reconceptualised as the study of law through literature and literature through law. Regardless of the precise wording, such a distinction (and, to be fair, the law in literature / literature as law distinction) highlights the two modes of analysis and the two linked foci. Such an insistence that law and literature are linked allows scholars to 'experiment in reconstructing the aesthetic in legal terms or the legal in aesthetic terms'.[59]

As might be expected, outside the law and literature movement, the articulation, reliance and applicability of the 'x as law/law as x' distinction have varied from field to field. Similar ideas have been propounded in other fields as many of the chapters that follow will explore. In some conceptualisations, the word 'in' is used for both parts of the distinction. For instance, drawing upon the work of Edward W. Soja,[60] Alexandre Kedar has distinguished between 'geography in law', that is, 'how geography and social space affect law and legal development' and 'law in geography', 'how law contributes to the social production of space, what is the role of law in constructing, organising and legitimating social spatiality'.[61] Similarly, David Delaney has made the distinction between 'Law in Space', the way in which 'situated legal practices, for example,

---

57. R L West, 'Literature, Culture and Law at Duke University' in A Sarat, C O Frank and M Anderson (eds), *Teaching Law and Literature* (Modern Language Association, 2011) 98.
58. J D Wright, 'Transcending Law and Literature: Literature as Law in Plato, Vico, and Shelley' (2017) 29(2) *Law & Literature* 291, 293.
59. R Weisberg, 'The Law-Literature Enterprise' (1989) 1(1) *Yale Journal of Law & the Humanities* 1, 4.
60. Soja distinguished two ways of looking at the relationship between law and geography: the first 'focuses on how geography or more broadly social space, social spatiality, affects law and legal development' examining how 'the law has always involved itself with the location of things, with disputes over turf, territories, boundaries, borders, jurisdictions'; the second deals with the reverse, 'how law shapes geographies', exploring how 'legal understandings and knowledge of law are plied to help in understanding the social production of space, how social spatiality is constructed and organized and expressed': E W Soja, 'Afterword' (1996) 48 *Stanford Law Review* 1421, 1425, 1426.
61. A Kedar, 'On the Legal Geography of Ethnographic Settler States: Notes towards a Research Agenda' in Jane Holder and Carolyn Harrison (eds), *Law and Geography* (Oxford University Press, 2003) 402, 406–407. See also R Sandberg, *Subversive Legal History: A Manifesto for the Future of Legal Education* (Routledge, 2021) chapter 7.

legislation or formal legal judgment, contribute to the shaping and reshaping of the spacialities of social life', and 'Space in Law', 'the analysis and/or critique of the work that spatial representations perform in legal discourse I will call Space-In Law'.[62] The use of the word 'as', 'in' or 'though' seems to make little difference. The point of the distinction is to underscore the interdisciplinary nature of the study – or even the transdisciplinary character of the study. Applying the distinction highlights how the study of law and literature is the work of both academic lawyers and literature experts and how the study of legal geography is similarly the product of both lawyers and geographers, for instance. This is shown by the way in which the Law and Religion academic John Witte Jr has described how 'a new interdisciplinary movement has emerged in the United States dedicated to the study of the religious dimensions of law, the legal dimensions of religion and the interaction of legal and religious ideas and institutions, norms and practices'.[63] The language may differ but the point remains the same: the study of 'law and x' involves the study of the legal dimensions of x as well as the examination of law from the perspective of x. This underscores that the 'law and' analysis is a two-way process.

However, the 'x as law/law as x' distinction variously articulated may ironically perpetuate disciplinary distinctions frustrating its inter- or trans-disciplinary potential. In the context of law and literature, Jarrell D. Wright suggested that the way in which law and literature 'is structured into two main branches that are based on relatively narrow understandings of the relationship between "law" and "literature"' has meant that the movement has 'tended more toward bidisciplinarity than interdisciplinary'.[64] The use of the conjunction 'and' has also been singled out for blame on grounds of perpetuating a binary and instrumental approach.[65] And there is significant tension between 'those who see law and literature as distinct fields with their own ways of finding meaning, and those approaching all texts as performative and open to multiple interpretations is usually construed as a battle of opposites'.[66] In the law and geography context,[67] Nicholas Bromley has criticised similar distinctions on the basis that they 'not only impoverishes inquiry into what is a complex and profoundly subtle relation, but also implicitly

62. D Delaney, 'Beyond the Word: Law as a Thing of this World' in Jane Holder and Carolyn Harrison (eds), *Law and Geography* (Oxford University Press, 2003) 67, 68–69.
63. John Witte, Jr., 'The Study of Law and Religion in the United States: An Interim Report' (2012) 14 *Ecclesiastical Law Journal* 327.
64. J D Wright, 'Transcending Law and Literature: Literature as Law in Plato, Vico, and Shelley' (2017) 29(2) *Law & Literature* 291, 292.
65. J Gaakeer, 'Law And Literature' in M Sellers and S Kirste (eds), *Encyclopedia of the Philosophy of Law and Social Philosophy* (Springer, 2022).
66. This can be conceptualised as 'formalists vs. subjectivists or foundationalist vs. anti-foundationalists': M J Schenck, 'Reading Law as Literature, Reading Literature as Law: A Pragmatist's Approach' (2013) 25 *Cahiers de Recherches Médiévales et Humanistes / Journal of Medieval and Humanistic Studies* 9, 25. This tension is evident in the work of Richard Posner which has responded to and rejected the claims of the Critical Legal Studies movement.
67. On which also see R Sandberg, *Subversive Legal History: A Manifesto for the Future of Legal Education* (Routledge, 2021) chapter 7.

constricts two self-contained categories of discrete objects'.[68] This criticism, however, does not mean that such distinctions be rejected. Rather, it means that emphasis in terms of law and geography should be made of how, in the words of David Delaney, 'the legal and the spatial, the discursive and the material, are inextricable'.[69]

It is also notable that the 'x as law/law as x' distinction does not comfortably apply to all 'law and' fields. This is something that will be explored by many of the chapters that follow. For instance, while it can be said that law and history involves the fusion of legal and historical analyses, it is difficult to follow the approach of other interactions to claim that law and history could include the study of history through the frame of law and the study of law through the frame of history. In terms of law and popular culture, whether the 'x as law/law as x' distinction applies depends in part on how the interaction is conceptualised. The distinction could be applied to law and popular culture as a whole in that this includes the study of popular culture from a legal perspective as well as the study of law as a form of popular culture. This second aspect could just about be applied to law and performing arts such as law and art or law and music. The study of law as a dramatic act and as a narrative could be examined through the study of the theatrical nature of the courtroom, for instance. However, this second aspect does not apply to some of the particular mediums that come under the law and popular culture umbrella. While television, film and graphic novels could be examined from a legal perspective, it would be difficult to see how law could be examined from any of these angles. The 'law as x' will rarely apply apart perhaps from in discussion of law as narrative where legal texts could be likened to these mediums in terms of style, format or authorship.

The 'x as law/law as x' may be more relevant to the study of law and culture where the field is divided not by discipline as this book proposes but instead by genre. The distinction would seem to apply to the study of law and drama or law and comedy. Such studies would include 'law as x' through the study law as a dramatic or comedic discourse. Studying 'x as law' could be interpreted narrowly as the way in which dramatic or comedic sentiments are given legal effect (and perhaps also the legal regulation of the manifestations of these arts) but could more fruitfully be broadened to include the study of the dramatic or comedic works from a legal perspective. This includes how such works include or exclude discussion of law, how they frame legal ideas and how their study can be both enriched by an appreciation of their legal dimension and how such texts can enrich understandings of law, justice and society. Similar conclusions can be reached in relation to the developing field of law and science fiction,[70] which has also emerged from the studies of law and literature and law and popular culture.[71] Although Kieran Tranter has argued that the 'general lawlessness' of much science fiction was

68. N Bromley, *Law, Space and Geographies of Power* (Guilford Press, 1994) xiii.
69. D Delaney, 'Beyond the Word: Law as a Thing of this World' in Jane Holder and Carolyn Harrison (eds), *Law and Geography* (Oxford University Press, 2003) 67, 71.
70. Though this raises the question of how science fiction is to be defined and also risks downplaying the importance of different mediums.
71. For an account of its development, see, e.g. K Tranter, *Living in Technical Legality: Science Fiction and Law as Technology* (Edinburgh University Press, 2018) 4–9.

a major reason why law and humanities scholars paid little attention to science fiction (given their preoccupation with 'law in literature'),[72] there is now ample evidence of the study of the legal aspects of science fiction texts – a study that can be referred to as the study of science fiction as law.[73] Law as science fiction, by contrast, could be used to refer to the study of how science fiction concepts, tropes and framings can be used to understand, critique and re-interpret laws (in the form of legal texts and also as legal discourse). It is also possible to conceptualise two 'law and x' distinctions as overlapping with one another. David S. Caudill has commented how, for instance:

> a fictional text about a scientists testifying in court is not only a literary representation of law (law *in* literature), as well as a literary representation of a scientist (science *in* literature) but the testimony of the scientist is both a legally significant event (law *as* literature) and a scientific text (science *as* literature) that can be analyzed using literary critical or rhetorical tools.[74]

The study of law and science, though clearly outside the scope of this present collection, provides evidence of why the 'x as law/law as x' distinction is useful. Like other 'law and' fields, law and science refers to the field of two distinct social systems[75] that nevertheless are forced to rely upon each other.[76] This is true of both legal practice – where science often provides or assists with evidence – and the academic study of law where a debate exists as to how scientific law should be.[77] As Cedric Charles Gilson has noted, 'law increasingly depends on science for determination of legal truth, so that its conclusions can be drawn more securely. [...] Law has a high expectation of science and scientists in this regard owing to the objectivity, rigour and precision extolled in its methods. It is disappointed when its evidence is doubtful, experts disagree or prove unreliable.'[78] Yet despite (perhaps because of) this dependence, law and science are seen as being distinct

72. Ibid 7.
73. Even according to the narrowest interpretation of science fiction as law, there is room to study laws explored in science fiction texts such as Asimov's 'Three Laws of robotics' and the 'Prime Directive' in *Star Trek:* ibid.
74. D S Caudill, *Stories about Science in Law: Literary and Historical Images of Acquired Expertise* (Ashgate, 2011) 6.
75. To borrow the terminology of Luhmann's social systems theory. Gilson who maintains that 'no theory approaches that of the systems theory of the sociologist Niklas Luhmann for accentuating the categorical disjunction of science and the law': C C Gilson, *The Law-Science Chasm: Bridging Law's Disaffection with Science as Evidence* (Quid Pro Books, 2012) vi.
76. M Freeman, 'Law and Science: Science and Law' in M Freeman and H Reece (eds) *Science in Court* (Ashgate, 1998) 1.
77. Ibid 3. 'There is some irony that, long before the interrelationship between law and science was explored, legal scholarship purported to model itself on the model of natural science': ibid 1.
78. C C Gilson, *The Law-Science Chasm: Bridging Law's Disaffection with Science as Evidence* (Quid Pro Books, 2012) iii.

in terms of scholarship and methodologies.[79] Michael Freeman noted that 'unlike scientific truth, law is created, not discovered' and that while 'natural scientists use data, [...] legal scholarship, by contrast, works with events'.[80] As Gilson put it, 'one is concerned with fact (science) and the other with legality (law).'[81]

Yet, as with other 'law and' fields, the different perspectives of law and science reveal much about themselves from one another. As David S. Caudill has noted, 'law is rhetorical, social and institutional involving ethical dimensions, credibility, cultural authority, and unstable interpretations. But so is science.'[82] In particular, the interaction between law and science reveals the way in which both are constructs. As Gilson noted 'that science is socially constructed is a matter of which law often is unaware of might find incredible'.[83] Grasping this is revelatory for law's understanding of science in that 'law should realise that science represents only a system of inquiry: it is not a privileged source of knowledge, however profound this appears from the outside'.[84] Moreover, this also underscores that the same is true of law. The 'x as law/law as x' distinction, then, not only highlights the differences but interdependencies between law and the other but also underscores the transformation that can be achieved by seeing law through the lens of the other and from seeing the other from the lens of law.

Conclusion

In the 1590s, the most distinguished playwright of all time William Shakespeare was working on the second part of his trilogy of plays on Henry VI. *Henry VI, Part 2*, concerned the events that led to the War of the Roses, focusing on the squabbling of the nobles. In Act IV, Scene II, Jack Cade who is leading a rebellion against the king is having a discussion with the murderous villain Dick the Butcher. They are discussing how they can take over and improve the country. At one point, in a line that will be much quoted and subject to a great deal of discussion as to its interpretation, Dick the Butcher turns to Cade and suggests:

> The first thing we do, let's kill all the lawyers.

***

79. M Freeman, 'Law and Science: Science and Law' in M Freeman and H Reece (eds) *Science in Court* (Ashgate, 1998) 1.
80. Ibid 2.
81. C C Gilson, *The Law-Science Chasm: Bridging Law's Disaffection with Science as Evidence* (Quid Pro Books, 2012) iv.
82. D S Caudill, *Stories about Science in Law: Literary and Historical Images of Acquired Expertise* (Ashgate, 2011) 140.
83. C C Gilson, *The Law-Science Chasm: Bridging Law's Disaffection with Science as Evidence* (Quid Pro Books, 2012) v.
84. Ibid iv.

Shakespeare's 'kill all the lawyers' line has been subject to a number of explanations ranging from seeing it as a criticism of legal bureaucracy and the way in which the law maintains the status quo to interpreting it as praise of how lawyers defend against the abuse of and seizing of power.[85] Though clearly a joke and a line uttered by a character that the audience is expected to find unsavoury, the popularity of the line underscores the image problem that lawyers have. Clearly 'thinking like a lawyer' is not always seen as a good thing.

There is considerable value to the doctrinal legal education that is central to what most Law Schools teach. It has the potential to be intellectually stimulating and to develop important transferable skills. However, it needs to be supplemented – some might say, corrected – by other methods. This chapter has argued that Law Schools still 'make tough law'[86] and that interdisciplinary correctives are needed in legal education to correct the prevalent 'legalism' perpetuated by doctrinal legal study. [87]

Shakespeare's 'kill all the lawyers' line and its positioning in one of his history plays underlines the value of a law and humanities approach. Law is ever present in textual, audio and visual arts; it is a constant across time and space. This means that the various 'law and' fields that draw upon humanities disciplines can provide a useful perspective upon law that questions, expands and reconstructs the understandings that are perpetuated by doctrinal legal studies. This can supplement/correct legal analysis and legal analysis can return the favour by bringing a new insight to bear upon the subject of study in the other discipline. This collection rests upon the premise that a law and humanities approach is mutually beneficial: placing law in the context of the humanities allows the humanities to transform our understanding of law and vice versa.

The aim of this volume is to provide an accessible introduction that introduces a range of 'law and' fields within the law and humanities umbrella. This focus on law and humanities is apt given that most interdisciplinary movements in law – which are much more common in research than teaching – tend to draw upon the social sciences. The terms 'interdisciplinary' and 'socio-legal' have become interchangeable, though it may be questioned sometimes how much such work draws upon literatures and methods from outside the Law School. Valuable though socio-legal approaches to law are, this volume contends that approaches from law and humanities can provide a different and equally necessary way of understanding and questioning law. This is despite the fact that it is not possible to neatly define what a law and humanities approach constitutes or entails. This chapter has argued that the heterogeneity of the approaches that come under the law and humanities umbrella is actually a definitional attribute. To study law

85. See D Kornstein, *Kill All the Lawyers? Shakespeare's Legal Appeal* (Princeton University Press, 1994) 26 *et seq.* As Ian Ward has pointed out, it was not that Cade wished to abandon the law but rather than he wanted to rewrite it. Although Cade authorised the destruction of the Inns of Court, he also asserted that he would rule by continuing to articulate the laws of England: I Ward, *Shakespeare and the Legal Imagination* (Butterworths, 1999) 140.
86. F W Maitland, *English Law and the Renaissance* (Cambridge University Press, 1901) 25.
87. R L West, *Teaching Law: Justice, Politics and the Demands of Professionalism* (Cambridge University Press, 2014) 114.

and humanities is to undertake a dynamic interdisciplinary interaction that defies canonisation and categorisation but which transforms both the understanding of law and of at least one other discipline.

This collection contends that introducing the field of law and humanities by exploring a range of 'law and' approaches in turn enables comparisons to be made between them and can underscore how this mutual blending is a key – if not the key – characteristic of law and humanities studies if it is understood as an inter- or even trans-disciplinary study. This can be usefully explored by examining whether and if so how the 'x as law/law as x' distinction is used in various 'law and' studies. The aim here is not to identify let alone stipulate a law and humanities method that can be taken but rather to show the range of disciplinary methods that a law and humanities study can take and to stress that a two-way process is required. The chapters that follow are organised alphabetically by discipline and are not designed to provide a comprehensive or exhaustive account of the number of 'law and' disciplines within the humanities. Moreover, each chapter provides an account of the respective 'law and' interaction from the author's (or authors') particular vantage point. There are other interactions we could have included, different ways in which we could have divided things up and every 'law and' field could have been examined in a multitude of different ways from a range of other perspectives. It is hoped, however, that each chapter will provide an accessible guide that provides one way of introducing the field and will show the value of a law and humanities approach. The intention is that the volume as a whole will underscore how a number of different methods, approaches and ideas that can enrich the study of law while also showing that a legal perspective can return the favour by transforming in turn the other disciplines studied.

Chapter Two

LAW AND ARCHAEOLOGY

Emma Nottingham

Introduction: Legal Archaeology – Methodology or Metaphor?

This chapter explores the intersection of the disciplines of law and archaeology, through the lens of the methodology of legal archaeology. Law and archaeology both involve physical and intellectual activity, and connections between law and archaeology can arise in different ways. Archaeologists need to follow law and regulations for managing archaeological sites, including how they carry out excavations and in relation to what they find. For example, there are laws which regulate the finding of artefacts classed as treasure,[1] certain historical sites are protected by the law[2] and a licence is needed for the excavation of human remains.[3] Materials or objects excavated during an archaeological dig might give insights about the law at a particular time or tell us something about historical relationships between people and the law. Much like other 'law and' movements, there are different ways in which we could depict the various interactions between law and archaeology.[4] We might examine 'law as archaeology', whereby law is analysed using what would usually be an archaeological approach, or 'archaeology as law', where archaeological research is conducted according to approaches that are more familiar to law researchers. We can also consider 'law of archaeology', exploring how archaeology is subject to legal regulation, or 'law in archaeology', investigating what an archaeological finding can tell us about law, or perhaps 'archaeology of law', which could involve analysis of law inspired by archaeological techniques.

This chapter is not concerned with all the possible ways in which the disciplines of law and archaeology interact but is primarily focused on exploring the methodology of legal archaeology, to consider whether we can learn more about its scope by looking to the discipline of archaeology itself, rather than simply using archaeology-related

---

1. Treasure Act 1996.
2. Ancient Monuments and Archaeological Areas Act 1979.
3. https://www.gov.uk/government/publications/apply-to-excavate-human-remains-for-archaeological-purposes (accessed 18.03.22).
4. For examples of work considering law and archaeology see, J Carman, *Valuing Ancient Things: Archaeology and Law* (Leicester University Press 1996); J Carman, 'Legislation in Archaeology: Overview and Introduction' in C Smith (ed) *Encyclopaedia of Global Archaeology* (Springer 2014) 4469; K P Smith and A Reynolds, 'Introduction: The Archaeology of Legal Culture' (2014) 45(5) *World Archaeology* 687.

terminology as a metaphor. Thus, the aim of this chapter is to outline the current understandings of legal archaeology alongside an examination of aspects of what archaeologists do, in order to highlight the extent to which the discipline of archaeology has synergies with legal archaeology. The purpose of this analysis is to enable us to consider the use of the archaeology language within this approach and help us to realise legal archaeology as an established and recognisable socio-legal methodology, rather than simply as a metaphor or as something that is absorbed into the canon of legal history.[5] This chapter argues that while there are overlaps with types of legal history and socio-legal studies more generally, it is worth treating legal archaeology as its own methodology. It therefore seeks to defend legal archaeology as an important and distinct approach to the study of law for both scholars and students, as well as urging law practitioners to appreciate the value that legal archaeology can bring to their practice. The chapter begins with an outline of the development of legal archaeology, how it has been used in the Law School both for academic research and for learning and teaching the law and how it challenges the doctrinal method as the dominant method in legal scholarship. It then explores connections between the disciplines of law and archaeology, to help us understand that the use of archaeology terminology is not simply to serve as a metaphor but can help us to realise legal archaeology as a credible socio-legal methodology which can draw new and important conclusions.

The Emergence of Legal Archaeology

Coined by Brian Simpson in 1995,[6] legal archaeology is a socio-legal methodology employed by scholars in order to undertake an in-depth, micro-level, contextual case analysis. Developed for both legal scholarship and as an alternative pedagogic teaching method, legal archaeology has received little academic attention, compared to other socio-legal methodologies. Yet it is an important and useful tool which may lead scholars and law students to different and new insights and thus it is worth taking the time to further explore its potential. In his book, *Leading Cases in the Common Law*, Simpson stated,

> [A] reported case does in some ways resemble those traces of past human activity—crop marks, post holes, the footings of walls, pipe stems, pottery shards, kitchen middens, and so forth, from which the archaeologist attempts, by excavation, scientific testing, comparison, and analysis to reconstruct and make sense of the past. Cases need to be treated as what they are, fragments of antiquity, and we need, like archaeologists, gently to free these fragments from the overburden of legal dogmatics, and try, by relating them to other evidence, which has to be sought outside the law library, to make sense of them as events in history and incidents in the evolution of the law.[7]

5. For discussion of Legal History, see Russell Sandberg's chapter on 'Law and History' in this volume.
6. A W B Simpson, *Leading Cases in the Common Law* (Clarendon Press 1995) 12.
7. Ibid.

An example of Simpson's legal archaeology is *Cannibalism and the Common law*,[8] a study of the well-known English case of *R v Dudley and Stephens*.[9] Simpson identified that, in spite of this case receiving considerable scholarly attention, opportunities to gain a 'real understanding' of the case were limited.[10] He outlined that '[t]here have been many accounts [...] in books periodicals, and newspapers; [but] few have added any real information, and most have been grossly inaccurate'.[11] Through a contextualised examination of historical sources found in archives and by consulting certain individuals including captains, academics and archivists,[12] Simpson provided an in-depth narrative and established the finer details of the case that had not previously been discussed and that might have otherwise been lost or forgotten. He provided 'a panoramic view'[13] of the case including the people involved, the places, the history and the setting, which led the court to discussions about the defence of necessity. Simpson also revealed that an earlier account of the case by MacCormick,[14] which was considered to be one of the most detailed studies prior to Simpson's, contained inaccuracies.[15]

When Simpson coined the phrase legal archaeology, the practice of studying cases in a contextualised way was not new, as there were already examples of other scholars who had engaged in this kind of work.[16] For example, Danzig's 1975 publication on the case of *Hadley v Baxendale*[17] has been considered one of the earliest known examples of legal archaeology. However, the research does not appear to have been conducted under this label.[18] In the twenty-first century, there have been further examples of legal archaeology case studies, but even some of this more recent research, which has all the hallmarks of a legal archaeology study, has not necessarily been defined as such or

8. A W B Simpson, *Cannibalism and the Common Law* (Penguin 1984).
9. (1884) 14 QBD 273 DC.
10. A W B Simpson, *Cannibalism and the Common Law* (Penguin 1984) x.
11. Ibid x, 306.
12. Ibid xi, 339.
13. M Dillon, 'A W Brian Simpson, *Cannibalism and the Common Law*' (1984) 24(4) *Santa Clara Law Review* 1019, 1021.
14. D MacCormick, *Blood on the sea* (Frederick Muller 1962).
15. A W B Simpson, *Cannibalism and the Common Law* (Penguin 1984) x.
16. For example, On *M'Naghten's Case*, 8 Eng. Rep. 718 (HL 1843), see N Walker, *Crime and Insanity in England* (Edinburgh University Press 1968) Ch. 5; On *Hadley v Baxendale* [1854] 9 *Ex*. 341, 156 Eng. Rep. 145, see R. Danzig, 'Hadley v Baxendale: A study in the Industrialization of the Law' (1975) 4 *Journal of Legal Studies* 249; On *Rylands v Fletcher* (1868) LR 3 HL 330, see A W B Simpson, 'Legal Liability for Bursting Reservoirs: The Historical Context of Rylands v Fletcher' (1984) 13 *Journal of Legal Studies* 209; On *American Banana United Fruit Co. Island RR*, 248 NY 339, 162 NE 99 (1928), see J T Noonan, *Persons and Masks of the Law* (1976), 65–151; On *Carlill v Carbolic Smoke Ball Co.* [1893] I QB 256, see A W B Simpson, 'Quackery and Contract Law: The Case of the Carbolic Smoke Ball' (1985) 14 *Journal of Legal Studies* 345.
17. (1854) EWHC J70.
18. D L Threedy, 'Legal Archaeology: Excavating Cases, Reconstructing Context' (2006) 80 *Tulane Law Review* 1197, 1198.

made any reference to the work of Simpson.[19] Some scholars appear to have associated legal archaeology with legal history. For instance, Ziff has considered legal archaeology to be akin to micro-history[20] and Threedy has described it as a 'subcategory of Legal History'.[21] Although there are obvious overlaps with some types of legal history, especially since legal historians do undertake legal archaeology projects, scholars such as Sandberg have observed that legal archaeology studies tend not to have been integrated into the legal history canon.[22] Accordingly Novkov has stated, 'not all history is archaeological in its approach'[23] and Donahue has maintained that, 'one does not have to be trained as an historian in order to use [legal archaeology]'.[24] Legal archaeology is one means by which we can research law and history, but it is distinct from other historical and legal methods. Moreover, while most examples of legal archaeology are historic, the methodology could be applied to cases whose judgement was published last week or even be used to analyse an on-going 'living' case, to help (re)conceptualise law in the present.[25]

Scholars have associated legal archaeology with the legal storytelling,[26] 'the narrative turn'[27] of legal scholarship and the law and literature movement.[28] Some researchers

19. M Chapman, *The Snail and the Ginger Beer: The Singular Case of Donoghue v Stevenson* (Wildy Simmonds and Hill 2009); D K Williams, *Defenders of the Unborn: The Pro-Life Movement before Roe v Wade* (Oxford University Press 2016).
20. B Ziff, 'The Great Onyx Cave Cases – A Micro-History' (2013) 40 *Northern Kentucky Law Review* 1, 46.
21. D L Threedy, 'Legal Archaeology: Excavating Cases, Reconstructing Context' (2006) 80 *Tulane Law Review* 1197; J Novkov, 'Legal Archaeology' (2011) 64(2) *Political Research Quarterly* 348, 351. For further discussion of Legal History see R W Gordon, 'Critical Legal Histories' (1984) 36 *Stanford Law Review* 57; D Ibbetson, 'Historical Research in Law' in M Tush et and P Cane (eds) *The Oxford Handbook of Legal Studies* (Oxford University Press 2005); A Musson and C Stebbins (eds), *Making Legal History* (Cambridge University Press 2012) and Russell Sandberg's chapter on 'Law and History' in this volume.
22. R Sandberg, *Subversive Legal History: A Manifesto for the Future of Legal Education* (Routledge 2021) 32.
23. J Novkov, 'Legal Archaeology' (2011) 64(2) *Political Research Quarterly* 348, 351.
24. C Donahue Jr, 'A Legal Historian Looks at the Case Method' (1991) 19 *Northern Kentucky Law Review* 17.
25. Ibid; A Shalleck, 'Pedagogical Subversion in Clinical Teaching: The Women & (and) the Law Clinic and the Intellectual Property Clinic as Legal Archaeology' (2003) *Texas Journal of Women and the Law* 113, 120.
26. P L Caron, Introduction: 'Tax Archaeology' in P L Caron (ed) *Tax Stories* (Foundation Press, 2009) 1; P L Caron, 'Back to the Future: Teaching Law through Stories' (2002) 71 *University of Cincinnati Law Review* 405; R L Rabin and S D Sugarman (eds), *Torts Stories* (West Academic 2003); R Lempert (ed), *Evidence Stories* (Foundation Press 2006); R Weisberg and D Coker (eds), *Criminal Law Stories* (Foundation Press 2012); D G Baird (ed), *Contract Stories* (Foundation Press 2007).
27. D L Threedy, 'Legal Archaeology: Excavating Cases, Reconstructing Context' (2006) 80 *Tulane Law Review* 1197, 1199–200, 1234.
28. P A Lombardo, 'Teaching Health Law - Legal Archaeology: Recovering the Stories behind the Cases' (2008) 36 *The Journal of Law, Medicine & Ethics* 589; W Twining, 'What is the Point of Legal Archaeology?' (2012) 3(2) *Transnational Legal Theory* 166, 170.

have referred to the legal archaeology style of analysis as 'the case method',[29] 'contextual case studies',[30] 'cases-in-context',[31] or they have depicted it as a method for case biography.[32] Yet several scholars make no mention of their methodological approach at all. Perhaps scholars are doing legal archaeology without realising, especially since the term has not yet become part of the mainstream knowledge of legal researchers. This has rendered it difficult to recognise legal archaeology as an established socio-legal methodology and to properly understand where it fits within the wider landscape of socio-legal research. Sandberg has suggested that legal archaeology has 'defied categorisation',[33] and Threedy has observed that 'few scholars have conceptualized the methodology as a field of study in its own right'.[34] She further suggested that legal archaeology 'remains a challenging and sometimes misunderstood approach to the study of law'.[35]

If it is not clear where legal archaeology research fits and if the exercise of legal archaeology can be carried out under a different label, or without any label at all, we might doubt whether we should even call this practice legal archaeology. Questions can also be raised as to why Simpson coined the phrase legal archaeology, and what gains there are, if any, from giving this approach its own identity and from using archaeology-related terminology in order to do so. In fact, we might see some justification in Twining's notable critique of Simpson's work in which he asked, 'what is the point of legal archaeology?'[36] However, as is argued throughout this chapter, archaeology terminology is not simply a metaphor but can help us to understand legal archaeology as a methodology for case study research. Thus, the terminology serves an important purpose for clarifying the researcher's approach and for grounding the research within an existing body of literature. It further helps the researcher to be explicit about the methodological choices that are being made or refrained from. Without the label of legal archaeology, the work and the researcher conducting the work, does not have the opportunity to become fully immersed into the existing body of literature in which they can benefit from the work of others before them. Situating research into a body of literature gives a researcher a foundation on which they can place their work. As is outlined

29. C Donahue Jr., 'A Legal Historian Looks at the Case Method' (1991) 19 *Northern Kentucky Law Review* 17.
30. D L Threedy, 'Legal Archaeology: Excavating Cases, Reconstructing Context' (2006) 80 *Tulane Law Review* 1197, 1199–1200.
31. J Vogel, 'Cases in Context: Lake Champlain Wars, Gentrification and Ploof v. Putnam' (2001) 45 *Saint Louis University Law Journal* 791.
32. C Jones and J Montgomery, 'Competing Narratives in a Case Biography: A Tale of Two Citadels' (2020) 47(3) *Journal of Law and Society* 412; M Franklin, 'Biography of a Legal Dispute' (1968) 46 *Syracuse Law Review* 1243.
33. D L Threedy, 'Unearthing Subversion with Legal Archaeology' (2003) 13 *Texas Journal of Women & Law* 133, 135.
34. D L Threedy, 'Legal Archaeology: Excavating Cases, Reconstructing Context' (2006) 80 *Tulane Law Review* 1197.
35. D L Threedy, 'Legal Archeology and Feminist Legal Theory: A Case Study of Gender and Domestic Violence' (2008) 29 *Women's Rights Law Reporter* 171, 192.
36. W Twining, 'What Is the Point of Legal Archaeology?' (2012) 3 *Transnational Legal Theory* 166.

later in the chapter, when we look to the discipline of archaeology to help us understand the potential of legal archaeology, we can immerse ourselves even more.

Legal Archaeology in the Law School

I have argued elsewhere that legal archaeology research is 'transformative' and 'changes the way you see all cases'.[37] It is therefore unsurprising that scholars have observed a profound impact on student learning.[38] Legal archaeology puts the human interest and experiences back into the study of Law, including the people, places and timing, which helps students to realise that no two cases are alike and that each one is variable, unique and subjective.[39] It provides the opportunity for more creative, organic and curiosity-based learning,[40] even putting fun and travel into the experience.[41] Shalleck suggests that legal archaeology gives students the opportunity to understand the chaos, inconsistency and ambiguity of stories, revealing the interaction between conflicting stories and how stories can be framed and reframed. Accordingly, she notes that legal archaeology encourages students to ask different questions and appreciate that significant and even subversive findings can be made when we are not confined to prioritising doctrine.[42] Exposure to the qualitative differences between a legal archaeology case study and a doctrinal case study teaches students that, when we invest the time to examine beyond the case report and delve into the wider context, there are different ways of analysing and constructing case facts.[43] Students therefore learn that we should not necessarily over-rely on published case reports or take them at face value. The learning experience may even go as far as questioning whether a case report should be considered to be a

37. E Nottingham, 'We Should all Get our Hands Dirty: Reflections on Why Lawyers Should Become Archaeologists' (2022) *Frontiers of Sociolegal Studies*. Available at https://frontiers.csls.ox.ac.uk/lawyers-as-archaeologists; E Nottingham, 'Digging into Legal Archaeology: A Methodology for Case Study Research' (2022) 49(1) *Journal of Law and Society* 16.
38. D L Threedy, 'Legal Archaeology: Excavating Cases, Reconstructing Context' (2006) 80 *Tulane Law Review* 1197, 1201.
39. Ibid 1200; E Nottingham, 'Digging into Legal Archaeology: A Methodology for Case Study Research' (2022) 49(1) *Journal of Law and Society* 16, 18 and 26.
40. J L Maute, 'Response: The Values of Legal Archaeology' (2000) 2000 *The Utah Law Review* 223, 229.
41. Ibid 226.
42. D L Threedy, 'Unearthing Subversion with Legal Archaeology' (2003) 13 *Texas Journal of Women and the Law* 133, 134; R Sandberg, *Subversive Legal History: A Manifesto for the Future of Legal Education* (Routledge 2021); A Shalleck, 'Pedagogical Subversion in Clinical Teaching: the Women & the Law Clinic and the Intellectual Property Clinic as Legal Archaeology' (2003) 13(1) *Texas Journal of Women and the Law* 113, 117–118.
43. A Shalleck, 'Pedagogical Subversion in Clinical Teaching: The Women & the Law Clinic and the Intellectual Property Clinic as Legal Archaeology' (2003) 13(1) *Texas Journal of Women and the Law* 113, 118, 130–131; D L Threedy, 'Legal Archaeology: Excavating Cases, Reconstructing Context' (2006) 80 *Tulane Law Review* 1197, 1220–1221.

primary source.[44] In addition, students likely encounter macro-level inquiries about how the legal system functions and therefore gain not only a more detailed understanding of a specific case at the micro-level and its context but a 'bigger picture' understanding of the operation of the common law and the doctrine of precedent.[45]

Scholars have explained that legal archaeology equips students with practical skills important for legal practice such as representing clients, inquiry into facts and effective presentation of cases.[46] There are different ways in which students can engage with legal archaeology in order to acquire such skills. They might undertake their own legal archaeology case study or they can examine existing studies. For example, scholars in the United States have set up classes or modules in which students actively undertake legal archaeology projects,[47] or alternatively some scholars have suggested that students could read a completed work and then revisit it when learning particular doctrines.[48] Shalleck has considered legal archaeology to be an effective pedagogic method in her clinical law modules, and Fernandez developed a module, entitled 'Legal Archaeology: Studies in Cases in Context', entirely dedicated to examining legal archaeology works.[49] Indeed, Threedy has identified that the contextual approach to cases has been incorporated into a number of first-year case books.[50]

Although legal archaeology as a learning and teaching tool has gained popularity among certain scholars, its use remains limited. Scholars who have engaged with legal archaeology research themselves and then integrated this into their teaching appear to be the main advocates of this approach. In UK Law Schools, legal archaeology is under-utlilised or most likely not engaged with at all. Lack of published research on legal archaeology in the UK makes it difficult to decipher perspectives on this approach as a teaching practice. It is likely that the time-consuming nature of legal archaeology research,[51] the pressure to cover many cases and topics within an area of law, the time

44. E Nottingham, 'Digging into Legal Archaeology: A Methodology for Case Study Research' (2022) 49(1) *Journal of Law and Society* 16.
45. For discussion on legal archaeology and the doctrine of precedent, see Ibid 29.
46. J L Maute, 'Response: The Values of Legal Archaeology' (2000) 2000 *The Utah Law Review* 223, 225; A Shalleck, 'Pedagogical Subversion in Clinical Teaching: the Women & the Law Clinic and the Intellectual Property Clinic as Legal Archaeology' (2003) 13(1) *Texas Journal of Women and the Law* 113, 118, 130–131; D L Threedy, 'Legal Archaeology: Excavating Cases, Reconstructing Context' (2006) 80 *Tulane Law Review* 1197, 1220–1221.
47. D L Threedy, 'Legal Archaeology: Excavating Cases, Reconstructing Context' (2006) 80 *Tulane Law Review* 1197, 1198 n5, 1202 n21; D L Threedy, 'Legal Archeology and Feminist Legal Theory: A Case Study of Gender and Domestic Violence' (2008) 29 *Women's Rights Law Reporter* 171, 190–191.
48. J L Maute, 'Response: The Values of Legal Archaeology' (2000) 2000 *The Utah Law Review* 223, 229.
49. https://archive.org/details/legalarcheologys2011fern/mode/2up (accessed 20.10.22).
50. D L Threedy, 'Legal Archaeology: Excavating Cases, Reconstructing Context' (2006) 80 *Tulane Law Review* 1197, 1199.
51. J L Maute, 'Response: The Values of Legal Archaeology' (2000) 2000 *Utah Law Review* 223, 223–224; J Novkov, 'Legal Archaeology' (2011) 64(2) *Political Research Quarterly* 348, 358; D L Threedy, 'Legal Archaeology: Excavating Cases, Reconstructing Context' (2005–2006) 80

it takes to redesign curriculums[52] and the need to adhere to Professional Statutory and Regularity Body (PSRB) requirements has meant that little room has been left for legal archaeology.

Tensions also exist for the academic researcher. In 1986, Twining stated that it would be a 'brave young legal scholar' who would risk tenure or reputation on doing legal archaeology.[53] In the modern-day context, at least in the UK, there is institutional pressure to produce quantities of high-scoring outputs for the Research Excellence Framework (REF). Legal archaeology, as a labour-intensive and time-consuming endeavour, might not be an appealing way to maximise the efficiency of meeting such targets.[54] Additionally, doctoral students might find it difficult to complete a legal archaeology project within the suggested three-to-four-year timeframe now common for PhD programmes in the UK, especially if their prior legal academic work has primarily been focused around traditional doctrinal approaches to analysing the law, which is the focus of most undergraduate law programmes and many Master's degree programmes. A new legal archaeology researcher might find it difficult to immediately find a network of legal scholars who appreciate the conduct of legal archaeology research, as focus on methodology is still relatively limited within legal studies.

Archaeology is a respected field of study which is also subject to pedagogic constraints and institutional research pressures. The discipline of archaeology has had to grapple with similar tensions and thus it may help legal archaeologists find further justification for their practice. Exposure to archaeologists and what they do will not only expand the interdisciplinary knowledge of a legal scholar but also enable researchers to better defend legal archaeology as an important and worthwhile venture which can yield excellent outcomes for both research and pedagogy. A researcher, or even a Law School, that is new to legal archaeology would therefore be advised to place value on what can be learnt from those outside of law, especially archaeologists and scholars who have experience of the complexity and indeterminacy of studying facts and lived experiences using original sources. The synergies between archaeology and law drawn

Tulane Law Review 1197, 1207; J L Maute, 'Response: The Values of Legal Archaeology' (2000) *Utah Law Review* 223, 223–224; P A Lombardo, 'Teaching Health Law, Legal Archaeology: Recovering the Stories behind the Cases' (2008) 36(3) *Journal of Law Medicine & Ethics* 179, 182; J Novkov, 'Legal Archaeology' (2011) 64(2) *Political Research Quarterly* 348, 358; D L Threedy, 'Legal Archaeology: Excavating Cases, Reconstructing Context' (2005–2006) 80 *Tulane Law Review* 1197, 1207.

52. J L Maute, 'Response: The Values of Legal Archaeology' (2000) 2000 *The Utah Law Review* 223, 228.
53. W Twining, 'Cannibalism and Legal Literature' (1986) 6(3) *Oxford Journal of Legal Studies* 423, 423.
54. J L Maute, 'Response: The Values of Legal Archaeology' (2000) 2000 *Utah Law Review* 223, 223–224; J Novkov, 'Legal Archaeology' (2011) 64(2) *Political Research Quarterly* 348, 358; D L Threedy, 'Legal Archaeology: Excavating Cases, Reconstructing Context' (2005–2006) 80 *Tulane Law Review* 1197, 1207. J L Maute, 'Response: The Values of Legal Archaeology' (2000) 2000 *Utah Law Review* 223, 223–224.

in this chapter might help to address some of the discomfort towards legal archaeology and provide reassurance of its value.

More than a Metaphor

Early use of the word 'archaeology' within legal archaeology discussions appeared to be focused on a metaphor for essentially digging into a case. Simpson's original metaphor referred to words such as 'excavation', 'scientific testing', 'comparison' and 'antiquity', all words commonly associated with the discipline of Archaeology.[55] It is not clear whether Simpson intended his archaeology-related terminology to simply be a metaphor or whether he was using this language to develop a new approach or methodology. It is possible that he was trying to differentiate his work from more mainstream ways of doing history, including some of his own previous historical work.[56] But it is equally possible that he was trying to create a movement in legal scholarship, towards more contextualised types of analysis which realise the benefits of not being constrained by doctrine. Campbell suggested that Simpson wanted to use his archaeological studies of leading cases to critique common law reasoning.[57] Even prior to Simpson, scholars engaging in this kind of work were likely trying to show something bigger and make observations beyond the case being studied. For instance, Danzig argued that reflecting on facts, timing and setting helps to 'comprehend the processes of doctrinal innovation, growth, and decay'.[58]

Simpson's legal archaeology research received high praise,[59] but this approach to studying cases was against the dominant doctrinal trend in legal scholarship and thus was also met with scepticism.[60] Despite being a supporter of the contextual study of law and fact analysis, more generally,[61] Twining criticised Simpson's legal archaeology for its distance from doctrine and lack of focus and questioned the relevance of the work beyond it being simply a piece of entertainment.[62] Simpson's work included little

55. A W B Simpson, *Leading Cases in the Common Law* (Clarendon Press 1995) 12.
56. A W B Simpson, *An Introduction to the History of the Land Law* (Oxford University Press 1961); A W B Simpson, *A History of the Common Law of Contract: The Rise of the Action of Assumpsit* (Oxford University Press 1987).
57. D Campbell, Book Review. *Landmark Cases in the Law of Contract* (2009) 30 *Journal of Legal History* 107, 109.
58. R Danzig, 'Hadley v Baxendale: A Study in the Industrialization of the Law' (1975) *The Journal of Legal Studies* 249, 250.
59. R C Berring, '*Cannibalism and the Common Law*; by A. W. B Simpson' (1985) 73 *California Law Review* 252; M J Prichard, '*Cannibalism and the Common Law;* by A. W. B Simpson' (1985) 44 *Cambridge Law Journal* 482.
60. D L Threedy, 'Unearthing Subversion with Legal Archaeology' (2003) 13 *Texas Journal of Women and the Law* 133, 144.
61. W Twining, 'Taking Facts Seriously' (1984) 34 *Journal of Legal Education* 22.
62. W Twining, 'Cannibalism and Legal Literature' (1986) 6 *Oxford J. of Legal Studies* 423, 424; W Twining, 'What Is the Point of Legal Archaeology?' (2012) 3 *Transnational Legal Theory* 166, 171; W Twining, 'Reading Law' (1989) 24 *Valparaiso University Law Review* 1, 10.

discussion as to the purpose of legal archaeology, as he did not draw explicit conclusions, which made clear the relevance of the study and left it to the reader to infer, nor did he provide any guidance on how to design this type of project.[63] However, in the twenty-first century, scholars have further explored the parameters of legal archaeology and sought to offer further explanation of the methodology following their own experiences of conducting legal archaeology projects. This more recent research shows the emergence of legal archaeology as a distinct, purposeful methodology, which helps to defend it from earlier criticism.

The work of Threedy is significant among scholars for contributing to the development of legal archaeology as a methodology in its own right. Threedy continued the metaphor advanced by Simpson stating, 'Just as archaeologists reconstruct a site from clues embedded in the earth, legal archaeologists reconstruct the context of a reported opinion from clues embedded in the opinion, the trial transcript, and other contemporaneous documents.'[64] Additionally, she stated that 'legal archaeology attempts to consider the relevance of the case as a historical artifact in society, as well as in the development of the law'.[65] Threedy's analogy of an archaeological site is a useful addition to Simpsons' original metaphor. However, most notable is how her research appears to have treated legal archaeology as more than a metaphor and as a distinct methodology for socio-legal research, which can draw new and important conclusions.[66]

Threedy has argued, '[l]egal archaeology is a type of qualitative empirical work that focuses on creating a thick, contextual case study of a single case.'[67] She has indicated that there are different categories of legal archaeology projects which, she argued, enable us to examine legal archaeology projects as scholarship. Accordingly, she suggested that there are descriptive projects. These might be the types of project which provide detailed accounts but do not necessarily draw explicit conclusions beyond the case being studied. Simpson's *Cannibalism and the Common Law*[68] could be considered one such example or *The Snail and the Ginger Beer*[69] by Chapman, an in-depth study of the famous English case of *Donoghue v Stevenson*.[70] Further, Threedy indicated that there are analytical projects, which can come in three different types: 'those that explore the theory of capability problems; projects involving the theory and practice of fact analysis;

---

63. E Nottingham, 'Digging into Legal Archaeology: A Methodology for Case Study Research' (2022) 49(1) *Journal of Law and Society* 16.
64. D L Threedy, 'Unearthing Subversion with Legal Archaeology' (2003) 13 *Texas Journal of Women & Law* 133, 135.
65. D L Threedy, 'Legal Archeology and Feminist Legal Theory: A Case Study of Gender and Domestic Violence' (2008) 29 *Women's Rights Law Reporter* 171.
66. D L Threedy, 'Legal Archaeology: Excavating Cases, Reconstructing Context' (2006) 80 *Tulane Law Review* 1197.
67. Ibid.
68. A W B Simpson, *Cannibalism and the Common Law* (Penguin 1984).
69. M Chapman, *The Snail and the Ginger Beer: The Singular Case of Donoghue v Stevenson* (Wildy Simmonds and Hill 2009).
70. [1932] UKHL 100.

and projects that explore interdisciplinary approaches to the study of law in society.'[71] Scholars have agreed that legal archaeology projects are important for not only establishing the minute factual details of the case but also for enabling scholars to make macro-level observations, such as how cases come about, how they advance through the legal system and how they fit together through the doctrine of precedent.[72] They might also reveal strategic actions, such as where a case has been brought as part of a political or social movement or where there is evidence of bias in the legal system. For example, Lombardo's research on the American case of *Buck v Bell*[73] demonstrated that the case was manufactured strategically in light of the parties' wider agenda: to establish the validity of the Virginia involuntary sterilisation statute.[74] Lombardo made clear that lawyers on both sides of the case, as well as the expert witness, had a connection to the eugenics movement, and thus the plaintiff, Carrie Buck, was exploited for the purposes of this wider agenda.[75]

As more legal archaeology projects have been undertaken, variations within the methodology have developed, arguably shaped by the researcher's background, interests and discipline(s). For example, Novkov aligns legal archaeology with American political development and historical institutionalism.[76] She has argued that legal archaeology helps to explain legal and political development and provides insight into legal institutions including how they produce state polices, by exploring culture at the ground level. Rather than being a metaphor for the work of archaeologists, Novkov advances a Foucauldian version of legal archaeology.[77] Threedy has sought to identify the common features between legal archaeology and feminism and has suggested that there are 'points of convergence' between the two[78] '(1) sharing an epistemological preference for contextualization and grounded theory, and (2) sharing a critical interest in how gender bias is embedded in our legal system'.[79] Gorman has followed the work and Threedy and advanced the phrase 'feminist legal archaeology'.[80] She also encompasses a geographic analysis, linking to socio-spatial ideas and analysing 'micro-geographies of legal reasoning', developing what she refers to as a 'social-spatial-legal' nexus.[81] This considers the

71. D L Threedy, 'Legal Archaeology: Excavating Cases, Reconstructing Context' (2006) 80 *Tulane Law Review* 1197.
72. E Nottingham, 'Digging into Legal Archaeology: A Methodology for Case Study Research' (2022) 49(1) *Journal of Law and Society* 16.
73. 274 U.S. 200 (1927).
74. P A Lombardo, *Three Generations, No Imbeciles: Eugenics, the Supreme Court, and Buck v Bell* (The John Hopkins University Press 2008).
75. Ibid.
76. J Novkov, 'Legal Archaeology' (2011) 64(2) *Political Research Quarterly* 348.
77. Ibid 349.
78. D L Threedy, 'Legal Archaeology and Feminist Legal Theory: A Case Study of Gender and Domestic Violence' (2008) 29 *Women's Rights Law Reporter* 171, 172.
79. Ibid.
80. C Gorman, 'Feminist Legal Archeology, Domestic Violence and the Raced-Gendered Juridical Boundaries of U.S. Asylumlaw' (2019) 51(5) *Environment and Planning* 1050.
81. Ibid 1054.

space in law where social issues operate and interact. She suggests that feminist legal archaeology provides a way to explore the cultural and historical significance of how the law shapes and is shaped by power structures which govern women's lives.[82]

Threedy has suggested that legal archaeology might not have previously been seen as a distinct approach because the studies span several different areas of Law and thus it is more difficult to decipher the methodological similarities.[83] Further to this, the variations in approach as a result of different disciplinary interests and perspectives may have further prohibited the visibility of the methodology. Although there are some differences in approach, the 'archaeology' aspect of each piece of research is most likely trying to achieve the same thing, to focus on the minute contextual details of a case in order to reveal new findings at both the micro- and macro-levels. By exploring the 'Archaeology' within legal archaeology further, with reference to the discipline of Archaeology itself, we can make visible the common thread(s) among legal archaeology studies.

Legal archaeology research in the twenty-first century has also offered more clarity as to how a researcher might conduct or design a legal archaeology project and further highlighted the value of this type of study. In previous research, I have put forward a four-phase framework to guide the process of investigation. This involves (1) 'surveying the ground', (2) 'excavating', (3) 'on-site interpretation' and (4) 'post-excavation analysis'.[84] The first phase involves selecting a case to research and the second involves digging into the case in order to find out as much information as possible about the case, perhaps from non-legal sources found in archival materials or through personal communication. The third phase involves an extensive reading and ordering of materials into a reconstructed case narrative. Fourth, the researcher should draw conclusions. This is not intended to be a strict framework but rather a phased approach which aims to add structure and organisation to the process so as to make the methodology more rigorous and transparent. I have suggested that this helps to defend the methodology from criticisms regarding the lack of focus, sensationalism and distance from doctrine. The framework allows a researcher to retain the variable and random nature of the case and realise its unique and subjective origins while encouraging the researcher to reach clear conclusions at both the micro and macro-level. The framework engages with the archaeology metaphor, making greater use of terminology that would be more familiar to an archaeologist. This aids a researcher with situating themselves into the field of legal archaeology. The impact of extending the metaphor in this way helps to give identity to this field of study and adding phases and detail to the process of investigation further justifies its existence as an important socio-legal methodology, which should occupy a place within mainstream legal studies and research.

82. C Gorman, 'Feminist Legal Archeology, Domestic Violence and the Raced-Gendered Juridical Boundaries of U.S. Asylum Law' (2019) 51(5) *Environment and Planning* 1050, 1054.

83. D L Threedy, 'Legal Archaeology: Excavating Cases, Reconstructing Context' (2006) 80 *Tulane Law Review* 1197.

84. E Nottingham, 'Digging into Legal Archaeology: A Methodology for Case Study Research' (2022) 49(1) *Journal of Law and Society* 16.

The 'Archaeology' in Legal Archaeology

The question of 'what is the point of legal archaeology?' advanced by Twining[85] might be further explored by looking to the discipline of archaeology itself. For the 'what is the point?' or 'why?' question is something that archaeologists have tackled in relation to their own research. For example, Johnson has argued, 'The question "why do we do archaeology?" is therefore bound up with the question "why is archaeology – the study of the past through its material remains so important to us?"'[86] Archaeological scholars generally agree that it is important,[87] but there are various justifications and conceptions for archaeology research as well as different methods for doing archaeology and different perspectives on where the discipline fits, i.e. is it a science, humanities or applied sociology?[88] Archaeology is closely intertwined with other disciplines such as history and anthropology, and the discipline of archaeology has had to consider how it overlaps with these areas and also how it can be differentiated so as to be worthy of being its own distinct field of study.

The origins of archaeology show connections with law. Archaeology developed from antiquarianism, the collection and study of artefacts, to understand the past. The Society of Antiquaries, established in 1586, sometimes known as the College of Antiquities, was the central forum for historical debate. Group members included heralds and lawyers, many of whom were educated at the Inns of Court.[89] Every Friday, the Society convened to consider questions of interest that had been raised at the end of the previous week's meeting. Group discussions involved etymological analysis (the study of the history and origins of words), an approach consistent with accepted practices of common law learning.[90] The group discontinued in 1607 following suspicions that the Society was subversive and trying to undermine royal authority. In 1614, four of the founding members resolved to re-establish the Society, enabling the antiquarian movement to continue. The modern Society of Antiquaries of London was re-founded in the early eighteenth century, and this period saw the first organised excavation. In the nineteenth century, the British Archaeological Association was founded, and the world's first archaeological conference took place in 1844.[91] In the first half of the twentieth century, archaeology

85. W Twining, 'What Is the Point of Legal Archaeology?' (2012) 3 *Transnational Legal Theory* 166.
86. M Johnson, *Archaeological Theory An Introduction* (2nd edn, Wiley-Blackwell, 2010) 1–2.
87. Ibid 1.
88. Everill considers archaeology to be a form of applied sociology. P Everill, 'Introduction to Archaeology: A Personal Perspective' in P Everill and K Burnell (eds) *Archaeology, Heritage, and Wellbeing: Authentic, Powerful and Therapeutic Engagement with the Past* (Routledge 2022) 27.
89. Ibid 217.
90. M Stuckey, 'Antiquarianism and Legal History' (1990) 218. Unpublished. Available at https://pure.southwales.ac.uk/en/publications/antiquarianism-and-legal-history (accessed 26.10.22).
91. For a helpful overview of the development of archaeology from antiquarianism in the sixteenth to nineteenth centuries, see P Everill, 'Introduction to Archaeology: A Personal Perspective' in P Everill and K Burnell (eds) *Archaeology, Heritage, and Wellbeing: Authentic, Powerful and Therapeutic Engagement with the Past* (Routledge 2022) 28–31.

was generally thought to be more of science. However, in the 1960s and the latter parts of the twentieth century, archaeologists became more concerned with epistemological thought and human history.[92] Some have considered this time as a turning point for archaeology forming as an explicit sub-discipline.[93]

Traditional approaches regarded the objective of archaeology mainly as the reconstruction of the past, whereas contemporary understandings have placed more emphasis upon connecting the discoveries made in an archaeological site to humanity, considering the implications of findings beyond the site. Current approaches to archaeology research are focused on production, preservation and presentation of archaeological knowledge and are generally thought to have two main purposes. First, to reconstruct the past and, second, to preserve past material remains. Much like the legal archaeologist, the archaeologist will not be wholly reliant on official written records, and values what can be learnt from other artefacts, which are likely to tell a different story to the official documents of that period, should any exist.

Both archaeologists and lawyers need to deal with factual indeterminacy and acknowledge that there are different versions of facts. As Courbin has stated, 'the pertinent facts are not, by definition, the only ones'.[94] Like legal archaeology, the discipline of archaeology has also evolved to place importance on drawing conclusions, rather than reconfiguring the past for the sake of new knowledge or history preservation. Archaeologists make connections, often through an ongoing reflexive process, which Hodder has referred to as 'reflexive excavation'.[95] Renfrew and Bahn have stated that '[t]he material the archaeologist finds does not tell us directly what to think [...] The objects that archaeologists discover [...] tells us nothing directly in themselves. It is *we* today who have to make sense of those things'.[96] Legal archaeology has shown similar evolutionary development. The earlier work of Simpson contributes to new and interesting knowledge, but more recent research is more explicit in its aim to interpret findings from a newly constructed narrative and connect these to the macro-level.

Archaeology is both a physical activity and an intellectual pursuit.[97] The process of excavation of an archaeological site involves careful observation of different strata (layers) of sediment, paying close attention to even subtle changes in the sediments and noticing where there are deposits. The process is time consuming and can be destructive. Technological developments have sought to limit the destructive nature of excavation, for instance, by helping researchers decide where to dig, at what depth, and

92. C Renfrew and P Bahn, 'Introduction' in C Renfrew and P Bahn (eds) *Archaeology The Key Concepts* (Routledge 2005) xi.
93. Ibid xi.
94. P Courbin, *What Is Archaeology? An Essay on the Nature of Archaeological Research* (University of Chicago Press 1988) 114–116.
95. I Hodder, '"Always Momentary, Fluid and Flexible": Towards a Reflexive Excavation Methodology' (1997) 71 *Antiquity* 691–700.
96. C Renfrew and P Bahn, *Archaeology: Theories, Methods and Practice* (5th edn, Thames & Hudson, 2008) 13.
97. Ibid 12.

whether we can ascertain what is going on beneath the surface without needing to dig. Carver has stated that 'excavators may dig one big hole or many small holes, and these strategies have varied – and still vary – according to the way that archaeologists imagine the past and visualise what lies under the ground'.[98] Although archaeologists will aim to limit their destruction during excavation, the findings following archaeological interpretation and analysis can be subversive.

Legal archaeology can also be thought of as both a physical and intellectual endeavour, as a case study of this kind is often an active pursuit. It can involve travelling to various places, speaking to different people and patiently wading through various documents. Legal archaeologists disrupt the official narrative of a case in the law reports but, much like the archaeologist, do not intend to destroy existing stories, for this would completely undermine the doctrinal method for case analysis. Rather a legal archaeologist seeks to show that there is another way of looking at cases and challenges the doctrinal method as the dominant method in legal study.

Conclusion: Law and Archaeology – Reflections on the Development of the Field and Discipline

Law and archaeology is an underexplored field, yet connections between the two disciplines have long existed. This chapter has sought to shed light on how the disciplines might interact in legal scholarship, through the lens of the methodology of legal archaeology. Regardless of whether Simpson intended to create a legal movement or a new methodology, his work on legal archaeology has been a catalyst for detailed contextual case studies, which challenges the doctrinal method as the default method for analysing cases. Through an analysis of the evolution of legal archaeology and a snapshot examination of the discipline of archaeology itself, this chapter has sought to make clear that legal archaeology is worthy of this label and defend its place as an established socio-legal methodology within mainstream legal scholarship. While legal archaeology might have begun as simply a nice metaphor or a convenient label, it has certainly evolved into a methodology in its own right which is capable of yielding new and important insights that would not be apparent from a doctrinal case analysis.

Reflecting on the discipline of archaeology, it may be helpful to view a legal case as an archaeological site, which we should look at within a landscape. Legal archaeology enables us to examine the site (i.e. the case) and also consider how that site sits within and alongside other monuments. The sites should not be seen in isolation and should be connected to phenomenological understandings of how people of the past experienced those sites. Context may provide clues about how things were at a particular time and by working through strata (layers) and interpreting deposits, we can understand how the sediment was formed and when and where there are changes in the sediment. Through this sensory process, a researcher can build a vivid and detailed storybook.

---

98. M Carver, 'Key Ideas in Excavation' in Colin Renfrew and Paul Bahn (eds) *Archaeology the Key Concepts* (Routledge 2005) 106.

Legal archaeology can be situated as part of the law as literature movement. A legal archaeology case study is essentially (re)telling a legal story, and the conclusions drawn from reconstructed narratives reflect the importance of how we tell stories and the words we use to tell those stories. The words lawyers use to present facts can influence the outcome of a case, how it progresses through the legal system and how cases fit together through the doctrine of precedent. Literary interpretation, analysis and critique are important techniques for developing a reconstructed case narrative. There could also be a role for law in literature analysis where relevant artefacts include literary texts, which the legal archaeologist will then use to search for legal insights. As an important tool for the creation of new and alternative case narratives, legal archaeology therefore equips socio-legal scholars with another interdisciplinary methodology working at the intersection of law and humanities. The possibility of new findings emphasises the need for interdisciplinary research in Law Schools. This chapter has been written with the aim of enhancing the academic and maybe even professional practice of lawyers and law students. It is hoped that by placing a spotlight on an intersection of two disciplines, often assumed to be distinct from one another, the minds of the archaeologist and the lawyer will be open to what they can learn from one another.

Chapter Three

LAW AND COMICS/GRAPHIC JUSTICE

Angus Nurse

Introduction: Intersections of Comics and Law

This chapter examines the development of law, comics and graphic justice as a distinct area of scholarly activity within the context of law and humanities study. The core focus of this chapter's discussion is the Anglo-American conception of law and comics studies, particularly that situated within the UK, North America and Australia. In these areas socio-legal studies, and law and humanities scholarship incorporating comics study has firmly established itself since the 1990s. This is not to ignore the existence of other, wider forms of comics studies which consider law and graphic justice, and, indeed, even within this chapter's discussion it is worth noting that law and comics and particularly 'graphic justice' scholars examine Japanese popular culture and manga comics.[1] However, this chapter's focus is on the Anglo-American and Global North *field* of law, comics and graphic justice study rather than a specific analysis of the texts and mechanisms contained within the discipline's academic focus and in Anglo-American and Global North comics production.[2]

Before exploring the development and nature of the law, comics and graphic justice field, some brief discussion of the nature of academic study of comics is necessary for context. The terms 'comics' and 'graphic novels' are sometimes used interchangeably and for the purpose of this chapter's discussion the distinction between a weekly or serialised comic and a standalone graphic novel or graphic novel series is largely irrelevant. Undoubtedly there are differences between the two, particularly in those instances where a graphic novel represents a standalone story or collected narrative specifically constructed for the graphic novel medium as opposed to a long-running comic series such as the X-Men, which explores more diverse narratives and a series of narratives over a longer period.[3] In the latter case, issues may be collected together

1. A Pearson, T Giddens and K Tranter (eds), *Law and Justice in Popular Japanese Culture* (Routledge, 2018).
2. It should be noted, for example, that there is arguably a burgeoning field of Global South and non-Anglo American comics including African comics and graphic novels, many of which deal with issues of race and the impact of colonialism alongside other distinct concerns. Examples include *Kwesi* by Loyiso Mkize (a superhero story) and *Lake of Tears* by Setor Fiadzigbey and Kwabena Ofei, which deals with child labour and child trafficking.
3. J Baetens and H Frey, *The Graphic Novel: An Introduction* (Cambridge University Press, 2015).

as a trade paperback or collection, which arguably is almost indistinguishable from a graphic novel. In this sense, comics can be either short or several hundred pages long and there is considerable variation in what is accepted as a comic or graphic novel.[4] However, for the purpose of this chapter's discussion, the medium of comics and field of comics study is the core focus of the academic inquiry, that of visual storytelling usually based within the sequential art-based comic book form.[5] Central to the idea of comic books and graphic novels is that they generally contain some form of pictorial and other images deliberately juxtaposed in a deliberately constructed sequence in order to convey information to the reader, most likely a 'sustained narrative'.[6] In mainstream superhero studies the narrative is often one situated in basic 'good versus evil' discourse, but beyond this standard narrative approach considerable opportunities exist to convey other types of information and even to allow readers to incorporate their own perspectives. As creator Scott McCloud states, 'the heart of comics lies in the space between the panels – where the reader's imagination makes still pictures come alive.'[7] Thus, readers may interpret comics' narratives differently and impose their own perspectives on what they read. Arguably when most people are introduced to comics at an early age, they are a form of escapist entertainment and accessible literature, albeit literature as popular culture. But comics have progressed from their early pulp origins to incorporate more complex law and order narratives and social commentary such that 'comics, perhaps, are many people's first glimpse at a social justice pedagogy in action'.[8] Accordingly, comics now attract academic attention and are both tools for research and research dissemination and objects of scholarly analysis.

Comics studies arguably emerged as a discipline with the publication of Will Eisner's 1985 *Comics and Sequential Art*,[9] followed by the publication of Scott McCloud's *Understanding Comics* in 1993.[10] Douglas Wolk's 2007 *Reading Comics* (subtitled *How Graphic Novels Work and What They Mean*) did much to develop the notion of academic study of comics in which he identified that 'comics are not a genre, they're a *medium*'.[11] Thus, Wolk cemented the ground paved by previous authors for consideration of comics as texts in their own right, worthy of scholarly analysis and opened the door for further study of the medium, its production processes, critical and consumer reception of comics and understanding the comics industry within its social and political context.

4. C Labio, 'What's in a Name? The Academic Study of Comics and the "Graphic Novel"' (2011) 50(3) *Cinema Journal*, 123. Available at: http://www.jstor.org/stable/41240728.
5. For clarity, there is a distinction to be made between comics and cartoons or comic strips and this chapter's discussion is concerned with the comic book and graphic novels rather than newspaper or magazine comic strips or cartoons.
6. D Wolk, *Reading Comics* (Da Capo Press, 2007).
7. S McCloud, *Understanding Comics: The Invisible Art* (Kitchen Sink Press, 2007).
8. S C Howard and R L Jackson II (eds), *Black Comics: Politics of Race and Representation* (Bloomsbury, 2013).
9. W Eisner, *Comics and Sequential Art* (Poorhouse Press, 1985).
10. S McCloud, *Understanding Comics: The Invisible Art* (Kitchen Sink Press, 2007).
11. D Wolk, *Reading Comics* (Da Capo Press, 2007) 12 (emphasis in the original).

Comics studies incorporates varied approaches to academic study of comics including the study of the comics form, content, comics production, the context in which comics are produced and are representative of social issues and the reception to comics.[12] In discussing the potential different types of comics studies that might exist, several key questions emerged:

> A key question is how insular or porous we see the field of Comics Studies becoming. Will Comics Studies be an exclusively academic discipline, a meeting point for all of those intellectually curious about comics or something in between? We might also ask which comics matter in this new Comics Studies and on what basis they matter. Is Comics Studies to be modelled on Art History or Literature, which have tended to embrace exemplary works, often masterpieces, while excluding much of what is produced? Is Comics Studies to be modeled upon Cultural or Media Studies where there is a desire to be more inclusive, to represent marginalized perspectives but also to reappraise works from the commercial mainstream?[13]

These questions apply to the field of law and comics but have arguably been answered through the development of comics studies in the decade since Jenkins' questions were posed as well as in the simultaneous development of law and comics and graphic justice scholarship as its own sub-discipline. Indeed, it can be said that some core themes have clearly emerged in the discipline of law and comics study which include 'the history and genealogy of comics; its inner semiotic structure and aesthetic properties; its cultural and social significance; and close scrutiny or evaluation of particular artists, works, stories and characters'.[14] Thus, scholars involved in the academic study of comics cover considerable ground in their analysis of comics as a medium through which law and legal topics can be explored. The significance of comics to law is genuinely multi-faceted and there is more to comics than just their content, but even within mainstream superhero comics 'narrative worlds navigate issues of right and wrong, morality, of retribution and vengeance, of methodologies of control'.[15] Indeed, comics situated within law and crime discourse touch on issues of power and responsibility, duty and moral choice, discussion of legal theory and articulation of specific legal concepts. Thus, comics and graphic novels have value as teaching tools, can be used to deliver messages to marginalised and vulnerable groups, can be important in respect of cultural and popular representation and can allow for the exploration of complex legal issues within an entertainment format potentially more digestible and accessible than academic texts and specialised forms of knowledge transfer (e.g. the legal press). Accordingly, like other forms of media

12. M J Smith and R Duncan (eds), *Critical Approaches to Comics: Theories and Methods* (Routledge, 2012).
13. H Jenkins, 'Introduction: Should We Discipline the Reading of Comics?' in M J Smith and R Duncan (eds) *Critical Approaches to Comics: Theories and Methods* (Routledge, 2012) 5.
14. L Gomez Romero and I Dahlman, 'Introduction – Justice Framed: Law in Comics and Graphic Novels' (2012) 16 *Law Text Culture* 3. Available at: https://ro.uow.edu.au/ltc/vol16/iss1/2.
15. T Giddens (ed) *Graphic Justice* (Routledge, 2015).

and popular culture, comics can be integral to how people develop their understandings of law, crime and justice issues. This is arguably an issue of significance in comics study and one integral to the development of law and comics as a growing discipline. Thus, comics scholarship has pedagogical importance such as 'bringing to life ideas such as the rule of law and the separation of powers that can springboard students into deeper understandings of these important concepts' as well as providing for an expansion of research approaches and methodologies that enhance and broaden legal scholarship.[16]

The Development of Law and Comics Scholarship

Law and comics scholarship and analysis of legal issues within comics are not readily distinguished from wider academic interest in comics, albeit a distinct study of comics within certain academic disciplines can be identified with certain publications.

In the context of contemporary analysis and academic discussion of law and comics, the publication of a 2012 issue of *Law, Text and Culture* edited by Luis Gomez Romero and Ian Dahlman is arguably a pivotal moment. The introductory paper to this special issue identified that 'comics are utterly gripped by issues of legality, order and justice, but their theoretical and ideological partnership has been conspicuously neglected in legal scholarship'.[17] Similarly, Giddens argued for the inclusion of comics to the interdisciplinary study of law noting that while comics and graphic novels routinely dealt with law and order issues and aspects of legal theory, the use of such sources in legal scholarship was largely absent.[18] In part, this reflected the reliance within legal scholarship on sources that would be accepted within traditional conceptions of legal scholarship and within disciplinary norms relating to research. Thus, even within law and literature studies a focus on 'acceptable' or recognised literature arguably negated the value of comics as sources for analysis and teaching. However, as Baron[19] notes, connections between literature and law are not always positive and raised both methodological concerns and a requirement to ensure that in engaging with literature and fiction, legal scholars are not merely bolting on interpretive techniques or using literature in an illustrative sense that is designed to support pre-existing paradigms. This also raises questions concerning the extent to which legal scholars need an understanding of methodological and theoretical considerations existent in other disciplines in order to properly apply interpretive techniques and engage with other disciplines. In addition, questions might be

---

16. Ibid 3.
17. L Gomez Romero and I Dahlman, 'Introduction – Justice Framed: Law in Comics and Graphic Novels' (2012) 16 *Law Text Culture* 3. Available at: https://ro.uow.edu.au/ltc/vol16/iss1/24.
18. T Giddens, 'Comics, Law, and Aesthetics: Towards the Use of Graphic Fiction in Legal Studies' (2012) 6(1) *Law and Humanities* 85.
19. J B Baron, 'Interdisciplinary Scholarship as Guilty Pleasure: The Case of Law and Literature' (1999) 21 *Law and Literature* 21.

asked concerning 'what kinds of interdisciplinary work represent 'rigorous' scholarship, as opposed to what one sceptic has called 'intellectual voyeurism?'.[20]

However, law and literature had already become a diverse and established discipline which had developed considerably from its fringe origins in the 1970s and 1980s to encompass 'reading and studying law as if it were a special "genre" of literature to be interpreted like any story'.[21] Minda's analysis identified that the likes of Dickens, Kafka and Melville, the acceptable 'classic' literature, had been edged out by the likes of Derrida, Foucault and Heidegger as law and literature scholars engaged with critical analysis of 'law's language as a cultural and literary artefact'.[22] In the law and comics field, varied scholarship exists such that the reading of comics and study of the comics form as a means of developing legal understanding sits alongside the study of comics' genres and individual narratives that illustrate specific legal and justice issues. Papers within the 2012 *Law, Text and Culture* special issue identify that law and comics scholars were engaging with issues beyond just the reading of legal language, to encompass topics including legal surrealism; the common law; failures in legal systems political and legal theory; good and evil, representations of trauma; and retributive justice.

Subsequently, the first one-day graphic justice symposium (funded by the Socio-Legal Studies Association) took place at St Mary's University Twickenham (UK) on Wednesday 11 September 2013. Several papers presented at the symposium were later collected in *Graphic Justice: Intersections of Comics and Law.*[23] This collection was published by Routledge's Glasshouse series, allied to the development of the Graphic Justice Research Alliance (GJRA), a network of scholars engaged in scholarship on the intersections of law and contemporary culture. GJRA scholarship uses comics and graphic fiction as critical resources to be employed in the academic study of law and as sources that broaden the understanding of law and justice within the human world. In this context, comics 'can contribute to legal debate in a number of areas, from doctrinal copyright law, to legal ethics, education, public discourse, and legal philosophy'.[24] Law and comics scholarship can engage with the analysis of individual comics and how particular narratives might articulate or explore contemporary societal concerns or specific aspects of the law and order paradigm. Comics creator Allan Moore identified that processes of globalisation and increases in media coverage and technology have altered our perceptions of ourselves and the society surrounding us to the extent that 'we make different demands upon the art and culture that is meant to reflect the constantly shifting landscape that we find ourselves in'.[25] Accordingly, in recent decades comics have responded to the change in market to consider more complex ideas and legal problems,

20. Ibid 22.
21. G. Minda, 'Law and Literature at Century's End' (1997) 9(2) *Law & Literature* 245.
22. Ibid.
23. T Giddens (ed), *Graphic Justice* (Routledge, 2015).
24. Ibid.
25. A Moore and D Gibbons, *Watchmen* (DC Comics, 1986).

thus providing more 'adult' and complex sources applicable to academic study and pedagogical approaches to comics' use as sources for redefining and understanding law.[26]

Following the creation of the GJRA, the first Graphic Justice conference, *Graphic Justice Discussions* took place at St Mary's University Twickenham (UK) in July 2017 (GJRA, 2017). Subsequent conferences have taken place at St Francis College, New York (2018); University of the Sunshine Coast, Australia (2019); Middlesex University London (virtual, 2020); and Federal University of Pampa, Brazil (virtual, 2022). The Graphic Justice stream is now also an established aspect of the Socio-Legal Studies Association (SLSA) annual conference and several individual graphic justice and law and comics conferences have also been held. As of 2022 graphic justice scholarship is arguably established with postgraduate and doctoral students pursuing work in the area of law, comics and graphic justice at various institutions and presenting this work at *Graphic Justice Discussions* and other conferences.

Intersections of Comics and Law: Disciplinary Perspectives

Contemporary law and comics scholarship, particularly that concerned with depictions of law and crime, is no longer confined to law as an academic discipline. Graphic justice scholarship has

> come a long way: from the doctrinal view of comics as regulatory objects within intellectual property law, through concerns of representation, education, communication and philosophy, across the complex role of comics in understanding crime and criminal justice and the tensions between reality and fiction, to the value of comics in understanding issues of a global significance: exceptional executive violence and international concepts of justice, and ultimately to the use of comics not simply as a tool or object of analysis, but as a meaningful and important participant in the protection of humans against mass harm.[27]

Accordingly, comics studies can provide for detailed analysis of mainstream legal issues in a manner easily digestible and understandable for undergraduate students. For example, comics scholars have discussed the issues of intellectual property and copyright using the medium of comics to do so. Barker's 2015 analysis of the complex intellectual property issues involved in a comic, for example, uses DC's Batman properties to discuss the protection granted to comics and engages with the expansion of fan fiction and fan fiction publishing outlets to consider issues of intellectual property and copyright in a manner perhaps more easily understandable than most textbooks. After all, most undergraduate students would be at least aware of the existence of Batman as a fictional character probably owned by a corporation or creator, even if they were unaware of the legalities of ownership between DC Comics, Warner Brothers film studio and the parent company Time Warner Communications. However, through a discussion of *DC*

26. T Giddens, *On Comics and Legal Aesthetics: Multimodality and the Haunted Mask of Knowing* (Routledge, 2018).
27. T Giddens (ed), *Graphic Justic* (Routledge, 2015) 6.

Comics v Towle[28] case study analysis moves from an abstract discussion of intellectual property issues to a tangible discussion of the extent to which 'the 'Batmobile' is to be regarded as a character – 'Batman' – and which benefits from individual copyright protection'.[29] Thus, law and graphic justice discussion applied to this case study articulates principles of copyright law and allows for analysis of the law's practical application.

The majority of contributors to the *Graphic Justice* edited collection identify as law academics.[30] However, Strobl and Philips' *Comic Book Crime*, published by New York University Press, 2013, is published within NYU's Alternative Criminology book series, edited by cultural criminologist Jeff Ferrell.[31] Analysis of presentations on law and comics at conferences and submissions to the Graphic Justice thematic collection at the *Comics Grid* identifies that law and comics scholars come from law, criminology, arts and communication, humanities and literature studies (among others).

Thus, law and comics scholarship expand beyond 'pure' law scholarship to encompass other disciplines, consistent with Giddens' argument for the inclusion of comics to the interdisciplinary study of law.[32] Other researchers contend that 'although comic books are far from manuals for how to run the criminal justice system, we can learn much about American Society by interrogating the ways in which cultural meanings about crime and justice are negotiated and contested within them'.[33] Thus, law and comics scholarship has also developed within the criminology discipline, which has embraced graphic justice conceptions and has integrated the study of comics within cultural criminology and crime media and culture study, as the next section discusses in more detail.[34] From a criminological perspective, 'popular culture brings to discourses about crime some attributes that scientific criminology cannot claim. One of these is an ability to speak to cultural anxieties'.[35] This includes popular fascination with the more sensationalised aspects of crime such as serial murder, sexual offences, child abduction and murder. But it can also extend to a more nuanced discussion of critical criminology and crime issues such as race, human rights, trauma and the effectiveness of law enforcement (see later discussion). As scholar Alison Young identifies 'far from being a minor aspect of the criminological enterprise, critical engagement with representations of crime and justice orient us as researchers towards the constitutive relation between subject and discourse'.[36] Thus, analysis of an image and interpretation of that image requires some understanding that the representation exists even in the context

28. 802 F.3d 1012 (2015).
29. K. Barker, 'Holy Blurring of Core Copyright Principles, Batmobile!' in Thomas Giddens (ed) *Graphic Justice: Intersections of Comics and Law* (Routledge, 2015).
30. T Giddens (ed), *Graphic Justice* (Routledge, 2015).
31. S Strobl and N Philips, *Comic Book Crime* (New York University Press, 2013).
32. T Giddens, 'Comics, Law, and Aesthetics: Towards the Use of Graphic Fiction in Legal Studies' (2012) 6(1) *Law and Humanities* 85.
33. S Strobl and N Philips, *Comic Book Crime* (New York University Press, 2013) 2.
34. G Martin, *Crime Media and Culture* (Routledge, 2018), J Ferrell, K Hayward and J Young, *Cultural Criminology: An Invitation* (Sage, 2015).
35. N Rafter and M Brown, *Criminology Goes to the Movies* (New York University Press, 2011).
36. A Young, *The Scene of Violence* (Routledge, 2010).

of a manifestly fictional representation. Thus, while readers clearly understand that Superman and Batman are not literally real, they will understand their representation as manifestations of the forces of good against the forces of evil. Beyond this surface representation, there are also conceptions on the different law and order perspectives portrayed in different comics, Superman's 'boy scout' persona versus Batman's more gritty, violent and vigilante-based approach to dealing with crime. Indeed, as society has changed so too have comics changed to consider more challenging law and order narratives. In particular 'many comics published in the aftermath of 9/11 explored and confronted the role of American heroes that find themselves in an age of anxiety surrounded by potential terrorist-centred criminal and global threats of epic proportions'.[37]

Accordingly, law, comics and graphic justice scholarship has developed into a field with diverse methodologies, occupying a range of areas of study, theories and approaches.

Contemporary Law, Comics and Graphic Justice Scholarship

While the field of law and comics has developed considerably in recent decades, it has arguably still to gain acceptance as a distinct area of study within legal academia. In part this may reflect the regulated nature of legal academia and the need to meet the professional requirements of the legal profession, qualifying law degrees which dictates that law degrees require the study of specified foundational law topics and compliance with established norms in legal academic research. Accordingly, law and literature and law and culture modules may be confined to electives on undergraduate law degree study or are limited to specialist postgraduate degrees, albeit law and media or culture, and law and society modules may also appear in criminology degrees (discussed later) and in non-qualifying law degrees. However, specialist law and popular culture modules are available at a number of universities as compulsory parts of law degree programmes and a few dedicated degrees also exist such as Ohio University's MA in Law, Justice and Culture. In addition, courses such as the MLitt in Comics and Graphic Novels at the University of Dundee provide for the study of specific genres and topics such as law and comics, and research in comics is facilitated through Dundee's Scottish Centre for Comics Studies. Elsewhere, comics studies or graphical narrative degrees are being offered by several institutions.

Within criminology, law and comics scholarship is most closely allied with cultural criminology, a sub-discipline of criminology and a growing field which examines issues of representation, meaning and politics.[38] Cultural criminology seeks to understand crime through the context of culture and cultural processes. Thus, in the field of criminology, cultural criminology courses and crime, media and culture courses also engage with comics and visual media scholarship, and in the UK they have been offered as part of undergraduate criminology degrees by several universities (e.g. Birmingham City

37. S Strobl and N Philips, *Comic Book Crime* (New York University Press, 2013) 61.
38. J Ferrell, K Hayward and J Young, *Cultural Criminology: An Invitation* (Sage, 2015).

University, University of Kent and Middlesex University). Indeed, there is an argument for a criminology of narrative fiction that advances a theory of the criminological value of fiction.[39] Arguably such a criminology already exists in the context of graphic justice as a criminology of visual narrative fiction in which 'the cultural meaning and symbolic importance of comic books represents a viable area of exploration for criminologists'.[40]

Contemporary law, comics and graphic justice scholarship is facilitated through a range of academic journals. A thematic Graphic Justice collection has been published by the *Comics Grid*, the journal of comics scholarship. At the time of writing this chapter, nine papers have been published in this collection between 2016 and 2021.[41] Papers in the collection cover a diverse range of issues including copyright and the question of whether Generic superheroes can be said to exist;[42] two papers on contract law, one concerning the validity of comics contracts[43] and a second concerning how comics can be used to adequately communicate the correct process of contract cancellation and whether comics can enhance understanding of the legal process;[44] the criminalisation of free speech;[45] and employment law via a case study of Danish labour contracts.[46] Keyword searches within the *Journal of Graphic Novels and Comics* identified 149 results using the keyword 'justice' and 175 results using the keyword 'law'. Analysis of these results identified that justice-based papers included articles (and interviews) covering issues such as vigilantism, LGBT rights, indigenous rights and anti-racism, anti-colonialism, genocide and the Holocaust, sexual abuse, state-sponsored sexual violence, gender-based violence and human rights. Analysis of the results for 'law' identified that papers identified via this keyword included articles covering issues such as comic book contracts; gender politics; representations of women and feminist discourse; representations of the Holocaust in comics and graphic novels; individual liberty and collective responsibility; crimes against humanity and international law, child soldiers and war narratives; and rape and analysis of legal issues surrounding rape and rape culture. Inevitably there is some overlap between the papers found using these keywords such that some papers are found using both search terms. However, for some of the topics identified in this preliminary analysis (e.g. international law and international crimes, rape and sexual violence) several papers are published within this specialist

39. M Rafe, *Criminology of Narrative Fiction* (Bristol University Press, 2021).
40. S Strobl and N Philips, *Comic Book Crime* (New York University Press, 2013) 5.
41. The Comics Grid, 2022.
42. A O'Connell, 'Generic Super Heroes: Can They Exist?' (2020) 10(1) *The Comics Grid: Journal of Comics Scholarship.*
43. M Giancasporo, 'Picture-Perfect or Potentially Perilous? Assessing the Validity of "Comic Contracts"' (2020) 10(1) *The Comics Grid: Journal of Comics Scholarship.*
44. M Botes, 'Using Comics to Communicate Leal Contract Cancellation' (2017) 7 *The Comics Grid: Journal of Comics Scholarship.*
45. A. Nurse, 'See No Evil, Print No Evil: The Criminalization of Free Speech in *DMZ*' (2017) 7 *The Comics Grid: Journal of Comics Scholarship.*
46. M N Høegh, M Stengaard and M Schmidt-Kessen, 'The Visualized Employment Contract. An Exploratory Study on Contract Visualization in Danish Employment Contracts' (2021) 11(1) *The Comics Grid: Journal of Comics Scholarship.*

comics journal. In their work that used 'a cross-section of two hundred contemporary American comic books published from 2001 until 2010', Phillips and Strobl identified that while superhero comics continued to dominate the comics field there had been a shift to more adult material in part as a consequence of a more mature readership that continued to consume comics well into adulthood and also as a consequence of social changes such as increased anxiety about rising crime rates and social disadvantage and the post-9/11 variance in the perceived terrorism threat.[47]

Methodologically, law and comics study contains a diversity that goes beyond the basic elements of doctrinal textual analysis that arguably dominates legal scholarship. Law and literature scholarship often studies law and legal meaning through analysis of literary texts[48] and this approach is certainly adopted by law and comics scholarship. Particularly, in that aspect of narrative and content analysis of individual comics and graphic novels that focus on the legal and justice themes contained within sequential narratives or that seek to employ allegorical analysis of individual comics, law and comics scholarship is arguably aligned clearly with basic approaches in law and literature scholarship. Accordingly, the analysis of X-Men comics as being about civil liberties and racism and ethical or philosophical perspectives allows for consideration of notions of rights and responsibility and the exercise of power via analysis of particular issues and storylines or even the series as a whole.[49] A Materialist or Marxist approach intended to 'reveal the operations of power and political motivations encoded within texts' can be applied to comics which are arguably political in respect of producing (or promoting) ideological and propogandist messages such as those in Captain America or Superman comics which articulate dominant American perspectives.[50] In this sense, doctrinal analysis and socio-legal analysis are arguably at play in identifying how the comics text operates in its original context as well as considering how it might align with what it is intended to convey (for example, Captain America's 1940s anti-Nazi messages, Superman's affirmation of dominant American political ideology and the rule of law). Thus, analysis of the comics text arguably goes beyond a surface reading of the good and evil narrative to consider the meaning of the text and the wider messages that might be conveyed. Law and comics scholarship has developed this type of textual analysis, arguably similar to that found in law and literature scholarship while expanding it to consider distinct legal and crime and justice themes through an analytical approach that considers both surface and secondary narratives.

However, law and comics scholarship arguably fits within a wider socio-legal discourse that considers the content and context of law and employs narrative methodology

---

47. S Strobl and N Philips, *Comic Book Crime* (New York University Press, 2013) 4.
48. R Posner, *Law and Literature* (Harvard University Press, 2009).
49. J McLaughlin, 'Philosophy: "The Triumph of the Human Spirit" in X-Men' in Matthew J Smith and Randy Duncan (eds) *Critical Approaches to Comics: Theories and Methods* (Routledge, 2012).
50. C Murray, 'Propaganda: The Pleasures of Persuasion in Captain America'Men' in Matthew J Smith and Randy Duncan (eds) *Critical Approaches to Comics: Theories and Methods* (Routledge, 2012).

as an analytical device to engage with meaning and relevance of law.[51] After all, the narrative method is well established as a means through which contested stories can be analysed and understood within adversarial justice systems. Narratives reveal the complexity of socially constructed notions of justice and allow for the analysis of conflicting and contested perspectives on what justice should or should not be, or the specifics of what constitutes justice in a particular case. However, narrative storytelling in legal scholarship arguably risks being confined to discourse around courtroom narratives and the behaviour of actors within adversarial criminal trials. But the method can be employed to examine wider issues and to analyse the narrational qualities of a wide range of legal discourse.[52] Artistic representations in comics can communicate the complexity of issues that cannot easily be communicated through other means, particularly in criminal law and retributive justice processes, and provide a 'safe' space through which challenging and complex legal and sensitive issues can be explored.[53] For example, Vertigo's *100 Bullets* comic, while ostensibly a revenge narrative, can also be used to discuss the notions of extreme restorative justice, vigilantism, corruption and the nature of retributive justice, complex ideas in crime and justice discourse.[54] Accordingly, law and comics scholarship allows for a more nuanced critical analysis of narratives and their importance to legal meaning that fits well within broader legal scholarship.

Wolff argues directly that 'law is narration: it is narrative, narrator and the narrated'. At its most basic level, legal cases are constructed from a variety of texts that can be read as a series of intertwining stories.[55] Establishing what happened, when, to whom and liability, arguably requires constructing, understanding and assessing a clear narrative to reach a judgement on the facts. In this regard, narrative storytelling can be distinguished from standard content analysis approaches as its function is both to identify the key narratives being developed and explicitly advanced by each side in a case and through critical analysis also construct appropriate alternate and wider narratives. Thus, in both law teaching and legal or socio-legal research, comics can be effective tools for narrative analysis and narrative constructed that advance legal understanding and critical analysis.

Conclusion: Future Directions

As this chapter indicates, the field of law and comics is now well established, with the Graphic Justice stream a near-permanent fixture of the SLSA annual conference, the

51. M Fludernick, 'A Narratology of the Law? Narratives in Legal Discourse' (2014) 1(1) *Critical Analysis of Law* 87–109.
52. A Nurse, 'Law, the Environment and Narrative Storytelling' in Naomi Creutzfeldt, Marc Mason and Kirsten McConnachie (eds) *Routledge Handbook of Socio-Legal Theory and Method* (Routledge, 2019).
53. H Baumeister, 'Drawing on Genocide' (2019) *Law and Humanities* 13.
54. A Nurse, 'Extreme Restorative Justice' in T Giddens (ed) *Graphic Justice* (Routledge, 2015).
55. L Wolff, 'Let's Talk About Lex: Narrative Analysis As Both Research method and Teaching Technique in Law' (2014) 35(1) *Adelaide Law Review* 3.

annual *Graphic Justice Discussions* conference run by the GJRA and presentations on law and justice within comics also appearing in law and society, cultural criminology and other more mainstream academic conferences and media. Several peer-reviewed outlets specifically aimed at comics studies engage with legal discourse and analysis, not least journals such as the *Comics Grid*, the *Journal of Comics and Culture* and the *Journal of Graphic Novels and Comics*, as well as academic book series such as Routledge's *Advances in Comics Studies*. Scholarship on law and comics is not confined to these specialist comics publications and law and literature discourse appears in the specialist legal literature and discourse surrounding law and humanities, law and popular culture, criminology, literature, media and popular culture studies more generally. Law and comics research and scholarship also appears within distinct cultural and socio-cultural studies in areas such as American studies, Japanese studies and even post-colonial studies. Accordingly, the graphic justice and law and comics movements have arguably expanded from the niche remit of comics studies to occupy a place within broader academic scholarship. Comics studies has also distinguished itself from the broader law and literature movement to encompass the study and analysis of specific legal issues, understanding of law and culture and study of the comics form itself, including that of legal issues in the production and ownership of comics.

In essence, the field has developed from the 'Holy Batman' scholarship concerned with the specific content of mainstream comics (i.e. US superhero books published by the big three comics publishers, Marvel, DC and Image) to engage with a more diverse range of scholarship and comics producers, including other mainstream and non-mainstream publishers, independent comics and non-superhero titles. Texts such as Phillips and Strobl's 2013 analysis show how comics and law scholarship can devote itself to a single area of legal/socio-legal analysis, such as crime and the criminal justice system and to consider how comics production and the field develop within the focus of a single 'legal' issue.[56] Even within this distinct approach, the scholarship on offer engages with issues of race, responses to terrorism, issues of genocide and analysis of how comics are used. These and related issues are increasingly examined with law and comics scholarship as are issues of legal pluralism.

The field of comics and graphic justice scholarship provides not just a forum for scholarship on the intersection of law and the liberal arts but also a forum for inquiry into the meaning of law, legal institutions and responses to legal problems as they relate to culture and the human good. Analysis of the existing and emerging law and comics scholarship identifies that such scholarship provides for academic explorations of the diverse ways in which law and legal institutions may express a cultural orientation to the human good, illustrate or explore particular issues of inadequacies in law and legal systems (broadly defined) and allow for critical analysis of the workings of law and understanding of legal systems. In recent decades, comics have 'needed to move beyond fight scenes and manifestations of superpowers to consider material more relevant to

56. S Strobl and N Philips, *Comic Book Crime* (New York University Press, 2013).

its older audience and less indicative of adolescent male fantasy'.[57] Accordingly, comics scholarship has 'grown up' as have comics themselves to consider adult issues and complex issues surrounding law and socio-legal understandings of law. Pedagogically, comics scholarship informs teaching of legal issues and also the creation and dissemination of research (including that presented using the medium of comics) to engage with legal issues.

The evidence of this chapter's analysis of law and comics scholarship and of the nature of publications within the discipline are that the future trajectory of law and comics scholarship is that of a diverse area of scholarship. Law, comics and graphic justice scholarship has expanded to consider a wide range of issues beyond mainstream superhero narratives and increasingly engages with the complexity of law, a range of international and specialist law issues and a socio-legal approach that considers law in its contemporary social context and its representation within popular culture and the visual storytelling medium.

57. A Nurse, 'The Family and the Fishing Net: Family Values and Dysfunction in Brief Lives' in Alexandra Dunne and Grainne O-Brien (eds) *Good Madness: A Collection of Essays on the Work of Neil Gaiman* (Inter-Disciplinary Press, 2014).

Chapter Four

LAW AND FILM

Steve Greenfield, Guy Osborn and Peter Robson

Sam Bowden:
A lawyer should represent his client.

Max Cady:
Should ZEALOUSLY represent his client within the bounds of the law. I find you guilty, counselor! Guilty of betrayin' your fellow man! Guilty of betrayin' your country and abrogatin' your oath! Guilty of judgin' me and sellin' me out! With the power vested in me by the kingdom of God, I sentence you to the Ninth Circle of Hell! Now you will learn about loss! Loss of freedom! Loss of humanity! Now you and I will truly be the same.

(Cape Fear 1991)

Introduction

There has always been a mild obsession with lists of 'best law/lawyer films' as a starter for any work using film in the study of law which can be found from the turn of the century up until the time of writing.[1] There are also Guides that exist to provide law teachers with material,[2] as well as accounts of how the justice system operates in practice.[3] In addition the role of ideology in film continues to be a theme.[4] Interest comes, too, from

---

1. A Jara, 'Lawyers in Film: 20 Great Movies About the Law' (2021) https://onward.justia.com/lawyers-in-film-20-great-movies-about-the-law/ (last accessed 7/12/22); T Nicolson, 'Your Honour, I Move to Recognise the Best Courtroom Dramas Ever Made' (October 2021) 20 *Esquire* https://www.esquire.com/uk/culture/film/a34155993/courtroom-movies/ (last accessed 7/12/22).
2. A Pannell, 'Law in the Reel World' (2012) https://lawinthereelworld.wordpress.com/2012/12/16/guide-to-law-and-film-resources/ (last accessed 7/12/22): M Asimow and J Silbey, *Law and Popular Culture: A Course Book* (3rd edn Vandeplas Publishing, 2020).
3. R Sherwin, 'Imagining Law as Film Representation without Reference?' in A Sarat (ed) *Law and the Humanities* (Cambridge University Press, 2009) 241.
4. N Mezey and M Niles, 'Screening the Law: Ideology and Law in American Popular Culture' (2005) 28(2) *Columbia Journal of Law and the Arts* 91–185; J Elkins, 'Popular Culture, Legal Films, and Legal Film Critics' (2007) 40(2) *Loyola of Los Angeles Law Review* 745; J Silbey, 'The Politics of Law and Film Study: An Introduction to the Symposium on Legal Outsiders in American Film' (2009) https://scholarship.law.bu.edu/faculty_scholarship/1065/ (last accessed 7/1/22).

slightly unexpected quarters.[5] The impact of film generally[6] as well as certain specific areas like race[7] is also encountered as is writing on strongly related areas.[8] Originally interest in the cinematic portrayal of law and lawyers tended to focus on the traditional American courtroom drama with specific attention on two classic films. First Sidney Lumet's 1957 film *Twelve Angry Men* and second Robert Mulligans 1962 offering *To Kill a Mockingbird.* It also started with American legal academics who had an interest in film as a cultural phenomenon. The two films, noted above, were selected by the American Film Institute as the two finest courtroom dramas, which was defined as 'a genre of film in which a system of justice plays a critical role in the film's narrative';[9] two iconic actors, Henry Fonda and Gregory Peck, standing up against all odds to support the idea of 'justice'. Both took up an unpopular stance demonstrating the importance of a fair trial against a backdrop of prejudice. The two films are powerful pieces of social drama with life-and-death decisions. However, Henry Fonda, as Davis Juror 8, in *Twelve Angry Men*, was not a lawyer but a member of the jury charged with determining the guilt or innocence of a young man accused of murder. The entire film is set within the confines of the jury room, while the backdrop for *To Kill a Mockingbird* is the explicit racism within the small Southern town of Maycomb, Alabama.

Given the quality and iconic status of these two films, it is hardly surprising that academics and especially legal academics with an interest in film would write about them. A key question though was whether legal films only comprised a limited set of courtroom dramas or whether there were alternative ideas and concepts that might be applied to produce a broader more coherent body of work. Furthermore, while these two films have a clear legal focus the political and social context is fundamental to the message of the film. The legal story is a vehicle for the portrayal of a wider social issue. As Cunningham notes: 'Twelve Angry Men goes beyond the well-intentioned "message

5. R Johnson, 'Getting Serious about Legally Blonde: The 2001 Comedy Shatters Expectations about What Makes a Good Heroine' (2022) https://divinity.uchicago.edu/sightings/articles/getting-serious-about-legally-blonde (last accessed 7/12/22); J Denoncourt, 'Using Film to Enhance Intellectual Property Law Education: Getting the Message Across' (2013) 4(1) *European Journal of Law and Technology* https://ejlt.org/index.php/ejlt/article/view/188/283 (last accessed 10/05/2023).
6. Film Inquiry, 'Law and Order: Examining Films that had an Impact on Legislation' (2018) https://www.filminquiry.com/law-and-order-films-legislation/_ (last accessed 7/12/22); T Kubrak, 'Impact of Films: Changes in Young People's Attitudes after Watching a Movie' (2020) https://www.ncbi.nlm.nih.gov/pmc/articles/PMC7288198/ (last accessed 7/12/22).
7. C Bond, 'Laws of Race/Laws of Representation: The Construction of Race and Law in Contemporary American Film' (2010) 11 *Texas Review of Entertainment & Sports Law* 219.
8. N Tsika, *Screening the Police: Film and Law Enforcement in the United States* (Oxford University Press, 2021).
9. The remaining 8 films were 3. *Kramer v Kramer* 1979, 4 *The Verdict* 1982, 5. *A Few Good Men* 1992, 6. *Witness for the Prosecution* 1958, 7. *Anatomy of a Murder* 1959, 8. *In Cold Blood* 1967, 9. *A Cry in the Dark* 1988 10. *Judgement at Nuremberg* 1961. https://www.afi.com/afis-10-top-10/.

picture" to make a remarkable cinematic statement about the nature of the limitations of the American jury system and of the American democratic process itself.'[10]

There are two distinct sources for films. First, fictional works of whatever type, and second, true-life stories though there is often overlap. A real-life event may form the basis for a book that is adapted into a film, for example, *10 Rillington Place*.[11] Alongside the adaption of fictional works true stories have provided a base for legal films. Tension and drama are more easily produced when there is a potential capital sentence at the end though there are significant examples such as *A Civil Action* (1998) and *Erin Brockovich* (2000) that were based on cases relating to claims of water contamination. In the UK true stories provided the basis for a number of significant legal films: *10 Rillington Place* (1971), *In the Name of the Father* (1993), *Let Him Have It* (1991), *Dance with a Stranger* (1985) and *Pierrepoint* (2005). Such films inevitably raise questions about historical truth and dramatic licence.

Lawyer turned novelist, John Grisham, injected new life into law films as his books were adapted for the screen. The first was *The Firm* in 1993 followed by *The Pelican Brief* (1993), *The Client* (1994), *A Time to Kill* (1996), *The Chamber* (1996), *The Rainmaker* (1997), *The Gingerbread Man* (1998) and *Runaway Jury* (2003). This in turn led to academic analysis of the material with Robson noting the twin approach:

> His works have alternated between thrillers and social issues works. Of his eleven novels six are broadly chase/thriller works whilst the other five are strongly centred on social issues. Not every one of his chase novels is devoid of social issues and there is some action in the social issues novels.[12]

These were undoubtedly legal films but not necessarily courtroom dramas though some have a significant courtroom element. Grisham's work turned the law and film gaze back towards the US legal system and Hollywood. One of the first issues to be addressed was how to define or recognise a legal film and essentially whether work could go beyond the classic courtroom drama. This attempt inevitably required engagement with theory and notably the tricky concept of genre. So, a starting point for law and film academics was a contemporary broadening and deepening of the research base with a push into other disciplines.[13] One of the difficulties for those embracing the challenge was the lack of an established base or framework though the blank slate was contemporane-

10. F R Cunningham and S Lumet, *Film and Literary Vision* (University Press of Kentucky, 1991) 109.
11. The film was based on Ludovic Kennedy's book, *10 Rillington Place* (Gollancz, 1961).
12. P Robson, 'Adapting the Modern Law Novel: Filming John Grisham' (2001) 28(1) *Journal of Law and Society* 147, 151. The same kind of split can be seen in his later works.
13. Examples of interaction with film theory include S Greenfield et al., 'Genre, Iconography and British LegaFilm' (2007) 36(3) *Baltimore Law Review* 371–391; S Greenfield, '*Solstorm:* Developing a Semantic/Syntactic Approach to Law Films' (2009) 39 *Stetson Law Review* 119. Media studies: M. Asimow et al., 'Perceptions of Lawyers? A Transnational Study of Student Views on the Image of Law and Lawyers' (2005) 12(3) *International Journal of the Legal Profession* 407. Psychology has also featured e.g., S Greenfield, 'State Executioner Pierrepoint: A

ously liberating. The absence of accepted boundaries has resulted in organic growth of the subject in a non-linear fashion with a range of interested parties contributing. This chapter first explores the internationalisation of the subject, through the analysis of national cinemas, which has been a very important and enabling dimension. It then considers possible trajectories for the subject though it needs to be stressed that there is great flexibility and scope for developments in different directions. For example, most recently work on vigilantes has blossomed.[14] New works to watch and comment on can always be unearthed and audio-visual works linked to a range of cultural artefacts in many ways.[15]

Engagement with Theory

A key development in the area has been the setting of film work within a theoretical framework. Originally this was configured as developing and applying ideas around genre and what constituted a law film to avoid the simple categorisation of law films being limited to courtroom drama or a trial film. One method was to expand the nature of the courtroom to include Military Tribunals and there is a healthy offering from *Paths of Glory* (1957) through *A Few Good Men* (1992) to *Mangal Pandey: The Rising* (2005) with variations such as the classic *Judgement at Nuremberg* (1961). *Pierrepoint* (2005) contains a scene where Albert Pierrepoint is sent to Germany to carry out the death sentences imposed by the court. It was argued that this group of films offered a different perspective on the relationship between the formality of law and the search for justice:

> Paradoxically, although they offer less of a model for court personnel behaviour, they seem to have more to say on the broader theme of the role of justice within the legal process. They take place in the context of a highly formalistic hierarchical structure of command and obedience. The very strictures on what kind of defence may be used in such a set-up means that the Court Martial can be seen as a metaphor for the operation of the law itself. The rigid rules under which soldiers serve and their need to adhere to these provide a version of inflexible law against which the interests of the individual can be counter-posed. These interests can be seen as justice.[16]

Although there are some parallels to be drawn with the more traditional courtroom films those focused on military tribunals are a small group with distinct common characteristics. There is a high degree of formality, obedience is a key concept, in terms of dress and process though without the impressive court buildings. They do though

---

Cinematic Portrayal of Moral Disen, Gagement' in P Hodkinson (ed) *The International Library of Essays on Capital Punishment*, Volume III (Ashgate, 2013) 391.

14. P Robson and F Spina (eds), *Vigilante Justice in Society and Popular Culture: A Global Perspective* (Fairleigh Dickinson University Press, 2022).
15. The British film *Cloudburst* (1951) was 'discovered' and used on the 2022 Cinematic Justice Module at Westminster with the overarching theme of vigilante justice.
16. S Greenfield, G Osborn and P Robson, *Film and the Law* (Cavendish, 2001) 42.

permit the political dimension of law to be more openly expressed and incorporated in addition to portraying significant historical events. For example, *Mangal Pandey* (2005) is set in the period of the First Indian War of Independence. For these reasons, they are often interesting stories about specific events in much the same way that *In the Name of the Father* (1993) has the 1970s IRA bombing campaign in England as its backdrop to the central theme of a miscarriage of justice. Focusing on a different setting was a way of expanding the analysis. This idea of going beyond the courtroom to find a courtroom was a novel interpretation of the genre. The shifting or alternative places of 'justice' included the boat in *Cape Fear* (1991) and even the streets in *Judge Dredd* (1995). This also opened up the route to exploring vigilante justice which has long roots in Western films from Death *Wish* (1974) to numerous contemporary examples such as *Promising Young Woman* (2020). Clint Eastwood's roles provide an overview of the development of this category of justice films from the Western (*High Plains Drifter* 1973) through the cop figure (*Dirty Harry* 1971) to the concerned citizen (*Gran Torino* 2008).[17]

Defining a law film has always been problematic once there is a move beyond the basic courtroom drama and a rather simple 'definition' was proposed in 2001:

> In order to qualify as a law film the following characteristic(s) must be present in some shape or form, the geography of law, the language and dress of law, legal personnel and the authority of law. This excludes films where 'justice' is enforced outside of any legal framework, for example, war films, social dramas and family sagas.[18]

The most difficult issue has been to separate justice from law and legal process as the idea and portrayal of justice appear across several different genres. An alternative method is to concentrate on the 'legal' personnel whether lawyers or judges, jurors or even those characters carrying out a legal function such as *Erin Brockovich* (2000). Concentrating on the lawyers themselves then opens up analytical frameworks exploring characteristics such as gender, sexuality and ethnicity.[19]

This raises the issue of whether it requires lawyers to be acting as lawyers or whether the professional status is incidental to the plot. It is arguable that a film such as *The Firm* (1993) which is centred around corruption need not be a law firm and could equally be Accountants or similar. *The Devil's Advocate*, which is similarly concerned with the organisation of a law firm, does include a number of court scenes though the genre is supernatural horror. Similar issues apply to films that fit into other genres such as

17. There were 4 sequels to *Dirty Harry, Magnum Force* (1973), *The Enforcer* (1976), *Sudden Impact* (1983), and *The Dead Pool* (1988).
18. S Greenfield, G Osborn and P Robson, *Film and the Law* (Cavendish, 2001) 24.
19. Kamir has written widely on issues of gender see for example O Kamir, *Framed: Women in Law and Film* (Duke University Press, 2006). See generally S Greenfield, G Osborn and P Robson, *Film and the Law* (2nd edn, Hart, 2010) chapters 14 and 15.

comedy though offerings such as *My Cousin Vinny* contain much in common with more 'serious' legal films.[20]

In addition to applying concepts such as genre to legal films visuality has been used as a theoretical framework in addition to the narrative. Drawing upon McArthur's work on gangster films that was rooted in the concept of iconography a structure was developed for legal films.

The starting point was the appearance of the characters themselves which was described as

> 1. The imagery surrounding the physical aspects of the principal actors and characters; this includes dress, physical presence, poise, attitude to other characters. The relationships between the key non-legal personnel and the legal personnel.[21]

The formality of court dress works well with gowns and wigs and this element was neatly satirised in *My Cousin Vinny.*

The second element is related to the pictures of the physical environment:

> 2. Images emanating from the milieu within which the characters are constructed. The courtroom itself and any allied surroundings such as law offices, judges' chambers and the jury room.[22]

The final part was the most innovative with the concept of the process of law as a tool:

> 3. In replacement of McArthur's technology we have identified the use of, and relationship to, the process of law itself. This seems to us to be the most apt comparison given that it is the application of law that is the "tool" at the lawyer's disposal.[23]

The framework worked effectively with British film as the first two elements had a strong presence in the traditional British offerings. It has proved less useful when exploring films from other jurisdictions that don't share the same iconography.

A further attempt to engage with film theory involved the application of Altman's syntactic/semantic structure to a single Scandinavian film, *Solstorm* (2005).[24] The motivation for this approach was to add to the analysis of law films:

---

20. Aside from *My Cousin Vinny* (1992) other notable examples of legal comedy include *Brothers in Law* (1957) A *Fish Called Wanda* (1988) and *Legally Blonde* (2001).
21. S Greenfield, G Osborn and P Robson, 'Genre, Iconography and British Film' (2007) 36 *Baltimore Law Review* 386.
22. Ibid 386.
23. Ibid 387.
24. S Greenfield, '*Solstorm*: Developing a Semantic/Syntactic Approach to Law Films' (2009) 39 *Stetson Law Review* 119. R Altman, 'A Semantic/Syntactic Approach to Film Genre' (1984) 23(3) *Cinema Journal* 6.

> By utilizing this theoretical framework, the Article evaluates both the descriptive and what might be termed the more ideological dimensions of Solstorm to determine whether the film, and other films not clearly within the genre, can be drawn within the boundaries of a law film.[25]

An alternative approach, to engaging with theory, has been to explore how law films have incorporated ideas and concepts from elsewhere reflecting the interest of the author.[26] The beauty of film is that it provides both a vehicle for theoretical analysis and a medium to portray theoretical concepts. While the engagement with theory has been limited the expansion of the research base has been greatly expanded through international investigation.

International Work

A key shift was the deliberate attempt by some writers to move away from the dominance of American-made films and American writers. British scholarship on British films, both in general and specialist areas, developed and themes started to emerge.[27] Some areas like Canada have been dominated by their neighbours in terms of film production, and the extensive Canadian scholarship by prominent writers like Schulz and Johnson and Buchanan has principally looked beyond their own borders but not exclusively.[28] There has also been discussion of issues traditionally out with the boundaries of

25. S Greenfield, '*Solstorm*: Developing a Semantic/Syntactic Approach to Law Films' (2009) 39 *Stetson Law Review* 119, 120.
26. See for example S Greenfield, 'Tobias Beecher: Law as a Refuge from Uncertainty?' in C Picart, M Jacobsen and C Greek (eds) *Framing Law and Crime* (The Farleigh Dickinson University Press, 2016) 455. S Greenfield, 'State Executioner Pierrepoint: A Cinematic Portrayal of Moral Disengagement' in P Hodgkinson (ed) *The International Library of Essays on Capital Punishment*, Volume III (Ashgate, 2013) 391. S Greenfield, 'Contrasting Depictions of Medical Serial Killers: Doctors Pétiot and Shipman from the Manic to the Mundane' in C Picart (ed) *Monsters, Law, Crime: Explorations in Gothic Criminology* (Rowman and Littlefield, 2020) 163.
27. S Greenfield, G Osborn and P Robson, 'Genre, Iconography and British Film' (2007) 36 *Baltimore Law Review* 386. P Robson, 'Vigilantes, the Law and Popular Culture – The British Experience' in P Robson and F Spina, *Vigilante Justice in Society and Popular Culture: A Global Perspective* (University Press Copublishing Division / Fairleigh Dickinson University Press, 2022).
28. R Johnson and R Buchanan, 'Strange Encounters: Exploring Law and Film in the Affective Register' (2009) 46 *Studies in Law, Politics, and Society* 33. R Johnson and R Buchanan, 'Getting the Insider's Story Out: What Popular Film can Tell us about Legal Method's Dirty Secrets' (2001) 20 *Windsor Yearbook of Access to Justice* 87. R Johnson, 'Justice and the Colonial Collision: Reflections on Stories of Intercultural Encounter in Law, Literature, Sculpture and Film' (2012) 9 *No Foundations: An Interdisciplinary Journal of Law and Justice* 68 http://www.helsinki.fi/nofo/NoFo9JOHNSON.html; R Johnson, 'Notes on Using Film to Engage with Philosophy of Law in the Arctic' in D Bunikowski (ed) *Philosophy of Law in the Arctic* (Rovaniemi, 2016); R Johnson, 'Intercultural Cinema and the (Re)Envisioning of Law: Exploring Life, Death and

law and film.[29] Australia has been rather luckier with a more dynamic film industry,[30] in turn, producing more work on locally produced film.[31] From individual essays in journals and collected works a shift from American material has occurred. The topics range from blockbuster films with implications for an understanding of justice[32] to those with a more modest international profile[33] as well as the colonial experience.[34] Some areas are rather more local.[35] Others address topics of great interest across the field of law and popular culture including ethnicity[36] and vigilantism.[37]

Law in *Atanarjuat* and *Before Tomorrow*' in T D Peters and K Crawle (eds) *Envisioning Legality: Law, Culture and Representation* (Routledge, 2016) 228.

29. J Schulz, 'The Cook, the Mediator, the Feminist, and the Hero' (2009) 21 *Canadian Journal of Women and the Law* 177. J Schulz, 'Law & Film: Where are the Mediators?' (2008) 58 *University of Toronto Law Journal* 233. J Schulz, 'The Mediator as Cook: Mediation Metaphors at the Movies' (2007) 2 *Journal of Dispute Resolution* 455; J Schulz, 'Contemplating Law, Film and Mennonites, Law', *Culture and the Humanities* https://doi.org/10.1177/17438721211026560 (June 27, 2021). J Schulz, 'Using Film to Teach ADR' in C Corcos (ed) *The Media Method: Teaching Law with Popular Culture* (Carolina Academic Press, 2019) 381–398. J Schulz and Y JiHyun, 'Monsters & Madwomen? Neurosis, Ambition and Mothering in Women Lawyers in Film' (2016) 16(3) *Journal of Law, Culture and the Humanities* 1.
30. B Goldsmith, S Ward and T O'Regan, *Local Hollywood: Global Film Production and the Gold Coast* (University of Queensland Press, 2010).
31. K Crawley and T D Peters (eds), *Envisioning Legality: Law, Culture and Representation* (Routledge, 2017), K Weinert, K Crawley and K Tranter (eds), *Law, Lawyers and Justice: Through Australian Lenses* (Routledge, 2020); K D Weinert, K Crawley and K Tranter, 'Australian Lenses on Law, Lawyers and Justice' in K Weinert et al. (eds) *Law, Lawyers and Justice: Through Australian Lenses* (Routledge, 2020) chapter 1.
32. P Crofts and H van Rijswijk, 'Picnic at Hanging Rock: Coming of Age as a Girl in the Gothic Colonial Institution' in K Weinert et al. (eds) *Law, Lawyers and Justice: Through Australian Lenses* (Routledge, 2020) chapter 6. K Tranter, 'Justice at the end of Fury Road' in K Weinert et al. (eds) *Law, Lawyers and Justice: Through Australian Lenses* (Routledge, 2020) chapter 13.
33. K Weinert, 'Romper Stomper: A Critique of Neoliberalism in Australia' in K Weinert et al. (eds) *Law, Lawyers and Justice: Through Australian Lenses* (Routledge, 2020) chapter 12. J Quirk and J Murphy 'Whose Country? Colonialism and the Rule of Law in Sweet Country and Charlie's Country' in K Weinert et al. (eds) *Law, Lawyers and Justice: Through Australian Lenses* (Routledge, 2020) chapter 3.
34. A Thalia and K Tranter, 'Taking a Lens to the Chase in Australian Settler State Colonialism' in K Weinert et al. (eds) *Law, Lawyers and Justice: Through Australian Lenses* (Routledge, 2020) chapter 4.
35. K Duncanson, 'Being Engaged in Colonial Critique by Mojo Juju's Native Tongue' in K Weinert et al. (eds) *Law, Lawyers and Justice: Through Australian Lenses* (Routledge, 2020) chapter 8.
36. D Callahan, 'His Natural Whiteness: Modes of Ethnic Presence and Absence in Some Recent Australian Films' in I Craven (ed) *Australian Cinema in the 1990s* (Frank Cass, 2001) 95.
37. L Pâquet, 'Vigilante Frontier Communities on Australian Screens: Bushrangers, Bikies, and Bogans' in P Robson and F Spina (eds) *Vigilante Justice in Society and Popular Culture: A Global Perspective* (Fairleigh Dickinson University Press, 2022) 794.

A survey of the directions of scholarship in *Film and the Law* in 2010[38] briefly noted a range of work being carried out in the non-anglophone world. In Germany, for instance, inspired by Stefan Machura, from German scholars in the twenty-first century there have been examinations of American law films[39] and engagement with major Hollywood fare from a German perspective.[40] There have also been reviews of the scope and methodology[41] of law and film scholarship.[42] The whole area of film in law-related areas such as war has also engaged the scholarly community, and in addition there has been a joint interest in both film and television.

It is clear that law and film also thrives in France with both courses and seminars as well as tangible evidence of a strong engagement with the field through traditional publications and the internet.[43] Similar themes crop up as have been encountered in the anglophone and German work such as the hegemony of Hollywood – the Atticus Finch effect. In 2015 a seminar on Law and Cinema suggested that the role of the United States also appears as dominant and involving nothing less than 'the Americanisation of the law'.[44] The themes of the literature have included the symbols of justice and their function both past and present including their representation in film.[45] Censorship and the controls on film link legal and cultural themes.[46] There have also been wide-ranging surveys with a French series, from the publishers Mare and Martin.[47] Within the overall

38. S Greenfield, G Osborn and P Robson, *Film and the Law: The Cinema of Justice* (Hart, 2010) 285.
39. M Kuzina, *Der amerikanischeGerichtsfilm: Justiz, Ideologie, Dramatik* (Vandenhoek and Ruprecht, 2000); S Machura and S Ulbrich, 'Law in Film: Globalizing the Hollywood Courtroom Drama' (2001) 28 *Journal of Law and Society* 21.
40. S Machura and S Ulbrich (eds), *Rechtim Film* (Baden-Baden, 2002); S Machura, 'German Response to 12 Angry Men' (2007) 82 *Chicago-Kent Law Review* 2; S Machura, 'Procedural Unfairness in Real and Film Trials: Why do Audiences Understand Stories Placed in Foreign Legal Systems?' in M Freeman (ed) *Law and Popular Culture* (Oxford University Press, 2005) 148.
41. S Machura 'An Analysis Scheme for Law Films' (2007) 36 *University of Baltimore Law Review* 329.
42. S Machura, 'Law and Cinema Movement' in C Picart, M Jacobsen and C Greek (eds) *Framing Law and Crime: An Interdisciplinary Anthology* (Rowman & Littlefield, 2016) 25.
43. Master Droit du Cinéma et de l'Audiovisuel https://facdedroit.univ-lyon3.fr/master-droit-du-cinema-et-de-l-audiovisuel-2 (last accessed 17/11/22).
44. Droit et Cinéma Printempts 2015 https://mafr.fr/en/enseignements/droit-et-cinema/ (last accessed 17/11/22).
45. W Mastor and L Miniato (eds) *Les figures du procès au-delà des frontières* (Dalloz, 2014). See also M Flores-Lonjou, 'Le jugefrançais mis en images: images officielles versus images documentaires', in e-legal, Revue de droit et de criminologie de l'ULB - http://e-legal.ulb.be/volume-n01/arrets-sur-images-les-representations-du-juge-au-cinema/le-jugefrancais- (12 October 2018, last accessed 17/11/22).
46. F Herve, *Censure et Cinema dans la France des Trenteglorieuses* (1945-1975) (Nouveau Monde, 2015); C Triolle, *Le contrôlecinématographiqueen France. Quand le sexe, la violence, et la religion font encore débat* (L'Harmattan, 2015).
47. https://www.mareetmartin.com/les-editions-mare-et-martin/les-collections/collection-droit-cinema (last accessed 17/11/22).

heading of *Droit et Cinéma* there have been monographs covering the family in film[48] individual directors, both French[49] and British,[50] TV comic amateur vigilantes,[51] the juridical thought of Sheldon Cooper from *The Big Bang Theory*,[52] Disney films[53] and interdisciplinary engagement with the humanities on specific themes.[54] Add to this a volume on police films[55] and the broad field of law and film has come a long way from the limited material from the early part of the twenty-first century.[56]

There is a fascinating blog, *Le Blog Droit et Cinéma,* which includes the analysis of traditional fare for cineastes such as *Rashomon.*[57] It has also explored the role of Isabelle Huppert in the controversial rape film *Elle*[58] as well as the feted vigilante film *The Revenants*[59] and the State *v* Family rights film *Philomena* (2013). Traditional concerns, such as censorship, appear as well as more unexpected topics such as the law in Star Trek. The directors' work examined ranges wide well beyond the standard coverage of law and film studies into the cinema of Hitchcock, Woody Allen and Clint Eastwood.

Spanish popular culture scholars have continued to focus almost exclusively on film rather than television. There has been a slight shift away from the earlier focus on Hollywood, which was noted in *Film and the Law.* There is also evidence that the interest in film goes beyond the academy into the legal profession. For example, the professional body for lawyers in Aragon, the Real y Ilustre Colegio de Abogados de Zaragoza, reveals in their Journal a series of presentations with accompanying literature, entitled *Ciclo de Cine Juridico.* These have covered *Matar a un ruiseñor* (*To Kill a Mockingbird*) in May 2019, *Doce Hombres sin Piedad* (*12 Angry Men*) in December 2019, *Acusados* (*The Accused*) in June 2020 and *Testigo de cargo* (*Witness for the Prosecution*) in December 2022.[60] There is also a book from commercial lawyers looking at a range of 13 films related to their field from classics like *Lloyds of London* (1936), *Double Indemnity* (1944), *Gilda* (1946) and *It's a*

48. M Flores-Lonjou and E Epinoux, *La famille au cinéma: Regards juridiques et esthétiques* (Mare & Martin, 2016).
49. F Defferrard, *Les lois de Michel Audiard: Liberté, Fraternité, Égalité* (Mare & Martin, 2021).
50. A Coutant, *Les loisd'Alfred Hitchcock* (Mare & Martin, 2018).
51. A Coutant, *Juridiquementvôtre: Brett Sinclair et Danny Wilde, un duo au service du droit* (Mare & Martin, 2020).
52. F Defferrard, *La pensée juridique de Sheldon Cooper ou Comment faire du droit avec The Big Bang Theory* (Mare & Martin, 2019).
53. Q Le Pluard and M Talbot, *Du droit dans Disney* (Mare & Martin, 2020).
54. M Flores-Lonjou, E Épinoux and V Lefebve, *Frontière(s) au cinéma* (Mare & Martin, 2019).
55. J Ollé-Laprune, *Le CinémaPolicierFrancais: 100 films, 100 réalisateurs* (Hugo Images, 2020).
56. C Delage, 'Image as Evidence and Mediation: The Experience of the Nuremberg Trials' in M. Freeman (ed) *Law and Popular Culture* (Oxford University Press, 2005) 491.
57. https://lesmistons.typepad.com/blog/au-quai-des-livres/ (18 May 2021, last accessed 17/11/22).
58. https://lesmistons.typepad.com/blog/au-quai-des-livres/ (30 August 2021, last accessed 17/11/22).
59. https://lesmistons.typepad.com/blog/au-quai-des-livres/ (14 November 2018, last accessed 17/11/22).
60. http://revista.reicaz.es/numeros-anteriores/n-012/cine-y-derecho/ (last accessed 27/11/22).

Wonderful Life (1946), to more modern films such as *Wall Street* 1987), *The Insider* (1999) and *The Social Network* (2010).[61]

The Tirant lo Blanch publishing house in Valencia had by 2022 produced no less than 69 volumes in their *Cine y Derecho* series. Commencing in 2002 there has been a steady stream of works. These can be divided into three broad categories – individual films, thematic works and overviews or guides. First, those which focus on a single film and are generally quite short with an average of 115 pages – the shortest 66 pages and the longest 240. They have covered a wide range of films and have been dominated by material from the United States. Of the 42 individual film monographs, 28 are on American offerings and only 1 on Spanish film. The remaining group examines British (6), Italian (3), French (1), Danish (1), Polish (1) and Palestinian (1). There is, in the volumes produced in the series, only one work on television.[62] The individual films covered ranging from classics are expected in a series dedicated to law and film like *Anatomy of a Murder* (1959), *Judgment at Nuremberg* (1960), *To Kill a Mockingbird* (1961) and *A Few Good Men* (1999); however, some of the early coverage was on less obvious films like *Blade Runner* (1982), *Three Colours Red* (1994), *The Scarlet Letter* (1995), *Macbeth* (1971), *The Matrix* (1999) and *The Shoes of the Fisherman* (1968).

There are 21 volumes centred on specific themes which range from the death penalty, torture, prostitution, rape, strikes and euthanasia to the rights of the child, films on life in the office and factory, prison films and the impact of Francoism. These are rather longer averaging some 240 pages, and there is also a volume from 2012 on the scholarship on law and film with a focus on migration.[63] They consist of essays by a collection of authors while straying from film, and one volume also offers a perspective encompassing literature and comics.[64] The approaches in these collections vary from a legal focus or a cultural assessment to a mixture. There is also a volume from 2020 on the impact of the image of To Kill a Mockingbird's protagonist, Atticus Finch – Nosotros, que quisimos tanto a Atticus Finch – what we love so much about Atticus Finch. This addresses, *inter alia*, the revisionist perspectives on the iconic defence lawyer.

The remaining six volumes involve overviews of the field of law in film. By their very nature they are longer averaging 350 pages. One of the earliest was a guide to law and film in 100 films from 2004.[65] It focused on films which encapsulated a specific legal concept rather than artistic quality and again US cinema dominated with 73 films with 9 from Spain. The remainder were from Italy (7), Great Britain (4), France (3), Japan (2), Colombia (1) and Germany (1). The films included standards like *Young Mr Lincoln* (1939), *12 Angry Men* (1957) and *Anatomy of a Murder* (1959) as well as less obvious films like the prison film *The Birdman of Alcatraz* (1961) and the notorious *Straw Dogs* (1971). The year

61. P Carballo-Calero, *Derechomercantil y cine* (Aranzadi, 2016).
62. M Presno Linera, *The West Wing: La Politica Como Promesa* (Politics as Promise) (Tirant lo Blanch, 2016).
63. M Cantero-Exojo, M Van Liew and J Suarez (eds) *Fotogramas para la multiculturalidad* (Tirant lo Blanch, 2012).
64. M Ramiro Avilés (ed) *Derechos, Cine, Literatura y Cómics. Cómo y porqué* (Tirant lo Blanch, 2014).
65. B Rivaya and B de Cima, *Derecho y Cine en 100 peliculas* (Tirantlo lo Blanch, 2004).

2006 saw the publication of a collection of essays providing a Cinematic Introduction to the Law, which consisted of individual areas of law being illustrated through film.[66] There is also a guide to the law in modern Spanish cinema – El Derechoenel Cine Español Contemporaneo (2009) – recounting the changes in Spanish social, political and cultural life since the arrival of democracy in 1975. This guide is provided by 20 different writers on how this can be seen through film.

Our heuristic division between individual films, themes and overviews does not accommodate every single volume perfectly. There is, for example, a volume on law in the cinema focusing on constitutional law that seeks to provide a guide to a broad theme.[67] The same kind of engagement with the underlying concepts in constitutional law as found in film is the theme of another 2012 volume.[68] Amore obvious example of a guide can be found in *A Judicial Handbook*: cinema for judges, which makes the case to study the seventh art as film offers the opportunity to observe different perspectives on the judicial process.[69]

The pioneering work of Benjamin Rivaya has been revised and expanded from its original 502 to an even weightier 659 pages though the title, however, remains Law and Film in 100 films.[70] The impact of film on people's understanding of the law is examined, and the book explores the field of the cinema of justice including film and legal theory as well as how law and film studies can be used. It seems that the world of film and law in terms of both publications and engagement is thriving in Spain. Law and film has also been subject to consideration in South America from Colombia to Peru and the coverage includes not only traditional Hollywood films but also local material.[71]

There is also extensive work in Italy and from 2017 there has been a series of 18 monographs from Editoriale Scientifica of Naples. Most of these are quite short with an average of just over 60 pages and only 4 in excess of 100 pages. These range across a wide range of topics from the threat to liberty under McCarthyism and neoliberalism in a modern world to taxation issues, bio-medical issues raised by films like *Blade Runner*, the Italian family in film, consumerism and the twentieth-century Balkan Wars.[72]

66. M Presno and B Rivaya, *Una Introducción Cinematográfica al Derecho* (Tirant lo Blanch, 2006).
67. A Ortega, M Ortega, M PresnoLinera, B Ruiz and O Benitez, *Derecho al cine: Una Introducciòncinematográfica al Derechoconstitucional* (Tirant lo Blanch, 2011).
68. F Picón (ed), *Proyecciones de Derecho Constitucional* (Tirant lo Blanch, 2012).
69. B Rivaya, *Un vademécumjudicial Cine para jueces* (Tirant lo Blanch, 2012).
70. B Rivaya, *Derecho y cine en 100 peliculas* (Tirant lo Blanch, 2021).
71. R de Mendizábal Allende, *Cine y Derecho: togas en la gran pantalla* (Chaplin Berenice, 2021). CO'Neill de la Fuente, *El derechova al cine: intersecciones entre la visiónartística y la visiónjurídica de losproblemassociales* (Universidad del Pacífico, 2017).
72. S D'Acunto and V Nuzzo, *Fotogrammi dal dominiodella lotta: L'occhio del cinema sullasocietàne-oliberista* (Editoriale Scientfica, 2017); F Amatucci and A Ciarcia, *Il cinema come evasione... fiscale* (Editoriale Scientfica, 2017); A Ciarcia, *Il cinema e le tasse* (Editoriale Scientfica, 2017); A Salvati, *Timema e Thanatos: Tasse e morte* (Editoriale Scientfica, 2017). R Catalano and C Vndenditti, *Questioni di biodirittonellafilmografia cyberpunk* (Napoli, Editoriale Scientfica, 2017); A Fachechi, *Storie di faciliconsumi* (Editoriale Scientfica, 2017), C DeFiores, *Il fragile scudo dellaCostituzione: L'occhio del cinema sullaviolazionedeidiritti al tempo del maccartismo* (Editoriale

There has also been work on how film represents immigration and medically assisted birth and more recently coverage of the representation of the legal process through the reflective lens of film.

There are also volumes focusing on individual films including the 1963 Italian film *Le Mani Sulla Città* about political corruption in the urban development process and the representation of law in the films of the Italian comic actor Totò.[73] Also the Steve McQueen version of Ibsen's *Enemy of the People* (1978) comes under the spotlight as well as the more conventional American courtroom drama *Fracture* from 2007.[74] Three very different films about Nazism are also examined, the Nazi propaganda historical drama *Jud Süß* (1940) along with the post-War Italian adaptation of the tale of the wandering Jew. Here this story of redemption, *L'ebreoerrante* (1948), is adapted to include the coverage of the Nazi concentration camps and the German Nazi propaganda documentary *Theresienstadt* (1944), which sought to show how the camps were happy and well run.[75] Despite the title of the series being *Cine e Diritto,* there has also been coverage of TV with a work on the US prison drama *Orange Is the New Black.*[76]

There is also a selection of films from some 500 deemed by the authors to be concerned with a legal theme. The coverage includes popular as well as classic Italian films in addition to international material.[77] A later collection of essays from 2020 covered several distinct issues from Italian comedy films between the 1970s to 1990s, multiculturalism in film, cinema and human rights to parenting and well-being, animal rights as well as animal rights and the film industry. There was also coverage of the 2,000 Canadian-American docudrama (*Il processo di Norimberga*).[78] Traditionally, there was a strong interest in Hollywood, although, more recently, there has been a focus on Italian films dealing with legal issues.[79] Such is the nature of the links between politics and law generally and in Italy, in particular, that some studies go beyond a narrow focus on the justice system including the Mafia.[80] Some titles which appear dedicated to film alone also cover other elements of the media. For example, the fascinating collection

---

Scientfica, 2017); M Vitucci, *La guerradietrocasa: Losguardo del cinema sulla Jugoslavia in fiamme* (Editoriale Scientfica, 2017).

73. F Flores, *Le manisullacittà. Il capitalismo: la democrazia in ostaggio* (Editoriale Scientfica, 2018); F Corso, *TotòIllavoro e ...la legge* (Editoriale Scientfica, 2019).
74. C Lanza and L Minieri, *+nemici del popolo* (Editoriale Scientfica, 2017); T Bene and G Spangher, *Un processo americano: Il caso Thomas Crawford* (Editoriale Scientfica, 2017).
75. A Argenio, *I film del nazismo: Süssl'ebreo, L'ebreoerrante, Terezin* (Editoriale Scientfica, 2017).
76. A Esposito, *Dalneroall'arancio: anatomiapenitenziaria di unaserie* TV (Editoriale Scientfica, 2017).
77. G Ziccardi, *Law in Film – 100 Years of Courtroom Drama and Judicial Melodramas) Il diritto al cinema (Cent'anni di courtroom drama e melodrammigiudiziar)i* (Giufre, 2010).
78. O Roselli (ed), *Cinema e diritto. La comprensionedelladimensionegiuridicaattraverso la cinematografia.* (Giappichelli Torino, 2020).
79. P Cattorini, *L'occhiocheuccide. Criminologi al cinema* (Franco Angeli, 2006); E Amodioc, *Esteticadellagiustiziapenale. Prassi, media, fiction* (Giuffrè: Milano, 2016); L Pannarale, 'La veritàdegliavvocati: un'indaginesul cinema italiano' (2021) *Sociologia del Diritto*, 3351.
80. A Mancino, *Il processodellaverità: le radici del film politico-in diziarioitaliano* (Kaplan, 2008); R Curti, *Italian Crime Filmography, 1968-1980* (McFarland Jefferson, 2013); M Ravveduto, *Lospettacolodella mafia. Storia di un immaginariotrarealtà e finzione* (Edizioni Gruppo Abele, 2019).

Innomedellalegge. La giustizianel cinema Italian in addition to considering why there has been no Italian courtroom drama contains essays on literature and television.[81] Again, as in Spain and France, there is the availability of courses on film and law such as the course *Communication, Crime, Deviance* (Comunicazione, Crimine, Devianza) at the University of Salento, which has been looking at films, as well as TV, for more than 10 years.[82] What can be seen is an increasingly rich body of work that has moved away from Hollywood in a myriad of directions.

Contemporary Topics and Future Trajectories

The development of law and film or cinematic justice has grown exponentially over the past 30 years and interestingly the focus on authorship started to shift away from the original base. This was due to the development of specific undergraduate courses investigating the law and film relationship and a desire to explore a multi-faceted research agenda. A key issue is how and where the subject might develop. Contemporary 'law films' are still being produced, for example, *Marshall* (2017), *Just Mercy* (2019), *On the Basis of Sex* (2018), *Dark Waters* (2019), *The Insult* (2017), *The Crime Is Mine* (2023), *The Judge* (2014), *Worth* (2020), *RBG* (2018), *Lucia de B* (2014), *Denial* (2016), *Loving* (2016) and *The Mauritanian* (2021), indicating the continuing appeal of the subject matter as a source of drama.

Contemporaneously new areas have been developed and one field that has exploded onto the screens is '*True Crime*' with a dedicated channel on Sky and a host of programmes on *Netflix* as well as material on all the established terrestrial channels. There are links here back to both documentaries and films based on true events. An interesting starting point is the psychological dimension that the viewer brings to the show and what is offered in return. As Goldman notes: 'the value of a work is measured by its capacity to engage fully and simultaneously all of our mental capacities— cognitive, emotional, imaginative, and perceptual.'[83] So, murder mysteries or whodunnits, or versions thereof, challenge the viewer's cognitive dimension, and we, the audience, engage to find the 'solution'. This cuts across different forms of media and explains the longstanding interest in the genre:

> Thus, the explanation of the mystery's appeal in terms of an intellectual puzzle or enjoyable game played between author and reader is partially correct, since the author is always challenging the reader to develop a correct interpretation of the story as a whole. This challenge or competitive game can be more or less complex, the puzzle solvable by the seasoned reader, as in most Agatha Christie novels, or not solvable by the reader (namely, me), as in mysteries by John Dickson Carr or Colin Dexter.[84]

81. G Vitiello (ed), *In nomedellalegge. La giustizianel cinema italiano* (Soveria Mannell, 2013).
82. https://www.unisalento.it/people/ferdinando.spina/didattica/1256842020/scheda.
83. A Goldman, 'The Appeal of the Mystery' (2011) 69(3), *The Journal of Aesthetics and Art Criticism* 261, 263.
84. Ibid 266.

There is scope to classify the different types of programmes that appear under the generic *True Crime* banner. First the fascination of the *Open Case,* for example, *Unsolved Mysteries* Netflix 2020 and specific examples such as *D.B. Cooper.* Here is something novel something we don't know the answer to, there is no neat and tidy solution. This piques audience interest:

> Perceptual curiosity refers to the driving force that motivates organisms to seek out novel stimuli, which diminishes with continued exposure. It is the primary driver of exploratory behavior in non-human animals and, potentially, also in human infants as well as a possible driving force of human adults' exploration.[85]

The audience is curious as to how this happened, why and who was responsible. The older and the more bizarre the greater the pull, Jack the Ripper stories are still ongoing with the search to unmask the 'true murderer'. Of course, the problem is how can the truth or guilt ever be established in historic cases, perhaps the speculation itself creates sufficient entertainment.

The second obvious class is cases based around *Wrongful Convictions* of which there is a long history through the BBC with *Rough Justice* (1982–2007). On Netflix *Making a Murderer* 2015 was filmed for over 10 years following the story of Steven Avery with a second season following up on the issues was screened in 2018. *The Innocence Files* is a 2020 Netflix production based on the work of the Innocence Project, which 'unravels missteps and deceit in a series of wrongful convictions, exposing the injustice inflicted on victims and the accused'.[86] Further examples can be found on the BBC with the 2016 two-part programme *Conviction: Murder at the Station*, produced in collaboration with the *Inside Justice* charity, which explored the conviction of Roger Kearney.[87] A historical approach has been applied in *Murder Mystery and My Family* with 5 series and some 50 episodes of cases, the oldest going back to 1839.[88] The focal point is a conviction and execution with some doubt cast over the safety of the outcome. The format is an interesting one, essentially a reinvestigation with a leading criminal KC on each side for the defence and prosecution, and the case determined by a judge.[89]

The third identifiable category relates to infamous criminals where there is no doubt over guilt but rather a fascination with their behaviour. The more extreme the outcome in terms of the violence level or the number of victims, the greater the audience's

85. C Kidd and B Hayden, 'The Psychology and Neuroscience of Curiosity' (2015) 88(3) *Neuron* 449, 450.
86. https://www.netflix.com/gb/title/80214563#:~:text=The%20Innocence%20Project%20unravels%20missteps,on%20victims%20and%20the%20accused (last accessed 03/05/2023).
87. https://www.theguardian.com/tv-and-radio/2016/sep/22/conviction-murder-at-station-review-miscarriage-justice-roger-kearney (last accessed 03/05/2023).
88. https://www.stokesentinel.co.uk/news/stoke-on-trent-news/staffordshire-boat-man-hanged-murdering-3575714 (last accessed 03/05/2023).
89. It led to a spin off series, *Murder, Mystery and My Family: Case Closed?* which over 4 seasons revisited some of the original cases and a book, K Farrington, *Murder, Mystery and My Family: A True-Crime Casebook from the Hit BBC Series* (BBC Books, 2019).

fascination. The phenomenon is explained by Harrison and Frederick who argue that the vicarious almost voyeuristic dimension can be explained by the link to horror:

> We live in a society that, as judged by dollars spent and ratings ascribed, places great value on horror as entertainment. Humans gravitate towards reading, hearing, and watching videos of fictional events, nonfictional events, and psychological phenomena that, if one experienced first-person, would undoubtedly cause harm.[90]

This explains the draw of programmes relating to punishment and death row, but there is also the search for a motive. So, programmes on murderous events such as 9/11 the Unabomber killings or the Boston Marathon bombing. Serial killers, such as Ted Bundy, Jeffrey Dahmer and Dennis Nilsen, also feature prominently.

The fourth group might be termed 'the twisted confessional' where convicted killers provide an 'insight' into their crimes. There is a major issue with this approach as it is clearly in the interests of the convicted murderer to present a more favourable perspective to the viewers, especially if there is a prospect of parole. As an example through intense prison interviews, Piers Morgan revisited the crimes of three convicted serial killers to learn more about their motives.[91] This format also included *Killer Women with Piers Morgan* and *Psychopath with Piers Morgan*. In the latter programme Morgan interviewed Paris Bennett, who at 13 years old raped and murdered his 4-year-old sister. He acknowledges his crime but seeks a form of redemption: 'Yes I did commit a monstrous crime but does that one mistake define my entire life [...] I don't think it does.'

A real danger emerging out of the true crime genre is glamourisation. As Mallet notes:

> My students and I often watch true crime documentaries as stimuli for discussion about criminal causation, or victim selection. Recently, a student in one such tutorial expressed admiration for notorious US serial killer Ted Bundy, even going as far as to say she was attracted to him – or at least Hollywood heartthrob Zac Efron's portrayal of him.[92]

The essence of these programmes is to raise curiosity and create drama, while truth (whatever that may be) is less important. Confession and repentance have their role, but a fundamental problem is that with murder there may only be one side of the story to be heard.

---

90. M Harrison and E Frederick, 'Interested in Serial Killers? Morbid Curiosity in College Students' (2020) 41(6) *Current Psychology* 1.
91. https://www.netflix.com/dk-en/title/80241003 (last accessed 10/05/2023).
92. X Mallet, 'Glamorising Violent Offenders with "True Crime" Shows and Podcasts Needs to Stop' *The Conversation*, August 16 2019 https://theconversation.com/glamorising-violent-offenders-with-true-crime-shows-and-podcasts-needs-to-stop-121806 (last accessed 10/05/2023).

Conclusion

At the outset of the development of law and film there was a limited range of material, largely what might be termed classic Hollywood films that had stood the 'test of time'. Figures such as Fonda's Juror No 8 and Gregory Peck's Atticus Finch were untouchable principled defenders of justice during a golden age of courtroom drama. Gradually this model altered as the lawyers were portrayed as more flawed and vulnerable, the alcoholic Frank Galvin in *The Verdict* (1982) and even the unethical such as Sam Bowden in *Cape Fear* (1991). A more complex and interesting portrait was appearing. Contemporaneously very high-quality works *inter alia. The Sopranos*, *The Wire*, *Oz* and others were being produced for the home viewing market. This has continued apace as *Netflix* and other streaming services have become increasingly important. *Breaking Bad* and the spin-off *Better Call Saul* have become very popular both with viewers and as a social media phenomenon. *Better Call Saul* is a dramatic vehicle concerning the law, lawyers and legal practice with a wide range of characters and issues. Ethics and principles fluctuate across storylines and within characters as the number of episodes (63 over 6 seasons) permits the development of complex characters and plot lines. The whole landscape of 'cinematic' justice has altered immeasurably and there are now many more opportunities to compare, contrast, investigate and analyse, but the downside is the sheer quantity of the material available. The fundamental issue of the vexed intertwining of law and justice is still present as it provides a dramatic framework around which stories can be built. An obvious solution to the problem of volume and trying to create overarching theories is to pick out a strand and even categories within that strand: for example, women protagonists in vigilante films. This ring-fencing is almost the opposite of where the subject started and does allow for more meaningful work to be developed. What is perhaps the most disappointing is the failure to develop the work focusing on audience reception and the influence of films. This is perhaps explained by the lack of social science research methods by those involved.

The focus, taken over the years by scholars in law and film, has changed from a rather functional approach, seeking to simply engage their students more effectively with doctrinal and practical issues. Typically, the interest was on what legal errors there were in specific films.[93] The relationship with the humanities is, thereafter, symbiotic or perhaps more accurately parasitic.[94] This stems from the critical methods that are

93. P Bergman and M Asimow, *Reel Justice* (Andrews & McMeel, 1996).

94. A Bottomley and N Moore, 'Law, Diagram, Film: Critique Exhausted' (2012) 23 *Law and Critique* 163; M de Zwart, B Richards and S Le Mire (eds), *Law and Popular Culture in Australia* (LexisNexis, 2015); C Douzinas, 'A Humanities of Resistance' in A Sarat, M Anderson and C Frank (eds), *Law and Humanities: An Introduction* (Cambridge University Press, 2009) 49; L Gies, 'Law as Popular Culture: Cross-Disciplinary Encounters' (2005) 19(2) *Continuum* 165; P Gisler, S Borella and C Wiedmer, 'Setting the Stage: Reading Law and Culture' in P Gisler, S Borella and C Wiedmer (eds), *Intersections of Law and Culture* (Palgrave Macmillan, 2012) 1; K Laster, *Law as Culture* (Federation Press, 2001); M Leiboffand and C Sharp 'Cultural Legal Studies and Law's Popular Cultures' in C Sharp and M Leiboff (eds) *Cultural Legal Studies: Law's Popular Cultures and the Metamorphosis of Law* (Routledge, 2016) 3; W MacNeil and P

central.[95] From the early days there had been interest in historical elements[96] along with some limited engagement with empirical approaches.[97] There has been little obvious engagement with literature which has operated in its own silo.[98] Much the same can be said about law and linguistics with its own specialist journal.[99] It is clear from the material noted above that the area of law and film has developed its own set of interests and criteria and has become self-sustaining and self-referential while drawing on some of the cognate areas of the humanities.

Hutchings, 'Law's Cultural Mediations: An Introduction by Way of Introduction' (2001) 10(2) *Griffith Law Review* 1.

95. G Binder and R Weisberg 'Cultural Criticism of Law' (1997) 49(5) *Stanford Law Review* 1149; S Sternet, B Meyler and M Del Mar (eds), *The Oxford Handbook of Law and Humanities* (Oxford University Press, 2019).
96. F Nevins, 'Through the Great Depression on Horseback: Legal Themes in Western Films of the 1930s' in J Denvir (ed) *Legal Reelism* (University of Illinois Press, 1996) 44.
97. M Asimow et al., 'Perceptions of Lawyers: A Transnational Study of Student Views on Law and Lawyers' (2005) 12 *International Journal of the Legal Profession* 407.
98. K Dolin, *Critical Introduction to Law and Literature* (Cambridge University Press, 2007); K Dolin, *Fiction and the Law: Legal Discourse in Victorian and Modernist Literature* (Cambridge University Press, 1999); K Dolin (ed), *Law and Literature* (Cambridge University Press, 2018); M Thornton, *Romancing the Tomes: Popular Culture, Law and Feminism* (Routledge, 2008).
99. *International Journal for the Semiotics of Law* (from 1988 to date – thus far 35 volumes).

Chapter Five

LAW AND GEOGRAPHY

Cristy Clark and John Page

Introduction: Studying the Legal in Legal Geography

Legal geography explores the interconnections between law and space, a field of study that relates law to context, while simultaneously revealing geography's legal footprints. The rich interconnections between law and space, and the diverse ways that each co-inform and co-constitute the other are legal geography's 'core objects of inquiry'.[1] In this chapter, we observe how this area of scholarship has evolved over nearly three decades, beginning in the mid-1990s, a generational confluence of law and geography that is neither a 'sub-discipline of human geography nor [...] an area of specialized legal scholarship' but rather (or, at least) 'a truly interdisciplinary intellectual project'.[2]

As a discrete 'intellectual project', legal geography features several defining characteristics. Core to its mission is to emplace law and to bring law to landscape. Legal geography likewise takes a broad sweep of form: from grand theory to the 'small';[3] from global observations of space, time and law to (sometimes very local) place-based case studies; and from explicit disciplinary articulation to an implied nuanced analysis. In the latter case, legal geography can play a significant, albeit often unacknowledged role in informing the scholarship.[4]

Writing in 1994, the foundational legal geographer Nicholas Blomley quoted Lawrence Friedman and David Harvey, who each in turn (yet separately) recognised the limitations of their own disciplines. Friedman argued 'law [...] is too important to be left to lawyers', while Harvey mirrored this sentiment word for word, noting that 'geography is too important to be left to geographers'.[5] Each gave voice to a gap that these two complementary disciplines had left lying on the field, a 'hidden to plain sight' lacuna of spatial relations where law fails to acknowledge the world it inhabits, and

1. I Braverman et al., 'Introduction: Expanding the Spaces of Law' in I Braverman and others (eds), *The Expanding Spaces of Law: A Timely Legal Geography* (Stanford University Press, 2014) 1.
2. Ibid.
3. D Delaney, 'Legal Geography I: Constitutivities, Complexities, and Contingencies' (2015) 39 *Progress in Human Geography* 96, 100.
4. See, for example, J Copeland Nagle, *Law's Environment: How the Law Shapes the Places We Live* (Yale University Press, 2010).
5. Cited in the Foreword to N Blomley, *Law, Space, and the Geographies of Power* (The Guildford Press, 1994).

geographers ignore or undervalue how 'social spaces, lived places, and landscapes are inscribed with legal significance'.[6]

In writing this chapter, we acknowledge our own disciplinary perspective on legal geography. We are both lawyers, variously critical property and human rights theorists. In many ways, unlike the 'progress report' that David Delaney penned from 2015 to 2017, when he wrote across three sequential journal articles of legal geography's evolution through a human geographer's lens,[7] our brief survey of the field is necessarily a legal interpretation. Rather than surmising what is the effect of law on geography, as Delaney ventures, we observe how geography has informed (and informs) the law. In other words, we seek to emphasise the *legal* in legal geography.

This chapter first sets out a brief overview of the evolution of legal geography, identifying a (non-exhaustive) number of critical works that serve as guideposts for its early development. These works include Blomley's *Law, Space, and the Geographies of Power* in 1994, two early edited books from the early 2000s, Delaney's theoretical enlivenment of the discipline in 2010, *The Spatial, the Legal, and the Pragmatics of World-Making*, and closing in its first-half with the landmark *The Expanding Spaces of Law* in 2014. It also observes legal geography's marked early engagement with urban issues, including spatial justice, enclosure, gentrification and what Mariana Valverde describes elsewhere as the 'everyday life of the (city) street'.[8]

Following this background survey of the literature and its early focus, the chapter then turns to more recent developments in legal geography, where the critical lens has expanded from urban spaces to highlight issues of environmental justice, the climate crisis and the ontological questions raised by deep considerations of humanity's legal relationships to place. In this section, the chapter considers legal geography's contributions to our understanding of the law, of its returning law to place; its revelation of the law's extant plurality; and its enrichment of the methodologies of legal scholarship. These are but several of the spatially informed skills required of legal scholarship as it grapples with the pressing ontological challenges raised by legal pluralism and the Anthropocene.

Formative Guideposts

While any 'history' of legal geography could extend back to the 1980s to pinpoint legal thinkers who 'found space without having found geography',[9] this chapter begins in

6. I Braverman and others (eds), *The Expanding Spaces of Law: A Timely Legal Geography* (Stanford University Press, 2014) 1.
7. D Delaney, 'Legal Geography I: Constitutivities, Complexities, and Contingencies' (2015) 39 *Progress in Human Geography* 96; D Delaney, 'Legal Geography II: Discerning Injustice' (2016) 40 *Progress in Human Geography* 267; D Delaney, 'Legal Geography III: New Worlds, New Convergences' (2017) 41 *Progress in Human Geography* 667.
8. M Valverde, *Everyday Law on the Street: City Governance in an Age of Diversity* (Chicago University Press, 2012).
9. I Braverman and others (eds), *The Expanding Spaces of Law: A Timely Legal Geography* (Stanford University Press, 2014) 2, for example, G Frug, 'The City as a Legal Concept' (1980) 93 *Harvard Law Review* 1057.

1994 with Blomley's *Law, Space, and the Geographies of Power*. This book is notable for its original critique of the common law (and particularly the modern common law of property), and its contextualisation of the shared histories and common synergies of both property and cartography that were early catalysts for each discipline's journey away from place and towards abstraction. It is also notable as a work that spoke explicitly of *legal geography* at a time when the nascent disciplinary project was rarely named.[10]

Law, Space, and the Geographies of Power was novel in many respects. Irus Braverman et al. describe it as 'agenda-setting' and 'arguably the founding treatise' of legal geography as an inter-disciplinary project.[11] Its concept of mapping law to place, its reminder that property was (and is) diverse, and its observation of the 'legal universe's […] centralizing and totalizing' logic that erased counter-stories of resistance,[12] were some of the spatio-temporal perspectives that have enriched the law of property with hitherto little-written tales of plurality, context and *critical* history.[13]

The concept of *mapping* law to place is alien to the law's modern conceit that it operates as a detached, neutral arbiter, a 'dis-embedded super-structure […] interpreted at the highest level of spatial abstraction'.[14] Reducing the law to mapped place, however, is a task that exposes this fallacy, one that few, if any, legal scholars have undertaken. As such, it becomes a task ripe for legal geographic analysis. In so doing in *Law, Space, and the Geographies of Power*, Blomley observes the significance of *absence* and what this says about the law's anti-geography bias:

> One important way in which space appears in law, ironically, is as an absence. [T]he spatial diversity of legal possibilities and meanings is erased by the assumed uniformity of legal norms and the aspatiality of legal knowledge, so central to legal decision-making and the 'rule of law.' Western legal reasoning is celebrated as utopic, divorced from the specificities and bonds of place and community[…]. According to the orthodox account: 'Law' cannot be customized to fit such circumstances as may actually arise; 'general principles' must outweigh specific considerations. This juridical common-sense however piles abstraction on abstraction. It is geographical nonsense, anti-geography.[15]

Gaps in maps become therefore not only a 'spatial deficiency' but are reinforced as a 'legal deficiency' too.[16] Legal geography calls out this 'geographical nonsense' and disrupts this closed loop, depicting another way to 'see' property such that inconvenient 'gaps' instead reveal the existence and location of other property types and landed practices away from the highly visible, bright lines of the private estate.

---

10. N Blomley, *Law, Space, and the Geographies of Power* (The Guildford Press, 1994).
11. I Braverman and others (eds), *The Expanding Spaces of Law: A Timely Legal Geography* (Stanford University Press, 2014) 5.
12. C Clark and J Page, *The Lawful Forest: A Critical History of Property, Protest, and Spatial Justice* (Edinburgh University Press, 2022) 102.
13. Ibid.
14. N Blomley, *Law, Space, and the Geographies of Power* (The Guildford Press, 1994) 77.
15. Ibid 53.
16. Ibid 54.

Such gaps also highlight the 'on-the-ground' reality that property and its laws were (and are) diverse. During the enclosure period, which reached its height in seventeenth- and eighteenth-century England, vast swathes of common lands were 'enclosed', unleashing massive social and economic change, and carving out a landscape that was a private property monotone, a 'world that was shaped and built and understood through private ownership, permanent site of all kinds, and exclusion'.[17] Blomley argues that this loss of property diversity sounded not only in the sheer acreage of diverse tenures enclosed but also in the loss of their potential to prefigure and re-imagine different ways of relating to space.[18]

This 'forgetting' of property plurality not only forecloses on the memories of past spatial relations but it also effaces and makes invisible *other* extant forms of non-private property, such as limited modern commons,[19] or the public estate.[20] To enclosure's proponents, the 'localized legal practices' and 'multiple jurisdictions operating at several spatial scales' were 'an affront to [the] unitary legal map'.[21] Yet legal geography reminds us of our diverse relations with land and space that are otherwise lost to plain sight.

Legal geography also makes plainer property's *other* narratives, tales of protest and resistance and alt-narratives of shared spatial legalities. As Blomley stresses, this interrelationship of law, power and spatial justice poses a 'question *central* to critical legal geography'.[22] He argues that the study of legal oppression necessitates 'an analysis of *opposition* to such oppression', a geography of protest which 'can be used to contest the closure of the legal map' by its enlivenment of 'alternative legalities [that] occupy the same jurisdictional space'.[23] Nearly three decades later, Blomley's advocacy for this central role continues: 'The violent injustices constituted by, and so often obscured by legal spatiality, not only persist, but often intensify. Naming and challenging the violence of such splices has never been more urgent. This, for me, is the work of legal geography.'[24]

Narratives of context, erasure and resistance all speak to the law's vexed, yet dynamic relationship to space and place. *Law, Space, and the Geographies of Power* set a benchmark for its scrutiny of spatiality and the law, a scholarly momentum that gained increasing traction in the years that followed, and which was captured in a snapshot moment by two key edited volumes that appeared at the beginning of the 2000s.

One common theme in these later collections stressed that space is neither inert nor apolitical. In 1994, Blomley observes that 'space no longer appears to have a subjective

17. T Dee, *Ground Work: Writings on Places and People* (Jonathan Cape, 2018) 53.
18. N Blomley, *Unsettling the City: Urban Land and the Politics of Property* (Routledge, 2004) 15.
19. C Rose, *Property and Persuasion: Essays on The History, Theory, and Rhetoric of Ownership* (Routledge, 1994) 199.
20. J Page, *Public Property, Law and Society: Owning, Belonging, Connecting in the Public Realm* (Routledge, 2021).
21. N Blomley, *Law, Space, and the Geographies of Power* (The Guildford Press, 1994) 76.
22. Ibid 56 (emphasis added).
23. Ibid 57.
24. N Blomley, 'Foreword: What is Legal Geography? Why, and Why Now?' in Bartel and J Carter (eds), *Research Handbook on Space, Place and Law* (Edward Elgar, 2021) xviii.

quality, but increasingly appears as an objective and pregiven surface […] something to be measured, contained, divided, manipulated, and crucially alienated'.[25] The trajectory 'has been to make space irrelevant' with the appeal of its 'aspatial language' and the 'homogenous rule of law'.[26] *The Legal Geographies Reader* and *Law and Geography* were edited collections that forcefully contested this legal aspatiality, arguing that space and legal claims to space are dynamic, co-constituted and unambiguously political.[27]

For example, in the essay 'Landscapes of Property', Blomley describes an inner-city neighbourhood in Vancouver, Canada, where the idea of space as blank or neutral is refuted by the facts on the ground. Rather law and geography intersect to co-constitute and transform the 'mean' and 'degraded' streets of the city's Downtown Eastside into a 'home' for its residents.[28] And instead of private property staking out a community's boundaries, local usages and practices effect a 'collective' claim to space that is both proprietorial and political:

> The physical landscape of the Downtown Eastside is locally owned […] in at least two practical ways. First collective investment in the physical landscape has occurred through histories of co-present *use and habitation*. Second the local landscape has been locally *produced* through collective action and political struggle […] The landscape is not silent but speaks to a history of struggle, occupation, and use.[29]

As Jane Holder and Carolyn Harrison surmise, 'context is everything'.[30] Law can only be understood, they argue, 'by reference to its place in, and relationship to, social, economic, political and ecological systems'.[31] Such a contextual approach shows that 'law's separateness', its supposed deafness to 'material, physical, spatial and cultural influences', is flawed. But their ambition is primarily to underscore law's *geographic* context, '[and] for good reasons, the very least of which is the paucity of research conducted […] under the "Law and Geography" banner'.[32]

The political dimensions of space, power and property were stark in Georgette Poindexter's essay 'Idolatry of Land', where the 'manicured' suburban lawn is proxy for private privilege, and where 'land as a communal good has been warped to limit the use of the good only to those presently in control':[33]

25. N Blomley, *Law, Space, and the Geographies of Power* (The Guildford Press, 1994) 91.
26. Ibid 107.
27. N Blomley, D Delaney and R T Ford (eds), *The Legal Geographies Reader* (Blackwell, 2001); J Holder and C Harrison (eds), *Law and Geography* (Oxford University Press, 2002).
28. N Blomley, 'Landscapes of Property' in N Blomley, D Delaney and R T Ford (eds), *The Legal Geographies Reader* (Blackwell, 2001) 123.
29. Ibid 124.
30. J Holder and C Harrison, 'Connecting Law and Geography' in J Holder and C Harrison (eds), *Law and Geography* (Oxford University Press, 2002) 1.
31. Ibid.
32. Ibid.
33. Ge Poindexter, 'Idolatry of Land' in J Holder and C Harrison (eds), *Law and Geography* (Oxford University Press, 2002) 205.

> The maniacal attention to lawn along the 'fenceless state' of suburbia can be used as a metaphor for the tension between the individual right to private property and the social interconnectedness of all property. It begs the question: who owns your front lawn – you or your neighborhood.[34]

These edited collections also foregrounded law's *relationality*. Penny English draws a link between the significance of place, and people's sense of belonging, and their personal and social identity.[35] People are 'knitted into a network of locales [...] a series of places through which people's life histories are threaded'. 'A place is not just a thing or an entity. Place is a relational concept.'[36]

While the emerging themes of legal geography may have become clearer by the end of the first decade of the twenty-first century, the seeming 'lack' of a theoretical basis for the disciplinary project was increasingly noticed. David Delaney's *The Spatial, the Legal, and the Pragmatics of World-Making* is frequently cited for its pioneering articulation of a basis for legal geographic theory.[37]

As Braverman and her colleagues observed in 2014, Delaney's monograph made three significant contributions to legal geography:

> [It] identifie[d] impediments to advancing the legal geography project, [...] the tacit alignment of the legal with discursivity and of spatiality with materiality, the generally disjointed or 'archipelagic' nature of legal geography, and the lack of distinctive theoretical frameworks that can be deployed across a range of contexts.[38]

The latter two 'impediments' are correlatives of a particular characteristic of geography's intersection with the law, the preponderance of the 'disjointed' or 'archipelagic' case study set amidst an absence of a clear (grand) theoretical framework that ties the scholarship together. In remedying such shortcomings, Delaney offered 'a set of neologisms', the 'most important of which are the *nomosphere*, the *nomic setting*, and the *nomoscape*'.[39]

Nomic settings are these individual or particularised case studies, while *nomoscapes* describe the assemblages of case studies and a consideration of their processes. Finally, it is the *nomosphere*, the overarching theoretical framework, which explains and contextualises. These coined expressions seek to address, or at least speak to, the inherent tension between the material and the theoretical. As we opine later in this chapter, our view is that legal geography's inclination should be to *extract* (from place-based context),

---

34. Ibid 204.
35. P English, 'Space and Time: The Genius Loci of Ancient Places' in J Holder and C Harrison (eds), *Law and Geography* (Oxford University Press, 2002).
36. Ibid 466.
37. D Delaney, *The Spatial, the Legal and the Pragmatics of World-Making: Nomospheric Investigations* (Routledge, 2010).
38. I Braverman and others (eds), *The Expanding Spaces of Law: A Timely Legal Geography* (Stanford University Press, 2014) 11.
39. Ibid 11.

not *abstract*. This is so because inevitably insights from other disciplines are necessary to enable or complete a theoretical approach to legal geography.

However, while not fully resolving the tension between theory and materiality, the concepts of *nomosphere*, *nomic setting* and *nomoscape* have been instrumental in identifying and distinguishing between:

1. The small-scale case studies (generally focused on *nomic settings* – the home, the court room, the street, etc.);
2. Attempts to 'connect the dots', drawing lessons from these case studies to understand processes and systems of power – those 'assemblages of *nomic settings*' or the '*nomoscapes*';[40] and
3. Ultimately, the need to draw on other disciplines in order to generate a broader theoretical framework that deals with issues of race, gender, class, neoliberalism and so on (helping to construct a 'fuller' *nomosphere*).

Indeed, Blomley later circumvents the need for legal geography to develop its own discrete theoretical framework, describing legal geography as a 'disposition' rather than a 'discipline',[41] a signifier that speaks to the richness and importantly, the utility of diverse (and outside) disciplinary insights.

This survey of earl(ier) literature concludes with another edited collection, *The Expanding Spaces of the Law: A Timely Legal Geography*,[42] a body of work that marked an inflection point of sorts in legal geography's ongoing development. As its title makes clear, the spaces of law continue to grow beyond their initial lines of enquiry and disciplinary approaches, from cross-disciplinary 'encounters' and inter-disciplinary 'common projects' to a 'third' truly trans-disciplinary 'mode',[43] one where scholars from beyond law and geography and from beyond 'Western' jurisdictions enrich and expand the field.[44] Its prescient essays include a study of 'thickening time' and the spatiotemporal dynamics in law, pluralist legal orders, the learning lessons of performative theory and the 'methodological turn' in legal geography.[45]

---

40. Also known in critical property theory as 'lawscapes': N Graham, *Lawscape: Property, Environment, Law* (Routledge, 2011).
41. N Blomley, 'Foreword: What Is Legal Geography? Why, and Why Now?' in R Bartel and J Carter (eds), *Research Handbook on Space, Place and Law* (Edward Elgar, 2021) xviii.
42. I Braverman and others (eds), *The Expanding Spaces of Law: A Timely Legal Geography* (Stanford University Press, 2014).
43. Ibid 5.
44. Ibid 9–12.
45. Respectively, F von Benda Beckmann and K von Benda-Beckmann, 'Places that Come and Go: A Legal Anthropological Perspective on the Temporalities of Space in Plural Legal Orders' 30–52; M Valverde, '"Time Thickens, Takes on Flesh": Spatiotemporal Dynamics in Law' 53–76; N Blomley, 'Learning from Larry: Pragmatism and the Habits of Legal Space' 77–94; and I Braverman, 'Who's Afraid of Methodology? Advocating a Methodological Turn in Legal Geography' 120–141, in I Braverman and others (eds), *The Expanding Spaces of Law: A Timely Legal Geography* (Stanford University Press, 2014).

The editors predict, and proffer, a number of ways, many 'already nascent in recent legal geographic scholarship',[46] into which legal geography can continue to grow. These include the 'particularities' or 'specificities' of power in space (and not merely its presence), addressing legal geography's privileging of space over time (through, for example, performance theory)[47] or moving beyond the human. The editors likewise argue it prudent to move beyond the project's 'nascent theoretical resources' to embrace other disciplinary influences (such as the humanities or physical geography),[48] and importantly, to re-think *the law* from a 'provincialized' Western mono-perspective to pluralist conceptualisations.[49] In surveying both the retrospective and the prospective, *The Expanding Spaces of the Law* detects and previews a paradigm shift, the subject-matter of this chapter's second half, and its study of the further 'expanding spaces of the law' into the legal spaces of Indigenous ontology, the emergence of environmental personhood, the climate crisis and cognate others.

Yet before leaving this discussion of formative guideposts, it would be neglectful to not observe the powerful context of the city and urbanism in this phase. Another Blomley monograph, *Unsettling the City: Urban Land and the Politics of Property,* exemplifies the city's then dominance of legal geographic discourse.[50] While this work traversed many of the themes already discussed, such as the law's pretence of objective neutrality, it did so through a particularly urban focus. 'Urban spaces are propertied spaces', Blomley observes,[51] 'where struggles over city space can be understood as part of the long-standing struggle to resist the enclosure of the commons, and carve out a right to place'.[52]

Resistance (to enclosure) was thus viewed through the lens of gentrification and its generational dispossession of inner-city residents, or through the 'push-back' of collective claims to under-used urban spaces (such as an abandoned department store or a neglected city park). In a similar vein, the rise of 'guerilla' gardening or urban community food gardens could be seen as collective claims or attachments to space. 'Cities are sites in which people live inside the [private] ownership model, but also depart from it',[53] as if the sheer density of people to place, and the intensified development pressures this unleashes, enables a clearer 'seeing' of property – in all its diversity and its continual 'state of contestatory becoming.'[54] Cities are 'terra populi',[55] Blomley asserts, comprising

46. I Braverman and others (eds), *The Expanding Spaces of Law: A Timely Legal Geography* (Stanford University Press, 2014) 13.
47. N Blomley, 'Performing Property: Making the World' (2013) 26 *Canadian Journal of Law & Jurisprudence* 23.
48. I Braverman and others (eds), *The Expanding Spaces of Law: A Timely Legal Geography* (Stanford University Press, 2014) 15.
49. Ibid 16.
50. N Blomley, *Unsettling the City: Urban Land and the Politics of Property* (Routledge, 2004).
51. Ibid xvi.
52. Ibid xix.
53. Ibid 15.
54. Ibid 53.
55. Ibid 93.

parcels of 'social property' and 'localized sets of relations conceived in terms of social interaction and effective bonds',[56] not blank slates ripe for gentrified re-development.

The urban dominance of earlier legal geographic scholarship led to Braverman et al. to comment in 2014 on 'another hitherto neglected zone of legal scholarship', the empty field of rural space.[57] Here, the work of Lisa Pruitt stands out, Pruitt's writing of diffuse 'rural lawscapes' and their 'relative absence of official legal actors and legal institutions.'[58] Pruitt argues that 'critical legal geographers have largely ignored the rural end of the urban-rural continuum, reflecting a rarely acknowledged urban normativity, not to mention urban hubris'.[59] As if underscoring this edited collection's breaking with the past, the project's 'default urban norm' was finally given voice and critical visibility.

Shifting Places and Laws

This shift away from the 'default urban norm' has led to a growing focus on environmental issues, including the 'impacts of environmental and climatic change on our material environments'.[60] Introducing their edited collection, *Legal Geography: Perspectives and Methods*, Tayanah O'Donnell et al. argue, '[m]ateriality of place should be as important to a legal geographer as the social dimension of place'.[61] This collection is particularly focused on how the physical features of land and waterscapes exert a distinct influence over the development of law, and law, in turn, 'has an enormous power to transform the material (including landscapes) through fixing, labelling, restricting and ordering'.[62]

In their chapter, 'Patent Landscaping for Vanuatu', Daniel Robinson et al. argue:

> Much of the study in the field of legal geography seeks to understand the co-constitution of both law and place, which is often discussed by legal geographers in regard to planning and environmental laws, through case law analysis and in studying laws in different places and contexts.[63]

---

56. Ibid 94.
57. I Braverman and others (eds), *The Expanding Spaces of Law: A Timely Legal Geography* (Stanford University Press, 2014) 22.
58. L Pruitt, 'The Rural Lawscape' in I Braverman and others (eds), *The Expanding Spaces of Law: A Timely Legal Geography* (Stanford University Press, 2014) 207.
59. I Braverman and others (eds), *The Expanding Spaces of Law: A Timely Legal Geography* (Stanford University Press, 2014).
60. T O'Donnell, D F Robinson and J Gillespie, 'An Australasian and Asia-Pacific Approach to Legal Geography' in T O'Donnell, D F Robinson and J Gillespie (eds), *Legal Geography: Perspectives and Methods* (Routledge, 2020) 9.
61. Ibid.
62. Ibid.
63. D F Robinson and others, 'Patent Landscaping for Vanuatu' in T Oanahinson and D F Robinson and J Gillespie (eds), *Legal Geography: Perspectives and Methods* (Routledge, 2020) 74.

They go on to explain, '[l]egal geography scholarship thereby offers scholars, and also activists, paradigmatic strategies for approaching the spatial and material dimensions of social and environmental justice.'[64]

These 'spatial and material dimensions of social and environmental justice' have been drawn into particularly sharp relief by the increasingly alarming impacts of climate change. Here, Tayanah O'Donnell et al. argue that legal geography's strength is in engaging 'with material dimensions of real-world problems by incorporating multiple methods, and a variety of disciplinary perspectives', including case studies 'complemented by a range of empirical, normative, discourse and doctrinal analyses'.[65] For example, Tayanah O'Donnell employs a case study analysis of a NSW Land and Environmental Court case ('the Vaughan Litigation')[66] '[l]aw's relationship with place, and the effects on social context, including in relation to climate change'.[67] The case concerned the maintenance of a seawall that protected private property from increasing extreme weather events at the expense of the public beach, and O'Donnell observes, '[t]he reciprocity of law and place is increasingly relevant in the age of the Anthropocene, in understanding how planetary boundaries can reshape social discourse'.[68] O'Donnell argues that this case, alongside others in the Land and Environment Court around climate change flood risk, 'demonstrates the increasing significance of climate change adaptation as a key context for legal geography scholarship, and the reciprocities between law and place that courts in some jurisdictions can illustrate'.[69] She concludes by arguing 'the disruption effect of climate change, to both law and to places, provides opportunities for transformative thinking in the nature/culture interface'.[70]

This growing environmental focus, along with legal geography's attentiveness to relationality and the political dimensions of space, power and property, has led to a wealth of place-based case studies focused on displacement, dispossession and spatial injustice – often centrally informed by the perspective of those engaged in active resistance. For example, Meg Sherval's work on the resistance of women in Australia and the UK to shale gas extraction highlights the way that this extractive industry's attempts to:

> exploit 'space as a resource [and as] a site of production' [...] invites a consideration of 'the local, the temporal and the relational' because the landscapes where these new material relations are proposed and currently taking place represent sites of power and contestation.[71]

---

64. Ibid.
65. T O'Donnell, D F Robinson and J Gillespie, 'An Australasian and Asia-Pacific Approach to Legal Geography' in T O'Donnell, D F Robinson and J Gillespie (eds), *Legal Geography: Perspectives and Methods* (Routledge, 2020) 7.
66. *Byron Shire Council v Vaughan [Proceedings 40344] NSWLEC*2009.
67. T O'Donnell, 'Legal Geography and Coastal Climate Change Adaptation: The Vaughan Litigation' (2016) 54 *Geographical Research* 301, 302.
68. Ibid 304.
69. Ibid 309.
70. Ibid 310.
71. M Sherval, 'Activating Rural Spaces in the Pursuit of Unconventional Energy and Justice' in R Bartel and J Carter (eds), *Research Handbook on Space, Place and Law* (Edward Elgar, 2021) 142, citing R Ghosn, 'Energy as a Spatial Project' 2 *New Geographies* 1, 7.

Sherval notes that accusations of 'NIMBYism' levelled at these activists miss the point that while place-based attachment is important to these struggles,[72] they are also sites of contestation around the larger public interest 'implications [of these extractive industries] for land, water, food, climate and energy futures.'[73]

Resistance to extractivism is also a theme in the 2021 paper by Martuwarra RiverOfLife et al., which employs a place-based case study to highlight the contest between the 'acceleration of invasive colonial "development"', including extractive industries, and the ongoing resistance of Traditional Owners to the threat this poses to the health of the Martuwarra/Fitzroy River and her peoples' (and by extension all Country).[74] In critically examining the role of law in this contest, they note:

> The currently dominant unsustainable extractive approach reflects a colonial framework that sidelines both Traditional Owners and the depth of Aboriginal legal and normative traditions. In doing so, this extractive approach also sidelines and disrespects both the Martuwarra itself, and the Yoongoorookoo story [Indigenous law].[75]

Legal geography's capacity to both reveal and critique the legal and political dimensions of both belonging and dispossession is being increasingly employed in relation to history, colonialism and resistance. Clark and Page, for example, draw attention to the history of ongoing resistance to the displacement and dispossession caused by enclosure – one that only makes sense through the combined analysis of both individual instances and the larger pattern of what David Harvey calls 'accumulation by dispossession'.[76] Building on Harvey, in his examination of the history of the political economy of land dispossession in India, Levien suggests the concept of 'regimes of dispossession' as a more effective way to 'emphasise the significance of state coercion to the process of dispossession, and to capture variation in patterns of dispossession over time and place'.[77] Here Levien argues, '[i]f dispossession is a social relation of coercive redistribution, the concept of regimes of dispossession helps us to capture how this relation varies over the different phases and uneven geographies of capitalist development.'[78]

Nicole Latulippe is similarly concerned with legal geography's capacity to help identify 'the particularly spatial dimensions of colonial power, those territorial processes, situated practices and material forms of dispossession that impede Indigenous land

72. M Sherval, 'Activating Rural Spaces in the Pursuit of Unconventional Energy and Justice' in R Bartel and J Carter (eds), *Research Handbook on Space, Place and Law* (Edward Elgar, 2021) 147.
73. Ibid 142.
74. M RiverOfLife and others, 'Yoongoorrookoo' (2021) 30 *Griffith Law Review* 1, 508.
75. Ibid.
76. C Clark and J Page, *The Lawful Forest: A Critical History of Property, Protest, and Spatial Justice* (Edinburgh University Press, 2022) citing D Harvey, *The New Imperialism: Accumulation by Dispossession* (Oxford University Press, 2003).
77. M Levien, 'Regimes of Dispossession' in N Graham, M Davies and L Godden (eds), *The Routledge Handbook of Property, Law and Society* (Routledge, 2022) 43.
78. Ibid 44.

relations'.[79] She argues that when it is grounded in Indigenous worldviews, legal geography can help to reveal otherwise hidden 'pathways of resistance and worldbuilding', thus helping to disrupt settler-colonial power.[80]

This is echoed by Melissa Nursey-Bray and Stephen Muecke, who emphasise the importance of drawing attention to 'strategies of resistance [...] enacted by Indigenous people who are actively "reconceptualizing the nomenclature of capitalist public space"'.[81] Moving (back) to the city and the capacity of Indigenous art to reclaim visibility, Nursey-Bray and Muecke observe the role that public spaces play 'in defining the social relationships in any specific location'.[82] In this context, (following Lefebvre) they describe the use of art by Indigenous peoples as 'the social production of space in cities',[83] and as a method of asserting sovereignty and pushing back against the 'spatial bias [that] has prejudiced Indigenous presence, legal and otherwise, within urban spaces'.[84] Nursey-Bray and Muecke thus argue that 'Indigenous street art has been, and continues to be, a powerful tool to reclaim, intervene and decolonize urban spaces and to assert lore over law'.[85]

Reflecting this ongoing expansion into the legal spaces of Indigenous ontology and law, Latulippe explains that she draws 'on the work at the intersection of Indigenous and settler-colonial studies, geography and law [to] write beyond dominant institutions to think with Indigenous law and relational worldviews about more peaceful relations between people and with the earth'.[86] Latulippe argues that 'Indigenous worldviews' understand that '[t]he non-only-human beings of Creation are agentic, willful, and intelligent [...] [and that t]he agency of land is rooted constitutionalism, the basis of Indigenous law. In other words, the earth is a living source of law'.[87]

79. N Latulippe, 'Indigenous Land Conflict and the Underlying Life of Laws: Lessons from the Ipperwash Crisis' in R Bartel and J Carter (eds), *Research Handbook on Space, Place and Law* (Edward Elgar, 2021) 174–175.
80. Ibid 175 (citations omitted).
81. M Nursey-Bray and S Muecke, 'Paying Attention to the Spaces in between: The Social Protection of Space and Indigenous Presence in Cities' in R Bartel and others (eds), *Research Handbook on Space, Place and Law* (Edward Elgar, 2021) 201 citing M R Smith, 'Indigenous Graffiti and Street Art as Resistance' in S Awad and B Wagoner (eds), *Street Art of Resistance* (Palgrave Macmillan, 2017) 252.
82. M Nursey-Bray and S Muecke, 'Paying Attention to the Spaces in between: The Social Protection of Space and Indigenous Presence in Cities' in R Bartel and others (eds), *Research Handbook on Space, Place and Law* (Edward Elgar, 2021) 200.
83. Ibid 196.
84. Ibid 197.
85. Ibid.
86. N Latulippe, 'Indigenous Land Conflict and the Underlying Life of Laws: Lessons from the Ipperwash Crisis' in R Bartel and J Carter (eds), *Research Handbook on Space, Place and Law* (Edward Elgar, 2021) 171.
87. Ibid 174.

Coming back to the importance of analysing opposition to oppression to enliven 'alternative legalities [that] occupy the same jurisdictional space',[88] Latulippe describes blockades as places 'where Indigenous and settler-colonial laws are "forced to meet": where Indigenous jurisdiction and law challenge putative authority of the settler-state to govern and derive benefits from Indigenous territories'.[89] Here she emphasises that 'Indigenous acts of civil disobedience' are acts of compliance with Indigenous law.[90]

Josephine Gillespie argues that this '[e]ngagement with legal pluralism by legal geographers is important in unpacking the complexities of law as an entity in the law–place–people dynamic'.[91] Daniel Robinson et al. adopt this approach of engaging with 'legally pluralist assertions of land rights claims' in their research into the land rights challenges facing the Moken, Moklen and Urak Lawoi Indigenous minority groups in post-tsunami Thailand.[92] Here they note that '[t]hrough customary norms and practices, rituals and ceremonies on common lands, these communities have established "place-laws" about sites and their uses'[93]

Linking this engagement back to critical property theory, Kirsten Anker explores how investigating the ways property language is employed in different contexts can highlight a deeper ontological plurality that is masked by the image of the 'bundle of rights'.[94] Here she argues that 'plural property presupposes a context of legal pluralism'.[95] She acknowledges that the term 'legal pluralism' 'has had multiple meanings ascribed to it',[96] and notes that she is particularly concerned with the definition that 'contests the idea that law is the normative product of the state alone, and that law can

88. N Blomley, *Law, Space, and the Geographies of Power* (The Guildford Press, 1994) 57: 'If geographers are to see law's landscape as that created by legal institutions, they should be able to see law in the landscape'.
89. N Latulippe, 'Indigenous Land Conflict and the Underlying Life of Laws: Lessons from the Ipperwash Crisis' in R Bartel and J Carter (eds), *Research Handbook on Space, Place and Law* (Edward Elgar, 2021) 170 citing S Pasternak, 'Blockade: A Meeting Place of Law' in P McFarlane and N Schabus (eds), *Whose Land Is It Anyway? A Manuel for Decolonization* (Federation of Post-Secondary Educators of BC, 2017) 33.
90. N Latulippe, 'Indigenous Land Conflict and the Underlying Life of Laws: Lessons from the Ipperwash Crisis' in R Bartel and J Carter (eds), *Research Handbook on Space, Place and Law* (Edward Elgar, 2021) 170.
91. J Gillespie, 'Challenges in Legal Geography Research Methodologies in Cross-Cultural Settings' in T Oanahspie, O F Robinson and J Gillespie (eds), *Legal Geography: Perspectives and Methods* (Routledge, 2020) 19.
92. D Robinson, D Drozdzewski and J Kaewmahanin, 'Enright, Land Territorialisation, Contestation and Informal Place-Laws of Indigenous Peoples in Phuket and Phang Nga, Thailand' in R Bartel and J Carter (eds), *Research Handbook on Space, Place and Law* (Edward Elgar, 2021) 159.
93. Ibid 160.
94. K Anker, 'Plural Property' in N Graham, M Davies and L Godden (eds), *The Routledge Handbook of Property, Law and Society* (Routledge, 2022) 31.
95. Ibid.
96. Ibid.

be comprehended solely according to statist precepts'.[97] Anker argues that attending to 'property in practice' necessitates 'a method for identifying property in ways that do not rely on formal state authorisation'.[98] In the context of conquered or colonised lands, the interactions between existing customary law and the colonial legal system are complex. Returning to the focus on resistance Anker argues that when Indigenous people assert territorial control over land through acts of reoccupation and the 'enactment and instantiation' of Indigenous law, they are demonstrating jurisdictional pluralism – 'an approach that focuses on struggles for the authority to "speak the law" (juris-diction) rather than on attempting to identify discrete collections or systems of norms'.[99]

The property law that is reasserted here can be contrasted with liberal property – which 'centres on the idea of individual autonomy and agency' – in that it 'is often contemplated from within a world of both human and nonhuman subjects, the spiritual or sacred character of the land, and relationships of respect and even kinship with nonhumans'.[100] This relational approach to land is the focus of Estair Van Wagner's analysis of a recent treaty-focused trial decision in Canada.[101] Here she describes 'glimpses of other ways of engaging with Indigenous relations with land through Canadian law',[102] and asks:

> Can consultation ever create spaces for the reimagining of property relations in particular places through 'truly inter-societal understandings' and 'reasoned, open, unconstrained and principles dialogue'?[103] Such radical reimagining will undoubtedly impact our understanding of private property in order to see how it can co-exist with, and within, the enduring environmental jurisdiction of Indigenous nations. Perhaps this is just the shift in perspective we require to take up Borrows' call to work towards our 'collective reconciliation with the earth'.[104]

This focus on Indigenous law and relational world views also extends to the examination of water, with legal geographers becoming increasingly engaged with exploring human relationships with living water. Laborde and Jackson, for example, emphasise the fundamental importance of revealing ontological and epistemic disjunctures

97. Ibid 31–32.
98. Ibid 34.
99. Ibid 39.
100. Ibid 37.
101. E VanWagner, 'Extracting Indigenous Jurisdiction on Private Land: The Duty to Consult and Indigenous Relations with Place in Canadian Law' in R Bartel and J Carter (eds), *Research Handbook on Space, Place and Law* (Edward Elgar, 2021) 182.
102. Ibid 191.
103. Citing G Christie, 'Aboriginal Title and Private Property' in K Morellato (ed), *Aboriginal Law since Delgamuukw* (Canada Law Book, 2009) 203–204.
104. E VanWagner, 'Extracting Indigenous Jurisdiction on Private Land: The Duty to Consult and Indigenous Relations with Place in Canadian Law' in R Bartel and J Carter (eds), *Research Handbook on Space, Place and Law* (Edward Elgar, 2021) 192, citing J Borrows, 'Earth-Bound: Indigenous Resurgence and Environmental Reconciliation' in M Asch, J Borrows and J Tully (eds), *Resurgence and Reconciliation: Indigenous-Settler Relations and Earth Teachings* (University of Toronto Press, 2018) 69.

between Indigenous understandings, and legal regulation, of 'living water' and the hegemonic way that 'modern water' is understood and regulated under settler-colonial law.[105] Here the authors critique 'the hegemonic ontology that underpins modern water policy and management' and advocate for the adoption of a framework of cosmopolitics to reveal diverse ontologies of water and 'highlight contests around epistemological authority between state and Indigenous narratives' of water politics.[106]

Similarly, Martuwarra RiverOfLife et al. explain that the imperative of recognising 'the pre-existing and continuing legal authority of Indigenous law, or "First Law", in relation to the River, in order to preserve its integrity through a process of legal decolonisation'.[107] Reflecting on the recent trend of legal recognition that has accelerated since 2017,[108] they go on to argue that '[r]iver personhood is understood as one pathway towards this outcome'.[109] Scholars have, however, also highlighted the risks of this 'rights of nature' approach, with Erin O'Donnell, for example, arguing, 'without deep, respectful engagement, such translations can also involve a re-interpretation (or appropriation) of Indigenous laws that may obscure or undermine the rights of Indigenous peoples'.[110] Elizabeth Macpherson et al. also highlight the risk of reinforcing 'western hegemony within liberal democratic frameworks that fail to account for legal pluralism'[111] – a risk that Anne Salmond describes as 'ontological submission'.[112]

While many argue that a deeper commitment to legal pluralism could be a mitigating force against these risks – coupled, necessarily, with a place-based approach to embedding relationality[113] – Virginia Marshall is less equivocal, describing rights of nature as 'a new tool of colonisation which would decouple Indigenous ontological relationships and laws and the inherent obligations to manage and care for the environment'.[114] Whether legal geography is up to the task of navigating this challeng-

105. S Laborde and S Jackson, 'Living Waters or Resource? Ontological Differences and the Governance of Waters and Rivers' (2022) 27 *Local Environment* 357.
106. Ibid 358.
107. M RiverOfLife and others, 'Yoongoorrookoo' (2021) *Griffith Law Review* 1, 508.
108. See, e.g., C Clark and others, 'Can You Hear the Rivers Sing? Legal Personhood, Ontology and the Nitty Gritty of Governance' (2019) 45 *Ecology Law Quarterly* 787; E O'Donnell, *Legal Rights for Rivers: Competition, Collaboration and Water Governance* (Routledge 2018).
109. M RiverOfLife and others, 'Yoongoorrookoo' (2021) *Griffith Law Review* 1, 508.
110. E O'Donnell, 'Rivers as Living Beings: Rights in Law, but No Rights to Water?' (2020) 29 *Griffith Law Review* 643, 644.
111. E Macpherson and others, 'Where Ordinary Laws Fall Short: "Riverine Rights" and Constitutionalism' (2021) 30 *Griffith Law Review* 438, 461.
112. A Salmond, 'Tears of Rangi: Water, Power, and People in New Zealand' 4 *HAU: Journal of Ethnographic Theory* 285, 302.
113. E Macpherson and others, 'Where Ordinary Laws Fall Short: "Riverine Rights" and Constitutionalism' (2021) 30 *Griffith Law Review* 438, 461; E O'Donnell, 'Rivers as Living Beings: Rights in Law, but No Rights to Water?' (2020) 29 *Griffith Law Review* 643, 662; E O'Donnell and others, 'Stop Burying the Lede: The Essential Role of Indigenous Law(s) in Creating Rights of Nature' (2020) 9 *Transnational Environmental Law* 403, 416.
114. V Marshall, 'Removing the Veil from the "Rights of Nature": The Dichotomy between First Nations Customary Rights and Environmental Legal Personhood' (2019) 45 *Australian Feminist Law Journal* 233, 234.

ing terrain remains to be seen, but its attention to place, to the power dynamics of law on the ground, and emphasis on interdisciplinarity and legal pluralism are all valuable assets for any scholar committed to making an attempt.

Conclusion: The Development of Legal Geography

This chapter chronicles the shifts in legal geography over three decades of time and space. From an early pre-occupation with urbanism and the city, this scholarly 'disposition' has expanded its remit into pressing contemporary issues, from the climate crisis to environmental justice, and from place-based, case-study 'lawscapes' to the complexities of legal pluralism and decolonisation in the settler-colonial state. Yet while the focus shifts, commonalities shine through. As a 'disposition', it is a project of multiple confluences, where insights from law, geography and increasingly beyond forge a critical perspective on place and space, and the law's impact on spatial ordering.

Legal geography's focus on *co-constitution* provides one answer to the question of 'law as [...] geography' or 'geography as [...] law' (a dialectic explored elsewhere in this edited collection) by arguing that law and geography mutually constitute each other – with the law operating to shape space and place (geography) through the regulation of how it is classified and understood, and our understanding of place and space (through geography) simultaneously operating to shape regulation (law). This concept of co-constitution is the focus of Graham's *lawscape*,[115] a neologism that Anker applies to a forested Mountain in Montreal, explaining that it 'speaks not just to the knowledge that law must have a material existence in some place, but also to the way that law authorises and enacts the mark of humans on the land'.[116] As she elaborates:

> On the Mountain, the law enacts culturally significant notions of this space as public, dedicated to urban leisure, [...]; it also produces the Mountain – complete with its reigning 100 foot Christian cross – a space within the territorial soverignty of a French-speaking province within the Canadian state. In turn, it is cultural mediated understandings of spaces like this one [...] that enable legal phenomena like property and jurisdiction to be meaningful in their modern sense.[117]

However, as Anker goes on to observe, these insights still work to maintain a binary between the concepts of law *and* geography (or regulation and place), while the idea of 'law *as* [...]' seeks to move beyond such a binary. This dualism, described by Max Weber as 'disenchantment'[118] – grounded in the division of 'mind from matter, human

115. N Graham, *Lawscape: Property, Environment, Law* (Routledge, 2011).
116. K Anker, 'Law as ... Forest: Eco-Logic, Stories and Spirits in Indigenous Jurisprudence' (2017) 21 *Law, Text, Culture* 191, 192.
117. Ibid.
118. Ibid citing M Weber, *Science as a Vocation* (Indianapolis Hacket, 2004) 12–13.

from non-human, cultural from nature'[119] – is most comprehensively challenged by Indigenous ontologies and laws, and the relational world views that accompany them (discussed above). Here Anker notes the 'grounded normativity' of such place-based practices, where the 'the land is the source of the law' and asks 'what it is to take forests, mountains, and rivers *as* law'.[120]

Other legal geographers have also asked what it means to take geography (place) as law, through the more effective recognition of Indigenous law and legal pluralism, the evolution of Western law and by unearthing those remnant, diverse strands of Western law that are already place-based and grounded inrelationality.[121] Macpherson, for example, asks how Western water law frameworks can evolve to 'meaningfully respect, reflect and re-enact relationships between water peoples and water places'?[122] Here she notes that relationality is just as relevant to the co-constituting processes of peoples relating to each other (and systems of law) as it is to the relatedness of people and place – thus highlighting the significance of power relations.[123] In writing of the '*lawful forest*' – those remnant, diverse strands of relational, place-based Western property law – Clark and Page similarly highlight the significance of power in these relational processes.[124] They also emphasise that in order to step back from the brink of the looming ecological crisis we may need 'to recognise, and to learn the lessons of [the lawful forest's] *other* ways of relating to land and space'.[125]

By centring context and relationality, legal geography makes plain the legal, spatial and power imbalances that pervade our lived environments, that both figuratively (and sometimes) literally concretise its injustices, and the resistances to this oppression. For the law, legal geography makes plain the 'nonsense' of its supposed abstraction, and its prized neutrality and detachment from place. What began as an attention to 'gaps in (city) maps' has entrenched itself as a discrete body of scholarly thought, a *critical* study of law's spatiality and space's lawful imprint.

---

119. K Anker, 'Law as … Forest: Eco-Logic, Stories and Spirits in Indigenous Jurisprudence' (2017) 21 *Law, Text, Culture* 191, 193.
120. Ibid 193–194 (emphasis added) citing C Black, T*he Land Is the Source of the Law: A Dialogic Encounter with Indigenous Jurisprudence* (Routledge, 2011); G Coulthard, *Red Skin White Masks: Rejecting the Colonial Politics f Recognition* (University of Minnesota Press, 2014) 60.
121. See, e.g., E Macpherson, 'Can Western Water Law Become More "Relational"? A Survey of Comparative Laws Affecting Water across Australasia and the Americas' (2022) 53 *Journal of the Royal Society of New Zealand* 1; C Clark and J Page, *The Lawful Forest: A Critical History of Property, Protest, and Spatial Justice* (Edinburgh University Press, 2022); S Jackson and others, 'River Rhythmicity: A Conceptual Means of Understanding and Leveraging the Relational Values of Rivers' (2022) 4 *People and Nature* 949.
122. E Macpherson, 'Can Western Water Law Become More "Relational"? A Survey of Comparative Laws Affecting Water across Australasia and the Americas' (2022) 53 *Journal of the Royal Society of New Zealand* 1, 2.
123. Ibid 2–3.
124. C Clark and J Page, *The Lawful Forest: A Critical History of Property, Protest, and Spatial Justice* (Edinburgh University Press, 2022).
125. Ibid 224–225.

Chapter Six

LAW AND HISTORY

Russell Sandberg[1]

Introduction: The Paradox of Law and History

Paradoxically, history is both everywhere and nowhere in legal education.[2] On the one hand, history is ubiquitous in law schools: most lectures and textbook chapters explore how a case law has evolved over time and students are used to citing legal materials penned centuries ago. Yet, on the other hand, history is often missing in legal study: students are not interested in the time and context in which the cases occurred; they are solely concerned with their relevance in terms of their task of determining what the law is now so that they can critique the law within its own terms in an essay question, apply it to an idealised if often embellished factual scenario to answer a problem question or memorise it as if it was trivia for the purpose of succeeding at a multiple choice test. As the legal historian Frederic William Maitland put it in his 1888 inaugural lecture at Cambridge, 'what the lawyer wants is authority and the newer the better; what the historian wants is evidence and older the better'.[3]

This paradox has affected the development of law and history as a subject of study. On the one hand, there is a magnitude of research that explores the development of law over time, often with an eye on the social, political and cultural contexts. Yet, on the other hand, the number of academics who identify primarily as experts in this field, as legal historians, is much smaller. There is, of course, significant variation from jurisdiction to jurisdiction. History seems to be taught more in civil law jurisdictions generally; within common law jurisdictions the development of legal history as a subject is more advanced in the United States.[4] There are also differences within jurisdictions. In England and Wales (which will be the focus of this chapter), a great deal of work that could be seen as coming under the umbrella of law and history has and is

---

1. Thanks to Dr Sharon Thompson and Dr Dan Newman for their feedback on earlier drafts of this chapter.
2. This chapter summarises and extends arguments originally made in R Sandberg, *Subversive Legal History: A Manifesto for the Future of Legal Education* (Routledge, 2021).
3. Frederic W Maitland, 'Why the History of English Law has not been Written' in H A L Fisher (ed), *Collected Papers of Frederic William Maitland, Downing Professor of the Laws of England* (Cambridge University Press, 1911) Vol. 1, 480, 491.
4. Though note developments elsewhere such as the publication of S McKibbin, L Connors and M Hames, *A Legal History for Australia* (Hart, 2021).

completed outside of law schools. History departments formerly led the way in terms of constitutional history, and more recently their attention has shifted to social history, which includes a significant focus on legal matters. Even within law schools, the number of people who consider themselves legal historians and who teach about and whose research focuses on legal history is dwarfed by the number of academics who write about law historically but would classify themselves as socio-legal scholars or identify themselves with a particular field of law. They, like many of those employed in history departments, would not see themselves as legal historians.

Law and history, therefore, has something of an identity crisis. The historical study of law is well established but is somewhat unfashionable. This is reflected in terminology. Although the label 'law and history' is sometimes used for associations, collections of papers and symposia, it is less common than equivalent labels such as 'law and literature' or 'law and religion'. 'Legal history' is the label often used but this is then typically reserved for the institutionalised specialised work of those within law schools who readily identify as legal historians.[5] This chapter will suggest that the reason for this is the continued influence of Maitland, who is often seen as the founder of the modern study of legal history in England and Wales. The following will examine how Maitland's work and example led to a divide between legal history scholarship and other legal-historical work. It will explore my suggestions for how this division can be re-conceptualised and how legal history can be understood as a necessary subversive corrective to the dominant doctrinal tradition in law schools. The conclusion will then return to the issue of terminology and the implications and merits of the 'law and history' label.

The Ghost of Frederic William Maitland

Although, as Ian Ward noted, legal historical work dates back much further, the idea of legal history as 'a distinct sub-discipline of law is rather more "modern"'.[6] In England and Wales, it can be can be traced back to the second half of the nineteenth century and to Maitland's body of 'seemingly miraculous writing', much of which was published posthumously, which has resulted in a 'superhuman myth engulfing him'.[7] For Ward,

---

5. For discussion of the difference between 'law and history' and 'legal history', see S Wilson, 'Value and Values in Higher Education: Some Reflections from the UK on the Subversive Dimensions of Historical Approaches in the Study of Law' in H Gibbon et al. (eds), *Critical Legal Education as a Subversive Activity* (Routledge, 2023) 149, 154.
6. I Ward, *English Legal Histories* (Hart, 2019) 11.
7. S F C Milsom, 'Maitland' (2001) 60(2) *Cambridge Law Journal* 265. Perhaps Maitland's best known work of legal history published in his lifetime was F Pollock and F W Maitland, *The History of English Law* (2nd edn, Cambridge University Press, 1968 [1898]). The first edition was published in 1895 with a second edition in 1898. His major posthumous publications notably include F W Maitland, *The Constitutional History of England* (Cambridge University Press, 1941 [1908]) and F W Maitland, *Equity, Also the Form of Action at Common Law* (Cambridge University Press, 1909). See also H A L Fisher (ed), *Collected Papers of Frederic William Maitland, Downing Professor of the Laws of England* (3 vols, Cambridge University Press, 1911). Maitland also authored works on political philosophy and biography

legal history 'was born of the same positivist impulse that drove forward modern historiography and historical writing'.[8] Maitland's reputation rests upon his method: he pioneered the use of primary legal materials subjecting them to the same level of scrutiny as modern-day legal sources. He was renowned for his introductions to numerous editions of primary materials prepared for the Selden Society and other organisations. The Selden Society, formed in 1886 with Maitland serving as its literary director until the end of his life, has been referred to as 'the living memorial which perpetuates not only the work but also the spirit of Maitland'.[9] His work scrutinised historical legal materials to the same standards of doctrinal scholarship and with the same approaches and assumptions as the modern law was beginning to be subjected to, with this period also seeing the rise of the textbook tradition. Like law itself, the doctrinal approach dominated legal history, and while other methods have become popular in the Post-War period, they have tended to exist outside the specialised field of legal history.

The authority and example of Maitland has meant that doctrinal approach has become synonymous with legal history. Yet, the rise of socio-legal and critical legal studies has meant that this understanding of legal history has led to criticism of such work. Legal history has been described as 'slowly and inevitably dying – or that it has been in a coma for the last 30 years, at least'.[10] David Sugarman has noted that belittling law and legal history has become 'fair sport among historians' who have often 'stigmatized law and legal historians (with some notable exceptions) as intrinsically unhistorical, given their preoccupation with reading the past in the light of modern legal doctrine'.[11]

As Sarah E Hamill has noted, the historical study of law has become a 'disparate and often jurisdictionally divided field'.[12] The basic distinction, to put it crudely, is between what may broadly be styled doctrinal and socio-legal approaches to the history of law. Doctrinal scholars who have followed Maitland into the archives and sought to apply doctrinal methods fall into the first camp, which has been referred to as the 'internal' or 'old' legal history[13] (although a number of other labels are used such as 'orthodox'[14] or

8. I Ward, *English Legal Histories* (Hart, 2019) 11.
9. T F T Plucknett, 'Frederic William Maitland' (1951) 26 *New York University Law Review* 10.
10. D Siemens, 'Towards a New Cultural History of Law' (2012) 2 *InterDisciplines* 18, 19.
11. He also noted a key reason for this: 'Divorcing history from law and legal history spoke to the self-identity of modern professional historians': D Sugarman, 'Promoting Dialogue between History and Socio-Legal Studies: The Contribution of Christopher W Brooks and the "Legal Turn" in Early Modern English History' (2017) 44(S1) *Journal of Law and Society* S37, S39.
12. S E Hamill, 'Review of Legal History' (2019) 28(4) *Social & Legal Studies* 538. For a detailed account of the development of Legal History see K J M Smith and J P S McLaren, 'History's Living Legacy: An Outline of "Modern" Historiography of the Common Law' (2001) 21 *Legal Studies* 251 and Michael Lobban, 'The Varieties of Legal History' (2012) 5 *Clio@Themis* 1.
13. E.g., D Ibbetson, 'What Is Legal History a History Of?' in Andrew Lewis and Michael Lobban (eds), *Law and History* (Oxford University Press, 2004) 33.
14. A Hunt, 'The New Legal History: Prospects and Perspectives' (1986) 10 *Contemporary Crises* 201, 202.

'classical'[15] legal history have also sometimes been suggested).[16] In the first camp, work explores the doctrinal development of legal ideas, concepts and institutions, and much of this work is the product of those within schools who are content to call themselves legal historians and whose work have led to the development of legal history as a specialist sub-discipline. It is the first form of the historically study of law – we may call it 'internal legal history' for convenience – that is the type most well known in law schools. It is the institutionalised sub-discipline of legal history that has spawned a number of specialist journals, societies and book series. Internal legal history is associated with the Cambridge legal historians who followed Maitland. It is preoccupied with the 'genealogy of legal doctrine'.[17] Its approach is 'internal to the extent that it is based on primary sources that are legal', that is, sources such as reported cases, actions in the plea rolls and yearbooks, statutes and early legal literature.[18] It examines 'law on its own terms', exploring 'the law that would have been recognized by lawyers in its times'.[19] As Michael Lobban noted, academic lawyers 'tend to focus their attention on the history of the legal doctrines whose contemporary manifestation they (or their colleagues) also teach'.[20]

This doctrinal study of the legal past is often seen as being what legal history is. It is a specialist doctrinal exercise in excavation. This is the approach taken in traditional legal history classes on the historical development of the common law as articulated in both the general and specific area of law student textbooks.[21] Such work has tended to focus more upon the role of the common law (as opposed to statute law) in civil law matters (as opposed to criminal law matters) during the medieval and early modern periods. Legal history is not generally seen as an interdisciplinary field or as a form of critique. This is not to deny, however, that there are scholars whose work uses history as a form of interdisciplinary critique of law. But their work has not entered the canon of legal history or at least is not seen as epitomising legal history as a sub-discipline.

---

15. J Rose, 'Studying the Past: The Nature and Development of Legal History as an Academic Discipline' (2010) 31(2) *The Journal of Legal History* 101, 117.
16. See also the work of Rosemary Hunter which distinguishes *legal* history, which 'focuses on primarily on statutes, cases and judges (and legal practice', and legal *history,* which 'explores the legal dimension of historical problems': R Hunter, 'Australian Legal History in Context' (2003) 21 *Law and History Review* 607, 613.
17. D Sugarman, 'Promoting Dialogue between History and Socio-Legal Studies: The Contribution of Christopher W Brooks and the "Legal Turn" in Early Modern English History' (2017) 44(S1) *Journal of Law and Society* S37.
18. J Rose, 'Studying the Past: The Nature and Development of Legal History as an Academic Discipline' (2010) 31(2) *The Journal of Legal History* 101, 118–119.
19. D Ibbetson, 'What Is Legal History a History Of?' in A Lewis and M Lobban (eds), *Law and History* (Oxford University Press, 2004) 33, 34.
20. M Lobban, 'The Varieties of Legal History' (2012) 5 *Clio@Themis* 1, 9.
21. J H Baker, *An Introduction to English Legal History* (5th edn, Butterworths, 2019), S F C Milsom, *Historical Foundations of the Common Law* (2nd edn, Butterworths, 1981), A W B Simpson, *An Introduction to the History of Land Law* (2nd edn, Oxford University Press, 1986), A W B Simpson, *History of the Common Law of Contract* (Clarendon Press, 1987), D J Ibbetson, *A Historical Introduction to the Law of Obligations* (Oxford University Press, 1999) and A Lyon, *Constitutional History of the United Kingdom* (2nd edn, Routledge, 2016).

This first camp is then contrasted with the second, peopled by legal scholars who would typically not refer to themselves as legal historians and those based outside the Law School. This is the 'external' or 'new'[22] legal history, also sometimes called 'socio-legal history'[23] or 'the social history of law'.[24] This studies 'the history of law as embedded in its context, typically its social or economic context; the history of the law in action'.[25] External legal history is 'not confined just to explications of doctrinal and institutional evolution [but] extends to investigation of the cultural factors, social forces and values, ideological and intellectual impulses and political and economic realities on the development of law, legal institutions and attitudes towards law'.[26] In this second camp, work explores how law exists as one of many social institutions and how law is shaped by (and shapes) other social institutions and society as a whole. Laura Cahillane has noted that 'in as much as the internal approach is described as doctrinal, we can refer to the external approach as looking at "the law in action" – almost a historical version of the socio-legal approach'.[27]

The internal and external approaches have had very different focuses. External legal history has engaged with periods and areas of law that were previously neglected in the legal history literature. Although David Sugarman has noted that the 'the boundaries of the subject have spread in almost every conceivable direction,'[28] certain areas and topics have achieved particular attention. Internal legal history focused on the medieval and early modern periods and the development of the civil law of property and obligations under the common law. By contrast, external legal history has focused on modern history,[29] with a particular focus upon criminal justice,[30] exploring the political, social, economic and cultural causes and effects of changes. The external camp also includes

22. A Hunt, 'The New Legal History: Prospects and Perspectives' (1986) 10 *Contemporary Crises* 201.
23. C W Brooks, *Lawyers, Litigation and English Society since 1450* (Hambledon Press, 1998) 179.
24. M Lobban, 'The Varieties of Legal History' (2012) 5 *Clio@Themis* 1, 20.
25. D Ibbetson, 'What Is Legal History a History Of' in A Lewis and M Lobban (eds), *Law and History* (Oxford University Press, 2004) 33.
26. J McLaren 'The Legal Historian, Masochist or Missionary? A Canadian's Reflection' (1994) 5 *Legal Education Review* 67, 70–71.
27. L Cahillane, 'The Use of History in Law: Avoiding the Pitfalls' in L Cahillane and J Schweppe (eds), *Legal Research Methods: Principles and Practicalities* (Clarus Press, 2016) 57, 61.
28. D Sugarman, 'Writing "Law and Society" Histories' (1992) 55(5) *Modern Law Review* 292, 299.
29. See, e.g., A H Manchester, *Modern Legal History* (Butterworths, 1980); W R Cornish and G de N Clark, *Law and Society in England 1750-1950* (Sweet and Maxwell, 1989) [A new edition of this was published as W R Cornish et al., *Law and Society in England 1750-1950* (2nd edn, Hart, 2019)] and the work cited by D Sugarman and G R Rubin, 'Towards a New History of Law and Material Society in England 1750-1914' in G R Rubin and D Sugarman (eds), *Law, Economy & Society* (Professional Books, 1984) 1.
30. There has also been a notable 'turn to history' in constitutional and international law as well as in the development of law and literature and legal biographies: D Sugarman, 'Promoting Dialogue between History and Socio-Legal Studies: The Contribution of Christopher W Brooks and the "Legal Turn" in Early Modern English History' (2017) 44(S1) *Journal of Law and Society* S37, S41.

a number of works that focus on gender,[31] as well as the importance of other non-legal developments.[32] The different focus of internal and external legal historians is striking. While Milsom exemplified the internal legal history's approach by asserting that 'the miserable history of crime in England can be shortly told. Nothing worth-while was created',[33] it has been claimed by an external legal historian that 'much of the existing contribution to legal history within socio-legal studies can be found concentrated in the field of criminal justice'.[34] This underlines how the two camps within legal history rarely talk to each other.

The basic difference between the internal and external approaches has been articulated by Robert W Gordon as follows:

> The internal legal historian stays as much as possible within the box of distinctive-appearing legal things; his sources are legal, and so are the basic matters he wants to describe or explain, such as changes in pleading rules, in the jurisdiction of a court, the texts assigned to beginning law students, or the doctrine of contributory negligence. The external historian writes about the interaction between the boxful of legal things and the wider society of which they are a part, in particular to explore the social context of law and its social effects, and he is usually looking for conclusions about those effects.[35]

Although this distinction is by no means clear-cut,[36] it is the emphasis and entrenchment of the differences between these two approaches to legal history which has led to its neglect.

---

31. See, for instance, L Gowing, *Domestic Dangers: Women, Words and Sex in Early Modern London* (Oxford University Press, 1996) and G Walker, *Crime, Gender and Social Order in Early Modern British History* (Cambridge University Press, 2009). Though see also Gwen Seabourne, *Women in the Medieval Common Law c.1200-1500* (Routledge, 2021).
32. Leading works include E P Thompson, *Whigs and Hunters* (Allen Lane, 1975); D Hay et al., *Albion's Fatal Tree* (Allen Lane, 1975). There has also been a focus on the history of the legal professions, though Brookes was critical of the lack of the literatures on the history of crime and the history of the legal profession 'either to communicate much with each other or to make a significant impact on the social and political history of the England between 1500 and 1800': C W Brooks, *Lawyers, Litigation and English Society since 1450* (Hambledon Press, 1998) 179.
33. S F C Milsom, *Historical Foundations of the Common Law* (2nd edn, Butterworths, 1981) 403.
34. L Charlesworth, 'On Historical Contextualisation: Some Critical Socio-Legal Reflections' (2007) 1 *Crimes and Misdemeanours* 1, 18.
35. R W Gordon, 'J. Willard Hurst and the Common Law Tradition in American Legal Historiography' (1975) 10 *Law & Society Review* 9, 11.
36. A number of areas of legal history scholarship are difficult to place within the internal-external distinction. This includes institutional legal history and the literatures on legal archaeology and legal biography. On legal archaeology see A W B Simpson, *Leading Cases in the Common Law* (Oxford University Press, 1995) and E Nottingham, 'Digging into Legal Archaeology: A Methodology for Case Study Research' (2022) 49(S1) *Journal of Law and Society* S16. On legal biography see W Cornish, *Life Stories and Legal Histories* (Selden Society,

External legal history has become much more fashionable than the internal doctrinal approach. As Sarah E Hamill put it, '"Good" legal history is no longer an endless "and then" of judicial decisions but a "why this at this time" approach. Legal historians are expected to read around the law and capture the contexts which shaped it.'[37] The tenor of this comment is telling: external legal history is regarded by its adherents as a necessary corrective to the internal approach which is dismissed if not as 'bad' history then at least as inferior. As Alan Harding provocatively put it, the external approach 'does at least try to be real history; to relate the development of law as a whole, and forwards, to the development of English society not to race backwards as a bundle of legal doctrines'.[38]

These criticisms and the caricaturing of the internal legal history mainstream have led to a hesitation on their part to engage in with the external approach. David Sugarman has accepted that 'it is difficult not to share the unease of many a historian' given the 'more *avant-garde* proponents of "newness"'.[39] The result has been that the internal legal historical approach – and legal history as a sub-discipline – has retreated from the mainstream of legal scholarship. As Lorie Charlesworth has noted, the domination of a 'a close-knit group of mostly (male) academics who took their law degrees from the Universities of Cambridge, Oxford and London where they occupy prestigious law chairs, some of which have always been designated for legal historians' has led to the area being unattractive to outsiders.[40] There has been a decrease in the appetite to produce doctrinal internal legal history in a way that is accessible enough for non-specialists in legal history. Sarah E. Hamill noted that 'strictly doctrinal histories play a much less significant role in legal history today than they did previously'.[41]

The antagonism between approaches results, at least in part, from the fact that external legal history has its roots in the same academic shifts that led to socio-legal

---

2015), D Sugarman, 'From Legal Biography to Legal Life Writing: Broadening Conceptions of Legal History and Socio-Legal Scholarship' (2015) 42(1) *Journal of Law and Society* 7 and the other essays published in that special issue; V Barnes, C MacMillan and S Vogenauer, 'On Legal Biography' (2020) 41(2) *Journal of Legal History* 115 and the other essays published in that special issue and the discussion in S Thompson, *Quiet Revolutionaries: The Married Women's Association and Family Law* (Hart, 2022) 49 *et seq.*

37. S E Hamill, 'Review of Legal History' (2019) 28(4) *Social & Legal Studies* 538, 540.
38. A Harding, *A Social History of English Law* (Penguin, 1966) 9. Christopher Brookes stated that 'thanks to the general interest over the past half century in so many aspects of social history, including questions about the political awareness and "agency" of the people outside the landed elite, any study of law that concentrates only on high politics is bound to seem unsatisfactory and myopic': C W Brooks, *Law, Politics and Society in Early Modern England* (Cambridge University Press, 2008) 9.
39. D Sugarman, 'Writing "Law and Society" Histories' (1992) 55(5) *Modern Law Review* 292, 300.
40. L Charlesworth, 'On Historical Contextualisation: Some Critical Socio-Legal Reflections' (2007) 1 *Crimes and Misdemeanours* 1, 27.
41. S E Hamill, 'Review of Legal History' (2019) 28(4) *Social & Legal Studies* 538, 540.

and critical legal studies. Ian Ward has noted that since the 1970s,[42] 'a broader interdisciplinary and contextual approach began to gain a foothold in the academy' and 'people started to matter'.[43] In history departments this 'critical turn' was manifest in the new social history that paid attention to the lived lives of ordinary people in the past and took a much more grounded approach. Law became a facet of this social history. As Smith and McLaren observed, the work of E. P. Thompson and his protégés at Warwick 'opened up interest in the legal history of the eighteenth and nineteenth centuries, encouraged scholars to consider how law was experienced within society and especially by the poor and unenfranchised, raising a host of awkward questions about the claimed objectivity and rationality of law in history'.[44]

In law schools, this same 'critical turn' manifested itself in socio-legal and critical legal studies which paid attention the importance of extra-legal factors upon legal change. However, for most socio-legal scholars, legal history (in its prevalent 'internal' guise) became regarded and attacked as an exemplar of the purely doctrinal approach. As David Sugarman pointed out, legal history 'attracted the suspicion of socio-legal scholars in that it underpinned and legitimated a preoccupation with the narrow technicalities of the law and the treatment of law as largely divorced from the society, politics, and economy in which it operated'.[45] This meant that for many advocating a socio-legal approach 'the moral was clear: the less history the better'. Such scholars generally 'set their sights on the present, and against the past'.[46] However, for the minority of socio-legal scholars who turned to history in their work (usually as a result of their quest to answer their research questions), the history to which they turned was not legal history but the new social history. It was this approach to history that proved attractive to the few socio-legal writers who embraced history. Rather than embracing the orthodox doctrinal internal approach of legal history, such scholars were inspired by the new social history that 'brought the relationships between law and class, race and gender

42. Smith and McLaren observed that it was possible to identify both internal and external approaches in legal history long before the 1970s but also noted that before that 'arguably the only out and out attempt at an "external" narrative account of the full span of English legal history was Alan Harding's *A Social History of English Law* (Penguin, 1966)': K J M Smith and J P S McLaren, 'History's Living Legacy: An Outline of "Modern" Historiography of the Common Law' (2001) 21 *Legal Studies* 251, 272.
43. I Ward, *English Legal Histories* (Hart, 2019) 11.
44. K J M Smith and J P S McLaren, 'History's Living Legacy: An Outline of "Modern" Historiography of the Common Law' (2001) 21 *Legal Studies* 251, 308.
45. D Sugarman, 'Promoting Dialogue between History and Socio-Legal Studies: The Contribution of Christopher W Brooks and the "Legal Turn" in Early Modern English History' (2017) 44 (S1) *Journal of Law and Society* S37, S38.
46. '[I]n England, history is still not as fully integrated within socio-legal studies as it is in, say, Canada and the United States': ibid S41.

to the fore'.[47] Socio-legal scholars interested in history embraced the methodologies of social historians.[48] As Sugarman noted:

> They were energized by history's reading of law as a social, political, and cultural formation that could only be understood over time; the contingency of particular legal arrangements; that ordinary people contributed by their conscious efforts to the making of history; and that law and legal practices were systematically structured by economic, cultural, and political power, thereby reinstating facets of the past that were otherwise marginalized.[49]

For Sugarman, this amounted to 'an important but largely unnoticed change in the character of the study of the history of English law: namely, its growing recognition that while legal doctrine is important, so too is the real impact of law on society'.[50] However, the reason why this change was 'largely unnoticed' was because legal history as a sub-discipline in law schools was largely unaffected: the specialist legal historians by and large continued to produce works of internal doctrinal legal history. It was the socio-legal scholars in law schools and the social historians outside the law school who were largely responsible for this new scholarship. Their differing backgrounds and perspectives as well as their often unwillingness to be regarded as legal historians meant that this new external approach neither became a key component of legal history, the legal sub-discipline, nor became a body of scholarship in its own right.[51]

---

47. J Phillips, 'Why Legal History Matters' (2010) 41 *Victoria University of Wellington Law Review* 293, 298. As Smith and McLaren observed, the work of E P Thompson and his protégés at Warwick 'opened up interest in the legal history of the eighteenth and nineteenth centuries, encouraged scholars to consider how law was experienced within society and especially by the poor and unenfranchised, raising a host of awkward questions about the claimed objectivity and rationality of law in history: K J M Smith and J P S McLaren, 'History's Living Legacy: An Outline of "Modern" Historiography of the Common Law' (2001) 21 *Legal Studies* 251, 308.
48. L Cahillane, 'The Use of History in Law: Avoiding the Pitfalls' in L Cahillane and J Schweppe (eds), *Legal Research Methods: Principles and Practicalities* (Clarus Press, 2016) 57, 61.
49. D Sugarman, 'Promoting Dialogue between History and Socio-Legal Studies: The Contribution of Christopher W Brooks and the "Legal Turn" in Early Modern English History' (2017) 44(S1) *Journal of Law and Society* S37, S38. This interest, however, has often not been reciprocated. 'While historians increasing resort to legal records and engage in law-related research, socio-legal scholarship is usually off their radars' (ibid S41). As Sugarman notes, 'the linkages between history and socio- legal studies are complex and paradoxical' (ibid S37).
50. Ibid S59.
51. As Sugarman has noted, law and history 'were competitors for academic legitimacy, cultural authority, student numbers, and material support, making boundary maintenance part of their raison d'être' (ibid S38). And history and socio-legal studies have different methods and assumptions: 'Socio-legal scholars may treat history as largely a repository of examples and data that they can draw upon for their own purposes. But historians may regard this as ransacking secondary sources in order to "theorize the facts", an exercise whose potential pitfalls include over-simplification': ibid S39–40.

The Subversive Spirit

A vicious circle has been created: the denigration of internal doctrinal legal history has meant that such work is being produced in a way that is unattractive to advocates of socio-legal studies. The prevalent perception of legal history as taught and researched in law schools remains predominantly internal and doctrinal. The external approach, though fashionable, has neither replaced nor co-exists with the internal approach as representing, let alone epitomising, how legal history is seen as an academic field. The internal-external division has had a significant detrimental effect upon the stagnation of the historical study of law in English law schools.

It is this impasse that has prompted my recent work on subversive legal history.[52] Rather than ignoring the distinction, it is preferable to recast it to stress that both of the two approaches which look at law from different angles are needed. Indeed, the strengths of one approach often help to rectify the weakness of the other approach. The particular, technical and grounded evidence unearthed by internal legal history complements and is complemented by the contextual, wider and interdisciplinary insights gleamed through external legal history. Internal and external responses should not be placed in opposition to one another; they are necessarily complimentary.

Drawing upon a remark by John Baker that 'Law flits uncomfortably between intellectual and social history',[53] I recast the internal-external division as instead highlighting the existence of two major traditions within legal history scholarship: one that examines law from an intellectual history dimension (exploring the development of legal ideas) and the other that looks at law from a social history dimension (exploring the development of interface between law and society). This stressed that legal history included 'at least' these two dimensions, that there was no clear dividing line between the two and that the two dimensions were 'raised in order to underscore that they are both valid and complementary to each other'.[54] Moreover, this articulation should not be taken as requiring both of the two approaches to be present at all times.[55]

The main argument of subversive legal history is that both of these approaches are needed and that history is a necessary corrective to the tendency in legal education to present law as being universal and progressive. While conventionally lawyers have used history as a means of stabilising the present, it could more usefully be used to subvert the present. As Rowan Williams has commented, 'good history makes us think again about

52. R Sandberg, *Subversive Legal History: A Manifesto for the Future of Legal Education* (Routledge, 2021).
53. J H Baker, 'Criminal Courts and Procedure, 1550-1800' in J S Cockbourn (ed), *Crime in England 1500-1800* (Methuen, 1977) 15.
54. R Sandberg, *Subversive Legal History: A Manifesto for the Future of Legal Education* (Routledge, 2021) 50.
55. The *Oxford Handbook of Legal History* takes a slightly different approach to what I proposed. It has a section dedicated to approaches to legal history which includes chapters on legal history as legal scholarship, social history, political history, intellectual history, doctrinal history, cultural history, economic history as well as a number of related chapters: M D Dubber and C Tomlins (eds), *The Oxford Handbook of Legal History* (Oxford University Press, 2018).

the definition of things we thought we understood pretty well, because it engages not just with what is familiar but with what is strange.'[56] The study of legal history shows that the law and legal institutions are not fixed, that every line drawn in the law and everything the law holds as sacred is arbitrary and that the environment that law students are socialised into is a historical construct. This makes legal history necessary in law schools but also means that it is frightening. The subversive nature of legal history means that it is unsettling to students and teachers socialised into believing that 'the law' is universal, natural, objective, progressive and inevitable and who see the scope for legal change limited by the evolutionary pathway that they are told is preordained.

This emphasis upon the radical and emancipatory potential of legal history is reflected in the work of none other than Frederic William Maitland himself. In a letter he wrote:

> The only direct utility of legal history [...] lies in the lesson that each generation has an enormous power of shaping its own law. I don't think that the study of legal history would make men fatalists; I doubt that it would make them conservatives. I am sure that it would free them from superstitions and teach them that they have free hands.[57]

This subversive spirit can also be found in Maitland's works. As Bell has noted, Maitland's work 'was never channelled in a single groove or pointed too single end; he has a lively, flexible mind that was always ready to follow a hint from the data that it happened to be processing'.[58] This included the questioning of received wisdoms and a 'spirit which causes one to go around looking for skeletons in closets which might be exposed'.[59] As Elton has noted, for Maitland, 'historical enquiry demanded the subversion of what had been said before'.[60] Yet, this subversive insight from the patron saint of English legal history has been forgotten.

Indeed, while Maitland's legacy of subjecting historical primary sources of law to the same doctrinal study rigour as modern law has been influential in terms of developing the internal approach to legal history, it is often overlooked that elements of the external approach can also be found in Maitland's scholarship. In other words, to use the language used in subversive legal history, Maitland's work blends both the intellectual history of law and the social history of law.[61] As Jonathan Rose pointed out, even his most

56. R Williams, *Why Study the Past?* (Longman and Todd, 2005) 1.
57. F W Maitland, 'Letter from Maitland to AV Dicey, c. July 1896', quoted in C H S Fifoot, *Frederic William Maitland* (Harvard University Press, 1971) 143.
58. H E Bell, *Maitland: A Critical Examination and Assessment* (Adams & Charles Black, 1965) 108.
59. He added, 'Perhaps it is putting it too strongly to imply that Maitland had a polemic spirit, but there is no doubt that when he thought he saw a historical truth, he hewed to the line and let the chips fall where they might': J R Cameron, *Frederick Maitland and the History of English Law* (University of Oklahoma Press, 1961) 65.
60. G R Elton, *F W Maitland* (George Weidenfeld and Nicolsonm, 1985) 21.
61. The intellectual history of law was also reformed by the work of SFC Milsom, often in the form of 'heretical' revisions of some of Maitland's works. See R Sandberg, *Subversive Legal History: A Manifesto for the Future of Legal Education* (Routledge, 2021) 31–32 and R Sandberg,

doctrinal work *The History of English Law*[62] 'focuses on institutional and doctrinal development, 'it is not purely legal, as he understands the relationship of law to a broader social and political context'.[63] Much of it involved 'political, social, and economic contexts' and this is even more true of his work as a whole which is 'his work is extensive, varied, and eclectic, abounding in ideas, insights, and concepts'. Maitland is acclaimed as 'the legal historian's historian'.[64] His work showed to historians the usefulness of looking at legal materials. He regarded legal documents as being 'the best, often the only evidence that we have for social and economic history, for the history of morality, for the history of practical religion'.[65] His work has been renowned not only by lawyers but by historians. For Michael Lobban, Maitland 'was one of the central figures who helped to turn the study of history into a professional pursuit'.[66] Ironically, although internal legal history developed as a small band of legal historians followed Maitland into the archives, Maitland can also be claimed as an inspiration for the interdisciplinary study of legal-historical materials and for a subversive approach. As Michael Lobban has pointed out, the proponents of both internal and external legal history 'would probably trace their professional genealogy to one man, F.W. Maitland'.

Conclusion: Beyond the Law School

The ghost of Frederic William Maitland continues to haunt the study of the interaction of law and history in England and Wales. His work has inspired the development of legal history as a specialist sub-discipline of law. This largely internal approach has been cocooned by institutional creations: research centres and groupings, book series, academic journals, learned societies and so on. Yet, in addition to this work, which can be understood to provide an intellectual history of English law, there also exists a significant but disparate literature that examines what may be labelled the social history of English law. Although some moves have been made to bring together these two groups of scholars, a community has not yet come into existence and there remains a gulf between those in law schools and those from other parts of the university. It is noticeable, however, that many of these researchers outside the traditional internal-focused cocoon shun the label of legal historian.

'The Time for Legal History: Some Reflections on Maitland and Milsom Fifty Years on' (2018) 180 *Law & Justice* 21.

62. F Pollock and F W Maitland, *The History of English Law* (2nd edn, Cambridge University Press, 1968 [1898]).
63. J Rose, 'Studying the Past: The Nature and Development of Legal History as an Academic Discipline' (2010) 31(2) *The Journal of Legal History* 101, 114.
64. K J M Smith and J P S McLaren, 'History's Living Legacy: An Outline of "Modern" Historiography of the Common Law' (2001) 21 *Legal Studies* 251, 261.
65. F W Maitland, 'Why the History of English Law Has Not Been Written' in H A L Fisher (ed), *Collected Papers of Frederic William Maitland, Downing Professor of the Laws of England* (Cambridge University Press, 1911) Vol. 1, 480, 486.
66. M Lobban, 'The Varieties of Legal History' (2012) 5 *Clio@Themis* 1, 4.

This raises the question of terminology and whether it is preferable to speak of 'law and history', a phrase that remains far from common but which has been adopted by some initiatives no doubt to highlight and achieve inclusivity. In terms of unpacking the term, reference can be made to the 'x as law/law as x' distinction discussed in the introduction. Such distinctions underscore the interdisciplinary nature of the study – or even the transdisciplinary character of the study.[67] It highlights how a 'law and' study is the work of both academic lawyers and experts in the other field. Law and history, therefore, could be used to refer to an interdisciplinary field where both lawyers and historians work. Adopting this approach of articulating and understanding to law and history would be advantageous given that legal history as a sub-discipline of law does not readily display the interdisciplinary let alone transdisciplinary character of many other 'law and' fields.

However, the application in the context of legal-historical study is problematic. While it can be said that law and history involves the fusion of legal and historical analyses, it is difficult to follow the approach of other interactions to claim that law and history could include the study of history through the frame of law and the study of law through the frame of history. Sarah Wilson has distinguished 'conventional *legal history*'s interest in the value of understanding law's own history for the present with *modern history*'s commentaries on the value of history for understanding society today'.[68] Although problematically presentist,[69] in that it sees both forms of history as useful in terms of understanding the present, Wilson's distinction may be used to highlight the centrality of law in legal history. It may be possible to distinguish between the study of 'history through law', the dominant internal history approach that focuses upon the development of law over time and 'law through history', the wider approach that understands law within the broader mix of historical change.

Although this could be used to distinguish the respective starting points of lawyers and historians,[70] such talk artificially separates legal history from the study of law by

---

67. See further R Sandberg, *Subversive Legal History: A Manifesto for the Future of Legal Education* (Routledge, 2021) chapter 7.
68. S Wilson, 'Value and Values in Higher Education: Some Reflections from the UK on the Subversive Dimensions of Historical Approaches in the Study of Law' in H Gibbon et al. (eds), *Critical Legal Education as a Subversive Activity* (Routledge, 2023) 149, 154.
69. Jonathan Clarke defines presentism as 'a privileging of the present' and writes that 'presentism in popular culture involves the reversion to a more restricted mental world', whereby the phrase 'that's old' no longer means 'that originated some time ago' but means 'that is vexatious' and 'that's history no longer means that is important because it has made us what we are' but means 'that is laughably irrelevant to us': J Clark, *Our Shadowed Present* (Atlantic Books, 2003) 2, 7.
70. This goes back to Maitland's inaugural lecture where he suggested that the lawyer and the historian used 'two different logics, the logic of authority, and the logic of evidence': 'what the lawyer wants is authority and the newer the better; what the historian wants is evidence and older the better': F W Maitland, 'Why the History of English Law has not been Written' in H A L Fisher (ed), *Collected Papers of Frederic William Maitland, Downing Professor of the Laws of England* (Cambridge University Press, 1911) Vol. 1, 480, 491.

other historians. It makes little sense to talk about two separate objects of study and distinguishing the legal and the historical as two frames of analysis seems somewhat superficial. It may be preferable, instead, to conceptualise legal history as a broad church, making it plain that it extends beyond the intellectual history of law to include the social history of law and indeed other forms of history. Key to this is understanding legal history (or law and history or whatever other label is preferred) as an interdisciplinary study: one that extends beyond the law school to include historians who work elsewhere. Indeed, perhaps in the same way that the historical dimensions of law are so central that for lawyers the historical study of law should be an integral part of what academic lawyers do,[71] it can be equally said that the ubiquity and usefulness of legal records means that law should be an essential component of what historians of various different branches do. It is not so much a question of trying to place legal history or law and history within the humanities but rather placing law within the humanities. If law is understood as part of the humanities, then this would underscore the necessity of history as part of the study of law and of law as part of the study of history. Perhaps, this is the legal-historical equivalent of the 'law as x', 'x as law' distinction popularised elsewhere.

71. This is the main conclusion of R Sandberg, *Subversive Legal History: A Manifesto for the Future of Legal Education* (Routledge, 2021).

Chapter Seven

LAW AND LITERATURE

Ian Ward

Introduction: The Shaping of Law and Literature

The purpose of this chapter is to introduce the study of 'law and literature', what it is and what it does. The first part will survey the critical landscape, revisiting the evolution and the associated 'strategies' of literary jurisprudence. The second part will then provide an illustrative case study. On this occasion we will indulge a little sorcery.

The interdisciplinary relation of law and literature is hardly new. The merest glance at the writings of Sophocles and Shakespeare confirms this much. The respective fates of Antigone and Shylock have lost none of their resonance down the centuries. The study of 'law and literature' as an academic enterprise has, however, assumed a renewed energy over the last couple of generations. Literary jurists commonly date this evolution to the pioneering work of James Boyd White in the 1970s and 1980s, which urged the appreciation that law expresses itself textually, and must therefore be read critically.[1] The better lawyer knows 'what reading means'.[2] A conclusion famously shared by Stanley Fish, who supposes that the 'practice' of reading legal and literary texts should be the same, as both take 'narrative' form.[3] Put simply, at its root, reading Milton's *Paradise Lost* is no different from reading *Donoghue v Stevenson*[4] or *R (Miller) v the Prime Minister*.[5] It is only context that makes the experience feel different.

Here we might contemplate an original, essentially functional, distinction in 'law and literature' scholarship: between law *as* literature, and law *in* literature.[6] Law *as* literature invites the lawyer to become a literary critic, to embrace the attendant challenges

1. See, for example, J Boyd White, *The Legal Imagination* (Little Brown, 1973), J Boyd White, *When Words Lose Their Meaning: Constitutions and Reconstitutions of Language, Character and Community*, (Chicago University Press, 1984), J Boyd White, *Heracles' Bow: Essays on the Rhetoric and Poetics of Law* (Wisconsin University Press, 1985), and J Boyd White, *Justice as Translation: An Essay in Cultural and Legal Criticism* (Chicago University Press, 1990).
2. J Boyd White, 'Law as Language: Reading Law and Reading Literature' (1982) 60 *Texas Law Review* 430–1.
3. S Fish, *Doing What Comes Naturally: Change, Rhetoric, and the Practice of Theory in Literary and Legal Studies* (Oxford University Press, 1990), 138.
4. [1932] UKHL 100.
5. [2019] UKSC 41.
6. I Ward, *Law and Literature: Possibilities and Perspectives* (Cambridge University Press, 1995), 4–22.

of textual indeterminacy. Law no longer becomes a matter of truth-seeking but of fashioning impressions. As Richard Rorty famously put it, the 'strong poet' is the hero of democracy, interpretive 'contingency' its resistance.[7] In practical terms, this means that the literary jurist must also appreciate the skills of the literary critic, hermeneutics, post-structuralism, historical materialism, deconstruction, reader-response theory and so on. Appreciation does not demand approval. But it does require an acceptance that there are different ways of reading everything – albeit the same different ways, for lawyers and everyone else. A conclusion that sits more comfortably with the student of literature, perhaps, than it does the student of law.

And a good point at which to acknowledge a defining characteristic of 'law and literature' scholarship, evident from its very inception. Its principal aspiration is didactic.[8] Boyd White's *The Legal Imagination*,[9] commonly regarded as the ur-text of modern 'law and literature' studies, was designed as an educative tool. Much of his ensuing work focused more closely still on rhetorical and interpretive strategies, urging the law student to read texts such as Plato's *Gorgias* and Lincoln's *Second Inaugural* in order to better understand how arguments might be won and lost.[10] The advocate as 'storyteller'.[11] Precisely the same can be said of Richard Weisberg, urging students to read Shakespeare's *Merchant of Venice* in order to better appreciate the moral complexities which underwrite ideas of justice, and Martha Nussbaum, recommending the poetry of Walt Whitman as a means to better comprehend the place of empathy and compassion in the courtroom, and the classroom.[12] The essence of 'poethics', as Weisberg terms it, lies in its attention to the plight of the "other"'.[13]

It is here that the idea of law *in* literature emerges, as a complementary poethical 'strategy'. Inviting the student to contemplate the deployment of law within literature, sometimes to entertain, sometimes to educate, commonly both. This is not to suppose that *Antigone* or *The Merchant of Venice* might somehow replace the writings of Hart or Dworkin or Raz in the study of legal morality, for example. But it is to suppose that it

---

7. R Rorty, *Contingency, Irony, and Solidarity* (Cambridge University Press, 1989), 61.
8. The didactic aspiration was commonly proclaimed in the early days of modern 'law and literature' scholarship. See C Dunlop, 'Literature Studies in Law Schools' (1991) 3 *Cardozo Studies in Law and Literature* 63, and I Ward, 'The Educative Ambition of Law and Literature' (1993) 13 *Legal Studies* 323.
9. J Boyd White, *The Legal Imagination* (Little Brown, 1973).
10. J Boyd White, *Heracles' Bow: Essays on the Rhetoric and Poetics of Law* (Wisconsin University Press, 1985), ch. 10, and J Boyd White, *Acts of Hope: Creating Authority in Literature, Law and Politics* (Chicago University Press, 1994), ch. 8.
11. See here R Cover, '*Nomos* and Narrative' (1983/4) 97 *Harvard LR* 4, and also P Williams, 'Alchemical Notes: Reconstructing Rights from Deconstructed Ideals' (1987) 22 *Harvard Civil Right-Civil Liberties LR* 401-.
12. See R Weisberg, *Poethics and Other Strategies of Law and Literature* (Columbia University Press, 1992), and M Nussbaum, *Poetic Justice: The Literary Imagination and Public Life* (Beacon, 1994), ch. 4.
13. R Weisberg, *Poethics and Other Strategies of Law and Literature* (Columbia University Press, 1992), 46.

might stimulate alternative perspectives. In a strange way, the use of a fictive text can make the attendant ethical dilemmas seem more real. In the preface to her *Tenant of Wildfell Hall*, Anne Bronte made much the same claim for her endeavour: 'My object in writing the following pages, was not simply to amuse the Reader […] I wished to tell the truth, for the truth always conveys its own moral to those who are able to receive it.'[14] As did Charles Dickens, in the preface to *Oliver Twist*. He might have created a story, but what occurs within its pages is a 'true' reflection of 'the best and worst shades of our common nature'. It is 'emphatically God's truth'.[15]

Another claim, necessarily related, is that of raising voices. Those of the 'other', most urgently. In Anne Bronte's case, it was the voice of the beaten wife, in Dickens's case, the beaten prostitute. In each case, it has been suggested, helping to raise a distinctive female 'consciousness' among a constituency of readers.[16] Reading is, after all, a 'shared process', an 'interactive experience'.[17] Here, of course, we are stretching the disciplinary reach a little further, not only into philosophy and ethics but into politics and history. In this instance, it is female voices raised against abuses inscribed in nineteenth-century English law. And it is certainly no coincidence that some of the most urgent and compelling 'law and literature' scholarship has been written from a feminist perspective.[18] But it might be any voices in any moment. Here again, there is no surprise in discovering that critical race theory has likewise embraced the 'strategies' of literary jurisprudence.[19]

The critical thing is that they are not legal voices, or at least not only. There are legal voices in literature, but they are scarcer and rarely edifying. Dickens writes in a few, invariably egregious. Shakespeare prefers to deploy pretend lawyers to sort things out, such as Portia in *The Merchant of Venice*. It is not simply that law and justice rarely seem complementary in literature, ancient or modern; it is more that the poetic imagination relishes their tension. There is no better metaphor for power, its savagery and its corruption, than the law. Thus Franz Kafka's *The Trial*, another of the ur-texts of 'law and literature' scholarship, is revered, not least, for its seemingly prophetic quality. A testament to modernity, and what follows. Of course, not everything that Kafka imagined has come to pass, at least not yet. But then predicting the future is always trickier than reading the past, and the present.

Similarly, we cannot be sure of the shape that literary jurisprudence will assume as it passes from generation to generation. Nor indeed should we want to know. We might,

---

14. A Bronte, *The Tenant of Wildfell Hall* (Oxford University Press, 1993), 3–4.
15. C Dickens, *Oliver Twist* (Penguin, 2002), 460.
16. L Surridge, *Bleak Houses: Marital Violence in Victorian Fiction* (Ohio University Press, 2005), 9–10.
17. J Boyd White, 'Law as Language: Reading Law and Reading Literature' (1982) 60 *Texas Law Review* 415, 425–6.
18. See, for example, M Aristodemou, *Law and Literature: Journeys from Her to Eternity* (Oxford University Press, 2000), M Williams, *Empty Justice: One Hundred Years of Law, Literature and Philosophy* (Cavendish, 2002), and S Heinzelman, *Riding the Black Ram: Law, Literature, and Gender* (Stanford University Press, 2010).
19. See, for example, P Williams, *The Alchemy of Race and Rights* (Harvard University Press, 1991).

though, bear in mind a couple of adages. The first is the Burkean 'prescription': that evolution is a sign of vitality. The second is Mark Twain's alleged observation: that while history rarely repeats, it does tend to rhyme. The 'law and literature' movement, in its more recent incarnation, has moved well beyond the stage of establishment, and has evolved in a variety of directions, commonly cutting across other disciplinary margins. The idea of 'law and humanities' has become common parlance, articulating an ever-broadening horizon. There is nothing to suggest that this will change. There again, as Rorty liked to affirm, in characteristically prosaic terms, 'only time will tell', nothing else can.[20]

Shapeshifting

As advertised, the purpose of the second part of this chapter is to witness some literary jurisprudence in action. We will look at two plays about witches. Societies have always worried about witchery, and just as commonly deployed, the law is at the sharper edge of its regulatory response. The shape of the perceived threat mutates, of course. But there is a common thread. Witches are terrifying, and they tend to latch on to a variety of ancillary anxieties which are specific to the moment.

Mother Sawyer's Case

We will start in 1602, with the troubled musings of Sir Edmund Anderson, Chief Justice of Common Pleas:

> The land is full of witches; they abound in all places, I have hanged five or six and twenty of them [...] Their malice is great, their practices devilish, and if we shall not convict them without their own confession, or direct proofs, where the presumptions are so great, and the circumstances so apparent, they will in short-time over-run the land.[21]

The threat was imminent, and the biblical injunction was clear enough, as William Perkins emphasised in his *Discourse of the Damned Art of Witchcraft*: 'Though shalt not suffer a witch to live' (Exod. 22:18).[22]

The governing law in the moment was found in the 1563 Act Against Conjurations, Enchantments and Witchcrafts. The Act made it a felony to 'use, practice or exercise any witchcraft', which led to the 'destruction of the persons or goods of their neighbours or any other subject'. Aimed thus, as Bishop Grindal affirmed, at the 'magic and conjurations' of papist priests, rather than the mutterings of village crones. Most importantly, it was aimed at instances of harm, of *maleficium*. Unless there was evidence of consequential 'destruction', a misjudged curse or a mis-mixed potion was more likely to result in an

20. R Rorty, *Contingency, Irony, and Solidarity* (Cambridge University Press, 1989), 189–98.
21. J Sharpe, *Instruments of Darkness: Witchcraft in Early Modern England* (Pennsylvania University Press, 1978), 216.
22. See T Borman, *Witches: James I and the English Witch-Hunts* (Vintage, 2014), 59, 101.

uncomfortable afternoon spent in the stocks. And this, according to the likes of Perkins, was the problem.

There was, hope, though, in the person of King James VI of Scotland, an expert on witch-hunting, even if he had said so himself, most famously in his treatise on *Daemonology*, published in 1587. The hope lay in the fact that James was the most likely successor to Queen Elizabeth. And so it came to pass. James did succeed to the English throne, in early 1603, and a year later gave his assent to a revamped Witchcraft Act. This did two things. First, it transferred jurisdiction for witchcraft trials to secular courts. It was after all a state crime, as Bishop Andrews recognised; the 'most notorious traytor and rebell that can be is a witch'. Second, the Act made it an offence to 'consult, covenant with, employ, feed or reward any evil or wicked spirit'. The idea of a Satanic 'compact', originally ventured by St Thomas Aquinas in the thirteenth century, had become widely accepted by the close of the sixteenth. 'All witchcraft', Perkins confirmed, 'is a league or covenant between the witch and the devil'.[23] The idea that the Devil might like to formalise his relationship with his various minions, by means of covenant, made sense to the lawyers too. This invited a softening of the evidentiary burden too. No longer requiring evidence of harm, or a confession, proof of witchery might now be surmised from a strange mark on the body, or a suspicious pet. A 'mousse, catte or some other visible creature', as Perkins helpfully explained. A 'familiar', the Devil's agency.

The fact that James had prioritised a new witchcraft statute spoke volumes. Interest in witches waxed and waned through the early modern period. Jacobean England was a waxing moment. Not simply because there were so many witches about but because there was so much excitement. Not least on stage. The list of plays about witchcraft in late Elizabethan and early Stuart England is long. For those who preferred a more metaphysical evening there was Marlowe's *Dr Faustus*. For those who craved the demonic thrill there was pretty much everything John Webster wrote. As well, of course, as perhaps the most spectacularly demonic of all staged Jacobean witches, the 'midnight hags' of Shakespeare's *Macbeth*. 'Double, double toil and trouble;/ Fire, burn, and cauldron bubble' (4.1.10–11).[24] Few literary witches have had better rhythm, or better ingredients: 'eye of newt, and toe of frog', a sprinkling of herbs and a 'pilot's thumb' (1.3.28). Or indeed greater ambition, the assassination of a divinely ordained king. It is impossible to read *Macbeth* out with the immediate political context. The succession to the English throne of a neurotic Scottish King who pretended to be an expert witch-hunter.[25]

---

23. In J Lumby, *The Lancashire Witchcraze* (Carnegie, 1999), 111.
24. References to *Macbeth* taken from the Arden edition, 1984.
25. 'Though this bark cannot be lost/Yet it shall be tempest tossed' (1.3.26); one of the many allusions that James might have picked up. What made the Berwick trials so personal to the King was evidence that the witches had deliberately raised a storm designed to drown James on his way back to England from Copenhagen with his new wife, Anna of Denmark. See G Wills, *Witches and Jesuits: Shakespeare's Macbeth* (Oxford University Press, 1995), 33–49, and R Wilson, *Secret Shakespeare: Studies in Theatre, Religion and Resistance* (Manchester University Press, 2004), 186–281.

And for those who fancied something a little earthier, if not quite sceptical, there was *The Witch of Edmonton*, a collaborative work written by Thomas Dekker, generally thought to be the lead author, William Rowley and John Ford. First performed in 1621, the immediate inspiration for the *Witch* was found in a 'true' account of the 'wonderful discoverie' and subsequent trial of an old woman named Elizabeth Sawyer. The account was written up by the Reverend Henry Goodcole, a chaplain at Newgate gaol, who developed a lucrative sideline in publishing 'true' accounts of the final days of various 'monstrous' women.

Goodcole's account of the case takes predictable shape, with a series of unexplained deaths; two infants, some cows and a woman named Agnes Ratcliffe. Rumours grow that old 'Mother' Sawyer might be responsible, and a local justice orders an investigation. A 'private and strange mark' is discovered 'on her body', and Sawyer is sent for trial. Ratcliffe's husband provides damning evidence, literally. His stricken wife had, in her final moments, accused Sawyer of having been the 'occasion' of her death.[26] Though acquitted of killing the children, Sawyer is convicted of having murdered Agnes. Goodcole's account concludes as any tale of Calvinist redemption should, with a contrite confession, after which Sawyer is hanged. At no point does Goodcole express a scintilla of doubt. Sawyer was guilty of a most 'diabolicall' crime.

And there is no demurrer in *The Witch of Edmonton*, at least not regarding Sawyer's guilt. But there are some critical, and oddly ambivalent, differences.[27] Most obviously, Dekker makes his 'mother' Sawyer a far earthier character.[28] A strategy which makes her deviance at once more relatable, and more unsettling.[29] She has in the end consorted with the Devil, through the medium of Dog, which becomes her familiar, not because she is innately evil or satanic, but because she has feels lonely and rejected:

> [...] Why should the envious world
> Throw all their scandalous malice on upon me?
> 'Cause I am poor, deformed and ignorant [...]
> Must I for that be made a common sink
> For all the filth and rubbish of men's tongues. (2.1.1–3, 6–7)[30]

26. In K O'Mahoney, 'The Witch Figure: *The Witch of Edmonton*' (2009) 24 *The Seventeenth Century* 244–5.
27. Making for an 'erratic medley of fact and fiction', according to Katherine O'Mahoney in ibid 254. A strategic form of 'scepticism', according to J Garrett, 'Dramatizing Deviance: Sociological Theory and *The Witch of Edmonton*' (2007) 49 *Criticism* 350.
28. 'Astonishingly sympathetic', according to E Cheng, in 'Marginalizing Women: Forced Marriage, Witchcraft Accusations, and the Social Machinery of Private Landownership *The Witch of Edmonton*' (2010) 36 *Concentric: Literary and Cultural Studies* 120.
29. See J Garrett, 'Dramatizing Deviance: Sociological Theory and *The Witch of Edmonton*' (2007) 49 *Criticism* 341–4, and M Pearson, 'A Dog, a Witch, a Play: *The Witch of Edmonton*' (2011) 11 *Early Theatre* 90–1.
30. References to *The Witch of Edmonton* taken from M Wiggins (ed), *A Woman Killed with Kindness and Other Domestic Plays* (Oxford University Press, 2008).

Again, when arraigned before the justice, Sawyer wonders why the 'eye' of the law is cast 'on me':

> Or any lean old bedlam? Reverence once
> Had wont to wait on age. Now an old woman
> Ill-favoured grown with years, if she be poor
> Must be called bawd or witch. Such so abused
> Are the coarse witches, t'other are the fine,
> Spun for the devil's own wearing. (4.1.121-6)

The inference is plain. In casting her out, Sawyer's neighbours have done the Devil's work for him. They rejected her, so she rejected them It might even be supposed that she has been prostituted. An insinuation laid in her preceding denunciation of those 'city-witches who can turn/ Their husbands' wares, whole standing shops of wares,/ To sumptuous tables, gardens of stol'n sin' (4.1.115–17). We might imagine some uncomfortable shuffling in the more expensive seats.

Among the lawyers especially:

> Is not that scold a witch? The man of law
> Whose honeyed hopes the credulous client draws,
> As bees by tinkling basins, to swarm to him
> From his own hive to work the wax in his;
> He is no witch, not he! (4.1.130–4)[31]

Lawyers, witches, dissemblers all. Precisely the kind of comment that gets Sawyer hanged, not just because she is a suspected witch but because she is 'too saucy and too bitter' (4.1.82). And too perceptive. It is after Sawyer has returned to the theme, wondering how many of her present accusers might have 'tempted maiden,/ With golden hooks flung at her chastity/ To come and lose her honour, and, being lost,/ To pay not a denier for't?' that the men conclude that they should 'no longer/ Hold conference with her fury' (4.1.147–8).

The play concludes with Sawyer assuming her guilt, and rather enjoying her notoriety. It does not conclude with much by way of redemption or, consequently, assurance. A generic repentance of 'all former evil', but a studied refusal to enumerate any instances (5.3.50). Neither does it conclude with a trial. The extent to which Sawyer may have benefited from due legal process is left to the imagination of the audience. Given the justice's earlier determination that there should be 'proofs [...] better armed', it might be assumed so (4.1.42). There again, Dekker deliberately chose not to write in a trial scene. Perhaps because, rumour aside, and a weirdly behaving dog, there was not much by way of evidence; just enough after 1604 perhaps, nothing like enough before.[32] They

31. For a commentary on this passage as a socio-economic critique, see J Garrett, 'Dramatizing Deviance: Sociological Theory and *The Witch of Edmonton*' (2007) 49 *Criticism* 355–8.
32. See ibid 352–8, supposing a concerted critique of 'judicial probity'.

all trudge 'home to Edmonton with heavy hearts' (5.3.167). The pervasive sense is one of contingency. A miserable old woman who allows herself to be duped into becoming the front of a diabolic enterprise. There is every reason to believe that the streets of Edmonton are abounding with women like Elizabeth Sawyer.

Tom's Case

Our second case invites us forward three and a half centuries, to 1976. A different environment, but with some predictable anxieties and some familiar prejudices. Our text is Caryl Churchill's play *Vinegar Tom*. Churchill has established herself as one of the foremost playwrights of her generation. Articulating a 'voice' that is 'oppositional' by inclination and political to its core.[33] And overly 'feminist' in its 'praxis'.[34] Among her critically acclaimed works can be counted *Cloud Nine* and *Top Girls*, and the mystical *The Skriker*, along with various rewritings of classical works such as Seneca's *Thyestes* and *A Mouthful of Birds*, inspired by Euripedes' *The Bacchae*. A Churchill play can assume a variety of forms, but as common as not it will reach back to make better sense of the present.

Vinegar Tom is conceived in this spirit, one of two plays which returned to early seventeenth-century England, to the same moment indeed in which Dekker and his co-writers were recasting the case of old 'mother' Sawyer. The other is *Light Shining in Buckinghamshire* – the title of which is taken from a Leveller tract of 1646.[35] In both cases, Churchill's purpose is to uncover resonances, between then and now, rhythms at least. In *Light Shining*, it is the fate of socialism. In *Vinegar Tom* is the condition of women. The idea that the female experience in late twentieth-century Britain might be engaged by means of reinvesting dramatic witch-scares was embraced by many 'second wave' feminist playwrights.[36] In an introductory essay to the published version of the play, Churchill reflected on the moment of its conception, England in 1976, when questions of 'religion, class' and most especially 'the position of women' were so peculiarly prescient.[37]

Churchill, typically, researched extensively before writing *Vinegar Tom*, days spent immersed in trial transcripts, as well as contemporary printed sources. It is around these materials that she weaves the story of four women and a cat who find themselves

33. E Aston and E Diamond, 'On Caryl Churchill', in E Aston and E Diamond (eds), *A Cambridge Companion to Caryl Churchill* (Cambridge University Press, 2009), 1.
34. J Reinelt, 'Caryl Churchill and the Politics of Style', in E Aston and J Reinelt (eds), *A Cambridge Companion to Modern British Women Playwrights* (Cambridge University Press, 2000), 174. A conclusion shared by E Aston, in her *Feminist Views on the English Stage* (Cambridge University Press, 2003), 18.
35. Also written in 1976. For a commentary on *Light Shining*, relating it to *Vinegar Tom*, see I Ward, *The Play of Law in Modern British Theatre* (Edinburgh University Press, 2021), 77–83.
36. Amongt similar contributions can be counted Sarah Daniels's *Byrthrite* and Bryony Lavery's *Witch-Craze*.
37. In C Churchill, *Plays 1* (Methuen, 1985), 129 [all internal references are taken from this text]. The same 'mood' is attested in Michael Billington's magisterial *State of the Nation: British Theatre since 1945* (Faber and Faber, 2009), at 241–2, 247–9.

caught amidst the witch-scare that swept East Anglia in the years immediately following the English civil war – the England of Matthew Hopkins, the notorious self-styled Witchfinder-General. The women are Joan, her daughter Alice, Alice's friend Susan and Ellen, a 'cunning' woman. The cat is the eponymous Vinegar Tom. Born of the same imagination that conceived the dog which seduced Elizabeth Sawyer, except that Tom really is a cat. There is plenty else that resonates too. A lot of odd coincidences, rumours and 'gossiping', and a lot of misogynistic prejudice (143).

Which, once again, makes for a world that is both oddly ordinary and terrifyingly extraordinary. A world in which the 'charms' of a 'cunning woman' are believed to prevent pregnancy, cure 'heartache' and impotence, lift existing spells and maybe even kill an unwanted lover, in which rats and spiders are 'imps' and cows are believed to be enchanted by cats, where suspects are pricked for marks, and where innocent women are strung up because they are supposed to have compacted with Satan. Ultimately, it is a world in which there are witches because witches are needed, more than ever. In a world 'turned upside down', as the contemporary ballad supposed, the fantastic can explain the otherwise inexplicable. When the accusers, Margery and Jack, visit Ellen the 'cunning' woman, they are invited to look in a 'cloudy glass'. They 'see' Joan, or rather they see what they 'come to see' (158).

Characters like Jack have a necessary function. There cannot be misogyny without men. Impotent and angry, Jack prefers to think that he is 'bewitched' by Alice, rather than being punished by God for his lust (152–3, 158–9). And then there is Packer, the 'famous finder of witches'. Packer may be a bit pricey, at 'twenty shillings a time', but he has an enviable record, having had 'above thirty hanged in the country round' (164, 168). A man after Chief Justice Anderson's heart, Packer knows that the fate of the 'kingdom' is at stake. If the diabolical 'infection' is not purged, England will be shortly 'overrun' with witches (167). It is Packer who 'pricks' Joan and Alice, assisted by Goody the 'searcher' who 'holds' them fast (165). Goody could have pricked too.[38] But Churchill prefers a man, in her prefatory comments keen to emphasise that the 'pricking scene is one of humiliation rather than torture', and all the more humiliating for being undertaken by Packer, 'an efficient professional, not a sadistic maniac'.[39] 'Miss' Betty, who refuses to marry as she should, is treated in much the same way by the Doctor, 'tied to chair' and bled and blistered in the hope that it will cure her rebellion, or at least terrify her into obedience (149).[40]

Alice has of course been pricked before, in the very opening scene, by the Man. The manner of penetration might be slightly different, but the humiliation amounts to much the same. The Man teases Alice with the thought that she has fornicated with the Devil. Alice has certainly come across devils before, all the various 'clergy and gentlemen' who, it might be surmised, have already pricked her (135). She is, it seems, the kind

38. It was not uncommon for 'searchers' to serve as 'prickers' too.
39. C Churchill, *Plays 1* (Methuen, 1985), 134.
40. For the Foucauldian resonance here, in the 'invasion' of their respective bodies, see J Reinelt, 'Caryl Churchill and the Politics of Style', in E Aston and J Reinelt (eds), *A Cambridge Companion to Modern British Women Playwrights* (Cambridge University Press, 2000), 178–9.

of girl that Sawyer had in mind when she berated her accusers, resigned to her abuse. And, like Sawyer, part of Alice might believe in the Devil too. Interested in 'potions' and charms', fascinated by stories of witches 'flying' (136-7). But the other part does not. Alice has not compacted with the Devil. She has just slept with a stranger. It might still be a 'sin', but it is not a satanic one. And neither is it new. She knows what a man feels like on top of her, she has 'been hurt by men' before, and she already has a child without a 'father' (135). Later Packer will condemn her for precisely this: evidence of a diabolic sexuality. The Man disappears from the play at the end of the scene, dismissing Alice as nothing more than a common 'whore' (137). But he has left his 'mark', and not just on Alice.

The abuse of Alice is the first in a sequence of violations which will be visited upon the women of *Vinegar Tom*. Along with sex comes marriage, and along with marriage comes wife-beating. Joan was beaten by her husband, and there are the same intimations in the troubled marriage of Margery and Jack (141). Susan views the fact that she has not yet been beaten as a miracle. Neither is it the only pain which sex and marriage imports. With three babies already and three miscarriages, Susan dreads the prospect of childbirth. So, she gets a 'potion' from Ellen the 'cunning' women in the hope that it might make her abort (147, 155–6).[41] Witchcraft manuals warned gentlemen about women such as Susan and Ellen and their connivances. It is why they had to be watched so closely.

Predictably Susan blames herself for her abortion and Alice for encouraging her: 'I'm wicked. You're wicked' (162). Shortly afterwards a hysterical Susan denounces Alice, relating how she 'did uncleanness' with the Devil and sought to learn 'wicked magic' from the 'cunning' woman Ellen (167). The evidence is damning, literally. It is not just that she killed her baby but that she 'cursed' it (167). Susan is accepting: 'I was a witch and never knew it. I killed my babies' (174). Joan is accepting too. 'I been a witch these ten years', she informs Packer, before she fantasises a series of past diabolical triumphs (173). There is defiance here, as there is in Alice's anger: 'I am not a witch. But I wish I was. If I could live I'd be a witch now after what they've done' (175). In the end Alice ends up where Sawyer ended up, leaving the play as she arrived: tormented by the irreconcilable temptations of scepticism and Satanism.

People say and do all kinds of things. Language can be liberating, but it can also be dangerous. Miss Betty wants to jump off a tree and 'fly' away from a marriage she dreads (140). She escapes the noose because she is 'Miss' Betty, and because the Doctor thinks he can make her 'better' (169). Joan is not so lucky. A casual curse is enough to send her to the gallows. She damns Margery's 'butter to hell' (145). Alice is brought down in the same way, chattering away as she sticks pins in a 'mud man'. It is just a bit of fun, she tells a horrified Susan, 'just words' (163). But it is again enough to hang them both.

41. For a commentary on Susan as 'failed mother', see Z Ravari, '*Vinegar Tom*: Women's Oppression through Patriarchal-Capitalist Dominations' (2010) 2 *Review of European Studies* 157.

The ambivalence of language finds its sharpest, most gruesomely ironic, expression in the penultimate scene, orchestrated by Kramer and Sprenger, the authors of the infamous *Malleus Malleficarum*, the ur-text of Reformation witch-hunting. Most women are witches because they are 'credulous' and have 'slippery tongues', and they like sex too much (177). They fornicate their way and gossip each other to the gallows. The presence of Kramer and Sprenger reinforces another critical theme in the play: the disruption of time and place. In the original production of the play, Churchill had them perform as an Edwardian music hall act. The songs which recur throughout the play serve much the same purpose: a 'kind of Brechtian cabaret' which, by 'catapulting the historical references in the drama into the present', serves to 'enable spectators to see both change and continuities'.[42]

Churchill closes the play with two songs, between which she places Kramer and Sprenger's performance. Both are intended to drive home the historical parallels. The first is the 'Lament for the Witches':

> Where have the witches gone?
> Who are the witches now?
> Here we are [...]
> Look in the mirror tonight.
> Would they have hanged you then?
> Ask how they are stopping you now.
> Where have the witches gone? (175–6)

One way they are 'stopping you now' is the same way women have always been stopped:

> The witches hanging the sky
> Haunt the courts where lawyers lie. (175)

The second song, 'Evil Women', is no less bitter and resonant. It concludes:

> Evil women
> Is that what you want?
> Is that what you want to see?
> On the movie screen
> Of your own wet dream
> Evil women
> Evil women
> Women. (179)

42. See J Reinelt, 'Caryl Churchill and the Politics of Style', in E Aston and J Reinelt (eds), *A Cambridge Companion to Modern British Women Playwrights* (Cambridge University Press, 2000), 23, quoting Sue Todd, who played Susan in the original production. The purpose of the songs was to disrupt, to be 'combative'.

The insinuation is patent. The 'evil' woman is a sexualised construct, and the constructors are men, priests, lawyers, farmers, wife-beaters, theatre-goers. It was in 1646, and 1621, and it is still.

Conclusion: The Poetics of Sorcery

As advertised, we have only had time to indulge the merest glance at 'law and literature' in action. Two plays, on a common theme, written at very different moments, but importing many of the 'strategies' common to literary jurisprudence. First, and most obviously, they tell us something about early seventeenth-century England, and more especially its regulatory response to the threat of 'abounding' witches. This, in its plainest sense, is the didactic aspiration. *The Witch of Edmonton* is a primary source which can enrich our understanding of how earlier generations of lawyers got the 'law-job' done.[43] Tempting us beyond the limitations of the 'legal' record, it puts some human flesh on the drier legal bones. Which is, of course, precisely what Churchill set out to do three centuries later. That she might cast a sceptical eye towards the legally inscribed prejudices of 1646 is hardly surprising. That Dekker and his chums did the same is more so. It is not that they make Elizabeth Sawyer a sympathetic character, but they do make her relatable. An ordinary woman trapped in a dreadful moment, who falls prey to her own weaknesses, and the terrified malevolence of those with whom she lives. And the law which has been conjured to destroy her.

Something else which *The Witch of Edmonton* did, and does, is raise the voice of Elizabeth Sawyer, and all those who suffered her fate. The poethical aspiration. Only rarely do we hear these voices anywhere else. It is a tempered voice, of course. Here it is the voice which Dekker, Ford and Rowley imagine, or rather, it is the voice which they discern in Henry Goodcole's imagination. The chronicler is always shaped by their own prejudices and impressions, whether they are clerics or dramatists, or lawyers. And no matter how much they might, like Anne Bronte, crave the telling of 'truth', they will all, in the end, tell their own truth. We might recall David Hare's observation, defending the art of *verbatim* drama: 'You find the driftwood on the beach, but you carve the wood and paint it to make it art.' It is a kind 'of sculpture'.[44] However reticent, dramatists are always responsible for the shapes they shift.

And the same is, of course, true of Caryl Churchill. Inspired by real cases perhaps, but still sculpting her own history. There is, of course, something else here, for *Vinegar Tom* is about now, as well as then. We do not really believe in witches anymore. We do though crave their presence, whatever shape they might take, and the terror they import. There is always a terrifying 'other' to dehumanise and repel. Reflecting on the writing of *Tom*, Churchill recalled a conscious decision to leave 'aside' a narrow reading of witchcraft, of the kind that might be confined by contemporary puritan prejudice, in favour of a more generic commentary on the practice of 'scapegoating'. She 'wanted to

43. The phrase 'law-job' was popular among American realist and critical lawyers.
44. Quoted in D Lane, *Contemporary British Drama* (Edinburgh University Press, 2010), 77.

write a play about witches with no witches in it; a play not about evil, hysteria and possession, but about poverty, humiliation and prejudice'.[45]

We will speculate another rhythm in closing. The most prescient 'other' today is of course the 'woke'. Not that anyone knows precisely what 'woke' means; indeed, it is the very shiftiness of the 'woke' which makes it so scary. But it seems to connote something that is progressive and resistant, and which finds a consciously cultural expression. Precisely the kind of thing which has terrified the Puritan imagination for centuries. In the absence of definitional certitude, it is perhaps easier to enumerate. A motley crew. BLM marchers, Brexit-deniers and the BBC, climate-change and trans-rights activists, social justice 'warriors' and immigrant 'invaders'. And their 'lefty-lawyers' too. And playwrights, of course, the uppity variety, especially, sceptical, ironic, resistant.

45. C Churchill, *Plays 1* (Methuen, 1985), 129–30.

Chapter Eight

LAW AND PHILOSOPHY

Daniel Newman

Introduction

This chapter looks at law and philosophy as it appears in the Law School. In contrast with some of the chapters in this volume, which consider emerging or prospective links between law and a humanities subject, law and philosophy are already closely bound together and have been a prominent part of the legal academy. They are bound by a shared interest in justice: probing relationships between state and citizen, unpicking the rules people are expected to live by and, centrally, exploring how to govern fairly. Concerns around justice are prominent philosophical concerns and play a central role in political philosophy, with justice central to debates in ethics as it looks at values, right and wrong action, obligations and rights. Within law, the field of legal philosophy takes its interest in what the law is and ought to be, which again brings justice concerns to the fore. Both political philosophy, which has tended to occur outside the Law School, and legal philosophy, from within, are typically brought together in the legal academy through the teaching of jurisprudence. Hence the connection between law and philosophy is firmly established with jurisprudence modules being common in Law Schools. And this impact of philosophy informs what is sometimes known as legal theory, which is the all-encompassing term for the approach that compliments and contrasts traditional black letter law.

Thus, legal theory derived at least in part from philosophy allows us to go beyond looking at the law in and of itself and ask bigger questions. As a teacher, for example, I use this theory to explore social justice, influenced by how such inquiry may explore the way law plays a role in structuring society to serve the ends of some, over others. For example, why do some people have their basic needs such as housing met while others do not? And what can be done to change things for the better? These questions can include asking how and why the law perpetuates certain structures of power. And thus, legal theorising can help us pursue issues of social justice – which can be such a powerful part of the legal academy and one of the topics that can most engage students.[1] This gives us a means to explore the role that law plays in stratifying society along the lines of class, race and gender to name but a few prominent divisions. A more holistic view

1. See F Gordon and D Newman (eds), *Leading Works in Law and Social Justice* (Routledge, 2021).

of justice is possible through thinking more deeply about the law as comes from taking on an insight from outside legal studies such as that informed by philosophy. This is the approach I take to my jurisprudence teaching and one that will inform this chapter. I want to think about what we teach students because jurisprudence helps us to shape the minds of legal scholars, and is a crucial part of the process of encouraging new lawyers to think about the meaning and function of the law. As such, we are teaching lawyers to be reflective, which is especially important considering the power of the law in underpinning social experience and therefore of lawyers in wider society.

While other chapters may look at law as another subject or that subject as law, what we will consider is how law and philosophy already work together to unpick issues around justice – and we will do this by taking brief inquiries into some of the most conspicuous areas. In this chapter, we will begin by considering insights from philosophy itself – particularly some prominent insights from political philosophy. We will then move to the dominant forms of legal philosophy that come from within the legal academy. We will then take a critical turn by looking at the way Critical Legal Studies pushes us to challenge some dominant assumptions and ways of doing legal theory. We will look at Feminist Legal Studies as a movement that seeks to add missing women's voices from legal theory. Next we will bring in Critical Race Theory to show how much of jurisprudence represents white interests. Postcolonial theory will be introduced to show the Western biases of the legal academy. We will finally conclude by thinking ahead to what law and philosophy, and theorising in the Law School, could look like moving forward.

Considering Justice from Outside the Legal Academy: The Insight of Political Philosophy

I will begin by looking at how concepts of justice are looked at within the field of philosophy itself. There are some branches of philosophy that are sometimes considered less applicable to legal scholars in the mainstream legal academy (though I am sure we could make an argument for any of them). I am thinking here of metaphysics with its questioning about the nature of reality or aesthetics looking at beauty and taste. Some areas of philosophy have more readily accepted relevance for legal researchers, such as epistemology – which we increasingly drill into postgraduate research students albeit from more of a social science than a humanities stance. Ethics, the study of right and wrong, feels highly pertinent for legal scholars and should really take a more overt role in what we teach law students. In the limited space I have for this chapter though, I will focus chiefly on political philosophy as the area that is perhaps most likely considered as germane for legal studies and our thinking about justice – and which appears as the most readily discussed literature from the field of philosophy on jurisprudence courses in the Law School. Political philosophy is often taken as the study of government, questioning the nature, scope and legitimacy of state institutions and those who act in their names.

Most discussions of political philosophy will be rooted in ancient society. Some of the earliest such attention might focus on ancient China – such as from Confucius and the sixth century before the Common Era onwards. Confucianism sets out a vision of a hierarchical, meritocratic government based on empathy, loyalty and interpersonal relationships. While Confucianism is the best known of ancient Chinese philosophy, other schools have often been ignored in the West. Here we should be aware of approaches such as agriculturalism (which sought a peasant utopian communalism and egalitarianism), Mohism (setting out a communal, decentralised government centred on frugality and asceticism) and Taoism (advocating a laissez-faire, small government and non-intervention).[2] The first dynasty of Imperial China, the Qin dynasty, was premised on Fajia (sometimes called Legalism). This was a highly authoritarian government based on draconian punishments and laws. But from its successor dynasty, the Han Dynasty, State Confucianism became the dominant philosophy and is certainly what legal scholars are most likely to be introduced to outside of China. The dominance of Confucianism lasted until the establishment of Communist government in the middle of the twentieth century of the Common Era. Thereafter, Confucianism was officially considered as a block to progress and fell out of favour in comparison to Mao Zedong Thought, an adaptation of Marxist-Leninist views of a one-party state that acts for the people and favours collectivism over private property. Confucianism has had a variable, albeit generally uneasy, relationship with the Chinese government since then – albeit recent discussion suggests that the ruling Communist Party is returning to elements of Confucianism, so it remains as a key example of how political philosophy of ancient times is still discussed today.[3]

Discussion could perhaps also focus on ancient Indian political philosophy – though these insights are less likely to appear in the Law School than those from ancient China. The *Arthashastra*, a treatise of political philosophy, can be picked out as a key moment here worth attention. It is believed to have been written sometime from the fourth century before the Common Era onwards.[4] The precise authorship is unclear, though it is thought to include a combination of scholars including the most well known of the potential scribes, Chanakya. This text outlines a vision of statecraft and how systems of government should work. It explores the issues of social welfare, the collective ethics that hold a society together and how those in power should use the state to initiate public projects, especially at times of challenge in which the public might suffer. Its ideas around the importance of an extensive bureaucracy in government to serve the people underpinned one of the largest empires in South Asia, the first to cover the region – The Mauryan Empire – in which Chanakya played a prominent role. With the growing prominence of India as a major player on the world political and economic stage in

2. For a fuller discussion of philosophy in China see T Jiang, *Origins of Moral-Political Philosophy in Early China: Contestation of Humaneness, Justice, and Personal Freedom* (Oxford University Press, 2021).
3. The Economist, 'How did Confucianism Win Back the Chinese Communist Party?' (2021) *The Economist* 23 June (available at <https://www.economist.com/the-economist-explains/2021/06/23/how-did-confucianism-win-back-the-chinese-communist-party>).
4. Kauṭilya, *The Arthashastra* (Aziloth Books, 2021).

recent times, the influence of the *Arthashastra* is again discussed showing still the importance of looking at such ancient texts.[5]

While I have started off with China and India, I note that, reflecting a Eurocentric bias, most discussions of ancient philosophy in Western Law Schools will tend to focus on ancient Greece. Here are generally supposed to be the roots of Western political philosophy.[6] In the fourth and third centuries before the Common Era, Plato is a prominent figure with his, Socratic dialogue, the Republic, in which he considers how a number of existing regimes have ruled and set out hypothetical examples of how government could operate differently.[7] In this work, he explores the order of the state, discussing the meaning of justice and considering whether the just is happier than the unjust in a society. A fundamental point of the text is his calling on us to define justice – and, in so doing, to understand that justice is worthwhile in and of itself. Justice is good not just because of the consequences that can follow from, for example, being found in conformity but purely because it is connected to the greatest good. Another prominent figure here is Aristotle, who studied under Plato and was concerned with the role that politics and the political community must play in bringing about the virtuous life for citizens. In the *Politics*, government exists to promote and foster virtue in a way that leads to the good life of its citizens with virtuous citizens who are prepared to live together under common laws and contribute to their community.[8] In the Western academy, such texts are generally considered the starting point of their political philosophy and are still extensively discussed today in philosophy as in Law Schools as a foundation for understanding governance, while the role that citizens should play in the polity has inspired many.

Following the ancient times, discussions in the Middle Ages will often be prominent in political philosophy – this is taken to represent the transition point between antiquity and modernity. And these are figures who can sometimes be encountered in Law Schools. The development of arguments from Christianity, following on from the insight produced in ancient Greece, will typically be the next port of call for many interested in tracing the history of political philosophy – especially in the West. Here we have figures such as St Augustine of Hippo, who sought to reconcile Plato with Christianity. In *Free Choice of the Will*, he argues that all human law – temporal law – must be consistent with God's law – eternal law.[9] As such, an unjust law is no law, should not be considered morally binding and can be ignored in good conscience. St Thomas Aquinas considered cardinal moral virtues like Augustine, but he had a different focus and, in turn, used these to develop a Christian Aristotelianism with the display of justice in human relationships, the most important character of the good person. Natural justice comes from God and must always take precedence over agreements constructed by people, so human law must never contravene natural law. Justice is a habit of a virtuous

5. An exploration of this legacy can be found in AS Chousalkar, *Revisiting the Political Thought of Ancient India: Pre-Kautilyan Arthashastra Tradition* (Sage, 2018).
6. P Cartledge, *Ancient Greek Political Thought in Practice* (Cambridge University Press, 2009).
7. Plato, *The Republic* (Penguin Classics, 2007).
8. Artistotle, *The Politics* (Penguin Classics, 1981).
9. Augustine, *On Free Choice of the Will* (Hackett Publishing Company, 1993).

character and, in being just, a person will be consistently committed to respecting the rights of others. These scholars are often considered the foundations of a natural law that sees a universal moral standard decreed from God.[10]

The importance placed in such Christian work on the Western political philosophy – and thereafter jurisprudential – canon has been criticised for ignoring the influence of Islam. For Panjwani, 'Islam's [...] role in shaping Western law has been almost ignored'.[11] Central to this thesis is the notion that scholars have accepted the Christian influence on medieval thinking around justice issues but have not acknowledged the role of Islamic scholarship. Panjwani explains:

> Western philosophers when they could read Greek realised just how much their interpretation of Aristotle and Plato had been influenced by Muslims. Indeed, Thomas Aquinas whose work still forms the basis of the philosophical doctrine of the Catholic Church tried to disentangle Aristotelian philosophy from Muslim philosophy and attempted to add in his system elements direct from Plato. However, his methods show distinct Muslim influences.[12]

As just one example of an Islamic thinker in this period of the Middle Ages who should be considered, we can look to Nizam al-Mulk, author of the *Siyasatnama*.[13] In this work, a vision of governance is outlined in which all classes should be given their due, and wherein the poor and the weak must be protected. Where possible justice is to be defined by both custom and Muslim law, and the ruler is held responsible to God. The denial of Islam's place as forwarding thinking in this area of political philosophy means to suggest ignorance from the Muslim world, in contrast to the supposed advances of the Christian. The relative absence of Islamic insight in the Western Law School is a testament to these prejudices.

The Middle Ages were followed by what Europeans often refer to as, the Enlightenment – the supposedly great 'Age of Reason'. This was a period of scientific discourse but also, crucially for our interests, political and philosophical discourse, from the late seventeenth to the early nineteenth centuries of the Common Era. The Enlightenment is widely accepted in the West as somehow crucial in the making of modernity. There was a great belief in the Enlightenment itself as the awakening of people's intellectual powers leading to more humane thinking and ultimately to a more fulfilled human existence. As Dipesh Chakrabarty shows, this notion of the Enlightenment is a mythical version of Europe infused with assumptions of European superiority and ignorance of non-European societies.[14] Despite this (or, rather, likely for just these reasons), Enlightenment

10. For an examination of their legacy see F Di Blasi, *From Aristotle to Thomas Aquinas: Natural Law, Practical Knowledge, and the Person* (St Augustine's Press, 2021).
11. I Panjwani, 'The Ignored Heritage of Western Law: The Historical and Contemporary Role of Islamic law in Shaping Law Schools' (2020) 54(4) *The Law Teacher* 562.
12. Ibid, 567.
13. N Al-Mulk, *The Book of Government or Rules for Kings: The Siyar al Muluk or Siyasat-nama of Nizam Al-Mulk* (Routledge, 2015).
14. D Chakrabarty, *Provincializing Europe* (Princeton University Press, 2000).

thinking takes a prominent place in the Western academy's approach to political philosophy and can be seen prominent in the Law School.

A series of hugely influential works from this age still hold revered places in the political philosophy canon – and are all likely to appear in jurisprudence courses. John Locke, John Stuart Mill, Thomas Hobbes and Jean-Jacques Rousseau are all held up for their contribution to thinking about humanity and, most centrally, people's rights. In *Two Treatises of Government*, Locke outlined his theory of civil society based on natural rights and contract theory.[15] He proposed that all human beings are created free and equal, that all individuals have a right to life, liberty and property, that there should be religious tolerance and that a government should be based on popular consent. *On Liberty* saw Mill discuss the nature of liberty, applying his utilitarian beliefs – the importance of actions that promote the greatest amount of good to the greatest number of people – to the state.[16] His essay tries to show the positive effects of liberty for people and communities as he links liberty to notions of social progress. In *Leviathan*, Hobbes set out his doctrine of the foundation of states and legitimate governments, creating an objective science of morality.[17] He considers the necessity of a strong central authority to avoid the evil of discord and looks at life without government – the state of nature – which would lead to all-out war as people compete together in feelings of entitlement to resources and benefits. *The Social Contract* by Jean-Jacques Rousseau sets out the basis for a legitimate political order within a republican framework.[18] Rousseau asserts that modern states repress the freedom that is citizens' birth right and that legitimate political authority comes only from a social contract agreed upon by all citizens for their mutual preservation. What we see emerge at this moment is a body of work that led to the rise of the liberal world view that still takes such a powerful role in political philosophy as it does in jurisprudence.

Legal Philosophy within the Law School

In this section, I will focus on legal philosophy – philosophising that has already been fully incorporated into the legal academy and that which takes place within the Law School. It tackles the foundational questions of law such as, what is law? These involve great overlap with ideas of justice (and morality and ethics). This scholarship is sometimes simply called jurisprudence – though some will resist that label. And, albeit alongside of some of the political philosophy we have already looked at, it is this material that is most typically taught to students in jurisprudence modules. Some refer to this scholarship as part of legal theory, although that label is opposed by those who feel it dilutes the field. I will concentrate the brief exposition in this section on the area of analytical jurisprudence that attempts to offer a general account of the nature of law, common

15. J Locke, *Two Treatises of Government* (Cambridge University Press, 1988).
16. JS Mill, *On Liberty* (Penguin Classics, 2003).
17. T Hobbes, *Leviathan* (Oxford University Press, 2008).
18. JJ Rousseau, *The Social Contract* (Penguin Classics, 1968).

features of laws and what separates law from other social phenomena. I will centre my exploration on three main schools of analytical jurisprudence, those that tend to dominate the legal academy: natural law, legal positivism and legal realism. The leading scholarship that still forms the foundations of much jurisprudence teaching is drawn from the twentieth century – and the most valorised figures in the Western academy all tend to be white, Western men so, while I want to note how deeply problematic that is, it is what will dominate here.

In our first school, natural law arguments as they operate in legal theory (as opposed to political philosophy with its own vision of natural law discussed earlier) suggest that law's authority comes, to varying degrees, from the moral merits of the legal standards. John Finnis is one such example of a natural law theorist – who develops ideas on natural law from older theories of Aquinas and of Aristotle. Finnis' concept of law is most clearly articulated in his book, *Natural Law and Natural Rights*.[19] Positive laws do not acquire their authority from their coherence and not because they come from an established process. Rather, the authority of law derives from morality. Law, for Finnis occupies the same place in the world as morality: an agenda through which people work out what they should do and what kind of person they should be. Law's role is to facilitate the common good by providing authoritative rules that offer answers to the problems that may arise from the pursuit of basic needs. The role of law for the common good means that people will obey laws even if they work against their own interests if the overall system of law is fair and works to support shared interests. Unjust laws may create obligations in a technical legal sense but fail to provide moral reasons to follow them: this is what legal authority must provide through its higher appeal to fair-mindedness.

Lon L. Fuller is another often-discussed natural law theorist, who differs from Finnis with his position that there is a prima facie obligation to obey all laws and that law is subject to a procedural rather than necessarily righteous morality. Fuller focused on the way law is guided by a system of rules, internal doctrines that constitute a morality. According to Fuller, certain moral standards – principles of legality – are built into the very concept of law, so that nothing counts as genuine law that fails to meet these standards. In virtue of these principles of legality, the law has an inner morality that imposes a minimal morality of fairness. He explores the relationship between law and morality, distinguishing between the morality of duty and the morality of aspiration. In *The Morality of Law*, he explained human behaviour as necessarily goal-oriented in the sense that people engage in an activity because it helps them to achieve some end.[20] Insofar as human activity is essentially purposive, particular human activities can be understood only in terms that make reference to their ends. Thus, since lawmaking is essentially purposive activity, it can be understood only in terms that explicitly acknowledge these purposes. This is a functionalist approach whereby there are general rules in place that help people orientate their activity.

19. J Finnis, *Natural Law and Natural Rights* (Oxford University Press, 1980).
20. LL Fuller, *The Morality of Law* (Yale University Press, 1977).

Legal positivism is a school premised on the notion that the existence and content of law depends on social facts and not on its merits: whether a society has a legal system depending on the institutions in place not on whether they satisfy more high-minded ideals such as justice. In Europe, Kelsen is the most recognised scholar working in legal positivism, with his pure theory of law looking to exclude the validity of natural law.[21] Kelsen sees law as a hierarchy of binding norms. The basic norm is a hypothetical norm from which all lower norms in the hierarchy of a legal system are understood to derive their authority. It from this relationship that other norms become binding. The first constitution, the basic norm, has a 'presupposed' authority: there are not infinite legal norms. But the reason for the validity of a norm must always be another norm, so a legal system must consist of norms all the way down until it reaches a transcendental norm. Accepting this basic norm is not to endorse it as inherently good but is rather the necessary precondition for a non-reductive account of law as a normative system. This is a process of legal validity rather than appealing to a non-human source such as a deity, nature or nation. His theory is not focused on evaluating those norms; he would separate 'legal science' from a 'legal politics' that would engage in such a process of moral appraisal.

H. L. A. Hart is the most prominent example of legal positivism in the Anglophone world and offers a counterpoint to Kelsen. He argues that law is a system of social rules. Hart rejected Kelsen's views on the transcendentalist nature of authority and disagreed that a normative social phenomenon, like law, cannot be grounded in non-normative social facts.[22] For Hart, the authority of law is social. The ultimate criterion of validity in a legal system is neither a legal norm nor a presupposed norm, but a social rule that exists only because it is actually practised. This norm is thus used to guide conduct. Law ultimately rests on custom: customs about who shall have the authority to decide disputes, what they shall treat as sources of law and how laws may be changed. The rule of recognition is an official custom and not a standard necessarily shared by the broader community. Law is normally a technical enterprise, characterised by a division of labour. Most peoples' contribution to the existence of law will entail little more than passive compliance; the existence of a legal system thus requires that the system's ultimate criteria of validity must be generally obeyed.

The final school to be considered here is legal realism, the view that a theory of law should be descriptive and account for the reasons why judges decide cases as they do because all law is made by humans and thus should account for reasons besides legal rules that led to a legal decision. Despite its prominent later development in Scandinavia,[23] Western Law Schools often focus on the North American branch of legal realism in which Oliver Wendell Holmes Jr is regarded as the leading influence on the development of the school in the United States. In *The Common Law* he explains that

21. H Kelsen, *Introduction to the Problems of Legal Theory: A Translation of the First Edition of the Reine Rechtslehre or Pure Theory of Law* (Clarendon Press, 1992).
22. HLA Hart, *The Concept of Law* (Oxford University Press, 2015).
23. See J Bjarup, 'The Philosophy of Scandinavian Legal Realism' (2005) 18(1) *Ratio Juris* 1.

'the life of the law has not been logic: it has been experience'.[24] He insists that judges, in deciding cases, are not deducing legal conclusions with inevitable, computer-like logic, but are influenced by ideas of fairness, public policy and prejudices – that these decisions are based on experience. Holmes rejects the idea that law could be something different from what is decided by the courts, that it is a system of reason somehow deduced from fundamental principles of ethics. Law is pragmatic and reflects the personalities and dispositions of those judges who make decisions. As such, law reflects its current social times and will change as prevailing values alter. The meaning of the law should not be pursued as if reading a book of mathematics, he noted, but rather can be found in looking at the people with power to make decisions.

Karl Llewellyn is another key figure in the legal realism movement, providing the most extensive US development of the ideas articulated by Holmes. For Llewellyn, realism was about trying to understand what was going on in the law and law needed to be explored by considering the practical reality by which judges would decide the outcomes of cases based on personal biases. He downplayed the importance of rules as only helping to predict what judges might do; 'that is all their importance except as pretty playthings'.[25] Per Llewellyn, a judge almost always has the latitude to characterise a decision in an earlier case in either a highly fact-specific way, to distinguish it from the present case, or in a way that abstracts from the specific facts of the earlier case, so as to make it binding in the present case. Thus, judges are never constrained by precedent. He felt that judges should be trained to explain how their decision was reached. He argued that instead of looking at the traditional rules to predict the outcome of the case, we should look at factors such as the role played by the personality of the judge, or the interaction of the facts with traditional concepts and typical fact situations and their outcomes.

A Critical Turn: Critical Legal Studies

The rest of this chapter will take a more critical stance. Some of these contributions will come from philosophers, some influenced by philosophy and some from outside and some from inside the legal academy. But all interrogate the theory that dominates in Law Schools to pick holes in how it is constructed, who it works for and who it works against. The rise of more critical theoretical approaches in the Western legal academy can be traced to the emergence of Critical Legal Studies in the second half of the twentieth century of the Common Era. The clue is in the name of course. Critical Legal Studies was critical of the Law School orthodoxy; they posed a fundamental challenge to mainstream jurisprudence. Allan Hutchinson and Patrick Monahan see the movement as 'mounting a full frontal assault on the edifice of modern jurisprudence'.[26]

24. OW Holmes, *The Common Law* (Dover Publications, 1991), 1.
25. KN Llewellyn, *The Bramble Bush: The Classic Lectures on the Law and Law School* (Quid Pro Books, 2012), 15.
26. AC Hutchinson and PJ Monahan, 'Law, Politics, and the Critical Legal Scholars: The Unfolding Drama of American Legal Thought' (1984) 36(1/2) *Stanford Law Review* 199.

In some ways, Critical Legal Studies picked up where the legal realism considered above had left off. For Alan Hunt:

> The intervening period between the realism of the 1930s and the emergence of critical legal studies in the late 1970s has been a series of unsuccessful attempts to recover from the shock of realism some basis for a legal theory which articulates an image of the objectivity of the legal process, even though the explanation offered by post-realism had to be more complex than that provided by a doctrine of rule-following.[27]

Critical Legal Studies follows the shock waves of legal realism and its challenge to more formalistic assumptions of jurisprudence that had grounded thinking in Law Schools for decades previous. Drawing on legal realism, they believed that what the law says it does and what it really does are two different things. For example, some laws claim to have the aim of protecting the interests of the disadvantaged. In reality, they often serve the interests of the power elites.

There was a dissatisfaction and a distrust of the law in the contemporary United States that came to a head in the late 1960s. Critical Legal Studies emerged in the radical US college environment of the period. This was the birth of the counterculture movement, an era of anti-establishment attitudes that was especially prominent on higher education campuses. It was the dawn of the teenager, a time of rebellion with the rise of drugs, rock music and protest. There were awakenings in gender and sexuality, we saw the peak of the Civil Rights movement and anti-war sentiment was at its height with the US invasion of Vietnam. It was in this climate of anti-authoritarianism, that Critical Legal Studies exists. The critical politics that surrounded these scholars seemed to contradict so many assumptions that American law was fundamentally just and the product of historical progress. In contrast, law emerged as a game in which the dice was heavily loaded to favour the wealthy and powerful. We have not discussed Ronald Dworkin – there just isn't the space to fit everyone in – but the movement could be contrasted with the liberal idealism of dominant jurisprudential establishment figures of the time such as him; they were convinced that law and politics cannot be separated.

They wanted to know how law could be so tilted to favour the powerful, given the prevailing explanations of law as working for fairness. They looked at the ways that law contributed to social hierarchies. Critical Legal Studies scholars would claim that apparently neutral language and institutions operated through law, masking relationships of power and control. The emphasis on individualism within the law – as we have traditionally taught in Law Schools – hides patterns of power relationships while making it more difficult to summon up a sense of community and human interconnection. From this base, Critical Legal Studies scholars covered a great breadth and depth of subject matter, though common threads can be identified. Scholars seek to demonstrate the indeterminacy of legal doctrine and show how any given set of legal principles can be used to yield competing or contradictory results. They undertake historical,

27. A Hunt, 'The Theory of Critical Legal Studies' (1986) 6(1) *Oxford Journal of Legal Studies* 1, 5.

socioeconomic and psychological analyses to identify how particular groups and institutions benefit from legal decisions despite the indeterminacy of legal doctrines. They expose how legal analysis and legal culture mystify outsiders and work to make legal results seem legitimate. What we see is the role of ideology behind the law and the way legal systems can act to serve certain powerful groups within a society while also realising that these dynamics can be challenged to claim back power for the marginalised.

Duncan Kennedy was one of the most well-known figures in the Critical Legal Studies movement and articulates clearly how the movement was moving beyond notions of objectivity or neutrality that have characterised jurisprudence. It is not possible to disentangle law from politics in analysis, and Critical Legal Studies theorists do not attempt to do so in their work. This was the first avowedly left-wing movement in the US legal academy. For Kennedy, this was the dawn of a 'new left intelligentsia [...] creating a radical left where once there were only variations on the theme of legitimization of the status quo'.[28] The radical nature of Critical Legal Studies can be seen in how it went beyond theorising – the movement was not restricted to scholarship, but it was entwined with activism. Kennedy explains this dual nature:

> Critical legal studies has two aspects. It's a scholarly literature and it has also been a network of people who were thinking of themselves as activists in law school politics. Initially, the scholarly literature was produced by the same people who were doing law school activism.[29]

The commitment to, both, theory and practice meant that Critical Legal Studies scholarship aimed to push a transformative agenda whereby scholarship is grounded in activism. Legal academics are sometimes dismissed as operating in an ivory tower detached from the lived reality of those outside. While that criticism can be challenged more broadly, what is certain is that the dismissal is especially difficult to make of Critical Legal Studies scholars. While sceptical of the operation of the law, they were at the same time interested how could law be a tool for social change. They give voice to new or previously less favoured social visions and argue for their realisation in legal and political practices in part by making them part of legal strategies.

Kennedy has documented some of the ways that the Law School, with its valorisation of the law as it stands, can work against social justice in his essay, 'Legal Education and the Reproduction of Hierarchy' – perhaps the foremost document of Critical Legal Studies.[30] For Kennedy, 'law schools are intensely political places', with the curriculum strictly ideological despite the insistence that law, legal judgements and the justice system as objective and meritocratic.[31] In this world, faculty will too often come across as

---

28. D Kennedy, 'Critical Labor Law Theory: A Comment' (1981) 4(3) *Berkeley Journal of Employment and Labour Law* 503, 506.
29. GJ Clark, 'A Conversation with Duncan Kennedy' (1994) 24(2) *The Advocate: The Suffolk University Law School Journal* 56–61, 56.
30. D Kennedy, 'Legal Education and the Reproduction of Hierarchy' (1982) 32(4) *Journal of Legal Education* 591–615, 591.
31. Ibid, 591.

politically impartial, hiding their passions and commitments, only occasionally revealing personal sympathies on particular cases that might excite them. In general, they present the law as instrumental, detaching legal craft from any wider social, political or cultural context. The Law School functions to produce lawyers who will reproduce the existing legal and political order, making it seem somehow inevitable. By this line, legal education reinforces class, race and gender and other inequalities in wider society. In the hope of resisting this and using the Law School to promote social justice, Kennedy proposes the practice of organisation around ideas, bringing together those who could challenge this hierarchy. There is a need to build a community based on engaging with the philosophies, the theories and the ideas of those who resist the injustices that exist in society. The way law works for the powerful does not have to be the case, claim the Critical Legal Studies scholars such as Kennedy. There is nothing intrinsic to the idea of law that should make it into a vehicle of social injustice. It is just that the scale of the reform that needs to be undertaken to realise social justice is significantly greater than what the mainstream legal discourse was ready to acknowledge.

Critical Legal Studies lasted for only a short time as a programme. According to Roberto Unger, the movement 'continued as an organized force only until the late 1980s [...] life as a movement lasted for barely more than a decade'.[32] Few will still identify themselves as Critical Legal Studies scholars, but there was an enduring influence, which will be seen in the critical approaches to legal theory that we will explore over the remainder of this chapter. While Critical Legal Studies challenges the objectivism and formalism of traditional legal theory that allows the powerful to shape and maintain discourses that sideline the marginalised other, there were limitations in Critical Legal Studies. Scholars would make calls for affirmative action in Law Schools to reflect cultural diversity, but the movement was restricted in its ability to provide liberatory insight into some of those most impacted by the unequal power relations that frame law. It was, after all, a largely white, Western movement – dominated, as with so much of the traditional jurisprudence it challenged, by men. What can be seen as the successor gender-, race- and nationality-based analyses soon went beyond Critical Legal Studies by founding their jurisprudence in the lived experience of oppression.

Feminist Legal Studies and the Voices of Women

Feminist Legal Studies – sometimes called feminist jurisprudence – is the study of the law from perspectives that centre the implications of the law for women. Feminist scholars raise questions about the meaning and the impact of law on women's lives. Feminist Legal Studies seeks to analyse and redress more traditional male-centric legal theory and practice. It focuses on the ways in which law has been structured that deny the experiences and needs of women. Feminist jurisprudence claims that the law functions for the patriarchy, that system of structural relations that oppresses women across society. Law and the legal philosophy that sets out to understand and explain it has presented

---

32. RM Unger, *The Critical Legal Studies Movement* (Verso, 2015), 24.

itself as rational and objective in a manner that makes claims for a gender neutrality in law. Law has been long presented as an institution that serves all while in practice only addressing and advancing the interests of men because women have been ignored.

This approach combines scholarship with activism. As such, Feminist Legal Studies is not politically neutral, as expressed by Patricia Smith:

> Feminist jurisprudence challenges basic legal categories and concepts rather than analyzing them as given. Feminist jurisprudence asks what is implied in traditional categories, distinctions, or concepts and rejects them if they imply the subordination of women. In this sense, feminist jurisprudence is normative and claims that traditional jurisprudence and law are implicitly normative as well.[33]

Thus, we get another huge challenge to traditional legal scholarship: despite previous assumptions, the legal academy is not neutral; it works for men against women and props up a legal order that, in turn, works for men and against women. So, in response, feminist scholars show that their legal scholarship should not be neutral: it needs to be partial to fight back and bring women's voices into our knowledge and understanding.[34] Feminist Legal Studies sees the workings of law as thoroughly permeated by political and moral judgements about the worth of women and how women should be treated.

There are varying schools of feminism, reflecting differences in emphasis or perspective in describing the many aspects and effects of patriarchy, differences in which problems to focus on, and differences in strategy for how best to overcome the problem of patriarchy.[35] One contrast that can be made is between the early liberal feminists that led the first wave in the early twentieth century, and the second wave from the 1960s, which included schools such as radical feminism. Liberal feminists focused on barriers women faced in the public sphere. It emphasised the similarities between women and men to argue for equal treatment for women. The law has been the arena through which liberal feminists believe they can achieve equality. Working on campaigns aimed at getting legal reforms enacted through statute has been their central activity. In the US Elizabeth Cady Stanton fought for the Married Women's Property Act of 1848 which considered women legally independent of their husbands and granted property of their own. In the UK, Emmeline Pankhurst founded the Women's Social and Political Union to fight for women's suffrage, and some women got the right to vote in 1918.[36] Despite these advances, women were still not equal in terms of most everyday issues – and there was a limit to how successful formal equality could be. Later radical feminist critics of liberal feminism from the second wave would argue that its individualist assumptions

33. P Smith, *Feminist Jurisprudence* (Oxford University Press, 1993), 10.
34. See, for example, R Hunter, C McGlynn and E Rackley (eds), *Feminist Judgments: From Theory to Practice* (Hart Publishing, 2010).
35. There are concerns over the value of 'labelling' schools of feminism, see M Maynard, 'Beyond the "Big Three": The Development of Feminist Theory into the 1990s' (1995) 4(3) *Women's History Review* 259.
36. Though not parity with men until 1928.

make it difficult to see the ways in which underlying social structures and values disadvantage women.[37] Liberal feminism relied on the liberal political view of a distinction between the public and private spheres – meaning that, if women are more commonly associated with the private sphere, they are often not inside the public sphere of state intervention. Legal changes ostensibly bringing women towards equality are insufficient to emancipate women because they fail to tackle the wider issues that have led to gender imbalance and male domination. Liberal feminists' insistence on equal treatment had made significant gains to women by the 1960s – it had gotten them greater access to education, employment and politics. However, liberal feminists had not challenged fundamental legal concepts and had not sought deep-rooted transformation of law, they only asked for its gender neutrality.

If laws reflect male experiences, making laws gender-neutral does not help women much. Equal treatment of socially unequal individuals does not result in real equality and, in many cases, only exaggerates the disparities. Radical feminism was a reaction to liberal feminism. They saw that apparently neutral rules could also generate inequalities, particularly since women's and men's societal circumstances were so different. Such differences demand different treatment – mere formal equal treatment could not sufficiently address existing structural and ideological inequalities. They look wider than the law; radical feminists seek to abolish the patriarchy in a struggle to bring liberation from a deeply unjust society by challenging existing social norms and institutions. Radical feminists locate the root cause of women's oppression in patriarchal gender relations, as opposed to legal systems. The root problem lies in the false impartiality of law as an entity. The superficially gender-neutral language of the law allows it to mask the extent to which it is permeated by male constructs and standards. Radical feminists believe that the rule of law and the values of gender neutrality, objectivity and formal equality mask the fact that they will always disadvantage women without challenging the broader inequity of the wider system. So, the radical feminist focus is not on specific inequalities supported by law but on the societal structure that forms the foundation for law and that law, in turn, legitimises.

Catherine MacKinnon was perhaps the foremost figure in the radical feminist movement during this second wave and has criticised liberal feminism as embracing maleness as a norm:

> Concealed is the substantive way in which man has become the measure of all things. Under the sameness standard, women are measured according to our correspondence with man, our equality judged by our proximity to his measure. Under the difference standard, we are measured according to our lack of correspondence with him, our womanhood judged by our distance from his measure.[38]

37. While chiefly associated with the first wave, liberal feminism has continued beyond as, for example, B Friedan, *The Second Stage* (Harvard University Press, 1998).
38. C MacKinnon, *Feminism Unmodified: Discourses of Life and Law* (Harvard University Press, 1988), 33.

Her work has focused on how the law upheld existing power structures in society that ensured men's dominance and women's subordination. Her 'dominance' approach is therefore not concerned with the Aristotelian formula of formal equality; rather its test is whether practices perpetuate subordination of women. Radical feminists argue for changes in the law and special treatment to deal with the inequalities of power, especially with regard to issues such as sexual violence against women. As such, it aims at substantive equality, beyond the limitations of liberal formal equality. MacKinnon sees the appropriation of women's sexuality by man as a central instrument of male dominance, the way women's sexuality is used against them.

An important topic here is pornography, said to be central to the institutionalisation of male dominance. MacKinnon saw pornography maintaining systematic sexual subordination. In her book, *Only Words*, she opposed the US constitution's first amendment interpretation of pornography that protected pornography as free speech.[39] MacKinnon rather considers it hate speech. But speech that had a concrete power, notably, to cause the rape and murder of women. Men expropriate women's sexuality and pornography acts to increase the sexual appeal of the subordination of women. In the 1980s MacKinnon (with Andrea Dworkin) campaigned to bring down the porn industry arguing:

> Pornography is central in creating and maintaining the civil inequality of the sexes. Pornography is a systematic practice of exploitation and subordination based on sex which differentially harms women.[40]

They offered a new law to act as a tool kit for sex equality: the anti-pornography civil rights ordinance. A civil protection that would put power in the hands of women (rather than a criminal sanction that merely gave more power to the institutions of a patriarchal state). And these ordinances were taken up in a handful of local governments across the United States.[41]

But, different schools of feminism have viewed pornography in varying ways – there is no one women's view and what emerged was a dispute known as the 'feminist sex wars'. MacKinnon and Dworkin's theory of sexuality has been attacked as one dimensional, as was their representation of women as victims. One such critique came from Robin West who can be found in another second-wave feminist school, cultural feminism – that looks to redefine and revalue supposed female attributes.[42] The anti-pornography approach denied women's sexual agency for her. West calls for a women-centred conception of

39. C MacKinnon, *Only Words* (Harvard University Press, 1993).
40. A Dworkin and C MacKinnon, *Pornography and Civil Rights: A New Day for Women's Equality* (Organizing Against Pornography, 1988), 99.
41. Although they all subsequently failed.
42. R West, 'The Feminist-Conservative Anti-Pornography Alliance and the 1986 Attorney General's Commission on Pornography Report' (1987) 12(4) *American Bar Foundation Research Journal* 681.

pornography that truly understands the diversity of women's perspectives and attitudes and thereon reaches conclusions properly grounded in women's experiences:

> Women's new-found voices have not yielded a monotonic chorus. We have begun to express our experiences of pornography, and one thing we have discovered is that our experiences of pornography are diverse and contradictory. However, in spite of the range of stories and values to which we have given expression, our voices have much in common. They are women's voices. The experiences of which they speak are women's experiences. Until recently, our experience was unutterably private, subjective, and 'other.' It demanded no audience. It commanded no language. It was unspeakably missing from every public position on the nature and value of pornography.[43]

West protests that the radical feminist stance on pornography ignored women's experience and was constructed without properly listening to women. She claimed that the anti-pornography stance had abandoned feminist practice by ignoring women's experiences that differed from their own such as lesbians who might have found in pornography a means to subvert heteronormative societal assumptions of sexuality. The plurality of women's voices must be heard – which in turn became the underlying basis of the third wave of feminism from the 1990s onwards that challenged existing feminist approaches that assumed cohesion or conformity of women's experiences.

The third wave of feminism would bring challenges to the mainstream of feminism such as black feminism,[44] which highlighted how white the movement was, and postcolonial feminism,[45] which drew out how it represented the knowledge and interests of Western women. We do not have space to explore these accounts but, to some degree, the following accounts of Critical Race Theory and postcolonial theory should give readers an understanding if they take the mainstream Feminist Legal Studies movement as subject to many of the criticisms made of mainstream jurisprudence more generally: a lack of representation and a white, Western view taken as standard. While bringing some missing voices in, mainstream feminist scholarship has been accused of compounding the marginalisation of other voices.

Challenging a White Academy: Critical Race Theory

The central thrust of Critical Race Theory is that racism is normal, not aberrational, in American society – and law has played a role in legitimising this.[46] Societies based on racism always create others against which the socially dominant cultural group is

43. Ibid, 711.
44. For example, K Crenshaw, 'Demarginalizing the Intersection of Race and Sex' (1989) 1 *University of Chicago Legal Forum* 139.
45. For example, CT Mohanty, 'Under Western Eyes: Feminist Scholarship and Colonial Discourses' (1988) 30(1) *Feminist Review* 61.
46. It can be applied in other contexts such as the UK, see B Malkani, *The Law of Racial Injustice* (Bristol University Press, 2024).

favourably contrasted. David Gilborn explains that, because racism is an ingrained feature of the social landscape, it looks ordinary and natural to people in the culture.[47] As with feminism above, there is a limit to what formal equal opportunity can provide. For example, laws that insist on treating black and white people alike can remedy only some of the more extreme forms of injustice; the ones that do stand out. It can do little about the 'business-as-usual' forms of racism – apparently more mundane yet no less devastating – that racialised people experience daily. By this line, racism is very difficult to overcome through law, and this poses a major challenge to many in the legal academy who would valorise and put their faith in law to achieve equality or fairness. It necessarily problematises the relationship between and law justice.

The Critical Race Theory label has been accepted and applied by a wide variety of scholars and analyses. All the same, it is possible to draw out some key arguments that apply to much of this school of thought to give a flavour of what has been produced by this approach to scholarship. Richard Delgado and Jean Stefancic are perhaps the foremost scholars to have documented Critical Race Theory in this manner.[48] In the Virginia Law Review they offer what they call an annotated bibliography of the subject. And though this survey is a quarter of a century old, and Critical Race Theory still a thriving field,[49] it provides us with a strong sense of what Critical Race Theory brings to jurisprudence and theorising in the Law School. They thus documented a dozen major themes as characteristic of work in Critical Race Theory.

First, a critique of liberalism. Critical Race Theory scholars favour a more assertive approach to social transformation as opposed to liberalism's more cautious approach. They pursue a race-conscious attitude to change rather than liberalism's embrace of colour blindness. They adopt methods that rely more on political organising, in contrast to liberalism's reliance on rights-based remedies. Second, storytelling, counter-storytelling and 'naming one's own reality'. Critical Race Theorists might use narrative to illuminate and explore experiences of racial oppression. Third, there are revisionist interpretations of American civil rights law and progress. These criticise civil rights scholarship and anti-discrimination law. Applying insights from outside the legal academy on race and racism to legal problems is the fourth theme. Fifth, the focus on intersectionality as the examination of race alongside other features such as gender, class, national origin and sexual orientation and how their combination plays out in various settings. For example, how the needs of a Latina woman are different from those of a black man, and how these play out in relation to the law. Sixth, essentialism philosophy – reducing the experience of a category to the experience of one sub-group. All oppressed people share the commonality of oppression; however, that oppression varies so the aims and strategies will differ for different groups. Non-white cultural nationalism and separatism

47. D Gillborn, '"Just the Right Amount of Racism" The Cultural Politics of Race and Reform' in Z Leonardo (ed), *Handbook of Cultural Politics and Education* (Sense Publishers, 2010), 381.
48. R Delgado and J Stefancic, 'Critical Race Theory: An Annotated Bibliography' (1993) 79(2) *Virginia Law Review* 461–516.
49. See, for example, M Alexander, *The New Jim Crow* (The New Press, 2010).

is the seventh theme. This includes black nationalism – exploring more radical views arguing for separation and reparations as a form of foreign aid.

Eighth in this list is a focus on legal institutions, critical pedagogy and minority lawyers in the bar. The ninth theme involves the concept of structural determinism, or how the structure of legal thought or culture influences its content. These are widely shared ideas or practices that determine significant social outcomes. Usually this occurs without conscious knowledge and, as such, legal systems do not typically provide redress. Tenth, white privilege refers to the myriad of social advantages, benefits and courtesies that come with being a member of the dominant racial group. For example, a security guard is less likely to follow a white person around a shop than they are a black person. Microaggressions are the eleventh theme. These are commonplace verbal or behavioural slights that communicate negative attitudes and hostility towards racialised peoples. Microaggressions are based on the assumptions about racial difference. The final, twelfth theme, is empathic fallacy; the belief that one can change a narrative by offering an alternative narrative in hopes that the listener's empathy will quickly and reliably take over. Empathy is not enough to change racism as most people are not exposed to many people different from themselves and people mostly seek out information that reinforces their own beliefs.

We will now unpick some of these themes to help provide a fuller understanding of how Critical Race Theory can work for legal scholarship. There would be wide agreement here that the system of white-over-colour ascendancy serves important purposes, both psychic and material. This is the notion of interest convergence. Because racism advances the interests of both white elites (materially) and working-class people (psychically), large segments of society have little incentive to eradicate it. Developed by Derrick Bell, one of the foremost Critical Race Theory scholars, this concept of interest convergence holds that white people will tolerate or encourage racial advances for black people only when such advances also promote the interests of white people.[50] Writing in the US context, interest convergence stipulates that black people achieved civil rights victories only when white and black interests converge. The signature example is *Brown v Board of Education of Topeka*,[51] which partially overturned *Plessy v Ferguson*.[52] *Brown* was a landmark US Supreme Court decision in which the Court ruled that state laws establishing racial segregation in public schools were unconstitutional, even if the segregated schools are otherwise equal in quality ('separate but equal'). This case paved the way for integration, was considered a major victory of the civil rights movement and became a model for many future impact litigation cases.

For Bell, the decision came about because it advanced white interests as well as those of black people. Specifically, desegregation raised the nation's prestige in world politics during the Cold War. By striking it down, the Court intended to improve the nation's

50. D Bell, '*Brown v Board of Education* and the Interest-Convergence Dilemma' (1980) 93(3) *Harvard Law Review* 518.
51. 347 U.S. 483 (1954).
52. 163 U.S. 537 (1896).

international image during the Cold War to make it seem democratic and the opposite of authoritarian. For example, with the United States and USSR both competing to court countries in Africa, how could the United States present itself as the 'leader of the free world' when black people in the country were so visibly unfree that African American children were not allowed to go to school with their white peers. This was image management. And could be suggested as a major reason why the decision was allowed and thus a significant audience for the decision came outside of the United States rather than from a concern to substantively improve the lives of the marginalised group within the country.

Brown becomes the Holy Grail of racial justice. Bell proposes that, despite the onerous burdens of segregation, many black schools functioned well. Brown's recognition of racial injustice in legal terms, without more substance to it, left wider societal racial barriers intact. In his book, *Silent Covenants,* Bell says that black school children would have been better served had the court in Brown rejected the petitioners' arguments to overrule *Plessy v Ferguson.*[53] While acknowledging the deep injustices done to black children in segregated schools, Bell argued the court should have determined to enforce the generally ignored 'equal' part of the 'separate but equal' doctrine. Instead of resolving the nation's racial dilemma, Bell supposes the *Brown* decision has made it more complex. Beyond the formal legal decision, we saw the wider structural impact of racism play out in society where there were gross disparities of financial and cultural capital. Rather than allow their children to mix at school, those white families who could afford to moved away from the inner-city areas – leaving behind black families who could not. This created a *de facto* school segregation. And it would be the white schools that were better resourced, attracted the top teachers and provided more opportunities for the children. And the black children would struggle in their poorer schooling but found it harder to blame the racism that had caused this because, in this realm, there was now apparently formal quality under the law so the white majority were less willing to accept such explanations.

Bell believes that racial disparities, wide and widening in every measure of well-being, overshadow the gains in status achieved by those black Americans who, by varying combinations of hard work and good fortune, are viewed as having 'made it'. Instead, what *Brown* did for many African Americans was legitimate the status quo. While they remained poor and disempowered, their status was no longer able to be claimed a result of denied equality. Rather, Bell suggests it allowed white populations to dismiss them as resulting from a personal failure to take advantage of one's defined equal status. In conclusion, Bell argued that *Brown v Board of Education* ultimately failed to remove barriers to equal education based on race. For Bell, hopes that it would do so were replaced by a disappointed acceptance that it unintentionally replaced overt barriers with less obvious but just as obstructive new ones. Black people in the United States, then, were given only symbolic encouragement that they could overcome discrimination by attempts at legal reform.

53. D Bell, *Silent Covenants* (Oxford University Press, 2020).

Critical Race Theory, then, questioned whether civil rights law was designed to benefit racialised peoples and even suggested that this formal legal equality might be a homeostatic mechanism to ensure that racial progress occurs at just the 'right' pace: change that is too rapid could be unsettling to the white population who benefited from racism, that which is too slow could prove destabilising through the protests of racialised minorities. Using this example, then, we can see just a little of the challenge Critical Race Theory poses to conventional accounts of the law in a legal academy that was dominated by liberal views of the power of the law to bring about formal equality.

Postcolonial Theory and Challenges to the Western Knowledge

A final set of critical theories that I want to consider are postcolonial theories of law. To some degree, postcolonial scholarship – as would befit a school that covers the majority of the globe, a huge array of cultures and perspectives – can be characterised by its diversity. It is thus not a centralised field of enquiry. For Wes Pue, this can make postcolonial theory hard to pin down:

> The spirit of the intellectual encounter between law and colonialism is of necessity interdisciplinary, diverse in perspective, and unbounded. Scholarship in the field does not – should not – fit into overly-neat disciplinary or perspective-bound categories.[54]

However, as per Eve Darian-Smith, while not a coherent intellectual field, what unites contemporary scholars of postcolonial law is that they all draw upon an intellectual legacy that emerged among non-Europeans in the decolonisation movement post World War II.[55] Postcolonial legal scholarship suggests that even when colonialism has officially ceased to exist, the injustices of material practices endure over time and frame emergent legal consciousness. Postcolonial theoreticians show how imperial laws served to cover up colonial violence and how injustice was legitimised through law. The law was used, for example, to deny indigenous populations in colonies their status as legal persons. The development of international law was also closely interwoven with colonialisation. Postcolonial legal studies today attempts to uncover and challenge colonial continuities in national and international law. Postcolonial legal studies look at the repercussions of colonialism and imperialism today. Law is a social and cultural construct which changes over time. During the period of colonialisation by European states, national and international law developed in a way that made it possible to legitimise slavery and genocide. And European law, with its often-racist elements, spread to many parts of the world in the course of colonialisation. There are then compelling reasons for bringing these theories into the Law School.

54. W Pue, 'Editorial' (2003) 1 *Law, Social Justice and Global Development*.
55. E Darian-Smith, 'Postcolonial Theories of Law' in R Banakar and M Travers (eds), *Law and Social Theory* (Hart Publishing, 2013), 247.

Diane Otto provides a clear overview of the challenges posed to legal scholarship by postcolonial theory:

> Critical postcolonial theory presents new and foundational challenges to law with respect to questions of power, hierarchy, wealth, poverty, diversity, equality, and justice. The term 'postcolonial' can be used in many senses. In international law its meaning has primarily had a celebratory 'sense, whereby the 'post' has been understood as marking an end to the long period of legally sanctioned European colonialism. In this meaning, the recognition of the right of colonized peoples to self-determination heralded the possibility of a more equitable world based on independence and equality for Third World states. Since the 1980s, however, the term postcolonial has also come to assume a critical meaning, as the promise of a fairer world seems as far as ever from realization and scholars and activists begin to probe more deeply in their efforts to understand why.[56]

This is an approach that, as with so much critical theory, would shake up orthodoxies in the legal academy.

There are different approaches to postcolonial theory that we could take up. For example, we could explore Third World Approaches to International Law as one of the most prominent and vibrant contemporary movements – one that brings Global South voices into the mix.[57] But we don't have space for to follow every thread and instead, I will focus on the role played by legal orientalism. Because this approach helps to set the groundwork for Third World Approaches to International Law and so much other contemporary scholarship by looking at the enduring legacy of European colonialism.[58] Orientalism is a key concept within the postcolonial studies movement. Orientalism is a way of seeing that imagines, emphasises, exaggerates and distorts differences of Arab peoples and cultures as compared to that of Europe and the United States. The concept comes from the cultural critic Edward Said, who was a leading figure in postcolonial studies and whose book Orientalism established a long trajectory of critical thinking about the subjugation of non-Western peoples.[59] He offers the concept of orientalism to refer to the ways in which European societies throughout the nineteenth century constructed their identity and self-understanding through imagining their difference to the Muslim world. The term came from art history, where it referred to Western depictions of the East. It often involves seeing Arab culture as exotic, backward, uncivilised and, at times, dangerous. For Said:

---

56. D Otto, 'Postcolonialism and Law?' (1999) 15 *Third World Legal Studies* vii–xviii, vii.
57. See, for example, BS Chimni, 'Third World Approaches to International Law: A Manifesto' (2006) 8 *International Community Law Review* 3.
58. For a recent critical appraisal of Third World Approaches to International Law see: NK Modirzadeh, '"[L]et Us All Agree to Die a Little": TWAIL'S Unfulfilled Promise' (2023) *Harvard International Law Journal* forthcoming.
59. E Said, *Orientalism* (Pantheon, 1978).

> The basic distinction between East and West as the starting point for elaborate theories, epics, novels, social descriptions, and political accounts concerning the Orient, its people, customs, 'mind', destiny and so on.[60]

Chiefly orientalism works to construct and exaggerate difference. The West created the cultural concept of the East. What we see, then, is orientalism accounting for an 'us-and-them' binary relationship in which Europeans intellectually divided the world into the occident and the orient. And orientalism sets a whole system of organising the world based on this division. People from outside the West were unable to express themselves as discrete cultures; they were lumped into one mass of other. Europeans could rename and redefine – and thereby control – oriental peoples (and their places, their ideas, their things) into imperial colonies. This stretched beyond the Middle East and Asia, as a variant of orientalism accompanied the whole imperial endeavour whereby the West contrasted their supposed civility with an assumed backwardness of all other cultures from Africa to the Americas. The understanding that results from our recognising orientalism forces us to think about how racial and cultural biases continue to inform globally dominant legal concepts and assumptions of Western legal superiority.

Typically nineteenth-century orientalist discourses about the East were negative and reinforced a presumed hierarchy of Western superiority and Eastern inferiority. European attitudes about Asian peoples could take the form of derogatory stereotypes. Europeans promoted themselves as modern, rational, moral and lawful in contrast to a projection of Eastern societies as premodern, irrational, immoral and lawless. This orientalism served a variety of purposes. The most obvious of these was that it helped confirm on the world stage the marginality of the East and the centrality of the imperial West. In relation to the law, for example, Western jurists argued that Eastern jurisprudential traditions were based on custom, ritual and religion, in contrast to the so-called rational and scientific legal systems of modern Western nations. Declaring non-Western legal systems inferior helped to justify European law and culture as an apparently superior civilisation, worthy of world leadership and dominance. Western law thus has orientalist assumptions writ through into its very being.[61] Orientalism can be seen in its essential structure, its process and its language. Legal orientalism thus endures in twenty-first-century international law and global legal relations. It underpins assumptions around the West's legal superiority over the Global South and has been deployed in a range of national and international legal forums such as asylum and refugee claims, as well as indigenous demands for recognition. Legal orientalism can be seen in the ways the West interprets law in the Middle East, particularly in the wake of the terrorist attacks on September 11 and in the invasion of Iraq with the United States taking on a role as the world's chief exporter of the rule of law.

---

60. Ibid, 10.
61. See, for example, E Beck and S Wahab, 'Orientalism, Oppression, and Contemporary Social Work' in JD Wright (ed), *International Encyclopaedia of the Social & Behavioral Sciences* (Elsevier, 2015), 428.

I would like to outline one example of legal orientalism that directly involves the United States to give us a firmer understanding of what can be involved. Orientalist rhetoric provided the rationale for Western nations such as the United States to marginalise Asian peoples. Teemu Ruskola shows how there has been a long history of American belittling of the Chinese legal system, premised on biases and prejudices that China is inherently backwards and lesser than the United States.[62] The Chinese legal system was dismissed for being based on traditional values such as the Confucian view that people are fundamentally good that predated the influence of the European Enlightenment that infuses the US constitution. Here we see the notion referred to earlier that the modern European ideas were inherently superior to older Global South ideas. The United States did not follow the European model of imperialism and set up colonies in China or join in the Opium War. Rather, it engaged in a different kind of imperialism: extraterritorial imperialism. The Treaty of Wanghia in 1844 meant US citizens in China could only be tried by officials appointed by the United States to enforce American law in China. This practice was built on a perception that Chinese administrative structures were archaic, and the country essentially lawless in comparison with the United States. And this idea filtered through to how the United States treated Chinese citizens too. The *Chinese Exclusion Act* (1882) suspended Chinese immigration and prevented Chinese people already living in the United States from ever being granted citizenship. Under the act, it was argued that Chinese people were non-legal subjects because they were incapable of understanding US law and so deserved to be excluded from the new republic. Chinese immigrants and their American-born families remained ineligible for citizenship until 1943 with the passage of the *Magnuson Act*.

With examples such as this, then, postcolonial legal scholars argue that the oppositional rhetoric between Western and Eastern legal traditions was essential for the development of the modern global legal order. European law – and American and international law that followed it – emerged historically through a perceived difference with non-Western legal concepts. Postcolonial theory pushes the legal academy to recognise the roots of this specific cultural history and the impacts they have had on those outside the West.

Conclusion

So, conclusions. It is hard to reach conclusions for such a diminutive overview (at this point, for example, someone grumbles – 'is that it, where's John Rawls?') of some massive themes in this well-established relationship between law and philosophy. But the main takeaway I want readers to have is the need to change up the jurisprudence canon. I want legal scholars to read something different from the white, Western men who have dominated jurisprudence – whether from within philosophy or law. Over recent years, we have seen moves to decolonise the Law School, which I think is hugely welcome.

62. T Ruskola, *Legal Orientalism: China, the United States, and Modern Law* (Harvard University Press, 2013).

This is often taken as shaking up reading lists. You can read many university websites that contain statements about decolonising the syllabus, which typically means moving away from the previous reliance on white, Western men.

Jurisprudence is a field prime for doing over with so many syllabuses reliant on white, Western men. That was certainly my experience of inheriting a jurisprudence module in my teaching. Many will protest at the importance of studying the classics and I am sure I annoy – much more knowledgeable – scholars of jurisprudence when I say that my approach was to rip the module up and start again. I just did not see the relevance in the way things were and found it deeply problematic teaching a diverse student body in a globalised world using the same male, pale and stale faces as the insight that law students were provided into deep thinking about justice. Much traditional theorising encourages abstraction or contains tacit values, which to me deny the fundamentally unjust nature of the society in which I teach students to think about the law. It would be to put to one side the reality that law has so often worked for oppression by those very groups who have been afforded the privilege of sitting around hypothesising about its greatness. I am sure the old guard has their place but, in the limited time I have with students, there are much more pressing and engaging ideas that I need to teach them. Ideas that can more readily help them come to grips with the injustice around us today.

And so I transformed my jurisprudence module from one reliant on exploring the famous *Hart v Fuller* debate or considering the work of Gustav Radbruch (another I ran out of space to include here) to one grounded in Feminist Legal Studies, Critical Race Theory and postcolonial theory. I always start the first lecture with a slide of a Google search I once did for 'leading jurisprudence authors' and how the results I received were a page full of head shots of white-presenting men. Then I explain what a limited view of the world this would give them and how, when we engage with such complex and multi-faceted issues such as the meaning of justice, we cannot rely on the limited and partial understanding that this one group could provide. We still encounter the ideas and the arguments of the traditional scholarship but we do so in the challenges posed to them by more critical theory, in the deconstructions that are offered from drawing on different standpoints. This is the way I have found that brings these debates to life and that makes them feel relevant.

Having taught it the old way and the new way, I can gladly report that student engagement is massively improved and the level of insight in our discussions is magnitudes greater. I would say that, of course: I am going to claim that my call was the right one and there is nobody else operating this keypad who can claim otherwise. But honestly, the classes are a dream: year-after-year since I made the change, I come away full of joy at how switched on and with it my students are when we grapple with unpicking law and its role in society. I see woke, empathetic and respectful contributions time-and-again: students who understand that there are a whole heap of different perspectives to take on board and listen to. They locate themselves and their experiences among the plethora of other views in a way they rarely did when we were just talking about what a bunch of white, Western men said. Because now, they understand that everyone should have a voice and that we only truly learn by looking for other contributions from those who have different positions in society to us.

I get more direct comprehension of how the students respond though as the module using reflective journals. By centring gender, race and nationality, I recognise that the issues we talk about are sensitive and emotive: they can really impact students and it tends to ask a lot of them, expecting students to bring themselves into our debates. Reflective journals are a means for them to deal with the stress or trauma that can accompany this, and a means through which students can come to understand themselves in a safe space. And, every assessment period when I come to read these journals I am blown away anew by how invested the students have become in our exploration of legal theory. I see students committed to change their behaviour in seeing themselves in a new light, full of fire at fresh injustice they have discovered, wrestling with existential disputes over their own identity, changing their relationships to others based on a new insight they have, excited to carry on researching all topics from different angles. This never happened when we just worked through the way the white guys saw morality.

That is all very exciting. But, decolonising the Law School means more than just adding some new readings. It entails an ongoing active process of decentring Eurocentricity and unlearning traditional Western modes of knowing and being. One of the foremost voices in decolonising the Law School is Folúkẹ́ Adébísí. Her book, *Decolonisation and Legal Knowledge*, is a must-read for anyone looking to engage in a fuller process of decolonisation for the legal academy.[63] The book explores the ways in which the foundations of law are entangled in colonial thought and the way that shapes how people are seen in ways that fundamentally work against social justice. It encourages legal academics to think about the ways we perpetuate colonial violence in our scholarship. And it also creates the space to rethink law and conceive of the legal academy in a way that can help us start to move towards something better, a legal studies that helps make the world a better place.

Adébísí also has a compelling blog, *African Skies*. Here, she writes most accessibly about decolonisation – what it means and how it should operate. I want to include some insight from the blog to inform our understanding of how decolonising the Law School should proceed – a reading that has had a large influence on me and my approach to legal scholarship. In an earlier essay, she writes:

> Decolonisation forces us to confront the history and effects of imperialism upon our academic practices in law. As legal academics, it is imperative that we explore what 'decolonisation' means for us and what the possibility of decolonised law means for the relationship between law and society. How do we become more aware of, and directly mention, how the law came to be, in tandem with a history of legalised dispossession and othering from humanity? How do we acknowledge how that history has influenced how law is taught, what law is taught, and what law is now, and who the law works for? How do we teach law as the study of social order, and elucidate how racial stratifications in the social are formed and maintained?'[64]

63. F Adébísí, *Decolonisation and Legal Knowledge* (Bristol University Press, 2023).
64. F Adébísí, 'Decolonisation and the Law School: Initial Thoughts' (2019) *African Skies* 22 July (available at <https://folukeafrica.com/decolonisation-the-law-school-initial-thoughts/>).

This essay is important to me as it sets the issues out clearly. These are questions I pose myself when thinking about how to construct a jurisprudence module. They are questions that I also put to my students at the start of the jurisprudence module. Reading lists are important, then, but they are not nearly the whole journey. Changing up the readings offered to students will only make a real impact if they are used as part of a more concerted process of decentring our whole approach to law and, for example, in jurisprudence to our notions of what justice is and could be – the way visions of justice will appear differently depending on the context. For me, this requires a commitment to putting into practice the insights of critical theory in jurisprudence hence moving away from traditional notions of what but, also, how we teach students. It is about epistemological change on a more fundamental level – to recover previously excluded knowledge from the margins and to consider our part in allowing them to be so disvalued.

Any attempt to become more critical as an ambition to realising a more progressive approach to legal studies is doomed to failure unless it gives voice to those who have for so long been excluded from what constitutes acceptable or relevant knowledge. From the same essay, we can understand some of the problems that can be encountered by piecemeal attempts to progress legal debate:

> Critical thinking is at the core of legal study, yet failing to engage with 'marginalised issues' is an impediment to achieving critical thinking. When we do not account for the concerns of various groups that have been 'othered', we fail to achieve the positive possibilities of legal study. When our curriculum delivery fails to contextualise the information we transmit, we contribute to this othering. We contribute to othering in many ways: when we teach Locke's ideas of the social contract theory without mentioning his legitimisation of slavery; when we hold out the concept of a fictional objective 'reasonable person' without acknowledging the gendered and raced and classist boundaries of its premises; when we teach in and revere buildings constructed with colonial profits and benefits derived from enslaving human beings; when our curriculum is skewed in favour of domination and privilege; and when our subjects are infused with male 'voices' [...] I could go on.[65]

It is not enough to add some non-white faces to a module, perhaps giving students a week to read about race as some interruption to our normal programming. There must be a more widespread and deep-rooted integration of alternative voices; they should not be presented as additions because that implies they are something to consider after the fundamentals have been tackled, a luxury to look at once we have completed the real work. Rather, the issues raised by decolonisation should be seen as infused in every aspect of our legal academy – they, and the injustice that results, are inescapable. As is the complicity of those of us who have legitimised this process, no matter how well-meaning we might think ourselves.

Adébísí talks about how we should feel discomfort in this process of decolonising. And we must be reflexive. For example, I am unhappy with the first half of this chapter featuring so many white, Western men who dominate discussions around law and

65. Ibid.

philosophy. I tell myself it was necessary because that is still the status quo as it presents thus it is needed to help readers understand the links. And further I convince myself that I include them first as we worked broadly chronologically and, also, because they are a point of departure for me as I build to the work that I think matters. But, do they all need to be included? And, should I have integrated all this critical scholarship from the start to avoid any notions of primacy? Also, should I be writing this chapter at all as someone who considers themselves an ally but is still just another white, Western man?

In writing this chapter, I wanted to give a short outline of some important work around law and philosophy but I could not do that in good conscience without pushing beyond the white, Western orthodoxy. Whether I have done that correctly, or whether I was the right person to do it, I do not know. All I do know is that I hope to encourage legal scholars to look beyond the male, pale and stale that has for so long been in the ascendancy. Because, I believe that the process of decolonisation in our Law Schools involves us changing up who we are turning to for our understanding of law. I want to turn to Adébísí's essay one more time, with her statement that:

> Therefore, we need to try out dynamic approaches to teaching and research and every other thing we do in the Law School. If we want a different world from what we see in the news and on our streets, we must be part of that change in the work we do as law teachers and researchers.[66]

In the spirit of looking forward to a Law School that works differently, I will conclude by offering one example of a scholar who I think should be brought from political philosophy into jurisprudence: Charles Mills. Now, Mills is not typically taught in Law Schools and little engaged with by legal academics. I am using the remainder of this chapter to provide the briefest of introductions to his scholarship in the hope of encouraging readers to dig deeper and use his analysis to inform their legal scholarship. Mills was a London-born, Jamaican-raised philosopher who encourages us to rethink Western liberalism for the way it is influenced by and carries forward the ideology of white supremacy. For Mills, philosophy has ignored fundamental issues of racial injustice in its academy and in the societies it undergirds.

Mills has developed a rigorous critique of liberalism, primarily focused on its centrality to mainstream political philosophy. This can be found across books such as *The Racial Contract*,[67] *The Contract and Domination*[68] and *Black Rights/White Wrongs*.[69] As we have discussed earlier, liberalism is focused around the belief that individuals are, and ought to be, recognised as free and equal beings. The self-understanding of most liberals would be that they advocate for and activate this belief in liberty for all. Here, the common interest in justice between philosophers and legal scholars comes out again because

66. Ibid.
67. CW Mills, *The Racial Contract* (Cornell University Press, 1997).
68. C Pateman and CW Mills, *The Contract and Domination* (Polity Press, 2007).
69. CW Mills, *Black Rights/White Wrongs* (Oxford University Press, 2017).

the law is a crucial means through a democratic society is to ensure that all individuals are free and equal.

A leading scholar applying Mills' ideas, Bain offers a valuable introduction to the work of Mills for legal scholars wherein she presents his work through the lens of social justice.[70] Her analysis draws out that contractarian liberalism is premised on protecting free and equal individuals from domination but that Mills shows us how domination is not peripheral to liberalism but, rather, central to it. For Bain:

> Mills offers us a non-ideal contractarian analysis that may really offer 'x-ray vision' into parts of society many would readily, if not always credibly, deny precisely because it pushes us to look at the world as it really is, to learn our history, and to be always on the lookout for the many ways that ignorance about matters of significant import to questions of social justice can be actively, resiliently produced.[71]

As per Bain, 'Mills completes the triumvirate of the "big three" of class, gender and race'.[72] His work locates the emergence of liberalism during the supposed Enlightenment period, which flourished against the backdrop of European expansionism through imperialist colonialism: thus, the establishment of the white supremacist world view. As we saw earlier with Critical Race Theory scholarship, we have a critique of a colour-blinded liberalism that, for Mills, is a fundamentally racialised liberalism: it is filled with tacitly white supremacist assumptions.

Following Mills, we can see that domination – for example, racism – is presented as an anomaly in the liberal democracy. Racism is an abhorrent but exceptional break to an otherwise just social order. The liberal world view sees individuals consciously or unconsciously displaying prejudicial biases that lead to discriminatory behaviours. However, Mills' work co-opts liberalism in a system of structural domination – along class, gender and also racial lines – that operates to enshrine and legitimise social injustice.

Bringing Mills into the jurisprudence canon will offer scholars a powerful weapon with which to challenge deeply rooted domination in the philosophy we engage with, but also in the application of the law and the wider society in which it functions. Mills' body of work provides a deep insight into the manner in which social justice in an illusive dream for many in the current liberal democratic system. He helps us understand, also, how we must change the way we understand a law so deeply tied to liberal idealism. This is a great example of how we can build on critical theory in making a positive combination of law and philosophy for the future lawyers we produce in the Law School. These are ideas that I want legal academics to take on board and that I think all law students must be exposed to in the hope of repurposing the legal academy for more progressive ends and in the fight for social justice that I as a legal scholar consider my main purpose.

---

70. Z Bain, 'A Very British Domination Contract? Charles W. Mills's Theoretical Framework and Understanding Social Justice in Britain' in F Gordon and D Newman (eds), *Leading Works in Law and Social Justice* (Routledge, 2021), 30.
71. Ibid, 42.
72. Ibid, 33.

Chapter Nine

LAW AND POPULAR MUSIC

Robbie Sykes and Kieran Tranter

Introduction: A Developing Tune

This chapter focuses on law and music, emphasising the engagement by law and humanities scholars with popular music. It is in five parts. The first part identifies a long-standing 'minor jurisprudence' concerned with the parallels and cross-fertilisations between legal theorising and musicology, most often depicting judging/lawyering as forms of creative performance. In the second part it is identified that these explorations parallel more doctrinal scholarship on the legal forms – especially copyright – that surround music in the popular space. The third part discerns an area of law and popular music scholarship that emerged in the 1980s and 1990s, formed from traces of textual signifiers in Critical Legal Studies (CLS) scholarship and the expanding of law and literature to a broader enterprise concerned with law and popular culture. The fourth part identifies law and popular music scholarship where music is seen as a challenge to the legal orthodoxy. In this work, there is the utilisation of popular music, particularly songwriters and their lyrics, as manifesting a cultural zeitgeist: the musician as the voice of a generation in protest against a legally embedded orthodoxy. The fifth part considers a trajectory within law and popular music of construing popular music as articulating a 'popular jurisprudence'. This focus has a connection with the earlier 'minor jurisprudence' of legal theory and musicology. It identifies in the cultural project of popular musicians – their lives, lyrics, videos, album art, political and cultural legacies, and social media presences – an articulation, and critique, of received legal forms. Through singing, dancing and creating in the mainstream, fundamental legalities are presented, questioned and reappropriated.

'Minor Jurisprudence' of Law and (Mostly Classical) Music

Law and music have a long-intertwined history. First Nations peoples of Australia describe essential legal relations with Country as 'songlines': that the proper relations between land, law and peoples are connected though song.[1] In the mythmaking of J. R. R. Tolkien's *The Silmarillion*, his world and peoples and the discord they experience are constituted from the singing of 'Great Music' by the godhead Eru and angelic-like Ainur.[2] However, the posited and doctrinal focus of the modern Western legal tradition has tended to be deaf to the potential foundational intertwining of law and music. Peter Goodrich has suggested: 'Just as music has historically paid little attention to writing, law – cold prose, serious social speech – has generally marginalised music.'[3] That is not to suggest that music has not been the subject of legal scholarship. Much of the early 'law and music' research could be seen as a 'minor jurisprudence'. The idea of a 'minor jurisprudence' – as a revelatory critique from beyond legal institutions[4] with their 'phantom of a sovereign and unitary law'[5] – is an invocative label for splinter discourses within legal thought, strands of reasoning and knowing that disrupt and creatively go outside mainstream concerns.[6] Describing the early legal theory and musicology literature as a form of 'minor jurisprudence' is a claim that we make knowingly. There seems to be an affinity between law and music and thinking about 'minor jurisprudence'. Christopher Tomlins, for example, prefigures an introduction on 'minor jurisprudence' by urging his readers to consider Elvis Costello and the Brodsky Quartet's version of 'Damnation's Cellar'.[7]

The forms and sounds of Costello and the Brodsky Quartet were not exactly the music that physiologist Henry J Watt had in mind in 1922 when he wrote 'Rule and Law in Music'.[8] Watt explores the role of rules and exceptions in composition: 'while it always falls to the composer to choose and create [...] he must obey the laws of music.'[9] Watt's conception of laws tends towards the natural sciences, of observable patterns, but what is significant is his formulation of rules. Parallel to the then-emerging critique of command theories of law, Watt engages with the nature of rules. For him, rules are guides that are complexly positioned in relation to the composer. They are external to

1. N Higgins, 'Songlines and Land Claims; Space and Place' (2021) 34 *International Journal for the Semiotics of Law* 723. On First Nation music as law, see also G Watt, 'Law Making Music' (2020) 14 *Law and Humanities* 26, 29–36 and K Dolin, 'From Orpheus to Yothu Yindi: Music and Legal Cultures' (2016) 12 *Law, Culture and the Humanities* 29.
2. V Flieger, *Interrupted Music: The Making of Tolkien's Mythology* (Kent State University Press 2005), xiii.
3. P Goodrich, 'Operatic Hermeneutics: Harmony, Euphantasy, and Law in Rossini's Semiramis' (1999) 20 *Cardozo Law Review* 1649, 1651.
4. P Minkkinen, 'The Radiance of Justice: On the Minor Jurisprudence of Franz Kafka' (1994) 3 *Social & Legal Studies* 349, 357–8.
5. P Goodrich, *Law in the Courts of Love: Literature and Other Minor Jurisprudences* (Routledge 1996), 2.
6. M Antaki, 'Making Sense of Minor Jurisprudence' (2017) 21 *Law Text Culture* 54; C Tomlins, 'Foreword: "Law as..." III—Glossolalia: Toward a Minor (Historical) Jurisprudence' (2015) 5 *UC Irvine Law Review* 239, 241–3.
7. Elvis Costello and The Brodsky Quartet, *Damnation's Cellar* (Warner Bros. Records 1993); C Tomlins, 'Law as....IV: Minor Jurisprudence in Historical Key: An Introduction' (2017) 21 *Law Text Culture* 1, 1.
8. H J Watt, 'Rule and Law in Music' (1922) 3 *Music & Letters* 349.
9. Ibid, 353.

the composer – *this combination sounds melodic* – but also internal; the composer knows, instinctively, what sounds melodic.[10] The composer has agency to comply, with awareness of the 'sanctions' for non-compliance. Embedded in Watt's account is both the then-emerging sense from jurisprudence in the inter-war period of the functions of rules to form legal systems and the relationship of rules to subjectivity and the 'bad man'.

While Watt and others were debating the legality of music,[11] the 'minor jurisprudence' of law and music was given a particular form by Jerome Frank. In 1947, Frank identifies parallels that correlate the creative tension between a composer and a performer with that of the legislature and judge: 'The legislature is like a composer. It cannot help itself: It must leave interpretation to others.'[12] Frank emphasises the essential creativity required to 'perform' the interpretative aspects of the judicial act. It is in this notion that there is a virtuosity to judging/lawyering that characterises the 'minor jurisprudence' of law and music. There are two characteristics to this scholarship. First, like Frank, the music under examination is generally classical, where the separation of labour between composer, conductor and individual performers can be identified. In the second characteristic, law is conceived as working with and interpreting texts.

A vivid example is Sanford Levinson and Jack Balkin, who, in an expansive review article, riff off the contributions to Nicholas Kenyon's edited volume *Authenticity and Early Music*.[13] They see in the 'Early Music' movement's quest for 'authenticity' an essence that proves contested and illusive, a problem parallel to the legal modernist desire to recapture an objective past through original-intent interpretative approaches.[14] For them, the performativity of law, both in the judicial act and in the practice of lawyering, should be more reflective of the present. Rather than trying to capture a past – of how something sounded, or what the founders intended – there should be a greater engagement with more immediate cultural circumstances. With the enthusiasm of the millennium, they suggest:

> For performance, whether legal or musical, is always situated in a culture and reflects the distinctive problematics of that culture. Thus, if ours is a modern culture, our interpretations, our subsequent performances of law and of music, must be understood in the light of the tangled and complicated experience of modernity and its gradual transformation into what is now called the postmodern.[15]

10. Ibid, 351–2.
11. M Meyer, 'Experimental Studies in the Psychology of Music' (1903) 14 *The American Journal of Psychology* 192; M Bauer, 'Natural Law: Its Influence on Modern Music' (1920) 6 *The Musical Quarterly* 469.
12. J Frank, 'Words and Music: Some Remarks on Statutory Interpretation' (1947) 47 *Columbia Law Review* 1259, 1264.
13. N Kenyon (ed), *Authenticity and Early Music: A Symposium* (Oxford University Press 1988).
14. S Levinson and J M Balkin, 'Law, Music, and Other Performing Arts' (1991) 139 *University of Pennsylvania Law Review* 1597, 1627–55.
15. Ibid, 1658.

In a later piece, published on the eve of the millennium, Balkin and Levinson expanded on their understanding of the law/music performative dynamism. Contemplating the choices and considerations implied and initiated by the performing of an offensive song,[16] they emphasised the importance of audience. It is in pre-empting and meditating on how an audience might react to an offensive lyric that the performativity also present in law is brought to the forefront.[17] Law work is performed in a context; there is an audience through which the judge/lawyer interacts: 'In the last analysis, the various audiences for performance – the people whom the performance moves, inspires, and affects – are the true judges of its fidelity and authenticity.'[18]

Levinson's and Balkin's performative contribution within the 'minor jurisprudence' of law and music was seemingly validated by Supreme Court Justice Sandra Day O'Connor when she argued that judging and the practice of law share with music a social performative dimension involving present and future audiences.[19] Indeed, Levinson's and Balkin's account of law and music has two important threads. The first: their musical exemplars begin to depart from the classical canon, with consideration of the performance of Gilbert and Sullivan's *Mikado*, jazz and Bruce Springsteen. The second is the invocative flexibility that can be revealed in their key insight on the performativity of law and music.

Sara Ramshaw has more recently developed how performativity in music illuminates the practice of law. Ramshaw proposed 'law as improvisation',[20] an explanation which identifies the 'aporia' – confounding and productive states – that suffuse all attempts to navigate the contradictory poles of law's textual sources and performative enactments, its general principles and specific cases, its precedents and innovations.[21] To illustrate and bear out this paradigm, Ramshaw brings together jazz – the exemplar of musical improvisation – and philosophical text, calling upon saxophonist Ornette Coleman and philosopher Jacques Derrida, an association that also occurred in person, and in *performance*, with the two appearing on stage together in Paris to present a combined format of playing and reading.[22]

The standard, simplistic account holds that musical improvisation is of the moment: instantaneous, unruly, lacking any internal architecture. However, as Ramshaw explained, improvisation plays out within structures that demand from performers an awareness of rules and expertise in working inside of their parameters. Improvisation is not just spontaneity but something that works through inescapable repetition, historical memory: its individuality dependent on, *given shape by*, the myriad restrictions – or,

16. J M Balkin and S Levinson, 'Interpreting Law and Music: Performance Notes on the Banjo Serenader and the Lying Crowd of Jews' (1999) 20 *Cardozo Law Review* 1513, 1526–8.
17. Ibid, 1549–57.
18. Ibid, 1571–2.
19. S Day O'Connor, 'Music and the Law' (2005) 18 *Western Legal History* 41, 44–6.
20. See also S Ramshaw, *Justice As Improvisation: The Law of the Extempore* (Routledge 2013).
21. S Ramshaw, 'The Paradox of Performative Immediacy: Law, Music, Improvisation' (2016) 12 *Law, Culture and the Humanities* 6, 16.
22. Ibid, 9–10.

as Derrida expressed it, 'laws' – of culture, genre, technology etc. that at once encircle creativity while creating its very preconditions.[23] Where Levinson and Balkin argued that law, when conceived of as a 'social practice',[24] does not have existence in text at all, but only finds an ontology in its being performed, this view of law as a one-way process of bringing text to life does not fully explain the interplay of text and enactment that characterise interpretation. For Derrida, law is a duality, being comprised of both a receptiveness to and an attempt at foreclosing the aleatory.[25] This interplay exposes that improvisation can only be identified because it arises from a backdrop of that which is already established (take, for example, a soloist playing melody over a chord progression), while, inversely, the performance of something already written uses its own pre-existence to conceal the improvisational nature of its being rendered for an audience. Improvisation and composition are symbiotic and inseparable: 'There are always traces of text in performance, composition in improvisation, and speech in music.'[26]

Ramshaw's putting forward the structured-unstructured-ness of improvisation as an account of the process through which judges and lawyers 'do' law, as a way of understanding the performativity of law and music, represents a continuality of the themes and tones that constitute the 'minor jurisprudence' of law and music since Watt in the 1920s. While the terminology changed, the core concern with the commonality of the art and artistry between the two fields remained the focus. What also persisted was an emphasis on classical musical texts and forms, but with an increasing embrace of more 'popular' musical genres like jazz or musical theatre. What was not strongly considered were the commercialised post-war musical genres like rock, pop, country, R&B or rap. There was mostly a continuity between the black-tie formality of the orchestra, opera or theatre and dealing with the 'black-letter' textuality of law work.

Popular Music as the Subject of Legal Scholarship

The sense that law and music could go beyond the 'black' was slow going, even though, in 1948, Frank would embrace his music-informed account of judicial interpretation as 'jazz jurisprudence'.[27] This did not mean that then-contemporary popular musical forms were absent from legal scholarship. Indeed, Alex Long has suggested that '[l] egal writers need little excuse to write about legal issues involving particular musical artists or genres'.[28] As early as the 1930s, there was scholarship that was concerned with copyright and the regulation associated with the broadcasting and recording of popular

23. Ibid, 10–12.
24. J M Balkin and S Levinson, 'Interpreting Law and Music: Performance Notes on the Banjo Serenader and the Lying Crowd of Jews' (1999) 20 *Cardozo Law Review* 15131518–19.
25. S Ramshaw, 'The Paradox of Performative Immediacy: Law, Music, Improvisation' (2016) 12 *Law, Culture and the Humanities* 6, 14.
26. Ibid, 12.
27. J Frank, 'Say it with Music' (1948) 61 *Harvard Law Review* 921.
28. A B Long, '(Insert Song Lyrics Here): The Uses and Misuses of Popular Music Lyrics in Legal Writing' (2007) 64 *Washington and Lee Law Review* 531, 532.

music and performers.[29] This doctrinal focus, where sheet music, tracks, recordings, images and performances as products and practices subject to legal interventions, continues.[30] Music and the recording and performing industries remain a significant economic driver and have generated, over the years, novel doctrinal conundrums for legal reflection. A clear example of how popular music and its distribution and consumption has given rise to novel legal concerns was the Napster litigation in the early 2000s.[31] By threatening to disrupt the business models of the established music industry, Napster and the litigation around it marked a key moment in the 'enclosure of the digital commons' and the emergence of a corporatised and proprietorial Web 2.0.[32] This doctrinal focus, particularly on copyright and the commercialisation of music, remains a theme within legal scholarship. Where Napster was doomed, subsequent content streaming services provide further consideration for legal scholarship.[33]

However, while ostensibly bringing together law and music, this body of doctrinal research ultimately is not really about law *and* music. The music dimension is flat and indistinguishable. These are studies on law and the enabling, and regulation, of consumer and later platform capitalisms. As a body of scholarship, the actual subject is intellectual property, contract and market regulation. The context might be popular music and its production, distribution and consumption, but not much is being said about the intimate and illuminating relationships between law and music that was evident in the 'minor jurisprudence' literature. Rather, law as a normative force in the organisation of power is emphasised. Law rules popular music.

29. C W Joiner, 'Analysis, Criticism, Comparison and Suggested Corrections of the Copyright Law of the United States Relative to Mechanical Reproduction of Music' (1939) 2 *Copyright Law Symposium* 43; I Propper, 'American Popular Music and the Copyright Law' (1940) 3 *Copyright Law Symposium* 164; MCohn, 'Music, Radio Broadcasters and the Sherman Act' (1941) 29 *Georgetown Law Journal* 407; H G Ball, *Copyright and Literary Property* (Banks and Co 1944), 448–69; L C White, 'Musical Copyrights v. The Anti-Trust Laws' (1950) 30 *Nebraska Law Review* 50.
30. See, for example, the contributions in A Harrison and T Rigg (eds), *The Present and Future of Music Law* (Bloomsbury 2021).
31. M Fagin, F Pasquale and K Weatherall, 'Beyond Napster: Using Antitrust Law to Advance and Enhance Online Music Distribution' (2002) 8 *Boston University Journal of Science & Technology Law* 451; R Shih Ray Ku, 'The Creative Destruction of Copyright: Napster and the New Economics of Digital Technology' (2002) 69 *University of Chicago Law Review* 263; L Marshall, 'Metallica and Morality: The Rhetorical Battleground of the Napster Wars' (2002) 1 *Entertainment Law* 1.
32. K Milberry and S Anderson, 'Open Sourcing Our Way to an Online Commons: Contesting Corporate Impermeability in the New Media Ecology' (2009) 33 *Journal of Communication Inquiry* 393.
33. E J Teague, 'Saving the Spotify Revolution: Recalibrating the Power Imbalance in Digital Copyright' (2012) 4 *Journal of Law, Technology and the Internet* 207; M Hogan, 'Upstream Effects of the Streaming Revolution: A Look into the Law and Economics of a Spotify-dominated Music Industry' (2015) 14 *Colorado Technology Law Journal* 131; J Gingerich, 'Is Spotify Bad for Democracy? Artificial Intelligence, Cultural Democracy, and Law' (2022) 24 *Yale Journal of Law & Technology* 227.

The Emergence of Law and Popular Music

However, the law ruling popular music revealed in the almost 100 years of doctrinal scholarship does not exhaust the intertwining of the two forms. Chronologically, there began to emerge from the 1980s scholarship that did more than just regard popular music as the subject for legal analysis. A key moment in the emergence of a more critical and reflective exploration of law and popular music is the CLS dialogue between Peter Gabel and Duncan Kennedy that borrowed its title from Chuck Berry's single 'Roll Over Beethoven'.[34] A text that inspires diverse reactions,[35] the schism rocked out by Chuck Berry, between an old, staid establishment and an exuberant counterculture, seemed to authorise and encourage scholarship that took more seriously popular culture within thinking about law.

A particular site of scholarship that seems to begin to move to the CLS's beat was the field of law and literature. In the 1980s and early 1990s, the focus on texts that denoted lawyers and lawyering began to expand. The law and literature movement bifurcated.[36] The first of these extensions was a sense that law is literature. In James Boyd White's words: 'Law is an art, a way of making something new out of existing materials – an art of speaking and writing.'[37] This notion of 'making', as emphasised by Levinson and Balkin, resonated with the 'minor jurisprudence' on law and music, a commonality that judging and lawyering, especially because of the processes of text generation, is a creative endeavour where understandings from creative enterprises – art, literature and music – can inform the practice and performance of law.[38] The second was an enlargement of law and literature to encompass law and popular culture.[39] Less emphasis was given to the insights of creative practice to the performance of law, and more on the representation, meaning and circulation of law, lawyers and legal concepts within the 'everyday'.[40] Film and television became legitimate sources for understanding an ambient culture of legality that projects, embodies and questions mainstream and institutional legal understandings.[41] This flowed over to consideration of music, and there

---

34. P Gabel and D Kennedy, 'Roll over Beethoven' (1984) 36 *Stanford Law Review* 1; Chuck Berry, *Roll Over Beethoven* (Chess Records 1959).
35. D Luban, 'Legal Modernism' (1986) 84 *Michigan Law Review* 1656, 1671–5.
36. R Weisberg, 'The Law-Literature Enterprise' (1988) 1 *Yale Journal of Law and Humanities* 1.
37. J Boyd White, *The Legal Imagination* (University of Chicago Press 1985), xiv.
38. S Levinson and J M Balkin, 'Law, Music, and Other Performing Arts' (1991) 139 *University of Pennsylvania Law Review* 1597, 1608.
39. S Macaulay, 'Popular Legal Culture: An Introduction' (1989) 98 *Yale Law Journal* 1545, 1552.
40. S Macaulay, 'Images of Law in Everday Life: The Lessons of School, Entertainment, and Spectator Sports' (1987) 21 *Law and Society Review* 185, 197–8; L Friedman, 'Law, Lawyers and Popular Culture' (1989) 98 *Yale Law Journal* 1579, 1598–603.
41. See for example C Dunlop, 'Literature Studies in Law Schools' (1991) 3 *Cardozo Studies in Law and Literature* 63, 68; S Machura and P Robson, 'Law and Film: Introduction' in Stefan Machura and Peter Robson (eds), *Law and Film* (Blackwell 2001), 3. See for example R E Rosen, 'Ethical Soap: *LA Law* and the Privileging of Character' (1989) 43 *University of Miami Law Review* 1227; P Bergman and M Asimow, *Reel Justice: The Courtroom Goes to the Movies* (Andrew and McMeel 1996).

started to emerge scholarship that did not merely reference popular music to be hip but to provide more detailed focus and thematising of popular music and popular musicians as reflections on law and as projections of popular legalities.[42]

Part of this taking popular music and law seriously was the emergences of compendium scholarship that identified where popular music lyrics had been referenced within judicial texts. These indexes established that the judiciary, as with legal scholars, do indeed let their 'freak flag fly'.[43] This work by Alex Long, and, more recently, Mark Klingensmith, tracks the artists whose lyrics have become enshrined in the texts of US court decisions, revealing a possibly not unexpected listening trend for the post-war predominately white judiciary with a preference for Bob Dylan and the Beatles.[44]

In addition to the compendium literature, more recent work on law and popular music has emerged. A well-established approach identifies within musicians and their lyrics a cultural zeitgeist. The musician engages with the political and is a challenge to the legally embedded orthodoxy. Desmond Manderson has suggested that this scholarship is characterised by 'a more complex engagement in which music and law are both seen as constitutively engaged in the structuring of social discourse'.[45] The popular musician is here positioned as legal critic.

Popular Music and Musicians as Legal Critics

Jennifer Jaff provided a founding text suggesting that popular music and musicians can be inspiration and a source of legal criticism.[46] She identified discontent with law and lawyers as revealed in the lyrics of popular music. Unlike orthodox legal scholarship's smug self-narratives of the justice of the rule of law, and lawyering as an ethical profession and public service, Jaff suggests through her survey of songs by *inter alia* Carly Simon, Don McLean, Bruce Springsteen, Joni Mitchell and Elton John, that popular musicians present 'law as unprincipled and paternalistic'[47] and 'lawyers as litigious and profit-motivated'.[48] The musician projects a culture of criticism towards the legal system and its officials.

---

42. B J Hibbitts, 'Making Sense of Metaphors: Visuality, Aurality, and the Reconfiguration of American Legal Discourse' (1994) 16 *Cardozo Law Review* 229, 327; C Weisbrod, 'Fusion Folk: A Comment on Law and Music' (1999) 20 *Cardozo Law Review* 1439.
43. A B Long, 'The Freewheelin' Judiciary: A Bob Dylan Anthology' (2011) 38 *Fordham Urban Law Journal* 1363, 370.
44. M W Klingensmith, *Lyrics in the Law: Music's Influence on America's Courts* (Lexington Books 2019); A B Long, '(Insert Song Lyrics Here): The Uses and Misuses of Popular Music Lyrics in Legal Writing' (2007) 64 *Washington and Lee Law Review* 531; A B Long, 'The Freewheelin' Judiciary: A Bob Dylan Anthology' (2011) 38 *Fordham Urban Law Journal* 1363.
45. D Manderson, 'Towards Law and Music' (2014) 25 *Law and Critique* 311, 313.
46. J Jaff, 'Law and Lawyer in Pop Music: A Reason for Self-Reflection' (1985) 40 *University of Miami Law Review* 659.
47. Ibid, 664.
48. Ibid, 666.

Within this particular focus, the preeminent musician as legal critic has been Bob Dylan.[49] Long identifies 'that judges frequently cite Dylan's lyrics does not necessarily mean that they always do so in interesting or effective ways'.[50] For the legal academy Dylan does seem more interesting. There have been three ways that Dylan is deployed as a legal critic. The first way examines the mentions of law, lawyers and injustice within the opus of Dylan's lyrics. For example, Michael L. Perlin has written on Dylan's lyrics as critical of American law, lawyers and procedure,[51] and Laurie Serafino has considered Dylan as narrating US legal history as a dialectic of struggle and revolution.[52] A development of this approach can be seen in Adam Geary's engagement with Dylan's lyrics as not just presenting a critique of the doctrines or practices of law, but as expositing a particular jurisprudential orientation towards a higher law: to be 'oppositional to the law is not to reject the law, but rather to believe in a more radical law'.[53] The second way is to focus on a critical legal reading emergent from the lyrics of a particular song. Perlin has examined Dylan's 1975/6 track 'Hurricane'[54] as a cypher for Rubin 'Hurricane' Carter's wrongful conviction and imprisonment.[55] In a similar manner, Renee Newman Knake identifies 'Blowin' in the Wind'[56] as encapsulating a sense of generational struggle reflected in the 1963 First Amendment Supreme Court decision of *NAACPv Button*.[57] The third way is to focus on the events in Dylan's life as a critical reflection on law. For example, the relationship between Dylan and Woody Guthrie as a lens on the tendency to idolatry demonstrated by judges in the common law tradition[58]

---

49. S J Levine, 'Symposium: Bob Dylan and the Law Foreword' (2011) 38 *Fordham Urban Law Journal* 1267, 1269; D C Newman, 'Law and Justice in Popular Music: Murder Ballads' (2018) 24 *European Journal of Current Legal Issues* https://webjcli.org/index.php/webjcli/article/view/596/798
50. A B Long, 'The Freewheelin' Judiciary: A Bob Dylan Anthology' (2011) 38 *Fordham Urban Law Journal* 13631370.
51. M L Perlin, 'Tangled up in the Law: The Jurisprudence of Bob Dylan' (2011) 38 *Fordham Urban Law Journal* 1395.
52. L Serafino, 'Life Cycles of American Legal History through Bob Dylan's Eyes' (2011) 38 *Fordham Urban Law Journal* 1430.
53. A Gearey, 'Outlaw Blues: Law in the Songs of Bob Dylan' (1999) 20 *Cardozo Law Review* 1401, 1422.
54. Bob Dylan and Jacques Levy, *Hurricane* (Columbia Recording 1976).
55. M L Perlin, '"Pistol Shots Ring out in the Barroom Night": Bob Dylan's "Hurricane" as an Exam (or Course) in Criminal Procedure' (2020) 48 *American Journal of Criminal Law* 253.
56. Bob Dylan, *Blowin' in the Wind* (Columbia Recording 1963).
57. 371 U.S. 415 (1963); R Newman Knake, 'Why the Law Needs Music: Revisiting NAACP v. Button Through the Songs of Bob Dylan' (2011) 38 *Fordham Urban Law Journal* 1303. See also on this specific lyric as critic R H Underwood, 'When the Law Doesn't Work' (2011) 38 *Fordham Urban Law Journal* 1495.
58. L Randy, 'Bob Dylan's Lawyers, a Dark Day in Luzerne County, and Learning to Take Legal Ethics Seriously' (2011) 38 *Fordham Urban Law Journal* 1323.

or, more denotive, Dylan's 2009 vagrancy arrest as illuminating policing prejudices against people with disabilities.[59]

These ways of using Dylan's lyrics or Dylan's life as legal critique have been replicated in relation to other popular musicians. Bruce Springsteen, with his themes of juvenile delinquency and the legal ambiguity of life in 'rust belt' America, has also been a locus of interest.[60] Springsteen, like Dylan, is regarded as the 'poet advocate', telling a story of others, the young, the poor, the outlaws, relaying these lives back to the legal system. For example, William Doyle used Springsteen's 1975 'Jungleland' to structure a narration of the death of a young boy from gang violence.[61]

These treatments of Dylan and Springsteen as critics of the law tend to home in on aspects specific to them as musicians. Predominately, this focus can be seen as a law and literature approach where the lyrics are read as critical texts. The alternative method is to focus on an event in the life of the musician. What is not overtly emphasised is the musicality of the musician. Whereas the 'minor jurisprudence' centres on musical performances as an analogy of judgement or lawyering, this approach seems quite 'literal'. The words of the musician/poet or an incident in the life of a popular musician as celebrity outlaw are the tools of analysis. This is quite an abstract and atomising way to engage with popular music and with musicians. What seems to be left on the mixing room floor is a more holistic consideration of popular music as a cultural phenomenon that includes – but also exceeds – solely the lyrics and celebrity run-ins with the law. There is the musicality – the beat, instruments, vocal tones and range, and collaborators. There is the dynamics of the band. The engagement with the recording and touring industries. The public personas and private lives. There is the visuality and iconography of popular music; the album covers, the music videos and the staging for shows. These combine to form an immersive aesthetics that gives nuances, complexity and life to popular music and potentially can inspire critical legal accounts.

An example that does draw more deeply on the immersive aesthetics of a popular musician is Ramshaw's analysis of Billie Holiday's 1949 acquittal for narcotics possession.[62] Ramshaw identified how Holiday's performances in the tracks such as 'Lover Man'[63] and 'My Man'[64] combined with a curated public persona as 'unlucky in love'

59. A Luber, 'Arrested Development: Bob Dylan, Held for Questioning under Suspicion of Autism' (2011) 38 *Fordham Urban Law Journal* 1385.
60. L Randy, 'The Lawyer as Poet Advocate: Bruce Springsteen and the American Lawyer' (2005) 14 *Widener Law Review* 867; A Smith, 'The Dignity and Humanity of Bruce Springsteen's Criminals' (2005) 14 *Widener Law Review* 787.
61. W P Doyle, 'Rats and Wounds in Bruce Springsteen's Jungleland: A Prelude to the Lawyer as Poet Advocate' (2005) 14 *Widener Law Journal* 731; Bruce Springsteen, *Jugleland* (Columbia 1975).
62. S Ramshaw, '"He's My Man!": Lyrics of Innocence and Betrayal in *The People v Billie Holiday*' (2004) 16 *Canadian Journal of Women and the Law* 86.
63. Jimmy Davis, Roger Ramirez and James Sherman, *Lover Man (Oh, Where Can You Be?)* (Decca 1944).
64. Maurice Yvain, Mardochee Charles, Albert Lucien Willemetz and Channing Pollock, *My Man* (Decca 1948); S Ramshaw, '"He's My Man!": Lyrics of Innocence and Betrayal in *The People v Billie Holiday*' (2004) 16 *Canadian Journal of Women and the Law* 86, 92–6.

cohered with her courtroom testimony to convince the jury of the authenticity of her claims, positively influencing their interpretation of the evidence in Holiday's case.[65] Ramshaw does more than just look at the lyrics of Holiday's songs as a critic of law. Rather, she engaged holistically with Holiday's performances, public personae, and private life to see in the acquittal a counter to the dominant legal narratives for black women in the United States.

Ramshaw's work on 'Lady Day' focused on Holiday's aesthetics and how her popular image was channelled by the defence team to influence the jury. David Caudill also looks at the aesthetics of a genre of popular musicians – country music singers – to criticise law schools.[66] Caudill drew attention not only to the various qualities of county music itself, such as styles of singing and lyrical content, but also to the aesthetics of the practices through which music is delivered and consumed, including styles of speech, artists' origins, stage presentation, artists' personal lives, dress and hairstyles. Country music 'stars' seek a sense of 'authenticity' to a tradition and traditional values that are presented as oppositional to the insincerity and selfishness of the present.[67] However, this is manufactured; a performed veneer, engaging with a tradition that is also in flux.[68] Caudill sees this as a cypher for law schools, in that they perform an aesthetic of an under-threat past of civility in the legal profession and a backward looking desire for old-time doctrinal legal scholarship that is under threat from less authentic 'law and' scholarships.[69]

In the musician as legal critic, popular music and musicians came to the forefront of law and music scholarship. The musician as a lyrist was predominately the focus. Dylan's criticisms of law in his songs, or Springsteen's storytelling of those outside of the law, provide the critical perspectives to show the injustice of legal institutions, rules and practices. Ramshaw provides a more holistic study, focusing on Holiday's aesthetics as revealed through her performances and her curated public persona, as allowing her to displace the prejudice and racial stereotyping of black women during her trial. The musician as legal critic does not exhaust law and popular music, however. There is also a thread that reads popular music jurisprudentially, looking beyond the musician as commenting on the social dimensions of law and turning instead to popular music as an animating, a bringing to life, of deeper legalities

'Major Jurisprudence' of Law and Popular Music

The 'minor jurisprudence' of law and music directly engaged with jurisprudence. This engagement was with the familiar jurisprudential concerns of the twentieth century of doing law as a system of rules and the 'technical' dilemmas of the proper ways to

65. Ibid, 105.
66. D S Caudill, 'Fabricating Authenticity: Law Students as Country Music Stars' (1999) 20 *Cardozo Law Review* 1573.
67. Ibid, 1576–7.
68. Ibid, 1586.
69. Ibid, 1586–7.

interpret written texts to be applied to the life-world.[70] However, there is more to the theorising of law than just understanding how judges and lawyers do law-work through performance and improvisation. And in this 'more', there is further scope for considering music.

A particular manifestation of this something more is Desmond Manderson's genre-breaking text *Songs Without Music*.[71] Manderson is not as preoccupied with issues of text and judicial interpretation, but rather the aesthetical and affectual dimensions of music as a parallel to the aesthetics and affectual dimensions of law. His 'Motet' chapter, for example, tracked the parallel development of the formalities of the English statute and the motet form of composition starting from the 1200s, identifying a common worldview of the creators for establishing cultural forms that compel obedience.[72] Manderson's *Songs Without Music* indicates a shift in priorities for law and music, a seeing the relationship not just as two professions concerned with text and performance, as has been a consistent fixation in the 'minor jurisprudence' tradition, nor the musician as legal critic, but as productive of cultural artefacts and practices.[73] Manderson provides a bridge from the earlier 'minor jurisprudence' of law and music to the popular jurisprudence focus evident in recent scholarship.

A recent strand within law and humanities has been the reading jurisprudentially movement.[74] Inspired by the form of analysis of popular culture undertaken by William P. MacNeil,[75] this approach has been less concerned with maintaining a singular focus on text, and more embracive of the visual and the everyday of mass and popular culture.[76] Furthermore, it has been less interested in the narrow textual jurisprudence of judges, lawyers and the interpretation of rules that was a feature of the 'minor jurisprudence' of law and music scholarship and the traditional focus of law and literature. As was anticipated by Manderson, this movement considers cultural artefacts and practices as distinct contributions to jurisprudence.

An example of reading popular music jurisprudentially is our work. We have attempted to show that the totality of a popular musician – and our focus has been on rock/pop artists – presents as not just a cypher of distinct jurisprudential contributions, but, in performance and aesthetics, presents a deeper critique of legal theoretical content. By staging a duet between a musician and legal theorist, we try to show that

70. R M Cover, 'Violence and the Word' (1986) 95 *Yale Law Journal* 1601.
71. D Manderson, *Songs Without Music: Aesthetic Dimensions of Law and Justice* (University of California Press 2000).
72. Ibid, 52.
73. Ibid, 31.
74. T D Peters, *A Theological Jurisprudence of Speculative Cinema: Superheroes, Science Fictions and Fantasies of Modern Law* (Edinburgh University Press 2022), 14.
75. W P MacNeil, *Lex Populi: The Jurisprudence of Popular Culture* (Stanford University Press 2007).
76. K Crawley, 'The Critical Force of Irony: Reframing Photographs in Cultural Legal Studies' in C Sharp and M Leiboff (eds) *Cultural Legal Studies: Law's Popular Cultures and the Metamorphosis of Law* (Routledge 2015), 186.

the rock star as a nexus of cultural signifiers – such as costuming, comportment, songs, media interviews and biography – can be understood as performing and commenting upon issues of jurisprudential significance.[77] One of the duets we stage is between John Rawls and Jimi Hendrix. We saw that they both

> had recourse to the abstract, using it to develop principles that, despite their virtuosic complexity, were unable to resonate with real social forces. In translating these imagined worlds into the concrete, their visions are revealed as hallucination. Rawls's envisioned society, as with Electric Ladyland, will remain forever 'up ahead.' Hendrix, however, recognized and grappled with the problem of abstraction in a number of his tracks; not seeing clarity and truth, but haze. Rawls's through Hendrix shows the dangerous attraction of abstraction to thinking justice.[78]

Another example of reading a popular musician as contributing to jurisprudence is Kristy Duncanson's examination of First Nations musician Mo'Ju's (then Mojo Juju) 2018 song, aesthetics, and film clip 'Native Tongue'.[79] Through a layered examination of Mo'Ju's clip, the words and musicality of the song, the costumes and staging, the angle and emphasis of the film shooting and the postproduction framing and animation, Duncanson suggests that it:

> grant[s] empathic access to an experience of the criminalizing and carceral marginalization of Western colonial law, which fragments the legal subjecthood of those whose bodies do not conform. At the same time, the video directly challenges parts of its audience and threatens to shatter the internal coherence of legal subjecthood, while also performing a continuation of culture and Indigenous sovereignty never ceded.[80]

Duncanson's appreciation of Mo'Ju's 'Native Tongue' as popular jurisprudence highlights the transformative possibilities of law and popular music. By engaging with the aesthetic totality of a popular musician's specific performance, she identified a strong location in First Nation sovereignty that cuts through colonialised legalities that objectify and exclude other bodies. Duncanson highlights the affective and emotional capacity of popular music to not just rationally convince but to sway. To misuse the original sense of a 'minor jurisprudence', it presents a major jurisprudence. Not the minor 'black' focus on the parallels between classical music and interpretative dilemma for modernist

---

77. R Sykes and K Tranter, 'You Gotta Roll/Rule with It: Oasis and The Concept of Law' (2016) 26 *Griffith Law Review* 571: R Sykes and K Tranter, 'The Rise and Fall of Ziggy Stardust and Natural Law' (2018) 31 *International Journal for the Semiotics of Law* 325.
78. R Sykes and K Tranter, 'A Just (Electric Lady) Land: Jimi Hendrix and John Rawls' (2017) 29 *Law and Literature* 383.
79. Mojo Juju, *Native Touge* (ABC Music 2018); K Duncanson, 'Being Engaged in Colonial Critique by Mojo Juju's "Native Tongue"' in K Weinert, K Crawley and K Tranter (eds), *Law, Lawyers and Justice: Through Australian Lenses* (Routledge 2020), 144.
80. Ibid, 145.

positivism nor the funky name dropping of CLS but a genuine opportunity for major insights into how law and its nomos makes life and living in the present.

The present of digital transformation has features where a major jurisprudence of law and music would be particularly strong. To make music, as was emphasised in the 'minor jurisprudence' of law and music, is inherently a fusion of *poiesis* and *techné*, of art and technical skill.[81] The music industry, particularly popular music, has always had a hard technological edge: from electrification of instruments to music videos to sampling and digital production. Further issues of authenticity and reproduction have consistently circulated. To separate the art from the technicity of playing instruments and manipulating the archive of past music has been an enduring problem. In a present of generative AI[82] and seemingly the further enclosure of human creativity by the technical, insights from a major jurisprudence of law and music have exciting potential to explore how technosocial systems that are forming normative orders for human life are emerging and how human life could flourish, dance and sing, within such orders.[83]

Conclusion

This chapter traced the changes in focus, themes and styles of law and music over a hundred years of scholarship. It highlights that consideration of law and music has been enduring. Initially law and music was considered within the 'minor jurisprudence' frame where the parallels between classical music performance and the common law judge were emphasised. This approach which draws parallels between music as a performance combining art with technique is an enduring concern for law and music scholarship. However, it not the only way that scholars have bought together law and music. An obvious locus of concern is the ways that law and regulation are disrupted by practices from the music industry and how copyright, consumer and market regulation need to change to be in step with the dynamic shifts within the music industry. CLS in the 1970s instigated another way to combine law and music – with a focus on popular music. Subsequent, law and popular music scholarship considered mainstream music and musicians, Bob Dylan especially, as articulating forms of legal critique, as voicing

81. E Kotzakidou Pace, 'The Techne of Music Theory and the Epistemic Domain of the (Neo-) Aristotelian Arts of Logos' in P F Broman and N A Engebretsen (eds), *What Kind of Theory Is Music Theory?: Epistemological Exercises in Music Theory and Analysis* (Stockholm University 2007), 133.
82. R Louie, J Engel and C A Huang, 'Expressive Communication: Evaluating Developments in Generative Models and Steering Interfaces for Music Creation' (2022) (Online) https://doi.org/10.48550/arXiv.2111.14951: J Smith, 'Human-AI Partnerships in Generative Music' (2022) *International Conference on New Interfaces for Musical Expression* (online) https://doi.org/10.21428/92fbeb44.1aaaf7ab
83. K Tranter, 'Sisyphus and the Present: Time in Modern and Digital Legalities' (2023) 36 *International Journal for the Semiotics of Law* 373.

and giving form in their lyrics and life critical accounts of the institutional prejudices and injustices of law and the legal system. This law and popular music focus has subsequently encouraged what we call a 'major jurisprudence of law and music': scholarship that draws upon Critical Legal Studies to consider music as a total cultural practice to understand and critique the fundamental normative orders that generate the present. We suggest that this orientation has opportunities in a present where normative orders are increasing being set through and by the digital.

Chapter Ten

LAW AND RELIGION

Russell Sandberg

Introduction: An English and Welsh Case Study

The interaction between law and religion differs considerably across time and space. At one extreme, there are theocracies where the religion is law and societies where religious hands shape the laws of the land. There are states where a religion or a particular religious group is afforded a protected position, be it by constitutional recognition of one religion or by the existence of concordats or treaties with them endowing upon the religion equal status to the state. Other societies bestow legal status with resulting benefits and burdens on to those that register or come within particular definitions. Others still provide for freedom of religion and belief, with protections being extended to non-religious world views and often expressed in international agreements. Some states see their role as facilitating and, where needed, regulating the religious marketplace and others see the role of the state as being neutral and/or taking a secular stance (two approaches that are not identical and not completely compatible). These are, of course, ideal types. These models rarely, if ever, exist in their idealised perfect form. In many places in many eras, several of these characteristics exist and interact uneasily. This is often the result of historical religion-state relationships failing to keep up with wider political, social and legal change. The interaction between law and religion is invariably in flux – always contestable, ever changing often in subtle sometimes unseen ways.

This chapter focuses squarely on the study of the interaction between law and religion in England and Wales in the early twenty-first century. Perhaps as a result of a lack of a single document amounting to a written constitution, a wide number and diverse variety of the ideal types described above apply in England and Wales today; often in non-ideal ways.[1] For much of its history,[2] English laws have been shaped by clerical hands and this continues to some extent today with bishops of the Church of England

1. For a general if now dated study see R Sandberg, *Law and Religion* (Cambridge University Press, 2011).
2. See, e.g., R H Helmholz, *The Oxford History of the Laws of England Volume I: The Canon Law and Ecclesiastical Jurisdiction from 597 to 1640s* (Oxford University Press, 2004) and N Doe and S Coleman (eds), *The Legal History of the Church of England* (Hart Publishing, 2024).

sitting in the House of Lords[3] and representatives of that church having a special protected position on the local bodies that determine how religion is taught in schools and the laws on collective worship in schools.[4] Education is but one example of a social function originally discharged by religions and enforced by church courts where the state has only relatively recently been active and this limits any attempt by the state to monopolise. The same is true of marriage,[5] while matters as diverse as divorce, defamation and wills are all examples of matters previously dealt with solely by ecclesiastical courts.[6] The Church of England remains the established church with a plethora of constitutional benefits and burdens varying from the role the UK Parliament still plays in the enactment of its laws to the way that the terms citizen, subject and parishioner are synonymous so that everyone in England has the right to attend, be married and be buried in their parish church.[7] In Wales, the Church was disestablished and set up on a voluntary basis by dint of the Welsh Church Act 1914[8] while in both countries other religious groups have been tolerated over the last few centuries with most disabilities removed without a clear legal framework developing.[9] A number of separate registration systems provide access to tax relief and the right to conduct marriages while attaining charitable status affords further financial benefits. And despite recent laws protecting freedom of religion or belief and the right not to be discriminated on grounds of religion or belief, many pre-existing legal provisions do not extend to non-religious beliefs, and where such beliefs are now protected, there is controversy and inconsistency as to how far this protection should extend. Talk of facilitating religious freedom and of state neutrality increasingly sit uneasily with historical legacies and the ongoing establishment of the Church of England.

This underscores the extent to which the interaction today between law and religion in England and Wales is shaped by its history. This chapter contends that the same is true of its study.[10] The development of law and religion as an academic field in law schools in England and Wales in the early twenty-first century has been shaped by the wider social context. In particular, the study of law and religion in England and Wales in the early twenty-first century has been shaped by the dominant and generally accepted narrative of secularisation that has seen the very existence of religion in the

3. See A Harlow, F Cranmer and N. Doe, 'Bishops in the House of Lords: A Critical Analysis' (2008) *Public Law* 490.
4. See R Sandberg, *Religion in Schools: Learning Lessons from Wales* (Anthem Press, 2022).
5. See R Sandberg, *Religion and Marriage Law: The Need for Reform* (Bristol University Press, 2021).
6. See R B Outhwaite, *The Rise and Fall of the English Ecclesiastical Courts 1500-1860* (Cambridge University Press, 2006).
7. For fuller discussion, see e.g., N Doe, *The Legal Framework of the Church of England: A Critical Study in a Comparative Context* (Clarendon Press, 1996) and J G Oliva and H Hall, *Religion, Law and the Constitution: Balancing Beliefs in Britain* (Routledge, 2017).
8. See N Doe, *The Law of the Church in Wales* (University of Wales Press, 2002) and N Doe (ed), *A New History of the Church in Wales: Governance and Ministry, Theology and Society* (Cambridge University Press, 2020).
9. Cf. J Rivers, *The Law of Organized Religions* (Oxford University Press, 2010).
10. See also the essays in R Sandberg, *Leading Works in Law and Religion* (Routledge, 2019).

public sphere as a problem.[11] This is because of the dominance of the acceptance of the idea of social differentiation: this is the idea that, while in previous eras religious authorities performed a variety of social functions, in a modern society a variety of social institutions now perform distinct social functions, with the state playing a central role. Social differentiation is understood as being a keystone of modern societies. This is the reason why the place of religion in the public sphere, the existence of religious schools, religious tribunals and so on are controversial. They offend modern society's expectation that the legal and religious are separated. The very idea of religions performing functions that now 'belong' to other social institutions, such as educating children or determining legal disputes, now seems archaic. This has shaped the assumptions at the very heart of the study of law and religion. The role of religion in the public sphere, and any fusion of the legal and the religious, is seen as being problematic and deserving of state interest. The focus of academics has been upon the role of the state and whether, how and why the state should accommodate religious difference when manifest in the public sphere. As Anthony Bradney has observed, law and religion scholarship has tended to assume and characterise the relationship between law and religion 'as a problem that is capable of solution'.[12]

This is a narrow understanding of what law and religion can involve, and although there are countless examples of work that do take a wider approach,[13] these remain exceptional. The growth of law and religion as an academic field in England and Wales in the early twenty-first century has been constrained by the dominant perspective that normalises the differentiation of religion and law and problematises any fusion of the two. The accepted and prevalent assumption of social differentiation – the idea that religious groups should only deal with religious matters – has underlined many of the political and social controversies surrounding religion in recent years, such as the wearing of religious dress, the operation of religious courts and clashes between freedom of religion and the prohibition of discrimination on grounds of sex and sexual orientation. These controversies have stimulated the development of law and religion as an academic area of interest but have also limited it given that the same assumptions that underpin these controversies have infected scholarship. The assumption of social differentiation that lay behind political controversies also shapes and constrains the outlook of law and religion as an academic endeavour. Much attention has been afforded to the moral panics of the day. The focus has been upon the interaction between religion and state law. The presence of religion in the public square and anything that goes against

11. See further R Sandberg, *Religion, Law and Society* (Cambridge University Press, 2014).
12. Anthony Bradney, 'Politics and Sociology: New Research Agenda for the Study of Law and Religion' in R O'Dair and A Lewis (eds), *Law and Religion* (Oxford University Press, 2001) 65, 68.
13. See discussions in R Sandberg, *Religion, Law and Society* (Cambridge University Press, 2014); F Cranmer, M Hill, C Kenny and R Sandberg (eds), *The Confluence of Law and Religion: Interdisciplinary Reflections on the Work of Norman Doe* (Cambridge University Press, 2016) and R Sandberg, N Doe, B Kane and C Roberts (eds), *Handbook of the Interdisciplinary Study of Law and Religion* (Edward Elgar, 2019).

the grain of social differentiation is regarded as a problem. This narrow focus has meant that interest in the study of law and religion has declined as questions concerning religion have become less central in the news agenda. Ironically, the political and social developments that led to increased legal attention being afforded to religion have led to the development of law and religion as a field but also the stalling of law and religion as a field. This chapter tells the story of the rise and fall of law and religion scholarship in England and Wales before briefly reflecting on what can be done to rejuvenate it.

A Short History of the Study of Law and Religion

Paradoxically, law and religion is a new academic discipline in England and Wales that relates to an age-old interaction. Part of the reason for this can be dated back to the English Reformation of the 1530s.[14] One often overlooked effect of the English Reformation of the 1530s was the sidelining of religious law. The termination of Papal jurisdiction was accompanied by a prohibition on the teaching of Catholic Canon Law at the Universities of Oxford and Cambridge.[15] The ban on the study of Catholic Canon Law did not result in the infant ecclesiastical law of the Church of England becoming a subject of study instead. Rather, it led to church law not being formally taught. Although lawyers in the Church courts (which continued to enjoy an extensive jurisdiction) continued to appeal to Roman canon law,[16] that and the developing new law of the English Church became solely subject of professional training at a learned society which came to be known as Doctors' Commons.[17] As the centuries wore on, the law of the Church was occasionally the subject of professional texts but almost no attention was given to the general interaction between law and religion.[18] Even when alternative forms of religiosity became lawful following the slow and piecemeal march of toleration, there was no discrete law on religious freedom to comment upon and no identifiable social problem. As Maitland expressed it in his lectures subsequently published as *The Constitutional*

14. For an account, see, e.g., R Sandberg, *A Historical Introduction to English Law: Genesis of the Common Law* (Cambridge University Press, 2023) chapter 9.
15. Injunctions were issued in 1535 which substituted lectures in Civil Law for lectures in Canon Law and in 1545 an Act (37 Henry VIII c. 17) allowed judgeships in the ecclesiastical courts to be held by laymen who were doctors only of Civil Law.
16. R Helmholz, *Roman Catholic Law in Reformation England* (Cambridge University Press, 1991). The Submission of the Clergy Act 1533 provided that the Roman canon law was to continue to apply unless it was 'contrariant or repugnant to the law, statutes or custom' of the realm or to the King's prerogative. See also N Doe, 'Pre-Reformation Roman Catholic Law in Post-Reformation English Ecclesiastical Law' (2022) 24(3) *Ecclesiastical Law Journal* 273.
17. See G D Squibb, *Doctors' Commons: A History of the College of Advocates and Doctors of Law* (Clarendon Press, 1977); P Barber, 'The Fall and Rise of Doctors' Commons' (1996) 4(18) *Ecclesiastical Law Journal* 462; D Pocklington, 'The Continued Relevance of Doctors' Commons' (2011) 166 *Law and Justice* 52.
18. See, e.g., in the twentieth century: W Dale, *The Law of the Parish Church* (Butterworths, 1932).

History of England, 'religious liberty and religious equality [was] complete'.[19] The powers of the ecclesiastical courts of the Church of England had 'very much declined'.[20] And the feeling was that there was very little to say about the interaction between law and religion at least in England.

This was still true by the mid- to late twentieth century. Legal textbooks seldom mentioned religion.[21] Moreover, what little literature existed rarely extended beyond the study of the law of the established church.[22] This changed, however, due to a curious mixture of personalities and politics. Developments in the 1980s and 1990s awakened interest in the law of the Church of England and treated it as the subject of academic analysis for the first time.[23] In 1987, the Ecclesiastical Law Society was formed 'to promote the study of ecclesiastical and canon law particularly in the Church of England and those churches in communion with it' and began to publish its own journal, the *Ecclesiastical Law Journal*, and organise its own conferences. An attendee at one early conference was Norman Doe, then a lecturer in law at Cardiff who had just completed a doctorate on how legal ideas and philosophies had formed in the fifteenth century.[24] Doe was intrigued as to where all the canon law he had found in his research had gone. These thoughts and the encouragement and support of the Ecclesiastical Law Society led to the establishment of the LLM in canon law degree at Cardiff University in 1991, the first degree to study the laws of the Church of England and Catholic Canon Law since the Reformation. Throughout the 1990s the focus of both the Ecclesiastical Law Society and the Cardiff postgraduate course broadened. The *Ecclesiastical Law Journal* published articles on the laws of other religions and faith communities and on national

19. F W *Maitland*, *Constitutional History of England* (Cambridge University Press, 1908) 520. It is worth noting that Maitland did dedicate a twenty-page section to 'The Church' which examined the legal historical development of the Church of England, the history of toleration, the present condition and powers of the ecclesiastical courts and the status of the established church: ibid 506–526.
20. Ibid 523. On which see R B Outhwaite, *The Rise and Fall of the Ecclesiastical Courts, 1500-1860* (Cambridge University Press, 2006).
21. J Rivers, 'The Secularisation of the British Constitution' (2012) 14 *Ecclesiastical Law Journal* 371, 372.
22. The 1975 edition of the Ecclesiastical Law volume of *Halsbury's Laws of England* (4th edn, vol 14, London, 1975), for instance, dealt with 'other religious denominations' as an afterthought.
23. Some canon law had been taught before 1991. From the late 1960s to 1981 Garth Moore offered a half paper on the canon law of the Church of England as part of the law degree at Cambridge. At Oxford seminars in canon law were conducted by Eric Kemp in the 1950s. See M Kotiranta, 'The Teaching and Study of Church-State Relations in the Nordic Countries, in the United Kingdom and in Ireland' in J Valle and A Hollerbach (eds), *The Teaching of Church-State Relations in European Universities* (Peeters, 2005) 105, 153. See also K Counsell, 'The Teaching of Canon Law in England and Wales: 1400-1996' (LLM in Canon Law Dissertation, University of Wales, Cardiff 1997).
24. Published as N Doe, *Fundamental Authority in Late Medieval Law* (Cambridge University Press, 1990).

and international laws affecting religion, while the success of the LLM programme led Cardiff University to establish its Centre for Law and Religion in 1998.[25]

Increasing political tensions about religion and racial integration also played a part. Although concerns about morality and differentness accelerated following the liberalisation brought about as a result of what Charles Taylor has referred to as the 'individuating revolution' of the 1960s,[26] it was the moral panics following the publication of the *Satanic Verses* that lit the fuse. In the last decade or so of the twentieth century, the place of religion in the public sphere began to be questioned. As historian Callum Brown argued, 'in the midst of overall decline in popular religiosity, British religion showed signs of increasing seriousness and militancy'.[27] This was a sign of weakness not strength: British Christianity became more militant as it contracted.[28] For instance, in addition to the rise of religious pressure groups and charismatic movements, 'British Catholicism showed a radically different approach to its position in British life': after the visit of Pope John Paul II to the UK in 1982, the domestic church stopped 'keeping its head down' and 'established a new spirit of political and ecumenical engagement by the Church in Britain', which was 'nurtured through media contact'.[29] The growth of the Internet helped to foster the 'growing opportunities for vigorous minorities' both liberal and conservative to 'argue their cases, achieve success and push forward agendas'. As Brown pointed out, 'this was an uneven and in some ways imperceptible process and one that only became really noticeable in the early twenty-first century'.[30] While previously religious fundamentalism was 'widely considered as almost irrelevant' in mainland Britain, by the close of the century 'a swing from racism to religious bigotry' meant that on the streets of English cities such as Bradford 'what were formerly classed as racist attacks were being re-counted as anti-religious attacks'.[31] The Al-Qaeda terrorist attacks in New York on 11 September 2001 and in London on 7 July 2007 provided a watershed moment. It was not the fear of religious extremism that was new: as sociologist Linda Woodhead noted, 'religiously-inflicted terrorism by the IRA had [...] been a much more serious threat in Britain for much longer than anything done in the name of Islam – yet this did not shake secular certainties'.[32] What was new was that these fears

25. See N Doe, 'The First Ten Years of the Centre for Law and Religion, Cardiff University' (2008) 10(2) *Ecclesiastical Law Journal* 222. For a further appraisal of Doe's contribution, see the essays in F Cranmer, M Hill, C Kenny and R Sandberg (eds), *The Confluence of Law and Religion: Interdisciplinary Reflections on the Work of Norman Doe* (Cambridge University Press, 2016) and J Witte Jr, 'Law at the Backbone: The Christian Legal Ecumenism of Norman Doe' (2022) 24(2) *Ecclesiastical Law Journal* 192.
26. C Taylor, *Varieties of Religion Today* (Harvard University Press, 2002) 80. See further R Sandberg, *Religion, Law and Society* (Cambridge University Press, 2014) chapter 5.
27. C G Brown, *Religion and Society in Twentieth-Century Britain* (Pearson, 2006) 297.
28. Ibid 314, 298.
29. Ibid 309.
30. Ibid 297.
31. Ibid 298, 313.
32. L Woodhead, 'Introduction' in L Woodhead and R Catto (eds), *Religion and Change in Modern Britain* (Routledge, 2012) 1, 9.

occurred against a backdrop of wider uncertainty; the motivations behind the terror were largely unknown and the fear of terrorism became indistinguishable from wider notions distrusting 'otherness'. Although, as Woodhead argues, attributing 'the atrocities in the name of Islam as the turning point' whereby religion was placed back on the agenda is too simple an answer,[33] the events of September 2001 changed the way in which the West thought and spoke about not only Islam but religion per se. The notion that religions were an invariably benign force for good became questioned and the fact that religious believers were loyal to forms of authority other than the state became to be seen as a problem.

This new context shaped the way in which religions operated in public life. Now religion became seen as a social problem and attention was afforded to it. This contributed to the creation of new laws most significantly those formally regarding religion as a human right actionable in domestic courts and laws expressly specifically prohibiting discrimination on grounds of religion or belief.[34] This abundance of new laws regulating religion was followed by a multitude of cases seeking to define the contours of the new religious rights and how the new laws interact (or not) with earlier provisions and older understandings. Several of these cases, especially those concerning the wearing of religious dress and symbols at schools and workplaces, became newsworthy. Meanwhile a lecture by the then Archbishop of Canterbury, Dr Rowan Williams, in which he acknowledged the existence of religious laws and religious courts such a sharia councils, became headline news, with the television news programmes graphically illustrating the item with footage of stoning.[35] These legal changes, and the headlines they were provoking, naturally led some law academics to pay attention to the interaction between law and religion or aspects of that interaction.

Prior to the years surrounding the turn of the millennium, law and religion could not be said to exist as an academic sub-discipline in England and Wales. There were no specialist journals, no research clusters and no academics that exclusively specialised in the area. As Anthony Bradney has noted, although there were occasional academic writings on particular topics, such work was 'spasmodic and disjointed'; there was 'no concrete and sustained debate about the proper relationship between religion and legal rules', and 'such articles and books as were produced failed to have any impact upon other more established areas of academic discourse'.[36] However, in the final years of the twentieth century and the opening decade of the twenty-first century, the law and

33. Ibid 8.
34. By virtue of the Human Rights Act 1998, the Employment Equality (Religion or Belief) Regulations 2003 and the Equality Act 2006 (now see the Equality Act 2010).
35. The lecture was subsequently published as R Williams, 'Civil and Religious Law in England: A Religious Perspective' (2008) 10 *Ecclesiastical Law Journal* 262.
36. Bradney gave the example of C Crowther, *Religious Trusts* (Oxford University Press, 1954); A Bradney, 'Politics and Sociology: New Research Agenda for the Study of Law and Religion' in R O'Dair and A Lewis (eds), *Law and Religion* (Oxford University Press, 2001) 65, 66.

religion literature blossomed.[37] An academic industry had come into existence.[38] There were now a plethora of law and religion journals,[39] book series,[40] many specialist conferences and symposiums, some centres and research groups[41] and several prolific national and international networks.[42] This was epitomised by the growth by the Cardiff Centre for Law and Religion, which celebrated its tenth anniversary in 2008 by formulating new networks that focused more on the interaction between religions and the state, the Interfaith Legal Advisers Network and the Law and Religion Scholars Network.[43] The legal study of this focus was not limited to Cardiff. Not many but some academics now identified their research interest as being law and religion. To a lesser extent, there were a few courses and textbooks dedicated to the subject, though it remained largely true that legal textbooks on areas such as public law, family law and employment law seldom mentioned religion and, although some work was published in mainstream general legal journals, scholarship in this field tended to be published in specialist journals, edited collections and monographs.

The development of law and religion as a field of study can therefore be regarded as a post-September 11th phenomenon. As Julian Rivers has noted there has been 'a new loss of consensus about the role and significance of religion'.[44] This resulted in legal changes and unease at existing legal situations and law and religion developed in order to study this. It may be objected, however, that it might appear overly convenient and simplistic to regard the post-9/11 tide of legislation and litigation as the main cause of this development of interest in law and religion. Maitland's assumption that religious freedom was 'complete' was questioned way before 9/11. Such tensions between secular authorities and religious convictions are a constant throughout history. Moral panics

37. A bibliography compiled for the Ecclesiastical Law Society's silver jubilee indicated that while between 1987 and 1997 there were on average 2–3 books published per year, this figure grew to an average of 6 books between 1997 and 2000 and to 10 books after 2007. This rise was even more accelerated in the case of edited books: R Sandberg, 'Silver Jubilee Bibliography: Ecclesiastical Law Publications 1987-2011' (2012) 14 *Ecclesiastical Law Journal* 149.
38. The language of 'industry' is derived from R Grillo, *Muslim Families, Politics and the Law* (Ashgate, 2015).
39. In addition to the *Ecclesiastical Law Journal*, these included the *Oxford Journal of Law and Religion*, *Religion and Human Rights* and *Law & Justice*. Although *Law & Justice* was founded in 1963 as a Christian Law Review (and titled as *QuisCustodiet?* until 1974), it has recently come to function as a law and religion journal.
40. Including two published by Routledge.
41. Such as the Centre for the Study of Law and Religion at Bristol and the Applied Study of Law and Religion Group at Oxford Brookes.
42. There are also a number of international associations such as the International Consortium for Law and Religion Studies (which met for the first time in 2009) and the European Consortium for Church and State Research (established in 1989).
43. These sat alongside the pre-existing and differently focused Colloquium of Anglican and Roman Catholic Canon Lawyers.
44. J Rivers, 'The Secularisation of the British Constitution' (2012) 14 *Ecclesiastical Law Journal* 371, 385.

that once concerned Catholicism have been superseded by moral panics about Islam. And the increase in academic writing might also be attributable to changes within law schools, whereby research has become more central to their mission and where there has been a move towards interdisciplinary work.

Yet, much of the work produced on law and religion in England and Wales suggests that there is some truth in this creation narrative. And this has shaped how law and religion has developed. The moral panics of the early twenty-first century have meant that attention has often been narrow with much attention being afforded to particular spots of conflict. While early works on the subject tended to be shaped around particular legal issues (how religion interacts with employment and charity law, for instance),[45] much work in the early decades of the twenty-first century focused on one area in particular (say, religious discrimination law[46] or international human rights laws on religion[47]), while other authors focused squarely upon the question of how the state accommodated religious difference[48] or developed an argument that law and religion (or aspects of it) constitutes a distinct field of study, an emerging sub-discipline in its own right.[49] Indeed, there remains a lack of identity and a suspicion that law and religion may not be more than the sum of its parts – an undeveloped Frankenstein's monster of other 'proper' legal areas.[50] A suspicion remains that what we are dealing with is not the development of a new area of study but rather a number of separate areas of interaction between religion and discrete, well-established areas of law. Most of the time the only connection that unites law and religion work is its focus on religion. Developments concerning religion in criminal law, discrimination law, human rights law, family law and so on can be understood solely in those terms. They are not interrelated to the degree that they ought to be understood as part of an overall body of law concerning religion. There is a question as to whether the study of law and religion amounts to more than the sum of its parts. It can still be questioned whether law and religion really exists.

There are some signs that law and religion is as well established (if not more established) than some other newly formed legal sub-disciplines like sports law or education law. This is evident in terms of the number of specialist journals, the establishment of bespoke book series and the thriving societies formed at both national and international levels. However, there are other signs that law and religion is less well established than

45. Epitomised by St John Robilliard, *Religion and the Law: Religious Liberty in Modern English Law* (Manchester University Press, 1984).
46. E.g., L Vickers, *Religious Freedom, Religious Discrimination and the Workplace* (2nd edn, Hart Publishing, 2016).
47. E.g., M D Evans, *Religious Liberty and International Law in Europe* (Cambridge University Press, 1997).
48. P W Edge, *Legal Responses to Religious Difference* (Brill, 2002).
49. See J Rivers, *The Law of Organized Religions* (Oxford University Press, 2010) and Sandberg, *Law and Religion* (Cambridge University Press, 2011) for slightly different examples of this.
50. Similar concerns have been raised in relation to family law as discussed by G Douglas, *An Introduction to Family Law* (2nd edn, Clarendon Press, 2004) 3–4 and in relation to Sports Law, see, e.g., M James, *Sports Law* (Palgrave Macmillan, 2010) 19 and S Gardiner et al., *Sports Law* (3rd edn, Cavendish, 2006) 88–91.

other sub-disciplines. Law and religion lags behind other sub-disciplines in terms of the number of courses taught and the quantity of works aimed at a student readership, for instance. Much law and religion work is being disseminated in ways and in places that limits it appeal to those already within the clique. There are, of course, exceptions especially where the particular law and religion scholar is also an expert in the wider area of law, such as Lucy Vickers's work on religious discrimination and Malcolm Evans's work on religion and international human rights law.[51] However, overall, law and religion writers on religion and criminal law, discrimination law, human rights law, family law and so on do not engage with or place their work within the wider context of those legal sub-disciplines.[52] There is a real risk of ghettoisation: there is a danger that law and religion scholars will speak only to one another and will be immune from and unable to shape wider debates within the discipline of law (not to mention the wider risks caused by the academic isolationism of law and religion scholarship that comes from such work being mainly situated in law schools). As Anthony Bradney has warned, the development of a common language may 'limit the possibilities or argument and conceal the realities of the subject-matter under discussion'.[53]

The development of law and religion as a niche clique is a consequence of the speed in which it developed as a field of study responding to the moral panics concerning religion that followed 9/11. Particular topics have dominated the field: an initial fixation with the law on religious dress and symbols has partially given way to new obsessions.[54] Patrick Nash has commented that there is no need for 'another rehearsal of dull material on done-to-death areas such as Muslim marriage and sharia councils', for instance.[55] What unites these obsessions is the way in which the agenda is set by the political and media controversies of the day and the seeing of the positioning of religion in the public sphere as being a problem that state law should fix. This highlights the risk that the development of law and religion seems dependent upon the continuation of political and social controversies surrounding the place of religion in the public sphere. Indeed, it is striking that as the number of legal changes affecting religion has slowed down in recent years, the field has shown some signs of stagnation.

The way in which law and religion developed as a field of study and the sheer pace in which this occurred have shaped the away in which law and religion scholarship has developed. By focusing on immediate changes and issues, by regarding them as discrete problems to be solved and by linking itself too firmly with the news agenda, law and

51. M D Evans, *Religious Liberty and International Law in Europe* (Cambridge University Press, 1997) and L Vickers, *Religious Freedom, Religious Discrimination and the Workplace* (2nd edn, Hart Publishing, 2017).
52. For a discussion of this in relation to family law see R Sandberg and S Thompson, 'The Sharia Debate: The Missing Family Law Context' (2016) 177 *Law & Justice* 188.
53. A Bradney, 'The Rise and Rise of Legal Education' (1997) 4 *Web Journal of Current Legal Issues* http://webjcli.ncl.ac.uk/1997/issue4/bradney4.html
54. However, some authors have shown that there remains more to be said on the issue: S Bacquet, *Religious Symbols and the Intervention of the Law* (Routledge, 2019); E Howard, *Law and the Wearing of Religious Symbols in Europe* (2nd edn, Routledge 2021).
55. P S Nash, *British Islam and English Law: A Classical Pluralist Perspective* (Cambridge University Press, 2022) 1.

religion has not developed a level of permanence or maturity within academia. It has developed as a legal interest and has ironically the very developments that have fostered and accelerated the field as a specialism (the number of specialist research groups, journals, conferences, book series and so on) have caused its marginalisation. Instead of dialogue with the legal mainstream, law and religion has developed at the margins of law schools and the focus has been mainly the pragmatic question of the extent to which and how religious difference should be accommodated by law. The very activities that have helped to constitute law and religion as a distinct entity have ironically curtailed its development by cutting it adrift from the legal mainstream. The partial development of law and religion as a legal sub-discipline has, therefore, created the worst of both worlds. On the one hand, the fact that law and religion is not sufficiently advanced as a legal sub-discipline means that there is still a lingering perception that it is not stronger than the sum of its parts; that it is a Frankenstein's monster of discrete areas of law that happen to interact with religion but which ultimately have little in common with each other and do not collectively constitute a legal framework. On the other hand, the attempt to formulate law and religion as a legal sub-discipline has meant that the field has become ghettoised with law and religion scholars increasingly just talking to one another and with their work becoming isolated from developments and trends within the wider areas of law that they are writing about. The way in which law and religion has developed has meant that it has developed as an activity largely situated within law schools and one that has by and large adopted a very narrow understanding of what 'law and religion' entails.

State of Decay

It was not just in England and Wales that the study of law and religion experienced a growth at around the turn of the millennium. In continental Europe and the United States, where aspects of law and religion had long been studied and taught, during recent years the subject matter has become increasingly controversial and the focus has evolved beyond the study of church and state. Other jurisdictions such as Australia and South Africa were more similar to England and Wales in that law and religion became established as an area of study for the first time, with research clusters and courses being set up and academics defining themselves as law and religion scholars.

In the English-speaking world, at least, it is the United States where law and religion scholarship is at its most advanced, with two prolific and world leading research centres: the Center for the Study of Law and Religion founded at Emory University in 1982 and the International Center for Law and Religion Studies established in 2000 at Brigham Young University. The Emory Center is responsible for more than 350 books on the topic with its director John Witte Jr himself having published 40 books.[56] In recent years, Witte has reflected upon how law and religion has developed in the United

56. For an appraisal of Witte's contribution see N Doe, 'Faith, Freedom and Family: An Introduction to the Work of John Witte Jr' (2022) 24(2) *Ecclesiastical Law Journal* 175 and the Symposium papers in (2023) 38(1) *Journal of Law and Religion.*

States, and this contrasts markedly with the experience in England and Wales. Witte has described how 'a new interdisciplinary movement has emerged in the United States dedicated to the study of the religious dimensions of law, the legal dimensions of religion and the interaction of legal and religious ideas and institutions, norms and practices'.[57]

Witte's interdisciplinary conceptualisation of law and religion studies has much in common with work on law and literature where a familiar distinction has been drawn between scholarship on literature as law – examining literature from a legal standpoint – and law as literature – examining law from a literature standpoint; that is, between 'the possible relevance of literary texts [...] as texts appropriate for legal scholars' and the application of 'the techniques of literary criticism to legal texts'.[58] Witte's schema suggests that similarly the interdisciplinary study of law and religion can be understood as involving both the study of law as religion (the study of how laws and legal mechanisms can be understood religiously) and the study of religion as law (the study of how religious texts and practices can be understood legally). Understood as an interdisciplinary endeavour, law and religion involves both reading law religiously and understanding religion legally. In the words of Witte, a 'dialectical interaction' between law and religion is required:

> This study is predicated on the assumptions that religion gives law its spirit and inspires its adherence to ritual and justice. Law gives religion its structure and encourages its devotion to order and organisation. Law and religion share such ideas as fault, obligation and covenant and such methods as ethics, rhetoric and textual interpretation. Law and religion also balance each other by counterpoising justice and mercy, rule and equity, discipline and love. This dialectical interaction gives these two disciplines and dimensions of life their vitality and their strength.[59]

For Witte, 'law and religion are distinct spheres and sciences of human life, but they exist in dialectical interaction, constantly crossing over and cross-fertilising each other'.[60] There is a need to study law and religion as two distinct spheres not only in how they interact with one another but also in how they see and reconstruct one another on their own terms. It is unclear, however, how prevalent Witte's identified approach is, even within US scholarship. A recent collection edited by David C. Flatto and Benjamin Porat became the first such work to be predicated upon this distinction and notably described this as 'a different perspective that has emerged in recent scholarship which regards law and religion as overlapping frameworks'.[61] For Flatto and Porat, this represents a move away from the dominant 'dichotomous paradigm' that has dominated law

---

57. J Witte Jr, 'The Study of Law and Religion in the United States: An Interim Report' (2012) 14 *Ecclesiastical Law Journal* 327.
58. I Ward, *Law and Literature: Possibilities and Perspectives* (Cambridge University Press, 1995) 3.
59. J Witte Jr, 'The Study of Law and Religion in the United States: An Interim Report' (2012) 14 *Ecclesiastical Law Journal* 327, 327–328.
60. Ibid 328.
61. D C Flatto and B Porat, 'Introduction' in D C Flatto and B Porat (eds), *Law as Religion, Religion as Law* (Cambridge University Press, 2023) 1.

and religion studies to date. Reaching a similar conclusion to Witte, the editors opine that this newer focus reveals that 'law and religion arguably share similar properties, and may have a symbiotic relationship'.

Regardless of how developed this 'law as religion, religion as law' approach might be in the United States, it is clear that it is considerably less established in England and Wales. Although there are notable exceptions, the study of law and religion on this side of the pond has not developed into such an interdisciplinary endeavour.[62] In England and Wales, law and religion has largely developed in law schools[63] and has focused on the 'legal dimensions on religion'; it has studied religion as law, how religious texts and practices can be understood legally. By contrast, little attention has been given to the 'religious dimensions of law' – studying law as religion, how laws and legal mechanisms can be understood religiously. The development of law and religion as a *legal* sub-discipline has itself gone largely unquestioned. While literature in other 'law and' areas have developed with close interaction with people, literatures and methods from other disciplines, academic lawyers have dominated the study of law and religion and the work in the field remains characterised by academic isolationism; throw-away references to work completed outside the law school is commonplace but the synthesis of work and approaches from other parts of the academy within works of law and religion scholarship remains exceptional.

Indeed, the main focus has been upon a very narrow understanding of the 'legal dimensions on religion'. Attention has been afforded to understanding how national and international laws regulate religion (which I have labelled as 'religion law')[64] and the challenges that religious conviction (both individually and collectively held) pose for the state. There has been some growing focus upon how religious groups use law to regulate their own internal affairs (which I have referred to as 'religious law'), but even there the focus in much of the literature has been very much upon debating the proper role of the state.

The legal nature of law and religion scholarship has narrowly construed and interpreted religion. Writing in the mid-1990s, Michael King accurately predicted that law would reconstruct religion 'essentially as those customs, rites and rituals which in the public domain come to symbolize statements of faith and holiness [...] as rights of worship and performance of ritual' and that law would likely see religion 'as constituting for law a set of rights' which would often result in judges 'seeing it in terms of some external authority' such as 'a law, God's law, Islamic law'.[65] These words have proved to be

62. See, further, R Sandberg, *Religion, Law and Society* (Cambridge University Press, 2014) chapter 1.
63. And there are important questions about the identity of the scholars who have done much of this work in terms of their religion, race, gender and geography as well as their own religion or belief
64. R Sandberg, *Law and Religion* (Cambridge University Press, 2011) chapter 1.
65. M King, 'The Muslim Identity in a Secular World' in M King (ed), *God's Law versus State Law* (Great Seal, 1995) 91, 108, 110.

prophetic and scholars have followed the legal construction of religion, mostly without recognising let alone critiquing this.

An exception can be found in the work of Suhraiya Jivraj which has criticised what she refers to as 'socio-legal law-and-religion scholarship' for 'conceptualizing religion in predominately theological terms such as belief/faith and practice' which 'tends to marginalize [the] racialization of non-Christianness' and understands religion 'as a contingent concept that can come to be produced within law'.[66] Jivraj argues that this is equally true of law and religion scholarship that accepts 'more complex notions of religious identity' in that these works perpetuate 'an onto-theological model of belief and ritual practice' that is 'so often left un-interrogated'.[67] She argues that a critical approach deriving from anthropology, religious studies and critical race studies is required that understands religion contextually and historically 'as contingent upon and as part of particular political, economic, and other circumstances' to 'challenge not only the onto-theological notion of religion through various methodological routes, but also the idea that there can be any fixed concept of religion at all'.[68] This, together with further critiques which have highlighted the lack of a feminist approach to law and religion studies,[69] underscores the problematic consequences of the isolated and limited way in which law and religion scholarship has developed.

Conclusion: The Need to Rethink Law and Religion

Any analysis of the interaction between law and religion, and the study of that interaction, needs to be specific to a particular time and place. The idiosyncratic and multifaceted relationship between law and religion in England and Wales today is the result of a complex cocktail of history, politics, ecclesiology, theology and wider socio-economic and cultural change. It is therefore unfortunate that this has not been captured in a rich body of academic scholarship. For most of the time, lawyers have paid inadequate attention to religious matters and the perceived dullness of church-state relations has meant that those who focus on religion elsewhere in universities have seldom focused on legal issues. The moral panics at the dawn of the new millennium provided an opportunity to redress this with much more popular and scholarly attention being afforded to religion generally and the development of new laws on religion and a plethora of high-profile cases leading to the quick development of law and religion as a sub-discipline in law schools with the institutional presence of journals, learned societies, book series and so on. Yet, this promise has been dashed. Law and religion still exists but has not developed in the way that it was expected to; indeed, it could even be said that it is a shadow of its former self.

---

66. S Jivraj, *The Religion of Law: Race, Citizenship and Children's Belonging* (Palgrave, 2013) 82.
67. Ibid 28.
68. Ibid 6–7.
69. S Thompson and R Sandberg, 'Multicultural Jurisdictions: The Need for a Feminist Approach to Law and Religion' in R Sandberg (ed), *Leading Works in Law and Religion* (Routledge, 2019) 179.

In terms of remedying this, the work of John Witte Jr together with the scholarship highlighted and collated by Flatto and Porat points the way forward. In short, we need to develop a fuller understanding of religion as law and develop an analysis of law as religion. However, this can only be achieved by acknowledging, questioning, de-constructing and re-constructing the dominant assumption of social differentiation. The ideas that law and religion exist in separation from each other and that in a modern society religion should only perform religious functions need dismantling.[70] Unlocking the legal dimensions of religion and the religious dimensions of law and liberating this understanding from dominant and taken-for-granted assumptions of secularisation should inevitably underline the need for interdisciplinary. The 'religion as law, law as religion' approach highlights how law and religion should be an interdisciplinary endeavour. This applies not only to the research and teaching within law schools but also to the including work by those outside law faculties. Seeing law and religion as an aspect of law and humanities is likely to be helpful here in that it provides examples of how the study of other interactions are inherently interdisciplinary if not transdisciplinary. Comparisons can be made with and lessons can be learnt from other law and humanities bedfellows. Yet, it is also important to appreciate a way in which religion differs from other humanities disciplines. Religion is also a form of identity and a source of inequality. It follows that the literatures and scholarly communities that have developed on law and race as well as law and gender may also point the way forward for law and religion studies.

It may be countered that this survey is unduly and unnecessarily pessimistic and that there are countless examples of work that breaks out of the mould of law and religion studies essayed here. Yet, as ever, exceptions prove the rule. It is noticeable that such groundbreaking work is seldom seen as an example of law and religion scholarship.[71] Those at the cutting edge seem to have abandoned the sub-discipline and its institutional trappings. The question is whether those who helped establish law and religion as an academic field need to follow them to the exit or whether it is possible to refashion and rethink law and religion.

70. Social systems theory may be helpful in this regard. See R Sandberg, 'A Systems Theory Reconstruction of Law and Religion' (2019) 8(3) *Oxford Journal of Law and Religion* 447.

71. See, for instance, the work of Patrick Nash (P S Nash, *British Islam and English Law: A Classical Pluralist Perspective* (Cambridge University Press, 2022)) which is at pains to distinguish itself from standard studies and Méadhbh McIvor, who employs a social anthologist approach (M McIvor, *Representing God: Christian Legal Activism in Contemporary England* (Princeton University Press, 2020).

Chapter Eleven

LAW AND TELEVISION

Jennifer L. Schulz[*]

Introduction: The Development of Law and Television

This chapter describes the burgeoning research area of law and television. I deliberately call law and television a research 'area' rather than a 'field' because it is not clear whether law and television is a field in its own right. More aptly, it is part of law and popular culture, which is a known, defined, interdisciplinary field. Popular culture refers to popular products manufactured for popular consumption: those forms of culture that are well liked by many people, are widely shared and are often used in everyday life. Popular culture includes TV shows, but it also includes films, novels, music and video games. When we think about television, we see that it changes over time, has a commercial nature, is class-, gender- and age-coded, varies in importance and popularity to different people in different regions and can be a source of escapism or fun. Any particular television show, whether watched on network television or streamed from a subscription service on a personal device, can have more than one meaning. The larger field of law and popular culture studies the nexus between popular products and law and argues that law can be understood as popular culture and popular culture as law. It is an interdisciplinary relationship where popular culture and law continuously meet and renegotiate one another. Law and television, as an area under the umbrella of law and popular culture, studies the relationship of law as culture and culture as law as manifested in the specific area of television.

In the early days of law and popular culture the term 'popular' was used to distinguish between 'categories' of culture. In the 1980s, popular culture was often defined in contrast to other types of culture, such as high or national culture.[1] A number of scholars played an important part in the development of law and popular culture. In 1986 Anthony Chase noted the failure of legal scholars to recognise and embrace the images

* The author wishes to thank Peter Robson for his leadership in law and television and his integral importance to her own work in the area.

1. For example, in Canada we have been saturated with images originating in the United States, while our Canadian images have needed the support of government institutions and quotas and have often been associated with 'high' rather than 'popular' culture. See J Leach, 'Reading Canadian "Popular" Television: The Case of E.N.G' in J Nicks and J Sloniowski (eds), *Slippery Pastimes: Reading the Popular in Canadian Culture* (Wilfrid Laurier University Press, 2002) 113.

of law and lawyers in popular culture as legitimate subjects of scholarly study.[2] Stewart Macaulay gave a noteworthy presidential address on 'Images of Law in Everyday Life' at the 1986 Law and Society Association conference[3] and Lawrence Friedman wrote an influential article in the 1989 *Yale Law Journal*.[4] All three encouraged the study of the quotidian experience of law and lawyers and the field of law and popular culture was born.[5]

Richard Sherwin says, 'The study of law and popular culture seeks to expand the traditional range of legal studies. It seeks to include what has often been omitted, such as the feelings, desires, conflicting impulses and wishes that circulate within the law.'[6] This field recognises that cultural categories shift over time,[7] and the class-ridden distinction between popular and high culture should be abolished.[8] Popular culture and high culture are both simply culture; one is not intrinsically better, more meaningful or more valuable than the other.[9] Drawing on Max Horkheimer and Theodor Adorno, who coined the term 'culture industry',[10] some scholars argue that popular culture is only devised to pacify the masses and accommodate them to the needs of capital,[11] while others argue that popular culture products are made by the people for themselves and are a form of resistance.[12] Today, law and popular culture scholars consider that

2. A Chase, 'Toward a Legal Theory of Popular Culture' (1986) *Wisconsin Law Review* 527.
3. S Macaulay, 'Images of Law in Everyday Life: The Lessons of School, Entertainment, and Spectator Sports' (1987) 21:2 *Law and Society Review* 185–218. A revised version of the presidential address Macaulay gave at the annual Law and Society Association conference in Chicago in 1986.
4. L M Friedman, 'Law, Lawyers, and Popular Culture' (1989) 98:8 *Yale Law Journal* 1579–1606.
5. See for example (1988) 98 *Yale Law Journal,* Special Issue on Law and Popular Culture.
6. R K Sherwin, 'Introduction' (1996) 30 *University of San Francisco Law Review* 891 at 898, Symposium: Picturing Justice: Images of Law and Lawyers in the Visual Media.
7. For example, Shakespearean plays, Italian opera and film noir were all originally examples of popular culture that are now considered part of 'high' culture. '*Film noir* started as despised popular cinema and within thirty years had become art cinema.' (J Storey, *Cultural Theory and Popular Culture* (3rd edn, Pearson, 2001) 11).
8. T Edensor, *National Identity, Popular Culture and Everyday Life* (Berg, 2002) 12. A Sarat and T Kearns say: 'Cultural studies has radically extend[ed] what counts in the analysis of culture beyond the realm of "high culture". It invites study of the quotidian world [...] products of "popular culture" have been legitimised as objects of study' in 'The Cultural Lives of Law' in A Sarat and T R Kearns (eds), *Law in the Domains of Culture* (The University of Michigan Press, 1998) 4. See also R. Johnson and R. Buchanan, 'Getting the Insider's Story Out: What Popular Film Can Tell Us About Legal Method's Dirty Secrets' (2001) 20 *Windsor Yearbook of Access to Justice* 87, 110: "Law is undeniably caught up in this mythic, world-making aspect of our ongoing collective project of constructing social meaning, so it is impossible to claim or reclaim for it some place of rationality apart from or above the (pop-cultural) fray."
9. J Storey, *Cultural Theory and Popular Culture* (3rd edn, Pearson, 2001) 169: 'That is not to say that one cultural text or practice might not be "better" (for what/for whom, etc., must always be decided and made clear) than another cultural text or practice.'
10. M Horkheimer and T W Adorno, *Dialectic of Enlightenment* (Amsterdam, 1947).
11. T Edensor, *National Identity, Popular Culture and Everyday Life* (Berg, 2002) 13.
12. J Fiske, *Reading the Popular* (Unwin Hyman, 1989).

both are true. Most popular cultural texts support the interests of dominant groups, but popular culture is also a site for contestations of meaning. We agree on the significance of popular culture for society[13] and that it impacts public legal consciousness.[14] We also agree that studying popular culture requires diverse approaches.

Popular culture can be defined anthropologically as material culture, performatively as symbolic practices, ideologically as the profit-based product of media and cultural industries and politically as the ways in which cultural practices are bound up with power. Thus, strict disciplinary boundaries are rejected in favour of interdisciplinary connections. In 1998 Rosemary Coombe argued that '[t]he relationship between law and culture should not be defined'.[15] Instead, 'An ongoing and mutual rupturing – the undoing of one term by the other – may be a more productive figuration than the image of relationship or joinder'.[16] In 2001 MacNeil and Hutchings echoed the importance of culture,[17] and in 2001 Naomi Mezey discussed the importance of law as culture.[18] Rather than studying law and culture together or side by side, Mezey's use of 'as' instead of 'and' suggests a mutually constitutive relationship where law constitutes culture and culture constitutes law. This means that popular culture artefacts such as television shows actually help to create law and that law is highly influential in the creation of popular TV series.

In 2004 Michael Freeman edited *Law and Popular Culture*.[19] This was a true law and popular culture collection spanning children's literature, television, film, novels, shopping malls and music, stemming from an international interdisciplinary colloquium the previous year. In 2007 Bill MacNeil published *Lex Populi: The Jurisprudence of Popular Culture*, arguing that leading issues of legal philosophy are to be found in popular artifacts and products.[20] Both of these volumes included chapters on television, but television was not their primary focus. In the early law and popular culture work focusing on visual media, films were much more commonly studied than television. Films had an elite status that television lacked, and, of course, films are easier to examine because they are shorter. Much greater research time and effort is involved in examining years and years of episodes of a television series. Whether it was felt that films had more gravitas than television, or movies were simply easier to examine because they comprised a

13. P Robson, G Osborn and S Greenfield, 'The Impact of Film and Television on Perceptions of Law and Justice: Towards a Realisable Methodology' in A Wagner and R K Sherwin (eds), *Law, Culture and Visual Studies* (Springer, 2014) 1021.
14. Ibid at 1022.
15. R J Coombe, 'Contingent Articulations: A Critical Cultural Studies of Law' in A Saratand T R Kearns (eds), *Law in the Domains of Culture* (University of Michigan Press, 1998) 21.
16. Ibid at 21.
17. W MacNeil and P Hutchings, 'Law's Cultural Mediations: An Introduction by Way of Introduction' (2001) 10 *Griffith Law Review* 1, Special Issue: Law's Cultural Mediations.
18. N Mezey, 'Law as Culture' (2001) 13 *Yale Journal of Law and Humanities* 35, 36.
19. M Freeman (ed), *Law and Popular Culture* (Oxford University Press, 2004) .A good compilation of earlier articles can be found in (2001) 48 *UCLA Law Review* 1305 at 1326.
20. W P MacNeil, *Lex Populi: The Jurisprudence of Popular Culture* (Stanford University Press, 2007).

finite two hours, film took up enough space in law and popular culture that it became its own distinct field.

Law and film first developed in the UK and then in the USA. Canada and Australia followed later. Pioneers in the field include Stefan Machura and Peter Robson, who edited *Law and Film* in 2001.[21] Members of London's Birkbeck School, Moran, Loizidou, Christie and Sandon, edited *Law's Moving Image* in 2004.[22] In 2005 Americans Sarat, Douglas and Umphrey edited *Law on the Screen*.[23] However, neither the British scholars nor the American group included television as part of 'moving images' or 'the screen'. As was typical for the 1990s and early 2000s, their collections only dealt with film. However, since many people learn a lot 'of what they think they know about law and lawyers from consuming popular legal culture',[24] and more people watch TV than movies, it is also important to investigate law and television.

Television is one of our most important storytellers. It provides its millions of viewers with exposure to lawyers, courts and judges that influence their thoughts and understandings about law. Law and television was begun by Robert M. Jarvis, Paul R. Joseph, Elayne Rapping and Michael Asimow in the USA, Barbara Villez in France and Peter Robson in the UK. They realised that ignoring television was a serious omission if one wanted to take seriously the nexus between popular images of law and lawyers and our understanding of law. Jarvis and Joseph edited *Prime Time Law: Fictional Television as Legal Narrative* in 1998, a descriptive set of essays about American law shows.[25] Elayne Rapping published *Law and Justice: As Seen on TV* in 2003[26] and Peter Robson wrote 'Lawyers and the Legal System on TV: The British Experience' in 2006.[27] Michael Asimow edited *Lawyers in Your Living Room! Law on Television* in 2009.[28] This collection is written in an accessible style and features forewords by actors famous for playing lawyers on TV. In 2009 Barbara Villez wrote *Television and the Legal System*,[29] and in 2012, Peter Robson and Jessica Silbey edited *Law and Justice on the Small Screen*.[30] Robson and Silbey did so to offset the much greater focus that still remained on film in legal popular culture. In 2014 Asimow, Brown and Papke edited *Law and Popular Culture: International*

---

21. S Machura and P Robson (eds), *Law and Film* (Wiley-Blackwell, 2001).
22. L Moran, E Loizidou, I Christie and E Sandon (eds), *Law's Moving Image* (Routledge-Cavendish, 2004).
23. A Sarat, L Douglas and M Merrill Umphrey (eds), *Law on the Screen* (Stanford University Press, 2005).
24. M Asimow and S Mader, *Law and Popular Culture: A Course Book* (Peter Lang Publishing Inc., 2004) 7.
25. R Jarvis and P R Joseph (eds), *Prime Time Law: Fictional Television as Legal Narrative* (Carolina Academic Press, 1998).
26. E Rapping, *Law and Justice: As Seen on TV* (NYU Press, 2003).
27. P Robson, 'Lawyers and the Legal System on TV: The British Experience' (2006) 2(04) *International Journal of Law in Context* 333.
28. M I Asimow (ed), *Lawyers in Your Living Room! Law on Television* (American Bar Association Press, 2009).
29. B Villez, *Television and the Legal System* (Routledge, 2009).
30. P Robson and J Silbey (eds), *Law and Justice on the Small Screen* (Hart Publishing, 2012).

Perspectives.[31] This collection included television but was not exclusively focused on it. Peter Robson and I continued to build the law and television research area with our two edited collections: *A Transnational Study of Law and Justice on TV* in 2016[32] and *Ethnicity, Gender, and Diversity: Law and Justice on TV* in 2018.[33] Robson and I sought to broaden the canon of American and British television shows most often studied.[34] Therefore, the contributors to our two edited collections contemplated law and television in Australia, Belgium, Brazil, Canada, Denmark, France, Germany, Greece, Israel, Italy, Poland, Spain and Switzerland, in addition to the USA and the UK.

Methodology

The research area law and television is quite new, so methodology is not as developed as in other areas of study within law and humanities. Many law and film scholars, myself included, switched our foci to television, mostly without considering whether television was sufficiently different from film that different methodologies and approaches might be required. This is relevant because in the 1990s, television and film *were* different. People still went to movie theatres as an 'outing'. Cineplexes developed comfortable, reclining chairs and started offering bar service in their VIP or more expensive theatres. Viewers also often went to movie rental shops, slowly walking through the aisles of VHS tapes, and later DVDs, trying to choose something to watch for the evening, thereby making the choice of the weekend film an outing in itself. Film actors and directors were thought to be of higher calibre than television actors and directors. While some TV actors made it into films, film actors did not work in television, unless their filmic careers had ended. Another difference related to the phenomenon dubbed 'must-see TV'. These were very popular television shows that viewers deliberately made sure they were home to watch, because these shows could only be watched once a week, on the nights they aired.[35] Must-see TV shows were then discussed the next day at work with friends and colleagues. When the TV show was over, it was impossible to find it anywhere else to watch, unless one physically recorded it on a VHS tape. In contrast to 'must-see TV', other less popular television shows were often simply on in the

---

31. M Asimow, K Brown and D Ray Papke, *Law and Popular Culture: International Perspectives* (Cambridge Scholars Publishing, 2014).
32. P Robson and J L Schulz (eds), *A Transnational Study of Law and Justice on TV* (Hart Publishing, 2016).
33. P Robson and J L Schulz (eds), *Ethnicity, Gender, and Diversity: Law and Justice on TV* (Lexington Books, 2018).
34. Canonical legal TV shows in the USA include *Law and Order* and its many spin-offs, many of David E. Kelley's legal programs (e.g. *Ally McBeal, The Practice*, etc.), *LA Law, Suits,* and *Perry Mason*. In the UK, the list includes: *Justice, Rumpole of the Bailey, Kavanagh Q.C., Judge John Deed* and *Silk*.
35. See M Danesi, *Popular Culture: Introductory Perspectives* (4th edn, Roman and Littlefield, 2019) who argues at 258 that streaming and binge-watching have fractured "the communal audience effect',' making television less influential as an agent of change than it once was, when viewers watched shows together on the same night and discussed them the next day at work.

background, as an almost-ignored soundtrack to daily life. Despite these initial differences between television and film, scholarly work on television and law does not really differ from work on film and law. Law and film scholars simply added television to their repertoire, working on the assumption that one could transition between the two media seamlessly.

And for the most part, that has proven to be true, especially now, when differences between film and television are far less evident. Viewers go to movie theatres far less often and watch or stream almost anything they want, whenever they want, on their devices or TV screens.[36] Gone are the days when actors and directors only worked in one medium and film was thought to be superior to television. Now we record any shows or movies we like, we binge watch, and the scripts and quality of episodic programmes are at least as good as, and often better than, movies. Importantly, the prominence of streaming services such as Netflix, Prime, Crave, Hulu, HBO etc. means that viewers can watch high-quality episodic and filmic programming from the comfort of their own homes, often on very large TV screens, whenever they wish. This has truly blurred the distinction between film and television, so it is not clear that the two media require different methodologies. This brings me back to my initial point. Law and television may not be a field in its own right since it does not have its own methodology.

Law and film and law and television academics are legal scholars who engage with moving images in their work. They often do so without delineated interpretative frameworks or any discernible methodology.[37] Especially in the early days of law and film and law and television, it was common to draw conclusions from movie or TV show plot summaries, without much else, or to point out all the instances where legal shows 'got things wrong'. Legal scholars who engage with film or television commonly make pedagogical use of their show, movie or programme, discussing what law students can learn for future practice.[38] Or, they make ethical use of on-screen images,[39] telling readers not to practice law the way on-screen lawyers do, but they do not employ any particular method in so doing. When there is an articulated methodology in law and television scholarship, it is usually very similar to what one finds in law and film work. Law and film methodology such as Orit Kamir's[40] is easily transposed to analyses of television

36. https://news.gallup.com/poll/388538/movie-theater-attendance-far-below-historical-norms.aspx; https://www.nytimes.com/2021/11/29/business/movie-theater-attendance.html; https://tucollegian.org/movie-theaters-are-dying-slowly-but-surely/
37. P Robson, G Osborn and S Greenfield, 'The Impact of Film and Television on Perceptions of Law and Justice: Towards a Realisable Methodology' in A Wagner and R K Sherwin (eds), *Law, Culture and Visual Studies* (Springer, 2014). See St Machura, 'An Analysis Scheme for Law Films' (2007) 36(3) *University of Baltimore Law Review* 329 for an example of law and film method.
38. D Black, *Law in Film: Resonance and Representation* (University of Illinois Press, 1999) states at 110: "Importantly, a great deal of legal scholarship on film serves a pedagogical purpose."
39. For example, see C Menkel-Meadow, 'Is There an Honest Lawyer in the Box? Legal Ethics on TV' in MiAsimow (ed), *Lawyers in Your Living Room! Law on Television* (ABA Press, 2009) 37.
40. O Kamir, 'Why "Law-and-Film" and What Does It ctually Mean? A Perspective' (2005) 19:2 *Continuum* 255 and O Kamir, *Framed: Women in Law and Film* (Duke University Press, 2006).

and Laura Mulvey's famous 'male gaze' is investigated by legal scholars, no matter what visual media they are discussing.[41] One finds feminist[42] analyses of both film and TV, as well as postmodern[43] and critical race theory explorations.[44] Thus, it appears that the assumption that law and film methodologies work for television is true.

Both law and film and law and television research are guided by a shared spirit and shared interest in popular culture's visual media.[45] Both have an effect on law students' opinions about lawyers.[46] Theoretical engagements are hard to come by in both areas.[47] Critiques have also been made that both research areas pay insufficient attention to the specifically cinematic or televisual aspects of the particular popular culture text under analysis. Lighting and music affect mood, guide attention and highlight or change perspectives. Jessica Silbey notes that the camera can provide distance for objectivity, close-ups for intimacy and emotion, and zoom shots for pointed

41. H Wheatley, 'Visual Pleasure and Narrative Television' (2015) 15:5 *Feminist Media Studies*, 896- and H Wheatley, *Spectacular Television: Exploring Televisual Pleasure* (I.B. Tauris, 2016) especially chapters 6 and 7.
42. J L Schulz, 'The Cook, the Mediator, the Feminist, and the Hero' (2009) 21 *Canadian Journal of Women and the Law* 177; J D'Acci, 'Television, Representation and Gender' in R C Allen and A Hill (eds), *The Television Studies Reader* (Routledge, 2004) 373; C A Corcos, '"We Don't Want Advantages" – The Woman Lawyer Hero and Her Quest for Power in Popular Culture' (2003) 53 *Syracuse Law Review* 1225 at 1239; S Caplow, 'Still in the Dark: Disappointing Images of Women Lawyers in the Movies' (1999) 20 *Women's Rights Law Reporter* 55; D Klein, 'Ally McBeal and Her Sisters: A Quantitative and Qualitative Analysis of Representations of Women Lawyers on Prime-Time Television' (1998) 18 *Loyola of Los Angeles Entertainment Law Journal* 259; C A Corcos, 'Portia and Her Partners in Popular Culture: A Bibliography' (1998) 22 *Legal Studies Forum* 269; and many others by Orit Kamir, Cynthia Lucia, Margaret Russell and Carole Shapiro.
43. J E Thomas, 'Legal Culture and The Practice: A Postmodern Depiction of the Rule of Law' (2001) 48 *UCLA Law Review* 1495 at 1503; R K Sherwin, 'Nomos and Cinema' (2001) 48 *UCLA Law Review* 1519 at 1529; R K Sherwin, *When Law Goes Pop: The Vanishing Line between Law and Popular Culture* (The University of Chicago Press, 2000).
44. I Perry, 'Cultural Studies, Critical Race Theory and Some Reflections on Methods' (2005) 50 *Villanova Law Review* 915; H Gray, *Watching Race: Television and the Struggle for 'Blackness'* (University of Minnesota Press, 1995); M. Russell, 'Foreword: Law in Living Color' (1998) 5 *Asian Law Journal* 1; C Smith-Khan, 'African American Attorneys in Television and Film: Compounding Stereotypes' (1998) 22 *Legal Studies Forum* 119; and I Bennett Capers, 'Afrofuturism, Critical Race Theory, and Policing in the Year 2044' (2019) 94 *New York University Law Review* 1.
45. P N Meyer, 'Will you Please be Quiet, Please? Lawyers Listening to the Call of Stories' (1994) 18 *Vermont Law Review* 567, 579.
46. M Asimow, S Greenfield, G Jorge, S Machura, G Osborn, P Robson, C Sharp, R. Sockloskie, et al., 'Perceptions of Lawyers: A Transnational Study of Student Views on the Image of Law and Lawyers' (2005) 12 *International Journal of the Legal Profession* 407–436 at 429.
47. D Black, *Law in Film: Resonance and Representation* (University of Illinois Press, 1999): 'In other words, there is no integral or necessary engagement with film history or the nature of film, but there is a pedagogical agenda' (at 123). For recent excellent pedagogical approaches, see: C A Corcos (ed), *The Media Method: Teaching Law with Popular Culture* (Carolina Academic Press, 2019).

commentary.[48] However, only recently are we seeing law and television scholarship that deliberately engages with lighting, shot duration and extra-diegetic sound.[49]

Watching a movie or TV show is different from reading a book, so law and film and law and television should investigate how movies and shows provide different information than text alone. The richness of sound, mood and moving images creates a different experience and that should be reflected in the academic writing on the topic. Johnson and Buchanan note that 'law and film scholarship has not drawn on film theory in quite the same way that law and literature scholars have drawn on literary theory'.[50] David Black agrees: 'film theory is not tapped by legal scholarship anything like the way literary theory is.'[51] Because the two research areas share methodology, this is true of law and television scholarship as well. Legal scholars who write about TV often do so without rich underpinnings in television theory and research. However, this is not fatal to the research area of law and television. Law and television scholars do not have to engage in the use of televisual theory because they do not address law *as* television the way law and literature scholars address law *as* literature. The two distinct foci identified in law and literature scholarship, namely examining law as literature (examining law from a literary standpoint) and literature as law (examining literature legally), do not apply to law and television. This is because legal scholars who engage with television are not using television *as* law. They are using television shows to examine lawyers, judges, ethical infractions, diversity in the legal profession, faith in the rule of law, justice and many other interesting things,[52] but not television *as* law. Law and popular culture scholars, a subset of whom focus on television, use television as they would any popular culture artefact, as a text through which to better understand, analyse, critique or reimagine law. This means that the fact that legal scholarship on visual media does not equate to film or television studies is okay. Legal scholars who write about television are engaging in legal scholarship, not television studies scholarship. (As such, it is unlikely that television scholars reference law and television literature in their work.) Legal scholars are, as this volume suggests, engaging in the larger project of law and the humanities or law and culture. Law and television is but one research area under this larger umbrella and shares much, if not most, of its methodology and theoretical underpinnings with law and film. Thus, we may be less inclined to insist on a bright line distinction between law and film and law and television.

---

48. J Silbey, 'Patterns of Courtroom Justice' (2001) 28 *Journal of Law and Society* 97, 107.
49. R Johnson and R Buchanan, 'Getting the Insider's Story Out: What Popular Film Can Tell Us About Legal Method's Dirty Secrets' (2001) 20 *Windsor Yearbook of Access to Justice* 87, 100.
50. Ibid 94.
51. D Black, *Law in Film: Resonance and Representation* (University of Illinois Press, 1999) 130.
52. For e.g. see K K Ho, '*The Simpsons* and the Law: Revealing Truth and Justice to the Masses' (2003) 10:2 *UCLA Entertainment Law Review* 275.

Conclusion: The Future of Law and Television

The primary intellectual contribution of law and television has been to underscore the importance of TV for people's understandings about law. On the one hand, there are the misperceptions – when viewers learn incorrect things about law from television. For example, due to the prevalence of American television in Canada, many Canadians incorrectly think that Miranda rights, as depicted on US legal shows, are available in Canada.[53] This is in fact not the case; Canadian suspects do not have a right to consult a lawyer before being questioned.[54] Many Canadians also do not realise that our lawyers wear legal robes in court the way British lawyers do, as opposed to business suits as depicted on American TV, and address judges by honorifics such as 'my lord' instead of 'your honour'.[55] On the other hand, law and television scholarship is much more nuanced than merely pointing out legal inaccuracies on TV shows. Law and television scholarship has proven to be an important source of jurisprudence.

Television contributes to its country's jurisprudence, or philosophy of law. Writers in law and television have shown that TV is an ideological institution that exists in relationship to its country's legal system.[56] What is shown on our screens makes legal meanings for us.[57] TV has an extremely wide influence. Not only does it reach millions of people, it is a constant source of entertainment; think about how much time we all spent in front of our televisions during the pandemic. As such, the jurisprudence of television is crucially important. People's beliefs about law, formation of ideas of justice, stereotypes and values are acquired through the help of TV. Hegemonic ideas on gender, sexuality and race are reproduced, challenged and negotiated on television.[58] As such, TV is of great import when it comes to understanding people's views on law and popular jurisprudence. Quite simply, TV has power. Power is, however, a neglected area in the scholarship. Law and television researchers have not engaged with the topics of power and production as much as they will in the future. While we know that everything stops in the court room when the lawyer turns on the TV, we do not understand the power of that phenomenon as well as we should.

53. J L Schulz, *Mediation and Popular Culture* (Routledge, 2020) 8, referencing *Miranda v. Arizona* 384 US 436 (1966).
54. *R. v. Sinclair* [2010] 2 SCR 310; 2010 SCC 35. The Supreme Court of Canada recently reiterated *Sinclair* in *R v Dussault,* 2022 SCC 16 at para 33: "On this point, it is worth reiterating what the *Sinclair* majority made clear: Detainees do not have a right to obtain, and police do not have a duty to facilitate, the continuous assistance of counsel. Although other jurisdictions recognize a right to have counsel present throughout a police interview, that is not the law in Canada."
55. J L Schulz, *Mediation and Popular Culture* (Routledge, 2020) at 8.
56. J D'Acci, 'Television, Representation and Gender' in R C Allen and A Hill (eds), *The Television Studies Reader* (Routledge, 2004) 374.
57. J L Schulz (2021) 'What is Cultural Legal Studies?' 44(2) *Manitoba Law Journal* 143, 148.
58. P Robson and J L Schulz (eds), *Ethnicity, Gender and Diversity: Law and Justice on TV* (Lexington Books, 2018) 8.

Another difficulty for law and television scholars is a lack of empirical data,[59] though this is a shared problem for all of law and humanities scholarship. We simply do not ever know for sure what effect a particular TV show has on audiences' understandings or thoughts about law. This is further complicated by the prevalence of streaming services. There is now so much to watch (in addition to regular TV services) that we cannot get a grasp on all of it. Adding further difficulty is the fact that streaming services, unlike network television, do not typically provide their viewership numbers or ratings. This makes it next to impossible to make definitive statements about correlation or effects between television and law because we cannot actually be sure who is watching what.

Despite these difficulties, law and television scholarship will continue to cover a wide range of interesting topics, such as the phenomenon of daytime reality TV shows focused on judging,[60] how TV shows can make queer people feel more comfortable,[61] what depictions of vigilantism around the world mean to TV viewers,[62] and how alternatives to court, such as mediation, better manage client feelings and expectations than litigation.[63] Researchers have begun to move away from the typical canon of American and British television shows to include a wider sample of TV shows from other countries,[64] and this trend should continue. It will be more and more common to discuss how law and television interacts with gender, race, class, religion, ethnicity, sexual orientation,

59. Some law and television scholars have attempted to gather empirical data. See for e.g. K Podlas, 'Testing Television: Studying and Understanding the Impact of Television's Depictions of Law and Justice' in P Robson and J Silbey (eds), *Law and Justice on the Small Screen* (Hart Publishing, 2012) 87–110; and C Sharp, 'Let's See How Far We've Come: The Role of Empirical Methodology in Exploring Television Audiences' in P Robson and J Silbey (eds), *Law and Justice on the Small Screen* (Hart Publishing, 2012) 111–132. See also A Lam, 'Making "ad Apples" on *The Bridge*: A Production Study of the Making of a Police Drama' in Peter Robson and Jessica Silbey (eds), *Law and Justice on the Small Screen* (Hart Publishing, 2012) 63–86. P Robson, G Osborn and S Greenfield state that 'further extensive empirical work is vital for the health of the film and television scholarship in this field' in 'The Impact of Film and Television on Perceptions of Law and Justice: Towards a Realisable Methodology' in A Wagner and R K Sherwin (eds), *Law, Culture and Visual Studies* (Springer, 2014) 1025.

60. See N S Marder, 'Judging Judge Judy' in M l Asimow (ed), *Lawyers in Your Living Room! Law on Television* (American Bar Association Press, 2009) 299 and T Lovell Banks, 'Judging the Judges – Daytime Television's Integrated Reality Court Bench' in Mi Asimow (ed), *Lawyers in Your Living Room! Law on Television* (American Bar Association Press, 2009) 309.

61. C Carter, '"Thank You for Making Me Feel So Comfortable in Your Home": Baroness von Sketch Queering Up Canadian Television' in L Zisman Newman (ed), *Women and Popular Culture in Canada* (Women's Press, 2020) 117.

62. P Robson and F Spina (eds), *Vigilante Justice in Society and Popular Culture: A Global Perspective* (Fairleigh Dickinson University Press, 2022).

63. J L Schulz, *Mediation and Popular Culture* (Routledge, 2020) 9. American television shows that depict mediation include: *The Good Wife, Fairly Legal, The Office, Orange is the New Black* and *Star Trek: The Next Generation.*

64. See analyses of Australian, Belgian, Canadian, Danish, French, German, Greek, Israeli, Italian, Polish, Spanish and Swiss TV in P Robson and J L Schulz (eds), *A Transnational Study of Law & Justice on TV* (Hart Publishing, 2016).

age and disability.[65] In the future, more legal writers should investigate how TV might help improve circumstances for women,[66] Indigenous peoples[67] and other marginalised groups, and how the pleasure, emotions and care depicted on TV are of vital importance to law.[68] Law and television is not its own research field because it lacks distinct methodologies and analyses, and it is not central to either legal academia or to legal practice. However, television shows that millions of people watch have impact and that is why legal scholars and humanities scholars will continue to study them. Law and television is, and always will be, a crucial, if not the most important, part of law and popular culture.

65. P Robson and J L Schulz (eds), *Ethnicity, Gender, and Diversity: Law and Justice on TV* (Lexington Books, 2018).
66. K Buczynski-Lee, 'Woman as Cabbage to Women as Prime Ministers and Presidents: Demanding Women's Rightful Space in the Film and Television Industry' in J A Scutt, *Women, Law and Culture: Conformity, Contradiction and Conflict* (Palgrave Macmillan, 2016) 109.
67. R Johnson, 'Intercultural Cinema and the (Re)Envisioning of Law: Exploring Life, Death and Law in *Atanarjuat* and *Before Tomorrow*' in T D Peters and K Crawley (eds), *Envisioning Legality: Law, Culture and Representation* (Routledge, 2018) 228.
68. R Johnson, 'Television, Pleasure and the Empire of Force: Interrogating Law and Affect in *Deadwood*' in P Robson and J Silbey (eds), *Law and Justice on the Small Screen* (Hart Publishing, 2012) 33 and J L Schulz, 'What is Cultural Legal Studies?' (2021) 44(2) *Manitoba Law Journal* 143, 150.

Chapter Twelve

LAW AND THEATRE

Barbara Hughes-Moore

Prologue, 'All the world's a stage [...]'[1]

A figure steps onto a stage.

Silence falls as she looks into the audience. And then she begins to speak. The words are ornate and she delivers them like prophecy. A story unfurls: of broken dreams and bad decisions, of rights and wrongs. The speaker will be judged; lives will be changed.

This is a scene which lawyer and thespian alike have played a thousand times or more. Indeed, the resemblances between law and theatre often start here: with a single orator skillfully putting their case before an audience. Like an actor, a lawyer must interpret a central text and use it to tell a convincing story.

In each discipline, language is king. Without language, how would we articulate our individual and collective rights? How would we codify norms and behaviours? In literature, the power of language predates the written word: long before we could write, we could recite. We would gather around a fire to recount tales we'd heard a thousand times, and fashion new ones besides. Language is primal: it takes us back to who we were before.

But even the finest words can fall flat. Law and theatre require an orator: more than that, they require a *conjuror* who can bring the words to life. This is the intervention which separates theatre from literature: a live, transforming presence. A *performance*. There is a magic to this space: things emerge from it differently to how they entered. Things may happen twice but they do not happen the same. It's not a paradox: it's show business.

Enough of the abstract, for now. We will return to it in due course. Instead, let's go back to the beginning.

Act One, 'And all the men and women merely players'[2]

Theatre's purpose, says Hamlet, is 'to hold [...] the mirror up to nature'.[3]

It can also show the law its true face. That, at least, seems to be a central tenet of law and theatre, which reframes legal actors as stage players and doctrinal issues as

1. W Shakespeare, *As You Like It* (1623), Act 2 Scene 7.
2. Ibid.
3. W Shakespeare, *Hamlet*, Act 3 Scene 2.

dramatic devices: the case its plot, the courtroom its stage. Law and legal matters have formed the two hour's traffic of many a stage, from *Oedipus Rex* to *Othello* and beyond. The courtroom itself is a theatrical space,[4] in which costumed lawyers wear wigs and billowing robes, take their assigned places and address an 'audience' of jurors. Law and theatre lays bare the common tongue of both disciplines: performance, textual interpretation, narrative storytelling. A lawyer will craft their case with a playwright's tools at their disposal: empathy, imagery, metaphor and symbolism.

While law and theatre does not straightforwardly mimic the law in/as literature dichotomy, which has now fallen somewhat out of favour,[5] its work can be broadly categorised in a similar way. Let's attend to each in turn.

Law in Theatre

This involves examining portrayals of law and legal concepts in theatrical works, for example, the depiction of ownership and property law in August Wilson's *The Piano Lesson*. Law provides a strong narrative for drama, and gives structure, urgency, context.[6] Plays like *Anatomy of a Murder* (1958) and *Witness for the Prosecution* (1953) exploit the dramatic conventions of the courtroom dynamic. Theatre can also be used to historicise the role of law, legal tradition and custom, such as the misogyny of the Salem witch trials as illustrated by Arthur Miller's *The Crucible* (1953), and to expose the subtextual and superficial meanings of legal rhetoric.[7]

Law as Theatre

This highlights the theatrical devices, conventions and techniques that legal practitioners and writers use, and engages with legal writings as a literary critic might a novel. Legal 'actors' occupy certain roles (Prosecution, Defence, Judge) and have certain lines of dialogue ('my learned friend [...]') This might involve examining rhetoric, dialogue, textual interpretation, performance and costuming, and evaluating legal trials as 'performances' of justice. The show trial is a classic example: the public trial of a defendant whose fate has already been decided, and making citizens 'complicit' in the retributive actions of the state.[8]

---

4. A Read, *Theatre and Law* (Bloosmbury, 2015), 19.
5. See, for example, J Gaakeer, 'The Future of Literary-Legal Jurisprudence: Mere Theory or Just Practice?' (2011) 5 *Law and Humanities* 185.
6. A Read, *Theatre and Law* (Bloosmbury, 2015), 9.
7. P Raffield, *The Art of Law in Shakespeare* (Bloomsbury, 2017); D Dunne, *Shakespeare, Revenge Tragedy and Early Modern Law: Vindictive Justice* (Palgrave Macmillan, 2016).
8. For example, Nuremberg Trials; Rwanda's Gacaca Courts. See A K Allo, 'The "Show" in the Show Trial: Contextualising the Politicisation of the Courtroom' (2010) 15 *Barry Law Review* 1, 41; M Arjomand, *Staged: Show Trials, Political Theater, and the Aesthetics of Judgment* (Columbia University Press, 2018).

The connections between law and theatre, however, blur these distinctions. Let's start with medium. In an orthodox sense, theatre is the product of a play, written by a playwright and performed by an actor. But theatre as principle and practice is more elusive. It resides in the live nerve of interaction, improvisation and interpretation. There may or may not be a script to follow. When brought to life by actors on a stage, the text (if there is one) shifts and changes. There is something transformative in this process: a transfiguring magic that animates the text.

Film achieves this through adaptation – but theatre is a live medium; it is ephemeral. Law, too, while choreographed, can be spontaneous. The interface of reality and fiction in a trial is messy and complex. Testimony might be true or false or somewhere in between; each juror might have a different take on the truth. A witness might break on the stand or a key piece of evidence be thrown out of court, though neither as frequently as *Law and Order* might have you believe. Narratives like this might give a false idea of the law's capacity for closure: a legal case might be solved within the span of a 45-minute episode – in reality, it could take months, or years, or not at all.

But what precisely do we mean by 'theatre'? Does it consist of plays, or also operas, musicals? Commedia dell'arte, improvisation or dance? Must there be a script, or a stage, or neither? And can theatre exist in a digital space? During the Covid-19 lockdowns, theatres closed their doors; if they kept operating at all, it was in the digital space. So when we dissect theatre into its component parts, we find very little that all 'theatrical' works have in common. In the humanities, mediums are slippery. Take, for example, classic courtroom drama *12 Angry Men*. The script was written for television, then adapted into the Oscar-nominated 1957 film starring Henry Fonda, and then premiered on Broadway. Is it a work of law and theatre, law and film, law and television, or law and literature – or all of the above? Does that distinction matter?

Naturally, legal processes are not always as transparent as artistic ones. But the courtroom trial is a public animal, and indeed that is where it harnesses its ritual power.[9] It is 'a dramatic thing put to legal use', as Richard Harbinger posits.[10] The legal trial must be performative, because it relies on recounting events that happened in the past: a contract that was signed, a murder that was committed. We can understand this, as they do in theatre, through the lens of phantasia: of recounting past events in a narrative form. Theatre, too, can add in the mimetic element which law lacks, that is, by re-enacting the events, so we see them with our own eyes.[11]

Theatre, too, can present ambiguity where the law cannot. Eliza's gasp at the end of the musical *Hamilton* might signal a dozen different things to a dozen different theatregoers. Is she glimpsing her husband's future? Has the fourth wall broken, and the audience finally come into view? Or is she merely taking her last breath? The actor's intention

9. P S Berman, 'Rats, Pigs, and Statues on Trial: The Creation of Cultural Narratives in the Prosecution of Animals and Inanimate Objects' (1994) 69 *New York University Law Review* 288.
10. R Harbinger, 'Trial by Drama' (1971) 55 *Judicature* 122. See also D Brion, 'The Criminal Trial as Theater: The Semiotic Power of the Image' inA Wagner and R K Sherwin (eds), *Law, Culture and Visual Studies* (Springer,2013), 329–359.
11. Ibid.

and the audience's interpretation might change with every performance. When Stanley Fish argues that 'interpretation is not the art of construing but the art of construction. Interpreters do not decode poems; they make them',[12] then the audience is as pivotal to 'creating' a play as the actors.

This complicity in the creative process is particularly apparent in plays with legal themes. Indeed, theatrical productions often use law to heighten and exploit the audience's emotions in ways that do not necessarily reflect the often staid proceedings of a formal trial scenario. Take, for example, David Mamet's controversial two-hander *Oleanna* (1992), in which a college student accuses her university professor of harassment. Its unsettling tagline warned its audience: 'Whichever side you take, you're wrong.' Likewise, in Suzie Miller's *Prime Facie* (2019), which follows a criminal defense barrister questioning her vocation after she is sexually assaulted, the main character speaks directly to the audience. One in three women will be assaulted in their lifetime, she tells us: 'Look to your left, look to your right: it's one of us.'

Drama can enable us to process these experiences, emotions, and to grapple with complex information in ways that law is not always equipped to do.[13] The connection between theatre and law is primal: it takes us back to tales around a campfire. Long before we fashioned our laws, we obeyed the law of narrative. The power of language which binds law and theatre together at the root. It is precisely to those roots to which I turn now.

Act Two: 'They have their exits and their entrances'[14]

In the beginning, there was the Word, and the word was Thespis.

He was the first actor in the Western world. The first 'thespian' and also the first 'hypocrite': from the Greek 'hupokrites', meaning 'mask-wearer', after the exaggerated *personae* donned in Athenian theatre. To act is to mask oneself in truth. To be or not to be? In theatre, the answer is both. While law and theatre remains a relatively spritely discipline, the connections between the two go back a long way. Ethical, moral and legal issues were explored in ancient Greek tragedies, comedies and 'satyr plays' (a combination of the two) as far back as 700 BC, often as tributes to Dionysus.[15] Thespis would have performed at the Dionysia. The ancient Athenian would attend the theatre as both a source of entertainment and as an act of citizenship, earning a day's wages for the privilege. As such, the theatre was a space in which the citizen could come to better understand herself and her community.[16]

12. S Fish, *Is There a Text in This Class?* (Harvard University Press, 1980), 326–327.
13. V Turner, *From Ritual to Theatre. The Human Seriousness of Play* (PAJ Publications, 1982), 110, 93, 12.
14. W Shakespeare, *As You Like It* (1623), Act 2 Scene 7.
15. S Goldhill, 'The Great Dionysia and Civic Ideology' (1987) 107 *The Journal of Hellenic Studies* 58–76.
16. L Winner, 'Democratic Acts: Theatre of Public Trials' (2005) 15 *Theatre Topics* 2, 149–169, 152.

These performances formed part of a broader social culture of 'theatricality' which seeped into the religious rituals, festivals and courtrooms of Athens. Plays such as Aeschylus' *The Oresteia* and Euripedes' *Medea* put their characters on trial, literally and metaphysically. Sophocles' *Antigone* interrogates the dichotomies of natural and divine law, of written and unwritten codes, of citizen and state;[17] *Oedipus the King* deploys its chorus as jury. Proto-satirist Aristophanes used *The Wasps* and *The Knights* to couch biting commentary within broad comedy. The glimpses afforded into the thoughts, motives and justifications of fictional characters doubtless informed citizens who were selected for court service, with individual *dikastes* (the Athenian equivalent of modern-day judges or jurors) often called to decide on dozens of cases throughout their lifetimes.[18]

Actors in ancient Rome, however, lacked any such status. Augustus' *leges Juliae* (18–17 BC) classified actors and sex workers as *infames* and excluded them from having equal rights.[19] Acting troupes that toured Europe following the dissolution of the Roman Empire were distrusted by the Catholic Church until the Middle Ages, when the advent of 'liturgical theatre' (the acting out of parables and Bible stories) nudged the profession towards social tolerance. It was only a nudge: acting remained disreputable even through the theatrical Renaissance of the Elizabethan period and the works of William Shakespeare, one of the mainstays of the Western literary canon (and therefore of law and literature, too). Shakespeare's plays, performed for and concerning royalty, received a modicum of legitimacy by James I, who gave his players the moniker 'The King's Men'.

Shakespeare showed a remarkable legal acuity in his work, from the trial scenes of *The Merchant of Venice* and *Measure for Measure* to the legal punnery of *As You Like It* and *Hamlet*. Whether he was trained in law remains unknown,[20] though one might speculate whether it explains his infamous dictum: 'Let's kill all the lawyers'.[21] His most famous fictional lawyer arrived several hundred years before women could practice law: Portia dresses herself as a 'doctor of laws' to prevent Shylock extracting the infamous pound of flesh from her fiancée's friend. Portia might claim that 'the quality of mercy is not strained' but Shakespeare seems to show little to the Jewish moneylender, whose portrayal has been interpreted as sympathetic to antisemitic to everything in between.

By the time Shakespeare arrived on the scene, Western theatre had detached from notions of citizenship, though the Athenian tradition of stimulating ethical debate survived in the form of the 'morality play', an allegorical drama with a moral (Christian)

---

17. J Fletcher, 'Citing the Law in Sophocles's Antigone' (2008) 41 *Mosaic: An Interdisciplinary Critical Journal* 79.
18. E M Harris, D F Leão and P J Rhodes (eds), *Law and Drama in Ancient Greece* (Bloomsbury, 2010), 1.
19. C Edwards, 'Unspeakable Professions: Public Performance and Prostitution in Ancient Rome' in J P Hallett and M B Skinner (eds), *Roman Sexualities* (Princeton University Press, 1997), 66–95.
20. D J Kornstein, 'Shakespeare the Unacknowledged Legislator' (1994) 66 *New York State Bar Journal* 50.
21. W Shakespeare, *Henry VI, Part 2*, Act IV.

lesson to teach. Its central character was usually an ordinary, flawed individual typified by the title character of *Everyman* (1530), the mirror image of the morally upstanding 'reasonable man' against whom defendants are still judged in criminal trials today.[22] Other morality plays took its characters in the other direction, as in Christopher Marlowe's *Doctor Faustus* (1592). Justice was often personified as a divine entity in these plays – see, for example, *The Castle of Perseverance* (1405–25) – but by 1553's *Respublica*, Justice had taken on many of the qualities of a secular Judge.[23] Legal realism, seemingly, was beginning to seep into the theatre.

As the Age of Enlightenment dawned, the theatre's judgement looked outward, at authority. Theatres had been closed by Cromwell in 1642, and reopened under Charles II, with the biting satire of Ben Jonson and John Webster, and increasingly extravagant sets and costumes. Music halls, operas[24] and melodramas[25] reached their peak in the Victorian era, with the dawn of 'modern' drama heralded by playwrights Henrik Ibsen and Anton Chekhov, and taken up into the next century by Bertolt Brecht and Konstantin Stanislavski.[26] Prestige had at last come to the profession – but at a price.[27] Oscar Wilde, the prolific playwright behind *Lady Audley's Secret* and *The Importance of Being Earnest*, became one of the most prominent turn-of-the-century 'celebrities'. He also became one of its most tragic pariahs when his own plays and writings (including his only novel, *The Picture of Dorian Gray*) were used to convict him under the brazenly homophobic Criminal Law Amendment Act of 1885.[28] The repression of one's sexuality and their 'unconscious' self was a key feature of Sigmund Freud, the father of psychoanalysis, and its founding text *The Interpretation of Dreams* (1899).

It was at this time that the search for meaning went inward once more.

---

22. See also 'the man on the Clapham omnibus' in *McQuire v Western Morning News* [1903] 2 K.B. 100 at 109 per Collins MR.
23. J W McCutchan, 'Justice and Equity in the English Morality Play' (1958) 19(3) *Journal of the History of Ideas* 40.
24. Including Gilbert and Sullivan comic operas like *The Yeoman of the Guard* (1888).
25. E.g., J Rosseau, *Pygmalion* (1770).
26. See R Brustein, *The Theatre of Revolt: Studies in Modern Drama from Ibsen to Genet* (Little Brown, 1964). Turn-of-the-century playwright George Bernard Shaw said in his preface to his 1905 play *Major Barbara*: 'I am, and have always been, and shall now always be, a revolutionary writer, because our laws make law impossible; our liberties destroy all freedom; our property is organized robbery; our morality is an impudent hypocrisy; our wisdom is administered by inexperienced or malexperienced dupes, our power wielded by cowards and weaklings, and our honor false in all its points.' See G B Shaw, *Complete Plays with Prefaces*, 6 vols (Dodd, Mead, 1962), 336.
27. D B Wilmeth and C W E Bigsby, *The Cambridge History of American Theatre* (Cambridge University Press, 1998), 449–450.
28. The Criminal Law Amendment Act 1885 criminalised sex acts between men in England and Wales; sex acts between women were not criminalised.

Act Three: 'And one man in his time plays many parts'

In 1917, Victor Shklovsky, Russian literary critic and futurist, published an essay entitled *Art as Technique.*[29] In it, he argued that art functions to make the familiar 'unfamiliar'. Art must be felt, not learned; understanding comes from feeling.

The theatre, too, prioritises sensation over perception. It is all part of the trick: the unique blending of the real and the unreal that occurs upon a stage. There is a peculiar decorum to the play of the theatre: If we watch a tragedy unfurl before our eyes, are we not complicit if we fail to step in? Or would that break the unwritten code, and split the thin veil between the worlds of the play and of our own? As Jiří Veltruský observes, theatre can destabilise the 'real' relations between humans and objects, making an object seem animated and a human seem lifeless.[30] Defamiliarising the familiar with such theatrical techniques may leave us in an uncanny valley. But it may also reveal a deeper truth.

This search for meaning led to the development of semiotics, through the work of Ferdinand de Sassure and Charles Sanders Peirce. As a study of signs and processes, semiotics was well suited to explore the linguistic intricacies of theatre and law, including analogy, metaphor and symbolism. In the 1930s and 1940s a group of theoreticians in Czechoslovakia collectively known as 'the Prague School' developed a theory of semiotics which conceptualised theatre as a producer of meaning[31] a system which could be analysed by examining a play's component parts such as use of language and tone, stage design, costume and spatial relations between actors and between actors and audience.[32] Along with elements of structuralism, this theory seems to have percolated through Anglo-American scholarship during the 1950s and 1960s, with writers like Harold Garfinkel, Robert M. Emerson and Abraham Blumberg using theatrical imagery to interrogate courtroom dynamics.[33] This was also an era which saw the publication of Erving Goffman's *The Presentation of Self in Everyday Life* (1959), a sociological study of human interaction using the language of theatre.

These images of law were repurposed in the 1970s by theorists like Pat Carlen and Douglas Hay, who characterised the courtroom as a quasi-theatrical, heavy 'symbolic'

29. Also translated as 'Art as Device'. See V Shklovsky, *Theory of Prose.* Translated by Benjamin Sher (Dalkey Archive Press, 1990), 6.
30. Jiri Veltrusky, 'Man and Object in Theatre' (1940) in P L Garvin (ed), *A Prague School Reader: Esthetics, Literary Structure, and Style* (Georgetown University Press, 1964).
31. See, for example, one of the founding texts of the Prague School: O Zich, *Estetikadramatickéhoumění/Esthetics of Dramatic Art* (Melantrich, 1931).
32. L Kleberg, *Theatre as Action: Soviet Russian Avant-Garde Aesthetic* (MacMillan, 1993), 40–41; see, for example, K Brušák, *Znakynačínskémdivadle/Signs in Chinese Theatre* (Slovo a slovesnost V, 1939), 91–98.
33. R M Emerson, *Judging Delinquents* (Chicago: Aldine, 1967); H Garfinkel, 'Conditions of Successful Degradation Ceremonies' (1956) 61(5) *American Journal of Sociology* 420; A Blumberg, *The Practice of Law as a Confidence Law and Society Review* (1967). Referenced in P Carlen, 'The Staging of Magistrates' Justice' (1975) 16 *British Journal of Criminology* 1, 48–55.

space designed to reinforce the hierarchy and authority of law.[34] Its architecture is built to isolate and intimidate. In the same decade, Brazilian theatre practitioner Augusto Boal reorients the citizen in law through an innovative arts-based pedagogy called the 'Theatre of the Oppressed': a type of interactive Forum Theatre in which actors stage a short play around a social issue and audience members (renamed 'spect-actors') intervene, critique and suggest solutions that can lead to a change in the law.[35] It brings citizenship back into the theatrical space in the biggest way since ancient Athens.

It was in the 1970s that law and literature emerged, as an offshoot of the US-based Critical Legal Studies movement which sought to critique the political, social and moral impact of law rather than simply teaching law as a set of rules. Spurred by Left-leaning American academics like Duncan Kennedy, and drawing on the work of Paolo Freire,[36] Critical Legal Studies aimed to challenge law's purported 'ideological neutrality' and demystify legal processes by pointing out unspoken biases, ambiguities and assumptions.[37] From forth these fatal loins sprung a slew of postmodern legal movements, including Critical Race Theory, feminist theory, Queer Theory and law and literature.

Law and theatre, like many 'law and's before it, emerged around 50 years ago with the publication of James Boyd White's *The Legal Imagination*, the catalyst and cornerstone of the formalised law and literature movement.[38] In it, White challenged orthodox interpretations of law as mere policy and politics, and claimed instead that law functions as a language which can be learned and mastered: 'The law makes a world. It is our task to acquire the art of reading and speaking the language of that world.'[39]

White's initial design was largely didactic: teach law students to write well through absorbing the skills, techniques and critical distance of literary critics, that is, through a process of literary osmosis. For the first few decades, the law and literature movement followed a similar pattern: gathering literary works as sources of legal analysis and critique. Theatre was here to begin with and provided the movement with some of its key foundational texts. Ask a non-lawyer to name a great legal play, and most will answer *The Merchant of Venice*. In law and theatre studies, ubiquitousness is an asset: it provides a touchstone from which (mostly) anyone can draw.

Law and theatre, however, did not emerge as a distinct entity for some time, or perhaps was simply not acknowledged as such. Since the formal inception of the movement, theatre has largely been subsumed within the monolith that is 'literature'. Law and

34. M S Ball, 'The Play's the Thing: An Unscientific Reflection on Courts Under the Rubric of Theater' (1975) 28(1) *Stanford Law Review* 81.
35. A Boal, *Theater of the Oppressed* (Theatre Communications Group, 1993), 132–133.
36. P Freire, *Pedagogy of the Oppressed* (Bloomsbury, 1970).
37. D Kennedy and K E Klare, 'A Bibliography of Critical Legal Studies' (1984) 94 *Yale Law Journal* 461.
38. J Boyd White, *The Legal Imagination: Studies in the Nature of Legal Thought and Expression, 45th Anniversary Edition* (Walters Kluwer, 1973/2018), xxii. Others trace it to Benjamin Cardozo's 1925 essay Law and Literature: B N Cardozo, 'Law and Literature' (1925) 14 *Yale Law Review* 699.
39. J Boyd White, *The Legal Imagination: Studies in the Nature of Legal Thought and Expression, 45th Anniversary Edition* (Walters Kluwer, 1973/ 2018).

literature was shaped by scholars based in the Anglo-American legal tradition, primarily in US Law Schools, who selected their foundational texts from the Western literary canon. In those first formative decades, core texts were sourced from the usual suspects: Shakespeare, Dickens, Kafka, Dostoyevsky. It was on their works, the 'Great Books' of mainstream literature, that Richard Weisberg built his theory of poethics[40] and Martha Nussbaum her concept of poetic justice.[41]

From there, literature became deployed as method and material in the lawyer's 'empathy' toolkit, a seeming extension of Wigmore's list of novels for lawyers:[42] read Dickens, to become considerate of your clients; read Kafka, to witness the absurdity of legal process. In these first tentative years, such works were seen to have a 'humanising' effect on law. Like a romance novel, literature was characterised as the eloquent, 'feminising' partner that could 'reform' the aggressive, 'masculine' law – but, as Greta Olson argues, this not only forces heteronormative, gendered roles on the discipline but fundamentally mischaracterises its radical capacity to critique and challenge exactly those kinds of binary divisions.[43]

Indeed, as previously discussed, law and theatre usually sidesteps the usual law in/as dichotomy. Instead, law and theatre is characterised more by discrete investigations of particular legal matters, using texts which still draw mostly from the Western literary well: assessing the law of binding contracts in *Doctor Faustus*,[44] using *Measure for Measure* to contextualise the history of nuptial agreements,[45] and illuminating common elements of tragedy in Sophocles' Theban plays and the House of Lords' judgement in *R v Dudley and Stephens*.[46]

These analyses tend to focus on well-known texts, drawing new insights in law using literature as a source of enquiry. I noted earlier that ubiquitousness is an asset to law and humanities-based work. Canonicity is king. It is also a limitation, because both literature and law have a history of privileging some voices and marginalising others, and of relying on certain authors almost to the point of obligation. This hierarchical thinking runs counter to the radical potential of theatre specifically, and the humanities more generally. Bringing theatre into law can provide critical distance – but not if it has become stuck in the same pitfalls: relying on a nostalgic, white-privileging Western canon with one foot in the past. Indeed, literature was deployed in rather narrow ways

40. R Weisberg, *Poethics and Other Strategies of Law and Literature* (Columbia University Press, 1992).
41. M C Nussbaum, *Poetic Justice: The Literary Imagination and Public Life* (Beacon Press, 1995).
42. R West, 'Submission, Choice, and Ethics: A Rejoinder to Judge Posner' (1986) 99 *Harvard Law Review* 1449–1456.
43. G Olson, 'Law is not Turgid and Literature not Soft and Fleshy: Gendering and Heteronormativity in Law and Literature Scholarship' (2012) 36 *Australian Feminist Law Journal* 1, 65–86.
44. D B Yeager, 'Marlowe's Faustus: Contract as Metaphor?' (1995) 2 *University of Chicago Roundtable* 599.
45. M Scott, '"Our City's Institutions": Some Further Reflections on the Marriage Contracts in Measure for Measure' (1982) 49 *ELH* 790.
46. I R Wall, 'Duress, International Criminal Law and Literature' (2006) 4 *Journal of International Criminal Justice* 724; R v Dudley and Stephens (1884) 14 QBD 273.

in the early days of the discipline. By venerating the same texts as the Western the literary canon, law and theatre (like its sister-disciplines) has a tendency to mimic it and its defects.[47]

Law and literature is not an inherently reductionist endeavour: by definition, it works to broaden out its sources into other realms, to mix genres, to borrow bits and pieces from other fields in a Frankenstinian feat of creativity. The emergence of 'law and performance' studies in the 1980s and 1990s, largely spearheaded by Jack Balkin and Sanford Levinson, shifted law and theatre back into the spotlight. 'Law, like music or drama, is best understood as performance', they argued: 'the acting out of texts rather than the texts themselves'.[48] Justice, after all, must be seen to be done. In pure Boyd White tradition, this was a law which lived and died on rhetoric. Law, too, was treading the boards again as a slew of early 2000s Broadway and West End revivals of classic legal plays in the 2000s instigated fresh conversations on law and performance: *Inherit the Wind, 12 Angry Men,* and *Witness for the Prosecution.* The old guard, marching again – but sometimes to move forward, you have to first go back.[49]

And it seemed to herald a sea change in the discipline as it moved across the Atlantic with UK-based law and theatre scholars like Ian Ward,[50] Paul Raffield and Gary Watt,[51] and Kate Leader[52] taking up the baton. Despite a few special issues here and there,[53] law and theatre did not coalesce into anything substantial for quite some time.[54] Books had previously been published on law and theatre scholarship, such as *Shakespeare and Law* (2008) and *Shakespeare's Imaginary Constitution* (2010).[55] But these, again, were discrete topics: they spoke to law and theatre generally, but through the lens of specificity (in both cases, Shakespeare). Journals like *Law and Humanities, Law and Popular Culture* and *Adaptation* provide specialist spaces for law and theatre scholarship, while some works occasionally find their way into orthodox legal or literary spaces, for example, in the form of special issues or individual pieces.[56] It was not until 2015 that the first comprehensive account of this interrelationship was released, in theatre practitioner Alan

---

47. J Resnik, 'Constructing the Canon' (1990) 2 *Yale Journal of Law and the Humanities* 221.
48. J Balkin and S Levinson, '"Law as Performance": Law, Music, and Other Performing Arts' (1991) 139 *University of Pennsylvania Law Review* 1597.
49. M Luther King Jr, Second Baptist Church in Detroit, Michigan February 28, 1954.
50. I Ward, *Law and Literature* (Cambridge University Press, 1995).
51. P Raffield and G Watt, *Shakespeare and Law* (Hart, 2008).
52. K Leader, 'Bound and Gagged: The Performance of Tradition in the Adversarial Criminal Jury Trial' (2007) *Philament* 11.
53. S Neild and M Leiboff (eds), 'Special Issue: Law's Theatrical Presence' (2010) 14 *Law, Text, Culture* 1–3.
54. J S Peters, 'Legal Performance Good and Bad' (2008) 4 *Law, Culture and the Humanities* 181; See J S Peters, *Law As Performance: Theatricality, Spectatorship, and the Making of Law in Ancient, Medieval, and Early Modern Europe* (Oxford University Press, 2022).
55. P Raffield and G Watt, *Shakespeare and Law* (Hart, 2008); P Raffield, *Shakespeare's Imaginary Constitution: Late-Elizabethan Politics and the Theatre of Law* (Hart, 2010).
56. See 'Law's Metaphors: Interrogation Languages of Law, Justice, and Legitimacy' (2016) 43 *Journal of Law and Society* 1.

Read's *Theatre and Law.*[57] The first overt law and theatre texts to examine this from a legal perspective are a 2018 collection on *Law and Performance*,[58] and lawyer-actor Marett Leiboff's *Towards a Theatrical Jurisprudence* in 2019.[59]

The latter is the first academic book to suggest the value of theatrical practice to law. Leiboff argues for a re-centring of the 'person' within law, through deploying theatre to reacquaint ourselves with the fleshy, bodily aspects that law often shirks. Colin Dayan talks about how the law 'consumes' people, dividing them into recipients of prejudice and recipients of privilege;[60] perhaps theatre can help us monitor this process. And (re) centring the person in law is something which theatre is uniquely equipped to do, from *The Last Days of Judas Iscariot* (2005), in which a purgatorial court battles for the immortal soul of history's most infamous traitor, to *Arguendo* (2013) in which the cast performs legal case *Barnes v Glen Theatre* (1991) verbatim.[61]

While analysis of methodologies of law and theatre remain scarce,[62] the field is undergoing something of a latter-day renaissance. Following Leiboff and Read, a wave of new theories and academic works, like Danish Sheikh's theatrical response to Section 377 litigation in India,[63] to Ian Ward's examination of law in contemporary British drama.[64] Sheikh built on this work by co-developing a year-long course 'Legal Theatre', which deployed theatre as a lens for examining gender and sexuality law, developing a legal pedagogy informed by theatrical techniques and queer theory.[65] Peter Goodrich meanwhile is at the forefront of what he terms 'jurisliterature', which examines how jurists write, persuade and mix textual styles and genres across cultures and traditions.[66] Law and literature courses are present in, though do not yet proliferate, UK and northern European Law Schools – not, at least, to the extent that they feature in American legal education.[67]

57. A Read, *Theatre and Law* (Bloomsbury, 2015).
58. A Sarat, L Douglas and M M Umphrey (eds), *Law and Performance* (University of Massachusetts Press, 2018).
59. M Leiboff, *Towards a Theatrical Jurisprudence* (Routledge, 2019).
60. C Dayan, *The Law as a White Dog: How Legal Rituals Make and Unmake Persons* (Princeton University Press, 2011).
61. *Arguendo* by Elevator Repair Service (2013), performed at New York's Public Theatre; *Barnes v. Glen Theatre*, Inc., 501 U.S. 560 (1991). This recalls the twentieth-century German 'Theatre of Fact' movement, in which court records and historical documents are performed verbatim.
62. See S Mulcahy, 'Methodologies of Law as Performance' (2022) 16 *Law and Humanities* 165.
63. D Sheikh, *Love and Reparation: A Theatrical Response to the Section 377 Litigation in India* (Seagull, 2021).
64. I Ward, *The Play of Law in Modern British Theatre* (Edinburgh University Press, 2022).
65. D Sheikh, 'Legal Theatre: Staging Critique in the Law School' (2020) 46 *Australian Feminist Law Journal* 115.
66. See P Goodrich, *Advanced Introduction to Law and Literature* (Edward Elgar, 2021).
67. There are law and theatre courses in Columbia and New York and modules on law and Literature with theatrical components have been taught at Derby, Warwick and Cardiff Universities.

There are innovators in this sphere. Scholars are using theatre to interrogate notions of justice, and how the law relates to race, gender and sexuality. Intersectionality, pioneered by Kimberlé Crenshaw, distils how oppressions do not stand alone but intersect: how, for example, a black woman faces discrimination both in terms of race and gender. Drawing on this, Amber Moore has assembled a canon of 'trauma literature', including such texts as *Macbeth* and *A Streetcar Named Desire*, as a means of developing intersectional new feminist pedagogies through which to address rape culture.[68] Other texts have broadened out to study the theatrical culture outside of the Anglosphere: examining the portrayal of Japanese contractual practices in Edo and kabuki theatre,[69] exploring an emerging concept of 'the self' in Chinese law through Chinese adaptations of Ibsen's *A Doll's House*.[70] Plays like Abigail Thorn's *The Prince*(2022) and *I, Joan*(2022) retell classic literary and historical stories from the point of view of queer, trans and gender non-conforming artists.[71]

Epilogue: [Exit, pursued by a bear][72]

The figure bows.

Her story being done, the audience gives her a world of sighs – and applause, always applause. The curtain falls; the play is done, but the story goes on.

Law and theatre remains imperfect, fragmented. It is grappling with all the things that Western legal-/literary scholarship grapples with, from diversifying the canon to unpicking the hierarchies to which we have become too accustomed. Is it enough for law and theatre to be just a subsidiary of law and literature, or can it strike out on its own? Should it? After all, law is a site of contradictions: a site of play,[73] and a site of violence, especially in regard to gender, class, sexual orientation and race.[74] It is also a site of politics, where people can find closure and critique without the imposition of law.[75]

68. A Moore, 'Creating a Canon for Change: How Teacher Candidates Demonstrate Readiness to Reckon with Rape Culture through Reading Trauma Literature' (2023) 34 *Teaching Education* 1.
69. S Landini, 'The Idea of Contract in Japanese Law and Culture' (2021) 3(9) *Japanese Society and Culture* 123.
70. K Tam, 'Law, Ethics and Gender: China's Quest for a Modern Selfhood as Reflected in its Adaptations of Ibsen's *A Doll's House*' (2018) *Fudan Journal of the Humanities and Social Sciences* 145.
71. See also C Charles, 'Panic in The Project: Critical Queer Studies and the Matthew Shepard Murder' (2006) 11 *Law & Literature* 225.
72. W Shakespeare, *AWinter's* Tale, Act 3 Scene 3.
73. J Huizinga, *Homo Ludens. A Study of the Play Element in Culture* (Beacon Press, 1950), 78.
74. R M Cover, 'Violence and the Word' (1986) 95 *Yale Law Journal* 1601, 1606–1607.
75. M Arjomand, *Staged: Show Trials, Political Theater, and the Aesthetics of Judgment* (Columbia University Press, 2018), 53, 179.

Theatre is not straightforwardly an ally, however: while it can provide a welcoming, inclusive space, it can also isolate and exclude.[76]

The principal aspiration of law and theatre is, or has been, illustrative. Examining the theatrics of the legal process lays bare its central subterfuge: authority through ceremony. Spotlighting the theatrics of the trial calls us to question exactly who is performing what, and for whose benefit? Even more than literature, theatre is the antithesis of law: to categorise is to lose its power.

But this lack of certainty may be the root cause of an imbalance within law and theatre scholarship. As a discipline, it is perhaps more fragmented than law and literature. There is a lack of certainty, of cohesion, that might be attributable to the slippage between genres. Stories travel across mediums; they overlap and contradict. 'Theatre' itself is a term that is hard to pin down; it no longer means a prop and a proscenium. Its bounds are infinite.

Oscar Wilde argued in *Dorian Gray* that 'to define is to limit'.[77] So often in law do we strive to define, to categorise and classify and codify. Doctrine verges so often on dogma. Theatrical works, in contrast, allow us to think beyond the law's constraints.[78] To silo theatre into neat compartments for law's good would be to go against its radical potential. Theatre does not merely refute definition: it actively challenges it. It means that the interface of law and theatre is a less a door and more a fissure: its truths seep in through the cracks. The theatre has given us Portia, Atticus Finch and Billy Flynn. Who might it bring in future?

'The body is memory', Marett Leiboff argues, in what might be the closest thing to a 'current' theory that law and theatre can lay claim.[79] Can the same be said of law? Perhaps it is enough for one discipline to throw light on another, as Bakhtin once said of languages.[80] In an increasingly dark world, we may be grateful for illumination. But theatre has radical potential. Only the court jester could speak frankly to the powers that be. And, after all, it was a play that once caught the conscience of a king.[81]

---

76. N Rogers, 'The Play of Law: Comparing Performance in Law and Theatre' (2008) 8(2) *Law and Justice Journal* 429.
77. O Wilde, 'The Picture of Dorian Gray' (1890) 271 *Lippincott's Monthly Magazine* 1.
78. M L Williams, 'Law and Literature/Literary Jurisprudence' in R Auchmuty (ed), *Great Debates in Gender and Law* (Red Globe Press, 2018), 185.
79. M Leiboff, *Towards a Theatrical Jurisprudence* (Routledge, 2019), 31.
80. M Bakhtin, 'Epic and Novel: Toward a Methodology for the Study of the Novel' in M Holquist (ed), *The Dialogic Imagination: Four Essays* (University of Texas Press, 1981), 43–62.
81. This is a reference to 'The Mouse Trap', the 'play within a play' in Shakespeare's *Hamlet.* Its title character stages this play before his uncle Claudius as a means of revealing his treachery ('conscience') to the Danish court. See W Shakespeare, *Hamlet*, Act 2 Scene 2.

Chapter Thirteen

LAW AND THEOLOGY

Norman Doe

Introduction: Towards Legal Theology[1]

In addition to the established field of law and religion whereby scholars study the interaction between religion and the law from a range of disciplinary perspectives,[2] attention should also be afforded to the interaction between the disciplines of law and theology.[3] Theology, the study of God, consists of a network of subdisciplines: in the Christian context,[4] these include biblical theology, moral theology, ecumenical theology and so on. Each branch of theology has its own distinctive object of study, methods and purposes. For example, pneumatology studies the Holy Spirit, practical theology uses the pastoral cycle, and liberation theology seeks to transform unjust societal structures that oppress the marginalised. Each branch of theology has its own distinctive community of scholars. It is a common view (though perhaps a contested one, as between the different church traditions) that the main purpose of Christian theology is to proclaim the Gospel of Christ. The branches of theology, in turn, are vehicles for each of this core purpose.

This chapter explores how legal theology could become a branch of theology with its own distinctive objects of study, methods and purposes. What follows explores these themes, how the subdiscipline of legal theology might be defined and developed in the context of the study of the systems of law, order, and polity, of churches across the Christian traditions that deal with, for example, forms of regulation, ministry (lay or ordained), governance (institutions and functions), discipline, doctrine, worship, rites,

---

1. The following heavily draws upon material from within: N Doe, 'The Category "Legal Theology" and the Study of Christian Laws' (2017) 32(1) *Journal of Law and Religion* 64–70, (c) Center for the Study of Law and Religion at Emory University 2017, published by Cambridge University Press, reproduced with permission.
2. On which see Sandberg's contribution to this volume on 'Law and Religion'.
3. Theology and law played a major role in the development by the Ecumenical Christian law Panel of the Statements of Principles of Canon Law (Rome, 2016) which was launched at the 11th Assembly of the World Council of Churches in September 2022. See N Doe, 'Juridical Ecumenism' (2012) 14 *Ecclesiastical Law Journal* 195; N Doe (ed), *Church Laws and Ecumenism: A New Path for Christian Unity* (Routledge, 2021).
4. For discussion of religious law inside and outside the Christian context see N Doe, *Comparative Religious Law: Judaism, Christianity, Islam* (Cambridge University Press, 2018).

property and external relations.[5] It does so as to the following: (1) The *object of study*: legal theology should at its core be about the relationship between theology and church law – more particularly, the relationship between church law and each of the other branches of theology. (2) The *method of study*: legal theology may involve the theological study of church law and/or the legal study of theology using standard juristic methods (such as text and context, critical, historical, analytical) as well as methods used in the other branches of theology. (3) The *purpose of study*: the development of a community of scholars collaborating with a view to its impact on ecclesial practice. In each section, the potential for legal theology will be discussed by reference to three other subdisciplines of theology. This chapter as a whole will underscore how theology is indispensable to a full understanding of the place of law in the life of the church, and law provides evidence to test the propositions of theology in the practical life of the church as this is translated through norms to action.

The Objects of Study: Topics for Legal Theology

The topics of well-established branches of theology may provide obvious objects of study for legal theology. Here are three examples—ecclesiology, dogmatic theology and biblical theology—that might also help us to locate legal theology.

Ecclesiology, the study of the church, explores the origins, nature and purposes of the church universal. Its methods include developing categories for the attributes of the church, such as one holy catholic and apostolic, and the people of God. One aim of ecclesiology is to understand what may be authentic, required, permissible or appropriate church structures, such as those in ministry, government, discipleship, evangelism, worship and teaching.[6] As such, each tradition has developed its own ecclesiology (also today the subject of ecumenical dialogue). Legal theology could be understood as a branch of ecclesiology. It is common today to see church law-order-polity as *applied ecclesiology*, and therefore to speak of a 'theology of church law' and 'theology in church law'.[7] The former is a doctrinal (perhaps speculative) exercise, and the latter is a more descriptive and perhaps scientific exercise. One aim of legal theology could be to develop these two categories through the study of such provisions in the regulatory instruments of churches as, for example, from the Orthodox tradition: a church (which may be part of a worldwide Patriarchate), exists 'to proclaim the Gospel of Christ, to teach and spread the Orthodox Christian Faith, to energize, cultivate and guide the life of the Church', to sanctify 'the faithful through Divine Worship', to build up 'the spiritual and ethical life of the faithful' and to serve as a 'witness of the message of Christ to all persons'.[8] Likewise, in the Protestant traditions, a Lutheran church exists as 'part of the whole Church of Christ', to 'declare the teachings of the prophets and apostles', 'to

5. See N Doe, *Christian Law: Contemporary Principles* (Cambridge University Press, 2013).
6. See, for example, A Dulles, *Models of the Church*, 2nd edn (Gill and Macmillan, 1987).
7. For a Roman Catholic perspective, see, for example, R Ombres, 'Canon Law and Theology' (2014) 14(2) *Ecclesiastical Law Journal* 164.
8. Charter of the Greek Orthodox Archdiocese of America (2003), art. 2.

confess [...] the faith' and to engage in 'worship and Christian service'.[9] Legal theology may be developed to test the claims of ecclesiology against the reality of church legal orders.

The object of study in dogmatic theology (or dogmatics) is the creeds or statements of faith (i.e. dogma, teaching, doctrines and confessions) of churches. It seeks a systematic arrangement of the articles of faith, or it is the branch of theology that deals with them. Dogmatic theology helps to test our own beliefs for coherence and rationality.[10] The dogmas, articles, confessions and so on of institutional churches (and of the traditions to which they belong) are the object of regulation (from their creation, through their redefinition, to doctrinal discipline in terms of assent to and dissent from them). Legal theology could test the dogmatic quality of church laws and should recognise also the normative quality of such dogmatic instruments as a means to regulate both belief and action. Typical of norms appearing in church juridical texts, which might inform such study, are those of the Methodist Church of Great Britain: 'The doctrines of the evangelical faith, which Methodism has held from the beginning, and still holds, are based upon the divine revelation'; the Methodist Church acknowledges this revelation as 'the supreme rule of faith and practice'; moreover, the Conference is 'the final authority within the Church with regard to all questions concerning the interpretation of its doctrines'; but it cannot alter fundamental doctrines.[11]

Biblical theology, or bibliology, takes a particular subject and explores what the Bible teaches on it. It emphasises the historical context in which the author wrote, may recognise that God self-reveals differently at different times in history and seeks to understand how this is demonstrated in the progression of the Bible. Bibliology explores the nature of the Bible as, for example, inspired Word of God and the development of the scriptural canon.[12] Legal theology could explore under this head the treatment of the Bible as an object of regulation within churches, such as how laws present the Bible (e.g. as the inspired Word of God), use it as a defining element of the juridical identity of a church, and how church legislators and others use the Bible as a material source for the creation of laws. For example, the Lutheran Church of Australia recognises 'the Holy Scriptures [...] as the only infallible source and norm for all matters of faith, doctrine and life'; its laws often cite passages from Holy Scripture;[13] and in the Lutheran Church Missouri Synod, if a rule contradicts scripture, it does not bind: 'no resolution of the Synod imposing anything upon the individual congregation is of binding force if it is

9. *Evangelical Lutheran Church in America: Constitution and Foundational Texts* (2003), chapters 1–4, 8.73.
10. See, for example, K Barth, *Church Dogmatics: A Selection* (Westminster John Knox Press, 1994).
11. 'Deed of Union', in *The Constitutional Practice and Discipline of the Methodist Church*, vol. 2 (Methodist Publishing, 2016), section 2, paras. 4–5, 213–24.
12. See, for example, J D Smart, *The Past, Present and Future of Biblical Theology* (Westminster, 1979).
13. Lutheran Church of Australia Inc., Constitution (2015), art. 2.1; see also ibid., art. 4.1, citing 1 *Corinthians* 6.

not in accordance with the Word of God or if it appears to be inexpedient as far as the condition of a congregation is concerned.'[14]

The Methods of Legal Theology

The dominant feature of several branches of theology is that of their method as applied to a particular theological topic or issue. These methods, too, may inform legal theology taking it beyond the standard juristic method in church law of description, explanation and evaluation.

This section provides three further examples – systematic theology, exegetical theology and pastoral theology – to shed light upon the possible methods of legal theology.

Like biblical theology, systematic theology uses the Bible as its main object of study. However, systematic theology offers distinct methods of biblical analysis, for example, to compare all of scripture so as to create a systematised statement on what the whole Bible says about particular issues. While biblical theology may see the divine self-revelation in a progressive manner, systematic theology seeks to present God and revelation in a way that transcends history and to construct a system of theological propositions that are internally consistent.[15] Legal theology might in its use of law and theology attempt to compare and relate all the laws of different churches and create a systematised statement on what all these laws provide about particular issues so as to transcend denominational affiliations. This method would have ecumenical merit in providing the total picture of juridical Christianity. It has been argued recently that, when compared, there are profound similarities between the basic elements of the normative regimes of the churches across the ecclesiastical traditions worldwide. From these similarities may be induced common principles of Christian law. When compared systematically, these regulatory systems also tell us much about convergence in action, based on common norms of conduct. While dogmas may divide churches, the profound similarities between their norms of conduct produce juridical convergence. This reveals that the juridical norms of the faithful, whatever their various denominational affiliations, link Christians through their stimulation of common forms of action. As laws converge, so actions converge. While there are key differences, similarities between the norms of conduct of churches indicate that their faithful engage in the visible world in much the same actions as other Christians. The articulation of principles of law-order-polity common to the churches: enables the reconciliation of juridical difference in the form of underlying principles of law; provides a stable ecumenical methodology through its focus on concrete textual data; offers a practical guide for Christian life; and defines that degree of achieved communion, as well as opportunities for and limits on future progress.[16]

---

14. The Lutheran Church–Missouri Synod, Constitution (2010), art. 7; The Lutheran Church–Missouri Synod, By-laws (2010), para. 1.7.
15. See, for example, P Tillich, *Systematic Theology*, 3 vols (University of Chicago Press, 1951–1963).
16. N Doe, *Christian Law: Contemporary Principles* (Cambridge University Press, 2013).

Exegetical theology seeks to 'bring out' truths of scripture by discovering what the message would have meant to its original audience (and author). It may address what a portion of Scripture says about a particular matter, and it uses the rules of exegetical analysis to draw out meaning. Its methods include hermeneutics, the historical and cultural context of the material, the literary style, original language and placing one passage with other passages. Once the original message, purpose and intent of a passage are determined, exegesis may also seek to apply that timeless truth of scripture to people today.[17] It would be fascinating to explore, for example, what impact principles of exegetical theology might have on the very practical norms currently used by churches to interpret their own laws; for instance, in the Roman Catholic Church, laws are 'to be understood in accord with the proper meaning of the words [...] in their text and context';[18] similarly, for Anglicans worldwide, if 'the meaning of laws remains in doubt recourse may be had to analogous texts, the purposes and circumstances of the law, the mind of the legislator, the jurisprudence of church courts and tribunals, the opinion of jurists, the principles of canon law and theology, the common good, and the practice and tradition of that church and of the church universal'.[19]

Pastoral theology (sometimes known as practical theology or applied theology) focuses on the day-to-day application of theology in the lives of Christians or churches and issues they face. A typical method is the pastoral cycle, in which the participant identifies a particular issue in life, reflects upon it theologically, deploys the results of that theological reflection and develops an action plan in relation to that issue. All areas of church regulation would be suitable for this theological method. For example, pneumatology, the object of which is the Holy Spirit (and its interaction with the world), would also be relevant here, not least in terms of how laws portray and accommodate the work of the Holy Spirit. From a field such as church discipline, the Methodist Church in Ireland provides 'Discipline in the Church is an exercise of that spiritual authority which the Lord Jesus has appointed in His Church. The ends contemplated by discipline are the maintenance of the purity of the Church, the spiritual benefit of the members and the honour of our Lord'. Moreover: 'All members and Ministers of the Church are subject to its government and discipline, and are under the jurisdiction and care of the appropriate Courts of the Church in all matters of Doctrine, Worship, Discipline, and Order in accordance with the Rules and Regulations from time to time made by the Conference' (the central governing body).[20] The application of each element of this understanding of church discipline in any particular disciplinary process could fruitfully involve identifying the mischief at hand, theological reflection on the gravity of the offense, the role of forgiveness and the decision whether to impose a just censure.

17. See, for example, F M Young, *Biblical Exegesis and the Formation of Christian Culture* (Cambridge University Press, 1997).
18. Code of Canon Law (1983), canon 17.
19. *Principles of Canon Law Common to the Church of the Anglican Communion* (Anglican Communion Office, 2008), principle 8.1-4.
20. Constitution of the Methodist Church in Ireland (1927), section 5.

The Purposes of Legal Theology

As we have seen, each branch of theology has its own purposes – though the purposes of some branches are more conspicuous than those of other branches (which may be classified as less substantive and rather more about method). Some branches of theology seek to transform not only ways of thinking and belief but also action in the world. This section explores three further subdisciplines of theology – natural theology, missiology and liberation theology – to show how these too may be adapted to the particular concerns of legal theology as it applies to the laws of churches.

The focus of natural theology is general or natural revelation.[21] It begins with observations of creation and suggests that, as God created in a way that is consistent with his own nature and character, so we might infer genuine truths and ethical positions from our observations. Legal theology should study not only relations between theology and positive law but the place of natural law thinking within the juridical framework of church life: whether there are principles of natural law overarching the legal systems of all churches across the Christian traditions, how these are ascertained, by whom and with what effect. In the ecumenical context, this has already been a focus of discussion in dialogue between the World Alliance of Reformed Churches (now the World Communion of Reformed Churches) and the Roman Catholic Church, that latter of which proposes that 'Reformed and Roman Catholics agree that discipleship to Jesus Christ entails the discernment of God's will regarding ethical issues and moral behavior'; moreover, both 'acknowledge the contribution of human reasoning to moral and ethical discernment, although theologians and ethicists within our communities have at times evaluated in differing or even contrasting ways that philosophical understanding of good and evil usually called the 'theory of natural law'. As is well known, Catholic teaching affirms the possibility of knowing right and wrong actions on the basis of natural law'.[22] A recent ecumenical exploration suggests that the Christian traditions worldwide share far more in terms of a common understanding of natural law thinking than this document implies.[23]

Missiology focuses on the study of mission: how the church should spread the Gospel and how the church should grow. One of its purposes is to convey how these matters should be conditioned by scriptures, cultures, psychology, trends, history and demographics.[24] Yet, there are few studies on how the laws of Christians address mission. However, regulatory instruments commonly make provision for mission. For example, the Standing Conference of the Canonical Orthodox Bishops in the Americas has

21. Moral theology, or Christian ethics, is also pertinent here.
22. *The Church as Community of Common Witness to the Kingdom of God: Report of the Third Phase of the International Theological Dialogue between the Catholic Church and the World Alliance of Reformed Churches* (1998–2005) (2007), para. 140.
23. See N Doe (ed), *Christianity and Natural Law: An Introduction* (Cambridge University Press, 2017).
24. See, for example L Newbigin, *The Open Secret: Sketches for a Missionary Theology* (William Eerdmans, 1978).

mission commissions 'to study the needs and opportunities of the jurisdictions in the external and internal mission fields of the Church, at home and abroad, to point out opportunities or failures, and to suggest areas in which necessary resources might be found'.[25] In the Ukrainian Orthodox Church in America, 'The diocesan bishop . . . is bound to propagate and expound Orthodox Faith and morals among all people within the diocesan boundaries'. To accomplish this, the bishop is obliged to 'ensure that his clergy make an Orthodox witness in their communities', 'establish missions for the purpose of propagating the Orthodox faith' and 'provide the necessary funds for missionary activity within his diocese'.[26] Here legal theology might engage how legal arrangements foster or frustrate the promotion of mission.

The focus of liberation theology is the plight of marginalised peoples. It proposes both a 'theology of liberation', that is, freedom from institutionalised injustice, and the 'liberation of theology' from the values of those who benefit from injustice. As to method, it is 'an interpretation of Christian faith out of the experience of the poor', that is, 'an attempt to read the Bible and key Christian doctrines with the eyes of the poor', and it relies on so-called proof-texts from scripture. One of its aims is to provide a theology-based program for social reform to liberate the marginalised from economic, political and other forms of injustice.[27] Legal theology could use the purposes of liberation theology – the transformation of unjust structures – as one of its own key purposes. The concepts of justice in liberation theology may provide yardsticks against which to measure the legitimacy of church laws, not least those that address the promotion of human rights in civil society and provision made by churches for social responsibility. Once more, the regulatory instruments of Christians worldwide address human rights and social justice. For example, as the Baptist World Alliance must defend human rights globally,[28] so, too, at national level Baptist Conventions and Unions recognise human rights and are 'to maintain religious liberty'.[29] Thus, the Baptist Union of Southern Africa accepts 'that no individual should be coerced either by the State or by any secular, ecclesiastical or religious group in matters of faith' on the basis of 'the right to interpret the Scriptures responsibly and to act in the light of his conscience'.[30] For the North American Baptist Conference, 'Christians, individually and collectivel [must] promote truth, justice and peace and] aid the needy and preserve the dignity of all races and conditions'.[31] The churches of the American Baptist Churches in the United States

25. The Constitution of the Standing Conference of Canonical Orthodox Bishops in the Americas (1961), art. 4.2; see also The Statutes for the Organisation and Functioning of the Romanian Orthodox Church, art. 106.
26. Statutes of the Ukrainian Orthodox Church in America (2015), art. 7.12.
27. See, for example, G Gutierrez, *A Theology of Liberation* (Orbis Books, 1973).
28. Constitution of the Baptist World Alliance (2016), art. 2.
29. Constitution of the Baptist Union of Southern Africa (1933, subsequently amended), art. 5.3.
30. By-Laws, para. 4.2.7.
31. Statement of Beliefs of the North American Baptists (2009), para. 8 (citing, for example, *Matthew* 5:13–16, Hebrews 13.5, Luke 9.23, Titus 2.12).

are to seek the mind of Christ on 'political, economic, [and] social' matters and express this 'to the rest of society'.[32]

Conclusion: The Potential of Legal Theology

This chapter has examined a number of subdisciplines within theology as part of an examination of how legal theology can develop. The 'fit' of legal theology to some branches of theology is more obvious than to other branches. Be that as it may, legal theology could be an interdisciplinary and collaborative branch of theology that draws on the objects of study, methods and purposes of other branches of theology. One of its tasks, therefore, could be to explore the relationship between these theological subcategories – their objects, methods and purposes – and the laws of churches across the various Christian traditions: that is, how these theological branches (their objects, methods and purposes) may be teased out in the context of the churches' substantive laws as they apply to ministry, governance, doctrine, worship, rites, property, ecumenism and the state and wider society. Such an exercise might include the aim of developing categories such as 'juridical ecclesiology', 'juridical ecumenics',[33] 'juridical dogmatics', 'juridical apologetics' and so on. It would also be worth exploring how legal theology might feature in theological education in terms of the formation of ministers. Above all, legal theology would provide an opportunity for theologians to offer insights into the theological foundations of church laws and for jurists to provide concrete evidence both to test theological propositions in the practicalities of ecclesial life and to shape them.

32. By-Laws of the American Baptist Churches in the USA (2012), prologue.
33. On which see N Doe, 'Juridical Ecumenism' (2012) 14 *Ecclesiastical Law Journal* 195; N Doe (ed), *Church Laws and Ecumenism: A New Path for Christian Unity* (Routledge, 2021).

Chapter Fourteen

LAW AND VIDEO GAMES

Ashley Pearson

Introduction

This chapter aims to position law and video games as an emerging and promising subfield of law and humanities scholarship. Video games, sometimes referred to as 'computer games', 'digital games' or 'electronic games', have garnered an immense following, captivating billions of players worldwide and generating nearly $200 billion in revenue in 2022 alone. Despite the widespread popularity and significant market presence of video gaming, law and humanities scholarship has largely overlooked the exploration of video games as rich cultural artefacts with legal entanglements. Or perhaps, if there has been interest, the modal peculiarities of video games have acted as a deterrent for legal scholars to tackle them as a site of analysis.

Fortunately, within the field of game studies or ludology, the discipline that primarily studies video games, there has been a rapid evolution of literature examining video games as objects of analysis. This vibrant body of scholarship offers valuable insights and approaches that can greatly complement and inform emerging law and video games research. This interdisciplinary dialogue between fields holds the potential to shed light on the complex legal dimensions of video games and enrich our understanding of intricate interplay between the forms. Or as Greg Lastowka puts it simply, 'those who study games and those who study law have things to learn from another'.[1]

How to Play: A Video Game Tutorial

While it may seem trite to provide an explanation of the video game medium within this chapter, assuming familiarity may do a disservice to potential entrants into the field who haven't yet had much exposure to the wonderful world of video games or may not have directly experienced their components for themselves. Unlike literature, art, music and film, video games occupy a somewhat niche space due to their historical reliance specialised hardware – such as a console or gaming PCs – for play. However, with the advent of smartphones, video games have become increasingly accessible to a wider audience.

Video games resist simple definitions due to the fluidity of their constituent parts – they are multimodal combinations that may contain aspects of code, art, music, text,

1. G Lastowka, 'Law and Games Studies' (2006) 1 *Games and Cultures* 25, 26.

cinematic cut scenes, gameplay mechanics and narrative, which are combined to engage a person in play.[2] Through these interactive experiences, players navigate virtual spaces, solve puzzles, combat enemies and manipulate avatars or in-game objects in pursuit of the game's objectives. These elements are typically displayed on a screen and can be controlled through various input devices, such as a keyboards and mice, game controllers, motion-sensing devices (or a combination of these elements), enabling users to directly interact with the game world.

The input device acts as a form of digital prosthesis that mediates the player's physical actions into contextually appropriate in-game actions. While seemingly mundane, the controller plays a vital role in distinguishing the video game format from other forms of entertainment media by providing a tangible apparatus of control.[3] Whether through direct control of avatars or characters (actorialised), or direct, transparent interaction with the game world (unactorialised), the materiality of the controller merges the physical and virtual realms, creating an embodied phenomenology of play in which real-world engagement with the input device is interwoven with, and difficult to separate from, their onscreen actions.[4]

One of the strengths of the video game as an immersive form is the inter(re)activity of the medium. This is not *just* to say that the player has, through the mediating input device, agency to 'influence the game state and game outcome'[5] as they play but also that the game itself is *reactive* to this input – providing sensory feedback to the player (visual, auditory, emotive, mimetic, haptic) as the player experiences the tactile outcome of the coded response that resulted from their input.[6] From player input to game reaction, the elapsed time is almost instantaneous which results in a feedback loop where the player and the game are perpetually reacting to one another. The incredible speed at which these symbolic (and increasingly simulative) gestures generate in-game feedback along with the iterative nature of the process creates a strong sense of identification between the player and avatar, to the point where the controlling apparatus fades into the background as the player and avatar coalesce.[7]

Through these iterative cycles of play and exploration using the tool of the avatar, the player learns what they *can* and *cannot* do within the specific video game context.

2. The word 'play' is used broadly here. While video games often intend to engage a person in play in the ordinary sense of the word, the purposes of games are vast and not able to be so easily captured by a single word.
3. P McDonald, 'On Couches and Controllers: Identification in the Video Game Apparatus' in M Wysocki (ed) *Ctrl-Alt-Play: Essays on Control in Video Gaming* (McFarland, 2013) 108.
4. L Papale, 'Beyond Identification: Defining the Relationships between Player and Avatar' (2014) 1(2) *Journal of Games Criticism* 1.
5. J Juul, 'The Game, the Player, the World: Looking for a Heart of Gameness' in M Copier and J Raessens (eds) *Level Up: Digital Games Research Conference Proceedings* (Utrecht, 2003), 7.
6. T Smethurst and S Craps, 'Playing with Trauma: Interreactivity, Empathy, and Complicity in *The Walking Dead* Video Game' (2014) 10(3) *Games and Culture* 269, 271–273.
7. R Klevjer, 'Enter the Avatar: The Phenomenology of Prosthetic Telepresence in Computer Games' in J Sageng, H Fossheim and T Mandt Larsen (eds) *The Philosophy of Computer Games* (Springer, 2012) 24–25.

The player learns that as Sonic they can be super speedy, as Samus they can morph into a ball, and that as Kirby they have seemingly endless lung power. In learning the affordances of the player-avatar and the game world, the player internalises the coded restrictions of the avatar body that they are provided. And as players determine their capacities for action, they also discover the coded restrictions that limit their interaction within the world.

Not uncommonly, the different forms of rule sets or type of interaction to be expected between player and code (platformer, fighting, rhythm, shooter) are used to describe genres of game as much as, if not more so, than the narratives, backdrop, or spaces (horror, fantasy, military, dystopian) within which the gameplay unfolds.[8] But the player does not experience the mechanics alone. All of this information is couched in a fusion of visual art, audio design and interactive storytelling that contributes to the player's immersion by creating atmosphere, heightening tension or evoking emotional responses. The combination of these aesthetic elements creates a multisensory experience that establishes a distinct identity for each game.

From this short overview alone of the most basic components of an ordinary video game – the game artefact's technical composition, the player's input device, the feedback loop, the limitations placed on the player via the avatar – we can glimpse the intertwined questions of agency, personhood, restrictions and violence that arise within the medium. Moreover, this overview assumes that everything is working correctly and as intended, without accounting for factors like unintentional bugs and glitches, cheating and exploits, user-made modifications, multiplayer dynamics or subversive play styles such as speed-running, all of which further complicate the player-game interaction.[9]

Playtesting: The Context of Law and Video Games Scholarship

Video games first became popularised from the 1970s, as coin-operated arcade machines such as *Computer Space* (1971), *Pong* (1972), *Space Invaders* (1978), *Pac-Man* (1980), *Donkey Kong* (1981) and *Tetris* (1984), became commercially available to play for the first time. From the mid-1970s, gaming companies began to release video console hardware that enabled video games to be played at home which further cemented their presence within the entertainment industry.

Almost as a rite of passage, developments in entertainment media have been accompanied by condemning reports about the effects that such media will have on the morality of society. Video games were no exception. Carly Kocurek proposes that *Death Race*

8. H Jenkins, 'Game Design as Narrative Architecture' in N Wardrip-Fruin and P Harrigan (eds) *First Person: New Media as Story, Performance, and Game* (MIT Press, 2004) 122.
9. For a general academic introduction to video games, I would recommend MJP Wolf and B Perron, *The Video Game Theory Reader* (Routledge, 2003); B Perron and MJP Wolf, *The Video Game Theory Reader 2* (Routledge, 2009); K Salen and E Zimmerman, *Rules of Play: Game Design Fundamentals* (MIT Press, 2003); J Juul, *Half-Real: Video Games between Real Rules and Fictional Worlds* (MIT Press, 2011); I Bogost, *Persuasive Games* (MIT Press, 2010); N Wardrip-Fruin and P Harrigan, *First Person: New Media as Story, Performance, and Game* (MIT Press, 2004).

(1976), in which the player controls a vehicle and receives points for running down pedestrians, triggered the first video game moral panic in the United States. She suggests that the game caused outrage not because it was violent but because the violence depicted was too close to real, non-fictional violence that was not 'already experienced as games at some level'.[10]

Despite the relatively simplistic stick-figure style graphics of *Death Race* and pixel art games that would follow for many years, academic studies on video games from the mid-1970s through to the early 2000s were dominated by scientific, psychological and socio-cultural studies that reflected the anxieties of moral panic. Through the prevalence of these studies, the active participation of the player in the creation of violence was culturally linked to heightened aggression and danger in real-world behaviours of players,[11] a connection which video game scholarship has struggled to shake for a long time.[12]

Early intersections of law and video game scholarships emerged within this context of moral panic, directing academic attention first and foremost to the *regulation of* video games rather than examining the ludic depth of video games as cultural artefacts. Before video games could be properly appreciated as worthy of deeper study by legal institutions and scholars, the various threats that they appeared to pose to existent legal paradigms needed to be acknowledged and addressed. Consequently, initial publications on law and video games focused on regulatory aspects centring on the ownership, transference, and theft of virtual property;[13] copyright;[14] the protection of video games

10. CA Kocurek, 'The Agony and the Exidy: A History of Video Game Violence and the Legacy of Death Race' (2012) 12(1) *The International Journal of Computer Game Research* 7.
11. NS Schutte, JM Malouff, JC Post-Gorden and AL Rodasta, 'Effects of Playing Videogames on Children's Aggressive and Other Behaviours' (1998) 18(5) *Journal of Applied Psychology* 454; CA Anderson and CM Ford, 'Affect of the Game Player: Short-Term Effects of Highly and Mildly Aggressive Video Games' (1987) 12(4) *Personality and Social Psychology Bulletin* 390; J Cooper and D Mackie, 'Video Games and Aggression in Children' (1986) 16(8) *Journal of Applied Social Psychology* 726.
12. Christopher Ferguson suggests that the perseverance of the framing of violent video games as a risk to society may have been further fuelled by external factors such as the political and economic benefits of moral panic. See CJ Ferguson, 'The School Shooting/Violent Video Game Link: Causal Relationship or Moral Panic?' (2008) 5 *Journal of Investigative Psychology and Offender Profiling* 25.
13. FG Lastowka and D Hunter, 'The Laws of the Virtual Worlds' (2004) 92(1) *California Law Review* 1; AV Arias, 'Life, Liberty, and the Pursuit of Swords and Armor: Regulating the Theft of Virtual Goods' (2007–2008) 57 *Emory Law Journal* 1301; OS Kerr, 'Criminal Law in Virtual Worlds' (2008) 1 *University of Chicago Legal Forum* 415; W Rumbles, 'Theft in the Digital: Can You Steal Virtual Property?' (2011) 17 *Canterbury Law Review* 354; H Postigo, 'Video Game Appropriation through Modifications: Attitudes Concerning Intellectual Property among Modders and Fans' (2008) 12(1) *Convergence: The International Journal of Research into New Media Technologies* 59.
14. J Stein, 'The Legal Nature of Video Games – Adapting Copyright Law to Multimedia' (2015) 2(1) *Press Start* 43.

from censorship as an expression of free speech; [15] and whether crimes can be committed in virtual spaces or perpetrated against avatars.[16]

While these publications occasionally touched on themes such as the phenomenological challenges of avatars and legal personhood, their primary focus remained on practical considerations rather than the possibilities that video games, as a cultural text, could offer in reimagining concepts of law in relation to the virtual. Although still within the context of developing regulatory frameworks, in 2006 Stephen Orr encouraged to look beyond content of video games and was one of the first legal scholars to consider the structure of the video game as a form legal analysis in and of itself.[17] Despite Orr's entreaty to engage, there was initially little to no response from the law side.[18] Game studies, however, was well-underway in developing its techniques to understanding the video game form.

A fundamental challenge that emerging scholars in this space must confront is determining an appropriate approach to studying video games as an object of inquiry. Referred to as the *ludology versus narratology* debate, this challenge occupied the 1990s to the early 2000s as game studies scholars grappled with the unique modal affordances of video games, and what aspect of a video game's analysis should take priority. The debate was later attributed to the game studies field (at the time) being 'cluttered with a series of misunderstandings and misconceptions'[19] since fundamental concepts such as narrative, gameplay, interactivity and ludology were 'couched in vague, broad terms'[20] that frequently exacerbated or misrepresented viewpoints.

At the heart of the debate were questions around interactivity, agency, play and whether these exigent characteristics of the video game medium were inherently

---

15. JM Balkin, 'Virtual Liberty: Freedom to Design and Freedom to Play in Virtual Worlds' (2004) 90(8) *Virginia Law Review* 2043; AC Yen, 'A First Amendment Perspective on the Idea/Expression Dichotomy and Copyright in a Work's "Total Concept and Feel"' (1989) 38 *Emory Law Journal* 393.
16. FG Lastowka and D Hunter, 'Virtual Crime' in JM Balkin and BS Noveck (eds) *The State of Play: Law, Games and Virtual Worlds* (New York University Press, 2006).
17. S Orr, 'Beyond Content: The Emergence of Video Games and their Diverse Effects on Legal Normativity as Seen Through the Lens of Jean Baudrillard' (2006) 5(1) *Canadian Journal of Law and Technology* 39.
18. Although Mantello does not situate his work within a law and humanities discipline but more so within international relations and media studies, his publication on the imagined 'witnessing' as a testimony to the legitimacy of state violence within *Battlefield* still has strong resonances with the field. See P Mantello, 'Legitimacy and the Virtual Battlefield: Putting the First-Person Shooter on the Witness Stand' (2013) 67(5) *Australian Journal of International Affairs* 638.
19. G Frasca, 'Ludologists Love Stories, Too: Notes from a Debate that Never Took Place' (2003) *Proceedings of the 2003 DiGRA International Conference: Level Up* (available at http://www.digra.org/wp-content/uploads/digital-library/05163.01125.pdf).
20. C Pearce, 'Theory Wars: An Argument against Arguments in the so-called Ludology/Narratology Debate' (2005) *Proceedings of the 2005 DiGRA International Conference: Changing Views: Worlds in Play* (available at http://www.digra.org/digital-library/publications/theory-wars-an-argument-against-arguments-in-the-so-called-ludologynarratology-debate/).

antithetical to the consideration of video games as a storytelling medium.[21] Story structure (usually) consists of a linear narrative with a pre-determined beginning, middle and end that is unchanged between repeated experiences.[22] The structure of video games, on the other hand, generates opportunities of play through interactive encounters that the player must respond to such as the strategies of another player, a puzzle to be solved, an objective to be achieved or a boss to be defeated.[23] The dialectic opposition of these structural characteristics means, as Jesper Juul states, that 'narration and gameplay, like oil and water, are not easily mixed'.[24]

The narratology perspective of the debate approached video game analysis from the standpoint that video games were a new expressive medium that had yet to discover its potential for storytelling.[25] The main alleged proponents of narratology side,[26] Janet Murray and Marie-Laure Ryan, privileged the narrative capacities of video games as a platform enabled stories that are spatial, embedded and emergent, to consider how the interactive function of video games may take better account for the player's participation and meaning-making within the storytelling process.[27]

The opposing ludologists, notably Espen Aarseth, Jesper Juul, Gonzalo Frasca and Markku Eskelinen, however, emphasised the unique qualities of video games as a medium, focusing on the technical aspects of game design, such as the creation of rule sets and gameplay mechanics that facilitated player interaction within the world. Incompatibility between game and narrative was highlighted by the frequent reliance of non-game elements such as cinematic cutscenes and scripted dialogue options in order to advance plot points or character development.[28] The ludologist approach was often seen as oppositional to the narratology perspective since narrative was categorised as extraneous to the function of games – putting the focus on form, not fiction.

21. G Costikyan, 'Where Stories End and Games Begin' (2000) 7(9) *Game Developer* 44.
22. Thisdefinition of narrative will not reflect all forms of stories, includinginteractive fiction or non-linear stories. However, the tension here ispredominantly between common, linear forms of narrative and its interactionwith games.
23. Rodriguez refers to these as moments of otherness. H Rodriguez, 'The Playful and the Serious: An Approximation to Huizinga's Homo Ludens' (2006) 6(1) *Game Studies: The International Journal of Computer Game Research* 2–3. Interactivity can be a loaded term within Game Studies. I would recommend the discussion on the relationship between interactivity and control by Aaron Smuts. A Smuts, 'What Is Interactivity?' (2009) 43(4) *The Journal of Aesthetic Education* 53.
24. E Aarseth, 'Genre Trouble' (2004) *Electronic Book Review* (available at http://electronicb ookreview.com/essay/genre-trouble/).
25. J Murray, *Hamlet on the Holodeck: The Future of Narrative in Cyberspace* (MIT Press, 1997).
26. I say 'alleged' because in later breakdowns of the debate, no clear narratologist figure emerged. The narratologist 'side' has been often since referred to as a hypothetical or imaginary antagonist to ludologist arguments.
27. ML Ryan, 'From Narrative Games to Playable Stories: Toward a Poetics of Interactive Narrative' (2009) 1 *Storyworlds: A Journal of Narrative Studies* 43.
28. G King and T Krzywinska, *Tomb Raiders and Space Invaders: Videogame Forms and Contexts* (IB Tauris, 2006). See also J Juul, *Half-Real: Video Games between Real Rules and Fictional Worlds* (MIT Press, 2006), 135.

Underlying the debate was the tentative navigation of how game studies, as an emerging field of inquiry, connected (if at all) with related fields of entertainment media, particularly film and literature. In Aarseth's words, the ludologist position was never to abandon narrative but rather to 'caution against and criticize the uncritical and unqualified application of terms such as "narrative" and "story" to games'.[29] If ludologists sought independence from the imposition of analytical techniques of other fields onto video games, then narratologists sought to avoid video game exceptionalism by relationally contextualising video games to other forms of media. The point is to not needlessly reject drawing upon existing analytical paradigms and established semiotics of other fields that video games could draw upon due to their inherent multimodality to enrich their analysis of the video game medium.

In the end, the debate was deemed something of a 'non-event' as game studies scholars seemed to take increasingly conciliatory and mutual positions that recognised that the separation of narrative and game elements was unproductive to a sincere analysis of the video game artefact.[30] Despite its ambivalent conclusion, the ludology-versus-narratology debate helped shaped the current interdisciplinary trajectory of game studies, which is one that acknowledges that neither gameplay nor narrative need be the *only* subject under analysis. Rather, narrative and gameplay have a 'contingent and arbitrary' relationship and relevant characteristics will emerge, clash, blend or recede depending on the individual game's design and how it plays.[31] Game studies emerged from the debate reinvigorated and reunited in their efforts to pursue and tackle the cultural juggernaut of the video game. Moreover, the extensive literature generated by the debate provides valuable insights for newcomers to the field.

Wild Legal Scholars Appeared! Development of the Law and Video Games Discipline

Truly interdisciplinary scholarship of law and video games that is both rooted thoughtfully in jurisprudence and legal tradition as well as engages meaningfully with the game studies literature has only really emerged within the last decade, in realm of the mid-2010s.[32] From that point to present, only a handful of papers had been published

29. E Aarseth, 'A Narrative Theory of Games' (2012) *Proceedings of the International Conference on the Foundations of Digital Games* (available at https://dl.acm.org/doi/10.1145/2282338.2282365).
30. Prominent examples of these conciliatory moves are J Murray, 'The Last Word on Ludology v Narratology in Game Studies' (2005) *Proceedings of the 2005 DiGRA International Conference: Changing Views: Worlds in Play* (available at https://inventingthemedium.com/2013/06/28/the-last-word-on-ludology-v-narratology-2005/); G Frasca, 'Ludologists Love Stories, Too: Notes from a Debate that Never Took Place' (2003) *Proceedings of the 2003 DiGRA International Conference: Level Up* (available at http://www.digra.org/wp-content/uploads/digital-library/05163.01125.pdf).
31. D Arsenault, 'Narratology' in MJP Wolf and B Perron (eds) *The Routledge Companion to Video Game Studies* (Routledge, 2014), 479.
32. To my knowledge, the earliest law and humanities engagement with video games are: C Newbery-Jones, 'Answering the Call of Duty: The Phenomenology of Justice in Twenty-First

prior to the release of *Law, Video Games, Virtual Realities: Playing Law*, which was the first concentrated collection to address the abiding gap within the field.[33]

As a nascent field within law and humanities scholarship, law and video games literature has not yet sufficiently developed and diversified to the point where discreet themes in the sub-field's development can be easily identified. But that is not to say that scholars within the game studies have not noticed the synergies that an analysis of video games and underpinning concepts of law as a cultural enterprise – such as concepts of identity and personhood, agency and power, violence and conflict, and morality and ethics – have to offer.

While the quasi-legal connections drawn would often benefit from a deeper theoretical knowledge of law, and particularly from engagement with cultural legal literature, game studies had already begun tentatively establishing connections and perhaps unknowingly creating some the foundations of cultural legal work tailored to a video game context. As a multidisciplinary field, we can and should draw upon the wisdom of partner-disciplines to assist in our own production of knowledge.

That is to also say that, in addition to game studies, we should lean on the extensive body of cultural legal scholarship that delves into the various components of the video game. While the video game stands unique as its own category, it often incorporates the semiotics and influences of other media forms. For instance, it may employ cinematography techniques to direct attention and elicit emotions, adopt specific art styles to create a particular atmosphere and utilise narrative storytelling methods. This edited collection serves as evidence of the profound activities of law and humanities scholarship that explore these evocative, aesthetic and cultural dimensions of law. By drawing insights from these existing fields, we can enrich our analysis of the video game medium.

Miguel Sicart characterises video games as ontologically both objects and experiences,[34] a sentiment shared by Espen Aarseth, who similarly describes them as having the qualities of 'both object and process'.[35] While the two are by no means extricable from one another, analytical emphasis on game as object or game as experience can produce different foci and can be used to loosely categorise some of the types of scholarship emerging from the law and video games discipline.

Century Video Games' (2015) 9(1) *Law and Humanities* 78; and M Barnett and CE Sharp, 'The Moral Choice of in FAMOUS: Law and Morality in Video Games' (2015) 24(3) *Griffith Law Review* 482.

33. D Mitchell, A Pearson and TD Peters (eds), *Law, Video Games, Virtual Realities: Playing Law* (Routledge, 2024).
34. M Sicart, 'The Banality of Simulated Evil: Designing Ethical Gameplay' (2009) 11(3) *Ethics and Information Technology* 191.
35. E Aarseth, 'Computer Game Studies, Year One' (2001) 1(1) *The International Journal of Computer Game Research* 2.

Code, Rhetoric and Form: The Power of Game as Object

Lawrence Lessig, in his influential 1999 book, *Code and Other Laws of Cyberspace,* likened code as having the power to regulate human conduct in a manner similar to legal systems. He argued that while an architecture of code determines what is permissible within a given system, it does not just constrain behaviour but enforces compliance, barring transgression of the regulated behaviour through its very composition. Although the book was not about video games but coded systems more widely, the structural comparison between video games and digital systems is sufficiently similar for it to have been applied analogically to games.[36]

Video games can be designed to serve all sorts of functions and objectives; they may focus on cooperation or competition with or against other players or the game AI, teach new skills or knowledge, provide a sense of comfort, present challenges to be overcome, allow for creative expression and much more. But above all, video games are most often designed with play in mind.

Play, according to Salen and Zimmerman, is the 'free space of movement within a more rigid structure'.[37] They suggest that the imposition of rules does not stifle play, but rather 'play exists both because of and despite the more rigid structures of a system'.[38] These rules are upheld by the material code that creates and regulates the architecture of the game and, in turn, evaluates the performance of players in reference to internal criteria for success or failure.[39] Code operates within the game as an apparatus of power and control over the player dictating finite options for what *is* or *is not* possible within the game space while providing the player with the illusion of agency and interaction.[40] Though James C Fisher has noted how analogies between code and law can conflate the compulsorality between the legal subject and law, and the player and the game: 'while the actions of the played character necessarily *conform* to the game design, they do not *obey* it.'[41]

As the player plays, they are positioned within the game world to identify not only *possible* actions but also *desirable* or *valuable* actions as communicated by the game state

---

36. M Sicart, 'The Ethics of Computer Game Design' (2005) *Proceedings of the 2005 DiGRA International Conference: Changing Views: Worlds in Play* (available at http://www.digra.org/digital-library/publications/the-ethics-of-computer-game-design/); Ian Bogost, *Persuasive Games: The Expressive Power of Videogames* (MIT Press, 2007).
37. K Salen and E Zimmerman, *Rules of Play: Game Design Fundamentals* (MIT Press, 2003).
38. E Zimmerman, 'Narrative, Interactivity, Play, and Games: Four Naughty Concepts in Need of Discipline' in N Wardrip-Fruin and P Harrigan (eds) *First Person: New Media as Story, Performance, and Game* (MIT Press, 2004), 159.
39. M Sicart, 'The Ethics of Computer Game Design' (2005) *Proceedings of the 2005 DiGRA International Conference: Changing Views: Worlds in Play* (available at http://www.digra.org/digital-library/publications/the-ethics-of-computer-game-design/).
40. M Sicart, 'The Banality of Simulated Evil: Designing Ethical Gameplay' (2009) 11(3) *Ethics and Information Technology* 193.
41. JC Fisher, 'Invisible Walls: Facts and Freedom in Coded Space' in D Mitchell, A Pearson and TD Peters (eds) *Law, Video Games, Virtual Realities: Playing Law* (Routledge, 2024), 59, original emphasis.

machine through reward or punishment for performing certain actions or behaviours. Games are a generally representational form, having adopted their own language built on intertextual symbolic norms that are inherited from common technological and gaming conventions. They signal players that defeating enemies or capturing territory gives the player points, money or beneficial perks, whereas the failure to complete a jump, anticipate an enemy move or time an input correctly may result in a negative consequence, avatar death or a game over.

Irrespective of the specific content of the stimulus, the player is trained through repeated exposure to enact certain behaviours in response to it when presented – the response to the symbol is not just visual or mental but also tactile.[42] The 'ongoing interaction between these representations and the embodied behaviour of the user that makes such images more than images',[43] it inscribes the act of play with a level of meaning that may serve as the first steps towards a procedural or simulative turn of cultural legal scholarship. Ian Bogost calls this inscription of value 'procedural rhetoric', stating that:

> video games do not simply distract or entertain with empty, meaningless content. Rather, video games can make claims about the world. But when they do so, they do not make it with oral speech, nor in writing, nor even with images. Rather, video games make argument with *processes*.[44]

These arguments are made more persuasive by the immersive properties of game.[45] Structurally, the perceived immediacy of the feedback loop removes space for reflexive or critical thought,[46] and the ease of identification between avatar and player, bolstered by the co-creation of on-screen meaning,[47] contributes to the easy adoption of certain ideological positions in response to stimulus. Moreover, it is not only what is *included*

42. S Penny, 'Representation, Enaction, and the Ethics of Simulation' *Electronic Book Review* (available at https://electronicbookreview.com/essay/representation-enaction-and-the-ethics-of-simulation/), 80.
43. Ibid, 83.
44. I Bogost, 'The Rhetoric of Games' in K Salen (ed) *The Ecology of Games: Connecting Youth, Games, and Learning* (MIT Press, 2008).
45. Melanie Green and Timothy Brock discuss how the players who are successfully 'transported' by the immersive properties of the video game are less likely to resist ideas presented to them. MC Green and TC Brock, 'The Role of Transportation in the Persuasiveness of Public Narratives' (2000) 79(5) *Journal of Personality and Social Psychology* 701; CN Burrows and H Blanton, 'Real-World Persuasion from Virtual-World Campaigns: How Transportation into Virtual Worlds Moderates In-Game Influence' 43(4) *Communication Research* 542.
46. A Pearson and K Tranter, 'Code, Nintendo's Super Mario and Digital Legality' (2015) 28(4) *International Journal for the Semiotics of Law* 825; see also M Csikszentmihalyi, *Flow: The Psychology of Optimal Experience* (Harper Perennial, 1990).
47. B Rehak, 'Playing at Being: Psychoanalysis and the Avatar' in MJP Wolf and B Perron, *The Video Game Theory Reader* (Routledge, 2003).

within the game but also what is *left out*, whether consciously or not, that can influence the adoption of these narratives by the player.[48]

To give an example, the game franchise *Civilisation* is a turn-based game strategy game in which the player seeks to explore the map, expand their colony, exploit other colonies and resources and exterminate threats. Through the core gameplay, *Civilisation* replicates ideologies connected to colonialism in the treatment of empty land as *terra nullius*, the framing of people and landscapes as resources or commodities, and the elimination of 'uncivilised' groups as the only means of progress.[49] The game converts the logic of settler colonialism into one of few actions available for the player to perform as they control the map and master the space, and in doing so, the game aligns conquering as correct or valuable.

Other notable examinations on the structural synergies between the law and the video game form include Dale Mitchell's demonstration of how legal and coded language can enable specific forms of power through the language games central to both forms[50] and a separate contribution to the field critiquing the apparatus of the Poke Ball as a representation of the technic of legal persona. Joshua Shaw has connected the act of moving throughout a game space as reminiscent of the performative nature of ordering through movement that occurs within the lawscape.[51] Ashley Pearson and Kieran Tranter have suggested that the video game medium naturalises entry into emerging techniques of digital legality, in which people become accustomed to seeing and representing themselves as data.[52]

Emotion, Aesthetic and Choice: The Power of Game as Experience

Video games are predicated on the machinic language of the code, yet the player does not encounter the game as an object but as an experience since they interface with the

48. R Fassone, *Every Game Is an Island: Endings and Extremities in Video Games* (Bloomsbury, 2018), 74.
49. C Leggot, 'Terra Nullius: Claiming Land on Civilization's Empty Earth' in D Mitchell, A Pearson and TD Peters (eds) *Law, Video Games, Virtual Realities: Playing Law* (Routledge, 2024), 269–289; ST Keynes, 'One More Turn: The Gamic Afterlives of *Johnson v M'Intosh* and Digital Settler Colonialism in *Sid Meier's Civilization VI*' in D Mitchell, A Pearson and TD Peters (eds) *Law, Video Games, Virtual Realities: Playing Law* (Routledge, 2024), 154–171; K Tranter, 'Playing the World Picture: Sid Meier's Civilization and the Law of Abstraction' in D Mitchell, A Pearson and TD Peters (eds) *Law, Video Games, Virtual Realities: Playing Law* (Routledge, 2024), 172–189.
50. See D Mitchell, 'Towards a Legal Ludology: Language Games, Playful Magic, and the Game of Law' in D Mitchell, A Pearson and TD Peters (eds) *Law, Video Games, Virtual Realities: Playing Law* (Routledge, 2024), 31–50.
51. J Shaw, 'A Minor Jurisprudence of Play: Becoming Jurisprudents through Play in the *Majora's Mask*' in D Mitchell, A Pearson and TD Peters (eds) *Law, Video Games, Virtual Realities: Playing Law* (Routledge, 2024), 190–210.
52. A Pearson and K Tranter, 'Code, Nintendo's Super Mario and Digital Legality' (2015) 28(4) *International Journal for the Semiotics of Law* 825.

processed audio-visual and tactile results of the code rather than the static code itself.[53] The game, as an object, runs the code that dictates the conditions of play. But players do not experience the code; they experience the game.[54] As such, procedural rhetoric can draw on a gamut of aesthetic, narrative, social and emotive artifice such as avatar perspective, cinematographic techniques in cutscenes,[55] the addition of music to smooth the transitions between changes in game state,[56] and creating social connections between other players of non-player characters (NPCs) to further immerse the player in the play space.

Some games, particularly educational or 'serious games', have deliberately employed procedural rhetoric as a way to connect to the embodied experience of law. For example, Jean Ketterling uses the aesthetic, emotive tools of the game *Borders* to re-orient the emphasis on logic and rationality within law toward empathy and justice.[57] The game portrays the experience of a Mexican immigrant trying to cross the American border without being captured by roaming guards and surviving in the harsh desert. Failed attempts of the player 'are documented via skeletons providing a sense of permanent consequence and symbolizing the lives lost to the Mexican desert'.[58]

The avatar, initially presented as a mere functional tool and an empty vessel for the player, actually encompasses a fusion of commingling subjectivities – 'the avatar is a collective, even before the player encounters it'.[59] Player-avatar identification, the act of performing as the avatar and the freedom to experiment with one's identity within the game space all contribute to shaping player behaviours.[60] Although developers strive to create immersive gameplay, lifelike graphics and captivating narratives that enable players to suspend disbelief and genuinely engage with the game world, it is important to recognise that complete detachment from reality is unattainable.

Running parallel to the idea that play may have ideological implications is that video games are still, ultimately, an experience of *play*. For Johan Huzinga, the author of the oft-referenced *Homo Ludens*, play is a non-serious, free and voluntary activity that occurs

53. R Fassone, *Every Game Is an Island: Endings and Extremities in Video Games* (Bloomsbury, 2018), 22.
54. There are, naturally, games that play with this distinction. See A Pearson, 'Decoding Legal (Un)certainty in *Doki Doki Literature Club!*' in D Mitchell, A Pearson and TD Peters (eds) *Law, Video Games, Virtual Realities: Playing Law* (Routledge, 2024), 111–130.
55. T Smethurst and S Craps, 'Playing with Trauma: Interreactivity, Empathy, and Complicity in *The Walking Dead* Video Game' (2014) 10(3) *Games and Culture* 269, 283–284.
56. T Summers, *Understanding Video Game Music* (Cambridge University Press, 2016), 60.
57. J Ketterling, 'Playing with *Borders*: Using Video Games to Bring Emotion into the Law Classroom' in D Mitchell, A Pearson and TD Peters (eds) *Law, Video Games, Virtual Realities: Playing Law* (Routledge, 2024), 133–153.
58. Description from the official *Borders* download page. G Alvarez and J DiGiacomo, *Borders* (available at https://gonzzink.itch.io/borders).
59. J Boulter, *Parables of the Posthuman: Digital Realities, Gaming, and the Player Experience* (Wayne State University, 2015), 43–45.
60. S Trepte and L Reinecke, 'Avatar Creation and Video Game Enjoyment' (2010) 22(4) *Journal of Media Psychology* 171.

within the *magic circle* which represents a conceptual boundary that separates the ordinary world from the immersive world of play created by the game.[61] Within the magic circle, the player's actions and decisions are contextualised within the game's universe and the consequences are confined to that world – temporarily suspending real-world norms and legal boundaries within the world of the game, to a limited extent.[62] The possible layers of engagement highlighted by the magic circle (inside and outside the game world, diegetic and non-diegetic) highlight the inherent artifice of the play state – troubling the relationship between serious moral considerations and the effectiveness of procedural rhetoric. While video games, with their technological mediation and input devices, create a more distinct magic circle compared to traditional games like chess or soccer, the distinction between play and non-play, even within video games, remains 'fuzzy and permeable'.[63]

Games such as the open-world *Grand Theft Auto*, with its capacity for the player to undertake the titular car thefts, bank robberies and even casual murder, invite jurisprudential reflection due to the illegality of the represented content. By incorporating opportunities for illegal or immoral action, these games allow for a nuanced exploration of the criminal experience to be interrogated and provide an embodied way to engage with concepts that may not be encountered frequently in reality. According to Zagal, games that feature ethical choices create a space for moral reflection, as the player's agency through the avatar places the responsibility for actions squarely on their shoulders.[64]

Games that explicitly tackle themes of justice, morality and ethics often employ a combination of procedural rhetoric and other strategies to immerse players within the game world. Graphic depictions of violence and brutality, and emotionally persuasive narratives of injustice target the procedural *experience* of the player and seek to persuade them of particular positions. These games may even try to absolve player concerns about engaging in unlawful activities, despite the conflict with ordinary legal norms that exist outside the game's fictional context. James Gilchrist Stewart has noted how *Grand Theft Auto V* has employed 'interpassivity' through satirical talk-back radio to critique the neoliberal frame of world within which the game is played. The game critiques in place of the player, allowing the player to enjoy the pursuit of financial gain

61. J Huizinga, *Homo Ludens: A Study of the Play-Element in Culture* (Routledge and Kegan Paul, 1949).
62. The 'Gamer's Dilemma' highlights the moral distinction that exists between different types of simulated wrongdoings depicted within video games. The common points of contrast are normative acceptance of virtual murder but not virtual paedophilia. This is one of the instances in which the magic circle is unable to sharply separate the two spaces.
63. K Salen and E Zimmerman, *Rules of Play: Game Design Fundamentals* (MIT Press, 2003), 94.
64. J Zagal, 'Ethically Notable Videogames: Moral Dilemmas and Gameplay' (2009) *Proceedings of the 2009 DiGRA International Conference: Breaking New Ground: Innovation in Games, Play, Practice and Theory'* (available at http://www.digra.org/digital-library/publications/ethically-notable-videogames-moral-dilemmas-and-gameplay/).

through crime guilt-free.[65] Similarly, in *Grand Theft Auto IV*, crime naturally emerges as the most lucrative and productive choice for the main character. However, as Luis Gomez Romero has point out, the player-avatar, Niko Bellic, will occasionally resist the player's decisions which attempts to hold them ethically accountable for their actions diegetically or within the game.[66]

In this way, the embodied experience of the player never seems to be entirely engulfed but rather oscillating between multiple frames of subjectivity and normative behaviour.[67] The presence of the magic circle establishes boundaries that may mitigate or limit the consequences of in-game actions or can also lead to a player disengaging from the immersive properties of the world completely, to instead use strategies that manipulate the game state to their advantage. Players may strategically save their progress before critical decisions or engage in metagaming where they optimise their play for maximum results rather than being persuaded by the narrative or moral implications of decisions.[68] Moreover, the magic circle analogy is insufficient for capturing the increasingly social and emergent game experiences that occurs in genres such as massively multiplayer online games (MMOs) and challenging the bordering of the virtual and material worlds that the magic circle puts forth.[69]

Examination of narrative and gameplay can be seen within Robbie Sykes's exploration of the tension of human responsibility and earth jurisprudence in *Final Fantasy VII*,[70] or in the analysis of *inFAMOUS* that privileges natural law principles over positivist ones through the way ethical decision making is encoded as 'good' or 'evil' within the game.[71] These examples, although direct, only scratch the surface of how law and justice manifest (or are noticeably absent) in the content and embodied experience of video games. In alignment with the jurisprudential variations in other law and humanities fields, it is acknowledged that legal meaning can extend beyond explicit markers of law and permeate the very structures, spaces and rhythms of life.

---

65. JG Stewart, '*Grand Theft* Neoliberalism' in D Mitchell, A Pearson and TD Peters (eds) *Law, Video Games, Virtual Realities: Playing Law* (Routledge, 2024), 251–268.
66. L Gómez Romero, 'Gaming at the Margins of Law or, Niko Bellic's (Critical) Theory of Justice' in D Mitchell, A Pearson and TD Peters (eds) *Law, Video Games, Virtual Realities: Playing Law* (Routledge, 2024), 213–235.
67. An exception to this might be when the player is engaged in a flow state. See M Csikszentmihalyi, *Flow: The Psychology of Optimal Experience* (Harper Perennial, 1990).
68. A common example of metagaming would be the discussion around whether to rescue or harvest *Bioshock's* Little Sister characters. From a metagame perspective, rescuing the Little Sisters gives the player a greater overall benefit, however this benefit is staggered throughout the game. Harvesting the Little Sisters provides a greater early-game advantage at the expense of the later-game gains.
69. D Hourigan, 'Emergent Systems: Virtuality, Legality, Formality' in D Mitchell, A Pearson and TD Peters (eds) *Law, Video Games, Virtual Realities: Playing Law* (Routledge, 2024), 96–110.
70. R Sykes, '"Those Chosen by the Planet": Final Fantasy VII and Earth Jurisprudence' (2017) 30(3) *International Journal for the Semiotics of Law* 455.
71. M Barnett and C Sharp, 'The Moral Choice of inFAMOUS: Law and Morality in Video Games' (2015) 24(3) *Griffith Law Review* 482.

In the realm of law and video games, publications embracing this nuanced approach have explored other ways in which the video game artefact can contribute to legal meaning. For instance, Anna Lukina and Shane Finn have noted the persistence of specific types of law, such as inheritance or service contracts, that exist within the backdrop of spaces of legal exception like the war-torn *Skyrim*.[72] Desmond Manderson has leveraged the aesthetics of neoliberalism as perfect, placid, empty space in *Push 'Em All* – a game that cleanses spaces of population and dissent from its populous.[73] Additionally, Annie Shum and Kieran Tranter have analysed *Pokémon GO* as the apotheotic culmination of visual jurisprudence, thanks to its augmented reality technologies and new way of mediated interaction with the world.[74]

What, perhaps, is currently lacking in the law and video games discipline is a comprehensive understanding of video games within their broader ecosystem of supporting structures and culture, which has significantly contributed to their popularity as a medium. This encompasses activities that exist on the periphery of the original gaming context or developer intention, such as cheating, modding, streaming, speedrunning and glitches. It also involves addressing the persistent issue of limited representation and diversity in video game player-avatars, particularly in terms of underrepresented groups such as women, people of colour, queer individuals and individuals with disabilities. Additionally, the discipline should anticipate the forthcoming revolution brought about by the expansion of simulative and embodied technologies like augmented reality and virtual reality. Furthermore, the non-diegetic frames that accompany gameplay, including menus, settings and avatar customisation, warrant attention and exploration.

Conclusion

This chapter has sought to welcome home the foundling discipline of law and video games into the law and humanities fold. Drawing inspiration from its companion discipline, game studies, this chapter seeks to bridge gaps and supplement existing literature with the view to providing newcomers a pathway into this burgeoning field of study.

Through an examination of the dynamic interactions between hardware and software, player and avatar, object and experience, this chapter has highlighted the unique duality of video games. Video games engage law as a structural, rigid, formalist medium governed by the underlying code that dictates the rules and conditions of interaction.

72. A Lukina and S Finn, 'Law Among Chaos: An Anti-Schmittian Reading of *Skyrim*' in D Mitchell, A Pearson and TD Peters (eds) *Law, Video Games, Virtual Realities: Playing Law* (Routledge, 2024), 236–250.
73. D Manderson, 'Game Over: On Emptying the Public Square' in D Mitchell, A Pearson and TD Peters (eds) *Law, Video Games, Virtual Realities: Playing Law* (Routledge, 2024), 290–308.
74. A Shum and K Tranter, 'Seeing, Moving, Catching, Accumulating: Pokémon GO, and the Legal Subject' (2017) 30(3) *International Journal for the Semiotics of Law* 477.

Yet, simultaneously, the medium offers an intensely aesthetic, spatial and emotive player experience that connects to the irrationality or non-seriousness of play.[75]

As with all law and humanities scholarship, the value of exploring the intersection of law and video games lies in its ability to unite law and culture, dismantling artificial boundaries and revealing the profound interconnectedness between them. This reveals that law is not an isolated construct but rather a living, breathing entity shaped by the forces of culture, structural violence and human imagination. By embracing the intersections of law and video games, we can expand our horizons and rethink the legal connections that lie beneath the surface of pixels and polygons.

75. J Huizinga, *Homo Ludens: A Study of the Play-Element in Culture* (Routledge and Kegan Paul, 1949).

Chapter Fifteen

CONCLUSION: SUBVERTING THE LAW AND HUMANITIES CANON

Sara Ramshaw

Part I: On the Question of Canonicity

One question that dominated many of the papers and conversations that took place at the 25th anniversary of the Association for the Study of Law, Culture and Humanities (LCH) annual conference, hosted by the University of Toronto in Canada on 22–23 June 2023, was whether there is (or should be) a law and humanities canon? I spoke directly to this question on a panel with James Martel and Hyo Yoon Kang on the first morning of the conference.[1] This question was picked up by many others during the two days, including past LCH president Susan Heinzelman in the plenary session entitled 'LCH at 25: Looking Back, Thinking Forward'.

The question of canonicity as it relates to law and humanities scholarship is very relevant to this current collection of essays edited by Newman and Sandberg as it attempts to add to, or intervene into, the established law and humanities canon (if there is one), and thus must be interrogated for the message and power it holds in that regard. In my conference paper, which closely followed the argument set out in my published Commentary, I imagined law and humanities not as a 'canon' per se but as a 'field without a canon', or a canon that resists canonisation. I argued that arts and humanities–based practices utilised in legal research and teaching expose the law and humanities 'canon' to its dual (and somewhat contradictory) nature, as that which continually strains towards a pre-established archive, but must also leap ahead fearlessly to properly defy disciplinary boundaries and move the field beyond siloed thinking. This, to my mind, is one of the preliminary aims of law and humanities interdisciplinary scholarship and pedagogy. These practices consist not of a stable collection of set texts but instead signify a process of experimentation that is ever in flux and alive to possibility. It is this process of discovering new arts and humanities–based practices that ensures law and humanities remains a vibrant, yet ever-changing, field for years to come.[2]

1. See H Yoon Kang, 'Is There (Should There Be) a Law and Humanities Canon?' (2023) 19(1) *Law, Culture and Humanities* 60; and S Ramshaw, 'Law and Humanities: A Field Without a Canon' (2023) 19(1) *Law, Culture and Humanities* 77.
2. Ibid., 79.

Canonisation, in its establishment of a field of intellectual thought that defines its parameters or the importance of certain texts and core issues at stake, invites community and consensus. In other words, those of us who consider ourselves 'law and humanities' scholars do so only because there have been key texts and scholars around which/whom we identify, thereby circumscribing law and humanities as a distinctive field of inquiry. That said, canons are also, by their very nature, exclusionary. Important voices and texts, especially outsider perspectives such as feminist and Indigenous voices, are often left out of or fall below the requisite standard for elevation to the status of canonical belonging. Canonisation is thus not without controversy. It invites us to ask who has the authority to determine or set the standard and what criteria matters for 'deciding what counts as "foundational texts that exemplify, guide, and constitute a discipline"'.[3]

James Martel, in his 2023 LCH conference paper on the question of a law and humanities canon, suggested that instead of getting rid of the canon altogether, which he thinks is impossible considering the archist[4] mindset governing social relations and academic practices, we should instead endeavour to *subvert* it. Newman and Sandberg's collection certainly goes far to destabilise the current North American focus[5] of law and humanities scholarship in that they have gathered voices from outside the United States and include disciplines often missing from law and humanities collections or handbooks such as theology, religion, geography, comic books and video games. Feminist voices are also quite strong throughout this collection, although racialised and Indigenous law and humanities scholars are still very much absent. Hyo Yoon Kang, in her conference paper (as well as her published Commentary),[6] finds the whiteness of law and humanities scholarship unsurprising given the racial composition of the humanities disciplines more generally. However, this is not without serious ramifications:

> To relate a social composition to an intellectual value, as a canon would do, would mean to normalize and give value to the fractured realities that is our present predicament. It would be a wrongful analogy to draw. And to assume the ability to speak and pass judgments of value in relation to a canon on behalf of the imagined other – imagined because they have been in considerable minority or not audible unless assimilated – would not be inclusive and global, but rather alienating and globalist.[7]

---

3. S Cummings, 'Law and Social Movements: Reimagining the Progressive Canon' (2018) *Wisconsin Law Review* 441, 442.
4. According to Martel, 'archism' is defined as a 'centralized and hierarchical political form that is a secularization of ancient Greek and Hebrew prophetic traditions'; it 'dominates contemporary politics through a prophet's promises of peace and prosperity or the threat of violence. Archism is met by anarchism, in which a community shares a collective form of judgment and vision': J Martel, *Anarchist Prophets: Disappointing Vision and the Power of Collective Sight* (Duke University Press, 2022) [Abstract].
5. H Yoon Kang, 'Is There (Should There Be) a Law and Humanities Canon?' (2023) 19(1) *Law, Culture and Humanities* 60, 74.
6. Ibid.
7. Ibid., 74.

Prior to the 2023 LCH conference, I asked my colleague and then acting dean of the Faculty of Law at the University of Victoria in Canada, Val Napoleon,[8] why so few Indigenous scholars attended the LCH conference, especially as Indigenous laws often make themselves known through arts and humanities–based practices, such as storytelling, songs, ceremonies, beading, drumming and visual art. Val responded by noting, among other reasons, the huge pressures placed upon Indigenous legal scholars at the moment, especially in the current climate of reconciliation and decolonisation, and their time is already filled with numerous other commitments in academia and beyond. Hyo Yoon Kang makes a similar point in relation to the inherent obstacles in creating a more inclusive law and humanities canon as it relates to the 'condition of academic labor and the structure of the academic "market"':

> There is a growing number of colleagues who teach and research in untenured positions and on temporary contracts, as universities increasingly rely on their labor. Outside and within the North American academe, academics are governed by a different institutional work load, career progressions, evaluation cultures and finances, many of which often translate into considerably less academic freedom, salary and financial resources, particularly for those who have not yet reached the professorial grade. Writing and research outside the tenure system and the North American academy underlie different political, structural and financial constraints, which influence the format, genres and scope of scholarship. These constraints are less visible, hence it is difficult to say how a canon could take into account these realities of differential conditions of intellectual work and their evaluative structures.[9]

In light of the above, it is obvious that the task of creating a more inclusive law and humanities canon (if there is one) is far more complex than first imagined. Also, as Hyo Yoon Kang notes,

> the desire to include critical or 'other' works within a canon may be well-meaning but could result in a paternalistic management of 'diversity' and a desire to assimilate other orders of worth into one's own. This could result in the subsumption of the critical potential and genuine alterity into a 'global' canon, which is driving the dominant group's tastes, ideologies and interests.[10]

That said, the task of asking the question of canonicity in the field of law, culture and humanities can be quite productive in that it highlights the tension between the canon as coherence and community, on the one hand, and archist and controlling, on the other. This tension, according to Susan Heinzelman in her 2023 LCH plenary paper, generates dissensus and resistance and opens the way for subversion to a canon that is

8. Val Napoleon is from northeast British Columbia (Treaty 8) and is a member of the Saulteau First Nation. She is also an adopted member of the Gitanyow (Gitksan) House of Luuxhon, Ganada (Frog) Clan.
9. H Yoon Kang, 'Is There (Should There Be) a Law and Humanities Canon?' (2023) 19(1) *Law, Culture and Humanities* 60, 74–75.
10. Ibid., 74.

both regulating and generating. Heinzelman calls for a non-traditional or non-canonical canon that is constantly under review and open to challenge. In other words, we must continue to pose the question of whether there is (or ought to be) a law and humanities canon.

Returning to Newman and Sandberg's *Law and Humanities* and its relation to the law and humanities canon more generally, I want to focus on some key contributions that this collection offers in terms of a challenge and/or subversion of the law and humanities canon (if there is one), while also gesturing towards its importance.

As Newman and Sandberg outline in their introduction, the aim of this collection is not to develop a distinct law and humanities method or approach but rather, in highlighting certain commonalities and differences, to assist those who study particular 'law and' fields to learn from one another and benefit from conceptualising their work under the law and humanities umbrella. The editors employ the 'x as law/law as x' formulation to signify the ways in which the interdisciplinary study of law involves cross-over between two objects or frames of analyses involving both the study of a non-legal discipline from a legal standpoint ('x as law') and the study of law from the standpoint of other disciplines ('law as x'). The use of the 'law and' approach throughout the collection is meant to signify 'how this mutual blending is a key – if not the key – characteristic of law and humanities studies if it is understood as an inter– or even trans–disciplinary study'.

Newman and Sandberg's collection also adds to law and humanities scholarship its introductory focus, making the field accessible for scholars and students who are exploring this area for the first time. Most importantly, to my mind, is the highlighting throughout that the 'law and' approach, read by the various authors as 'law as x/x as law', is more than simply a metaphor, but is itself a methodology. This is a point that, as Emma Nottingham notes in her chapter on 'Law and Archaeology', can be 'transformative', and change the way students, lawyers, judges and legal academics see law, especially case law. Nottingham's musings on the benefits of this methodology in the area of legal archelogy are equally true in relation to other areas of law and humanities research and pedagogical practices:

> [Law and humanities] puts the human interest and experiences back into the study of Law, including the people, places, and timing, which helps students to realize that no two cases are alike and that each one is variable, unique and subjective. It provides the opportunity for more creative, organic and curiosity-based learning, even putting fun and travel into the experience.

Nottingham goes on to note that such an approach offers students 'the opportunity to understand the chaos, inconsistency and ambiguity of stories, revealing the interaction between conflicting stories and how stories can be framed and reframed'. As such, law and humanities 'encourages students to ask different questions and appreciate that significant and even subversive findings can be made when we are not confined to prioritizing doctrine'.

It is tempting to theorise law and humanities metaphorically, especially in the realm of law and music, for example. Pointing to the '[t]he disciplinary difference between the two fields of endeavor',[11] Desmond Manderson admits to employing music primarily metaphorically in his ground-breaking text *Songs without Music: Aesthetic Dimensions of Law and Justice*.[12] In other words, music was 'employed more for rhetorical than analytical purposes'.[13] Gerald J. Postema's 'Melody and Law's Mindfulness of Time' provides another example of this approach. For Postema, 'melody', while an appropriate model of law's characteristic normativity, is viewed to be so only as metaphor:

> Compared with other images frequently deployed in the history of jurisprudence to illuminate law's normativity, melody has one signal advantage: *No one will be inclined to take it literally*. No one will be tempted to look for music from courtrooms, solicitors' offices, parliament chambers, or police precincts.[14]

Postema treats law and music as separate and distinct disciplines, disciplines that may have certain aspects in common and certain things to teach each other, but only metaphorically and certainly not as inevitably interactive.[15] My interdisciplinary research in the area of law and music challenges this view in that I demonstrate that both law and (musical) improvisation share the same *structural* tension in that their meaning rests on the aporetic relation between singularity and generality, repetition, and alteration. Borrowing from Jacques Derrida,[16] this shared tension is what I call in my work 'the law of the extempore' or 'justice as improvisation'.[17]

By signalling the methodological strategies that law and humanities scholarship employs, Newman and Sandberg's collection adds to and/or subverts the law and humanities canon (if there is one) in meaningful and important ways.

Part II: Interrogating the 'And' of Law and Humanities

As this collection of chapters is structured upon the 'law and' model, it is necessary to interrogate what is meant by this 'and' and whether such allows for any subversion of the canon, as advocated by James Martel.[18] In her Commentary on whether there is (or

11. D Manderson, 'Making a Point and Making a Noise: A Punk Prayer' (2016) 12(1) *Law, Culture and the Humanities* 17, 18.
12. D Manderson, *Songs without Music: Aesthetic Dimensions of Law and Justice* (University of California Press, 2000).
13. D Manderson, 'Making a Point and Making a Noise: A Punk Prayer' (2016) 12(1) *Law, Culture and the Humanities* 17, 19.
14. G J Postema, 'Melody and Law's Mindfulness of Time' (2004) 17(2) *Ratio Juris: An International Journal or Jurisprudence and Philosophy of Law* 203, 208–209 (emphasis added).
15. D Manderson, 'From Hunger to Love: Myths of the Source, Interpretation and Consititution of Law in Children's Literature' (2003) 15(1) *Law and Literature* 87.
16. J Derrida, 'The Last Interview' (2004) *SV*, 8.
17. See, for example, S Ramshaw, *Justice as Improvisation: The Law of the Extempore* (Routledge, 2014).
18. J Martel, *Anarchist Prophets: Disappointing Vision and the Power of Collective Sight* (Duke University Press, 2022).

should be) a law and humanities canon, Hyo Yoon Kang writes about the 'and' of law and humanities as a 'montage' in which

> every piece has a double identity of a whole *and* a part of a whole. The montage is composed of many 'ands.' If we approach law and humanities as an evolving montage, the question is: what is the glue that makes the montage stick together? The literal adhesive is the 'and.'[19]

Desmond Manderson's interrogation of the 'and' of 'law and literature' is applicable here.[20] Manderson asks, 'What exactly does "and" mean? Does it hold its two terms separately or together? Does it identify a mere juxtaposition, a supplement or sub-set, or a fusion?'[21] One answer is to think of law and humanities as 'two separate genres' in which the non-law discipline 'provides the insights that law does not, speaking in a different voice and appealing to a different register'.[22] Law, in other words, is theorised as an entity persistently separate and distinct from that which it is being compared, be it literature, music or otherwise.[23] Each sphere may have 'certain aspects in common' with the other and be able to teach the other 'certain things', but their separation 'treats them as fit subjects for comparison but not interaction'.[24]

Tina Piper calls this the 'translational/descriptive' methodological approach, or the 'law *as*' method, which employs the humanities 'as a metaphor for understanding, describing, and characterizing aspects of law that are challenging to comprehend'.[25] It is translational in that concepts more at home in various humanities disciplines are applied to 'describe law in external terms, rather than in words purely internal to its discourses'.[26] The reverse is also possible in that legal concepts and tools can be utilised to understand various humanities disciplines. This is especially true as it relates to normative legal concerns such as justice, democracy, resistance and ethics.

A second possible approach outlined by Manderson has law being thought of as a 'sub–set of literature' in which 'law is treated as a branch of *rhetoric*, an aspect of narrative whose history, force and meaning are amenable to a literary analysis'.[27] This is a method that has been advanced by Peter Goodrich and James Boyd White, for

---

19. H Yoon Kang, 'Is There (Should There Be) a Law and Humanities Canon?' (2023) 19(1) *Law, Culture and Humanities* 60, 63 (emphasis in original).
20. D Manderson, 'Making a Point and Making a Noise: A Punk Prayer' (2016) 12(1) *Law, Culture and the Humanities* 17, 18.
21. Ibid., 18.
22. Ibid., 18.
23. D Manderson, *Songs without Music: Aesthetic Dimensions of Law and Justice* (University of California Press, 2000), 31.
24. Ibid.
25. T Piper, 'The Improvisational Flavour of Law, the Legal Taste of Improvisation' (2010) 6(1) *Critical Studies in Improvisation* 15, 2.
26. Ibid.
27. D Manderson, 'Making a Point and Making a Noise: A Punk Prayer' (2016) 12(1) *Law, Culture and the Humanities* 1718 (emphasis added).

example.[28] Third, literature can also be viewed as 'sub–set of law'.[29] Manderson's writings on children's literature[30] are an example of this approach in which the literary constitutes legal values and subjectivity. As Manderson writes, 'It is not that these genres *influence* the law, but that they *are* the law.'[31]

All three approaches are united in their placement of law *next to* the humanities. Manderson argues that such an approach is common in 'law and' scholarship, such as law and literature or law and music.[32] A different approach is to view humanities not as a subject or object but as a 'way of knowing'[33] or a 'way of seeing'.[34] According to Manderson, 'law and' scholarship aims to juxtapose two *nouns*, while a better approach would be to explore law and humanities as two *verbs*.[35] Such would assume that there is already present between law and humanities 'a relationship of *inevitable interaction*'.[36] The humanities, in other words, 'is already in the law'.[37] Manderson calls this 'law *with*'[38] while Newman and Sandberg designate it as the 'x as law/law as x' approach. Regardless of the formulation used, the connector – 'and', 'as', 'with' etc. – creates a relational association between law and the humanities, which recognises some commonality between the two concepts or disciplines.[39] Not purely translational, the approaches utilised by the authors in this collection refuse applications of the humanities to law as metaphor. They also do not prescribe that law *should* be more humanistic. Nor is their aim to demonstrate the formal impact of the law on the humanities. Instead, the law and humanities approaches utilised throughout re-imagine law and justice as fundamentally 'humanistic' in nature.[40] To conclude, Hyo Yoon Kang's discussion of the importance of the 'and' in law and humanities bears repeating:

---

28. See P Goodrich, 'Rhetoric and Law' in MJ MacDonald (ed), *The Oxford Handbook of Rhetorical Studies* (Oxford University Press, 2014), 613; P Goodrich, 'Antirrhesis: Polemical Structures of Common Law Thought' in A Sarat and TR Kearns (eds), *The Rhetoric of Law* (University of Michigan Press, 1994), 57; and JB White, 'Imagining the Law' in A Sarat and TR Kearns (eds), *The Rhetoric of Law* (University of Michigan Press, 1994), 29.
29. D Manderson, 'Making a Point and Making a Noise: A Punk Prayer' (2016) 12(1) *Law, Culture and the Humanities* 17, 18.
30. D Manderson, 'From Hunger to Love: Myths of the Source, Interpretation, and Constitution of Law in Children's Literature' (2003) 15 *Law and Literature* 87.
31. D Manderson, 'Making a Point and Making a Noise: A Punk Prayer' (2016) 12(1) *Law, Culture and the Humanities* 17, 18 (emphasis in original).
32. D Manderson, *Songs without Music: Aesthetic Dimensions of Law and Justice* (University of California Press, 2000), 31.
33. Ibid., 30.
34. Ibid., 31.
35. Ibid., 31.
36. Ibid., 31 (emphasis added).
37. Ibid., 31.
38. This borrows from Manderson's discussion of 'law with aesthetics', or the aesthetic dimensions of law and justice: ibid., 33.
39. P Fitzpatrick, *Modernism and the Grounds of Law* (Cambridge University Press, 2001), 59.
40. C Douzinas, 'A Humanities of Resistance: Fragments for a Legal History of Humanity' in A Sarat, A Anderson and CO Frank (eds), *Law and the Humanities: An Introduction* (Cambridge University Press, 2009), 49.

> In the field of law and the humanities, the meaning of 'and' acts as the glue, which hold together the field as an un-disciplined montage of different disciplinary insights. If a value can be derived from the 'and,' it would be an *open-ended value plurality*, an attribute which is better mediated passively rather than positively authored.[41]

Thus, the importance of the connector 'and' is its 'value plurality', which welcomes a diversity of complex questions and opens up the possibility of even more law and humanities associations and conjunctions.[42] This collection of essays intervenes in the law and humanities canon (if there is one) through its reading, interpretation and critical engagement with diverse humanities disciplines and sub-disciplines.[43] By focusing on the 'and' of law and humanities scholarship, it bridges and connects a wide range of scholars and scholarship and pushes the field in diverse and interesting ways, ensuring that law and humanities scholarship remains relevant and important for years to come.

41. H Yoon Kang, 'Is There (Should There Be) a Law and Humanities Canon?' (2023) 19(1) *Law, Culture and Humanities* 60, 74, 66 (emphasis added).
42. Ibid., 75.
43. Ibid.

INDEX

Milton Keynes UK
Ingram Content Group UK Ltd.
UKHW012211191223
434677UK00003B/54

9 781839 990366